How to Do
Everything
with

M
Visio® 2002

Elisabeth Knottingham

Osborne/**McGraw-Hill**

New York Chicago San Francisco Lisbon
London Madrid Mexico City Milan New Delhi
San Juan Seoul Singapore Sydney Toronto

Osborne/**McGraw-Hill**
2600 Tenth Street
Berkeley, California 94710
U.S.A.

To arrange bulk purchase discounts for sales promotions, premiums, or fund-raisers, please contact Osborne/**McGraw-Hill** at the above address. For information on translations or book distributors outside the U.S.A., please see the International Contact Information page immediately following the index of this book.

How to Do Everything with Microsoft® Visio® 2002

1234567890 CUS CUS 01987654321

ISBN 0-07-213365-1

Publisher:	Brandon A. Nordin
Vice President	
& Associate Publisher:	Scott Rogers
Acquisitions Editor:	Megg Bonar
Project Manager:	Dave Nash
Acquisitions Coordinator:	Alissa Larson
Technical Editor:	Ellen Zander & Scott James
Production and Editorial:	Apollo Printing and Typesetting
Illustrators:	Lyssa Sieben-Wald, Michael Mueller, & Alex Putney
Series Design:	Mickey Galicia
Cover Design:	Greg Scott
Cover Series Design:	Dodie Shoemaker
Cover Illustration:	Tom Willis & Joseph Humphrey

This book was composed with Corel VENTURA™ Publisher.

Dedication

To Zen

You have changed my life,
thank you.

Love always,
-L

About the Author

Elisabeth Knottingham lives and breathes in the digital world. This is her third book and her second about Visio. Elisabeth has written about nearly every type of software and has been developing software for the World Wide Web since before it even existed. She teaches classes in a wide variety of subjects ranging from Web development to software documentation to metaphysical history. With degrees in Physics and English, she can carry on a conversation with a literary critic and a mad scientist at the same time.

Elisabeth lives in rainy Seattle with her husband and two large and very helpful cats in their new home. In her non-existent spare time, Elisabeth writes fiction. She is currently working on software documentation for a company in the Seattle area.

Contents at a Glance

Contents

Acknowledgments

A book this large is not possible without a huge amount of help from a dedicated team. Everyone from Microsoft to Osborne/McGraw-Hill has been vital in making this book happen. I'd like to extend my sincerest thanks to everyone who helped me create the book you hold in your hands (both named and unnamed), because without the support of these fine people this book would never have happened.

Thank you to:

John Hedtke, he got me into this craziness of writing books, and that is something I'll never forget. You continue to be an inspiration for me, John. Thank you.

Charlie Zaragoza, for his help with everything Visio. Charlie is not only a great stash of information, but he's a great man as well.

Lonnie Foster, my husband, for supporting both of us while I wrote this, for helping with the move that happened in the middle, for helping create the code in chapter 9, for cat wrangling, and as always for loving me far more than I could ever hope to deserve.

Rebecca and Guy Champ, for being there, no matter the country or time.

Britton Steel, for being one of the best managers I ever had, for giving me the chance to write the Visio print documentation, and for being a friend and inspiration. Congrats on your new home!

Thank you to the huge list of people from Visio including:

Dail Bridges and Jeff Hannibal, the masters of all things Visio Documentation. The exposure to the product and the work you put into making it better is amazing.

Nanette Eaton, for insight and without whom this book would have been much harder.

Scott James, my information contact and an all around great guy. Not only would this book have been worse without you, but also your support and help were unmatched.

A special thanks to all the outstanding people at Osborne/McGraw-Hill:

Megg Bonar, our acquisitions editor, for editorial duties that will continue to amaze for years, even from the far reaches of Utah.

Alissa Larson, our editorial assistant, for keeping track of all the details, handling all the image nightmares, and making sure we got it all done.

David Nash, the project manager, for making sure that we had a schedule, and that eventually we even made it.

Lyssa Wald, for fixing the image nightmares in time to make it to press.

Alan Zander, for technical editing, and comments that truly made the book better.

Jan Benes, our project editor, without his dedication and perseverance you would not be holding these pages in your hand.

As well as the rest of our production team—this book would never have been completed without each and every one of you.

A big thanks to Sweet Spirit Candles, for keeping the light on while all this was being created. You guys are the greatest.

And lastly, thank you to the readers, for without you there would be no need of books.

Without all these people, and many more, you would not be holding this book. Our heartfelt thanks to all who saw us through this project; we owe you more than words can say.

Introduction

Welcome to *How To Do Everything with Visio*. This book shows you how to use Visio to create diagrams of all shapes and sizes.

Why This Book Is for You

How To Do Everything with Visio is for anyone who wants to use Visio to its fullest. Readers who are unfamiliar with Visio will be able to learn about the features and options it offers to create professional-looking diagrams. Readers who are already familiar with the program will learn about the powerful new features in Visio Standard as well as learn about some features and options in Visio. Everyone will able to further their productivity with Visio and be able to tailor-make Visio solutions for their own diagrams.

> **TIP** *If you're simply considering Visio and haven't yet purchased it, you can evaluate the software at http://www.microsoft.com/office/visio.*

If you already have Visio to create diagrams, the process-oriented approach of this book makes it excellent for an easy reference guide to features that you haven't used before. Experienced users will find discussions on how features can be used together to create more complicated Visio solutions.

How This Book Is Organized

This book is divided into eleven chapters and two appendices, outlined below:

Chapter 1, "Visio Basics," introduces you to Visio. It shows you how to install Visio Standard and discusses its general and various options and basic features. You'll learn how to install and configure the program, the basic screen layout, and understand the product's general options and features. You'll also learn about printing and saving your Visio drawings.

Chapter 2, "Creating Your First Diagram," introduces you to creating Visio diagrams. You'll learn how to create a drawing with the basic template using the standard shape tools, such as stencils, connectors, and templates. You'll also learn how to print your drawing through a discussion of basic printing options. You'll be shown how the drag and drop feature works as well as how to draw lines and add text to Visio drawings. You'll also be shown how to use the text rotation, drawing, freehand, shapes, view, and pointer tools.

NOTE   *Chapters 3, 4, 5, and 6 include projects at the end of the chapter showing you how to use Visio to create outstanding diagrams.*

In Chapter 3, "Going Further," you'll continue exploring Visio tools. You will learn techniques to create custom objects, layers, backgrounds, pages, and other advanced tools. This chapter demonstrates how to create an overall look for a presentation using these tools. You'll learn how to insert graphics and how to use them as an important way to make your drawing look personal and meaningful.

Chapter 4, "Using Stencils and Templates," discusses the many kinds of stencils and templates that come with Visio. You'll learn how to bring up a stencil, choosing it from the list of stencils that ship with Visio. You'll be shown how to modify a stencil with either standard or custom objects created in Chapter 3. This chapter also teaches you how to create a stencil in Visio. You'll learn how a template works and how to choose one from the list of templates that come with Visio. You'll see how a template and stencil work together and be able to choose new stencils to go with your template from a list showing which stencils come with which templates. You'll learn how to modify an existing template and how to create a template of your own.

In Chapter 5, "Creating Flowcharts," you'll learn how to choose the right flowchart template and how to use the special features of connectors and SmartShapes objects to make your flowcharts work beautifully. You'll learn how to create an organization chart or a flowchart from a database, as well as how to create database information from a flowchart.

Chapter 6, "Getting Your Point Across Graphically," shows you how to use Visio to convey information graphically in presentations and on paper. You'll learn how to use the project scheduling templates in Visio, as well as how to work with these templates to manage your business. You'll also learn how to work with the Office Layout template, using it to create office diagrams and to generate inventory and ownership reports. You'll learn how to create charts, forms, and graphs, as well as how to add maps to your diagrams. You'll also learn how to create a slide show in Visio, how to use color schemes, and how to add comments to shapes.

Chapter 7, "HyperLlinking, HTML, and XML," discusses how Visio is completely Internet compatible. You'll learn how to set links between pages or documents within Visio and to documents outside Visio. You'll learn how to use Visio with HTML and the Internet. You'll learn how to save your diagrams as XML. This chapter shows you how to create hyperlinks in Visio diagrams as well as how to create HTML documents in Visio. You'll see how this would be useful for creating Web pages and for linking to Web documents and HTML Help.

Chapter 8, "Using Visio with Microsoft Office," teaches you how to use Visio with Microsoft Office products. You'll learn how to place a copy of your current drawing into an Office document and how to dynamically link Visio diagrams to Office 2000, Office 97, and some Office 95 products for automatic updates when anything changes in either the drawing or the Office document. This chapter discusses linking and embedding Visio diagrams with Word for Windows, as well as going from Excel data to a Visio diagram. It also discusses how to use the PowerPoint color schemes in Visio.

Chapter 9, "Creating Custom Shapes and Solutions," shows you how to create original shapes, both by modifying existing shapes and by creating new shapes from scratch. You'll also learn how to define custom properties for shapes, how to use and alter ShapeSheets, and how to integrate Visual Basic for Applications into your Visio diagrams.

Chapter 10, "Using Visio Professional for Engineering, CAD, and Building Planning Diagrams," introduces you to Visio Professional. You'll learn how to make the most of the precision drawing tools, how to work with CAD drawings, and how to create engineering drawings. You'll also learn about the facilities management tools that come with Visio Professional.. This chapter also includes a discussion of the added stencils and templates that come with this version.

Chapter 11, "Network Diagrams, Software Development, Web Diagrams, and Reports with Visio Professional," discusses the highly technical advanced features that come with Visio Professional. You'll learn how to use the advanced computer templates in Visio Professional, including the network and software development templates. You'll also learn how to diagram your web site, and manage web site design, using Visio Professional templates. Lastly, you'll learn about the reports that have been added to Visio Professional to help you manage all the added templates.

Appendix A, "Stencils and Templates," lists all the shapes, stencils, and templates that come with Visio Standard and Visio Professional as well as special features about each template.

Appendix B, "Resources," contains a selection of Internet and other online resources for Visio users.

Conventions Used in This Book

This book has several standard conventions for presenting information:

Defined terns are in *italics*.

Keyboard names appear in SMALL CAPITALS. If you're supposed to press several keys together, the keys are joined with a hyphen. For example, "Press CTRL-F1" means to hold down the CONTROL KEY (CTRL) and press F1.

There are three types of notes in the text:

 *A note is simply a comment related to the material being discussed.*

 *A tip is a technique for doing things faster, easier, or better in Visio.*

 *A caution is a warning to prevent you form doing something that could result in a loss of data or cause you problems.*

Other Books of Interest

If you aren't already familiar with Windows 98 and will be using it with Visio, you may want to buy *The Complete Reference Windows 98,* by John R. and Margaret Levine (Osborne/McGraw-Hill, 1998), a complete guide for Windows 98. If you're using Windows 2000, you might consider buying *Windows 2000 : A Beginner's Guide* by Martin S. Matthews (Osborne/McGraw-Hill, 2000), an inclusive, starters guide to Windows 2000. If you're using Windows ME, you might consider *buying How to Do Everything with Windows, Millennium Edition* by Curt Simmons (Osborne/McGraw-Hill, 2000), a complete guide to Windows Millennium Edition.

For More Information

For news and information about other products of interest to Visio users, check out Visio's Web page at:

http://www.microsoft.com/office/visio

There you can evaluate Visio as well as get troubleshooting tips.

Chapter 1

Visio Basics

How to...

- Find out what's new in Visio 2002
- Install Visio
- Understand the Visio screen

This chapter shows you how to install Visio and introduces you to its basic features and screen layout. You'll learn about the new features in Visio 2002. You'll learn how to install and configure the program, and be acquainted with the various options and features of Visio.

What Is Visio?

Visio is a drawing application that helps you easily create professional-looking business diagrams. Visio, by Microsoft Corporation, comes in two editions: Standard and Professional. This book covers both editions, but it focuses primarily on Visio Standard. The Professional builds on the Standard by taking all the information contained in Standard and simply adding more options and features.

 *While the whole book covers the basic concepts in chapters 10 and 11 cover Professional specifically.*

Visio Standard comes with dozens of templates and stencils to help you draw great diagrams easily, as well as ways to automate repetitive drawing tasks. Professional has several extra features that aid with common business tasks, and has some features to help engineering and facilities professionals create detailed schematics.

 *For simplicity's sake, throughout this book Visio Standard will be referred to simply as Visio. Professional will be referred to as Visio Professional.*

What's New in Visio 2002

The newest version of Visio, Visio 2002, includes several new or enhanced features over previous versions. This section outlines these changes.

Improvements and Additions to the Drawing Types

Visio has worked hard to make the diagrams you create look better and work easier with other types of diagrams. Here are just some examples of the features that have been enhanced:

- Organizational Charts now look smoother, have better reports, are easier to layout, and allow you to alter the fields displayed to show more information than ever before.

- Timeline and Gantt charts easily export and import information from one another. For example, using Information in a timeline to create a Gantt chart, and vice versa.

- Office Layout includes more shapes than ever before, and the shapes have increased movement and options, many of which are available from the new right-click shortcut menus on each shape.

- 3D directional maps have been added, allowing you to create colorful directional maps applicable to small areas and other locations requiring detailed documentation.

Visio 2002 Professional also includes dozens of updates, most notably the addition of much of the information that was in Visio Technical in previous versions. Visio 2002 Professional also has enhanced Web Site mapping and greatly expanded support for Software Development. Building Plans and Process Engineering have also been greatly expanded and enhanced.

Tighter Office Integration

Visio is now part of the Microsoft family of products, which gives it the benefit of much tighter integration with Office products. This tighter integration means Visio 2002 has the new Office 10 look, including menus that have the same personalization options that make Office applications easy to learn.

Visio also shares common functions with Office. You can take advantage of a new built-in AutoCorrect features, familiar keyboard shortcuts, and the Office spelling checker. It's easy to move among applications now that Visio 10 displays the same Open, Save, and Save As dialog boxes used in Office 10. Plus, Visio 10 now provides integration with Office clip art when installed alongside Microsoft Office.

NOTE   *To learn more about using Visio with other Office products, see Chapter 8, "Using Visio with Microsoft Office."*

New Web Interface Features

Visio has always worked well to create graphics for the Internet, but Visio 2002 has new advanced features to create web pages completely independent of any other software. You can now use Visio's Save As Web Page feature to turn your diagrams into web pages with the click of a mouse. Visio has also added an integrated XML format for deployment of Visio diagrams in a variety of new and different environments.

Visio also works with the web in other new ways. Visio's Find Shape feature automatically searches the web for shapes that meet your criteria, and Visio's automatic updates make sure you keep your copy of Visio as current as possible.

Installing Visio

Visio is easy to install. It comes on a CD-ROM, and it is compatible with Microsoft Windows 98, Windows 2000, Windows NT, and Windows ME.

CAUTION   *Installing Visio may require rebooting your system, so save all the files you have open and close all programs before you start to install Visio.*

Installing Visio usually takes about 20 minutes. The installation of Visio has two parts: installation of the Microsoft installer files and installation of the Visio system files.

To help installation go smoothly, follow these simple guidelines:

- Close all programs other than Windows currently running on your system. Visio needs to update some system files that other programs use, and it can't successfully install when they are running.

- Make sure you have your CD Key code handy. The installation program asks for the code before it will let you finish installation.

- Make sure you have at least 200 Megs free on you computer before you start the installation process. Your installation of Visio may not take this much, but it gives the installer enough space on your system to complete its job.

- Make sure you have critical Visio files and your system files backed up somewhere other than your computer. If the setup fails for any reason this will let you get your system back up and running.

■ If you can, connect your computer to the internet via a modem or network connection before you install Microsoft Visio. This will make it easier to activate your product when you first open Visio.

NOTE *Microsoft recommends you have at least 110MBs free to install Visio Standard and at least 170MBs free to install Visio Professional. Both require that you have a CD-ROM drive.*

During Installation you'll need to fill in the Visio product ID number, which is included in the Visio packaging. You should place the product ID sticker on the CD-ROM case for ease of retrevial.

Installing Microsoft System Files for Visio 2002

Visio works closely with other Microsoft products, including Microsoft Windows and Microsoft Office. The first part of the Microsoft Visio installation involves registering and setting up communication with Microsoft system files.

To start the installation of Visio, insert the CD-ROM into your computer's CD-ROM drive. The installation should start automatically. If the installation doesn't start automatically, select Run from the Start menu and then type **D:/setup** (where D is the drive letter of your CD-ROM drive), and click OK.

The first installation screen is shown in Figure 1-1. Microsoft Visio needs to add and then run all the installer files to update your system.

After the first installation screen in Figure 1-1, you'll see another preparation screen telling you that it is creating the files necessary to install Visio. When the

FIGURE 1-1   Preparing to Install

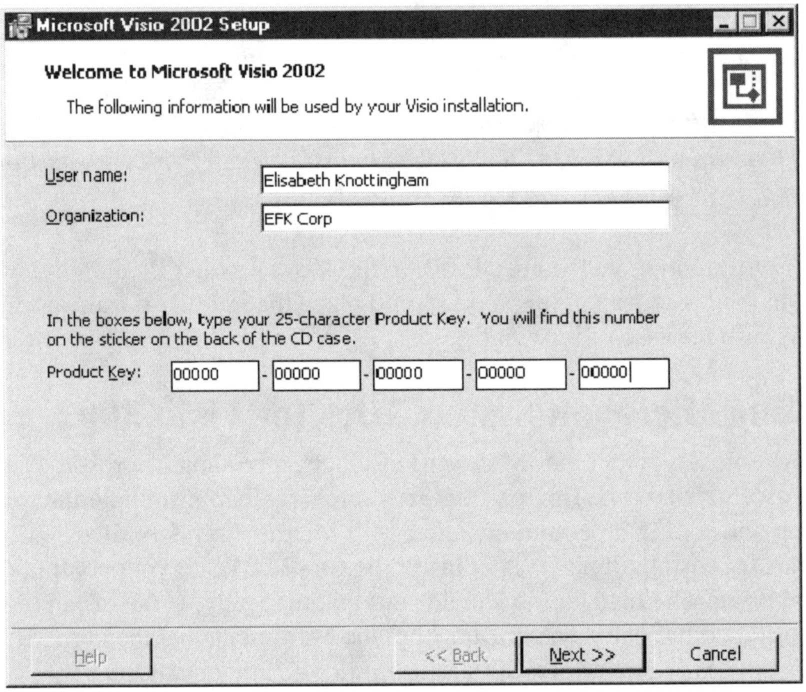

FIGURE 1-2   Entering Organization and Name Information

preparation screens are finished, you'll see the screen shown in Figure 1-2, asking you to enter your name and organization. Fill out this screen as correctly as possible since this is the information that attaches to every Visio file you create, and others who view those files will see the information. The Installation Manager automatically fills in the name of the registered user of the computer and the company name (if one was provided when installing Windows).

When you're finished entering the information, click Next. The next installation screen appears, as shown in Figure 1-3. This is the Microsoft End User License Agreement. This is a standard agreement stating that you promise to use the product only on the computer you purchased it for. When you've finished reading the License Agreement, check the I accept the terms in the License Agreement box and then click Next.

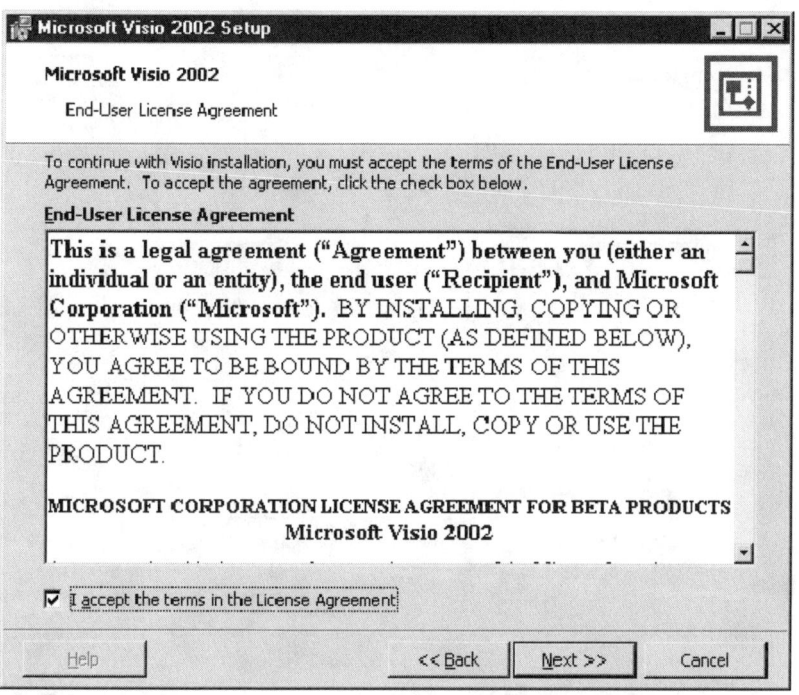

FIGURE 1-3   Microsoft End User License Agreement

Installing Visio Program Files

After you accept the terms of the license agreement, installation of the Visio program file begins. You'll see the Visio Installation Manager screen, as shown in Figure 1-4, telling you it is ready to install Visio. To continue, click Install Now.

 *Your system may require Visio to update some system files, so there may be a few more screens to your installation than the standard installation shown in this chapter.*

Once you tell Microsoft Visio to start the installation, you'll see a screen similar to the one in Figure 1-5, showing a progress bar. The progress bar shows several different stages of installation, one after the other.

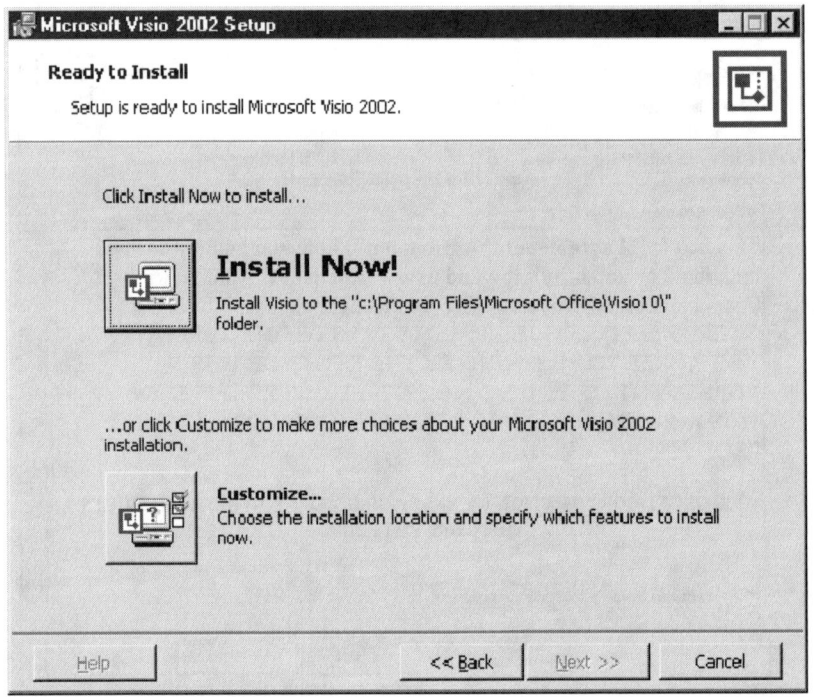

FIGURE 1-4 Install Visio Now

Once the installation of Visio program files is complete, the Installation Manager displays an Installation Complete screen, telling you the program files were installed to the hard drive, as shown in Figure 1-6.

After you're finished reviewing the Installation Complete screen, click Ok. This concludes the installation of Visio.

Customizing your Visio Installation

If for some reason the basic Visio installation does not suit your needs, you can choose to customize your Visio installation.

There are several reasons for you to need a custom installation of Visio:

- If you are installing a laptop or other computer with limited hard drive space.

- If you want to install every file Visio will ever need, you'll want to do a complete installation.

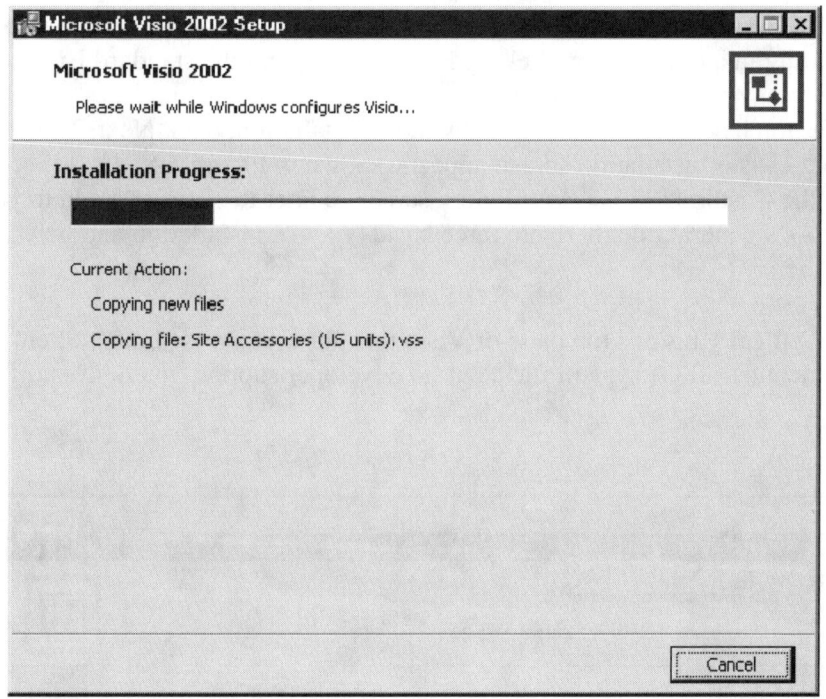

FIGURE 1-5 Progress of the Visio installation

- If you need to alter where Visio installs the files on your computer.

To customize the Visio installation, follow the standard installation procedure until you come to the Install Visio Now screen, show in Figure 1-4. On this screen, choose Custom.

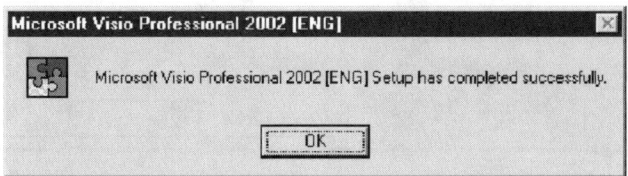

FIGURE 1-6 Installation Complete

The next screen you see is the Visio Installation Location screen seen in Figure 1-7. Use this screen to change the location of your Visio installation by either typing in a new path or clicking Browse and using the standard Browse window to navigate to the location.

Once you have set the location for Visio's installation, click Next. The Customize Visio Installation screen appears, shown in Figure 1-8.

Use the Customize Visio Installation screen to alter the files you add to your system. As a general rule there are three basic types of installation and how you can get them:

■ **Typical** Installs the parts of Visio that are usually used most often. This includes all the system files, but no developer support, and leaves off a few

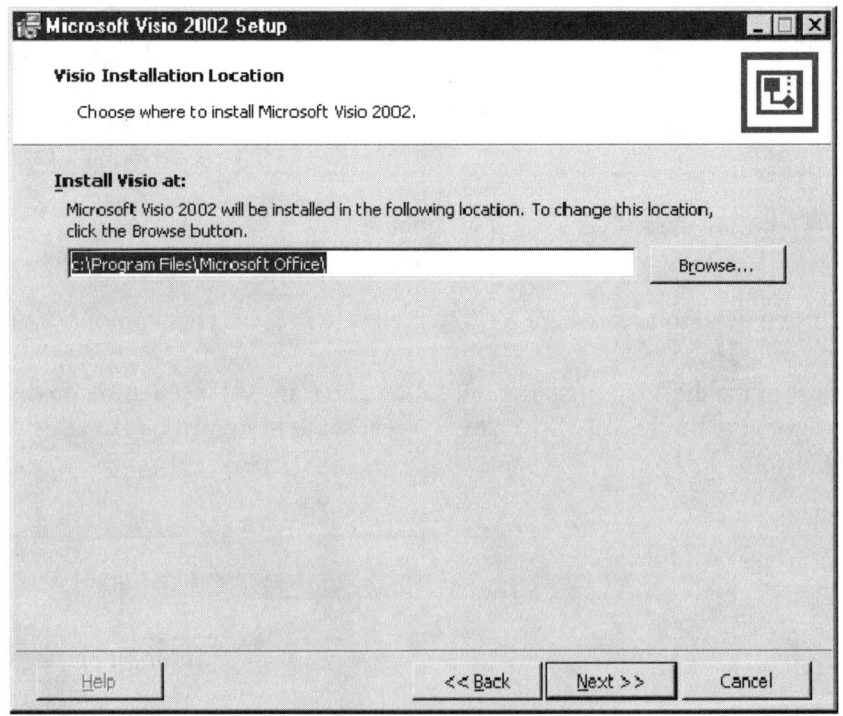

FIGURE 1-7   Visio Installation Location

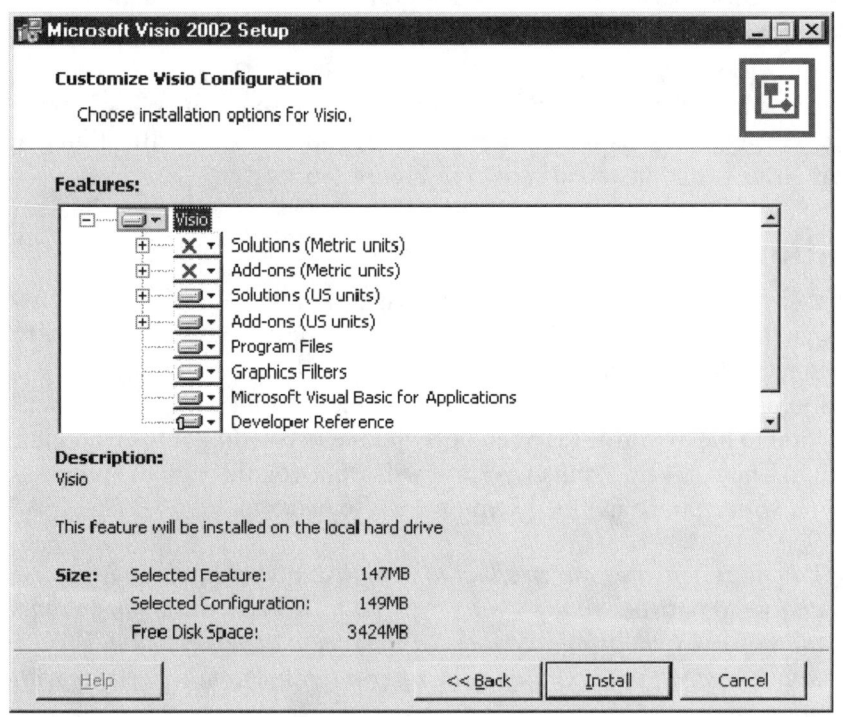

FIGURE 1-8   Customize Visio Installation

macros. The Customize Visio Installation screen is set to this installation by default.

■ **Compact**   Installs just the Visio program files. You can achieve this installation by removing the add-ons and some of the solutions.

■ **Custom/Complete**   Installs everything that comes with Visio. You can achieve this installation by making sure everything available in the Customize Visio Installation screen is selected.

NOTE   *Visio now allows you an almost infinite number of installation options. Using the Customize window gives you access to more ways to install that ever before.*

 *It is best to perform a Complete installation of Visio if you have enough space on your hard drive.*

When you are finished selecting the parts of Visio to install, click Next. The progress screen appears as shown in Figure 1-5, and then the notification that Visio has successfully installed shown in Figure 1-6.

Activation

Your installation is not complete until you have activated Visio. Activation happens the first time you open Visio. When Visio opens the first time after installation, the Activate Product Wizard appears to help you though the installation process. You can activate Visio by the internet if your computer has a connection to the World Wide Web or by phone if you do not have an internet connection. The Activate Product Wizard will walk you through the process, and supply you with a phone number if you need it to activate.

 *You must activate your product to complete installation, and if you do not choose to activate your product the first time Visio starts, do so quickly thereafter by choosing Activate Product from the Help menu. Visio will go into Reduced Functionality mode after a limited number of uses without activation.*

Getting to Know Visio

After you've installed Visio, you can start the program by going to the Windows Start menu and selecting Microsoft Visio from the list.

The first time you start Visio after installing, you will be asked to activate your product.

When you open Visio, you'll see the Choose Drawing Type window, shown in Figure 1-9.

On the left side of the Choose Drawing Type window are categories for each type of Visio drawing. In the center are the drawing types in the category you have selected from the list on the left. On the right side are four other ways to start drawing, including opening an already existing drawing, and creating a new drawing from a drawing that already exists.

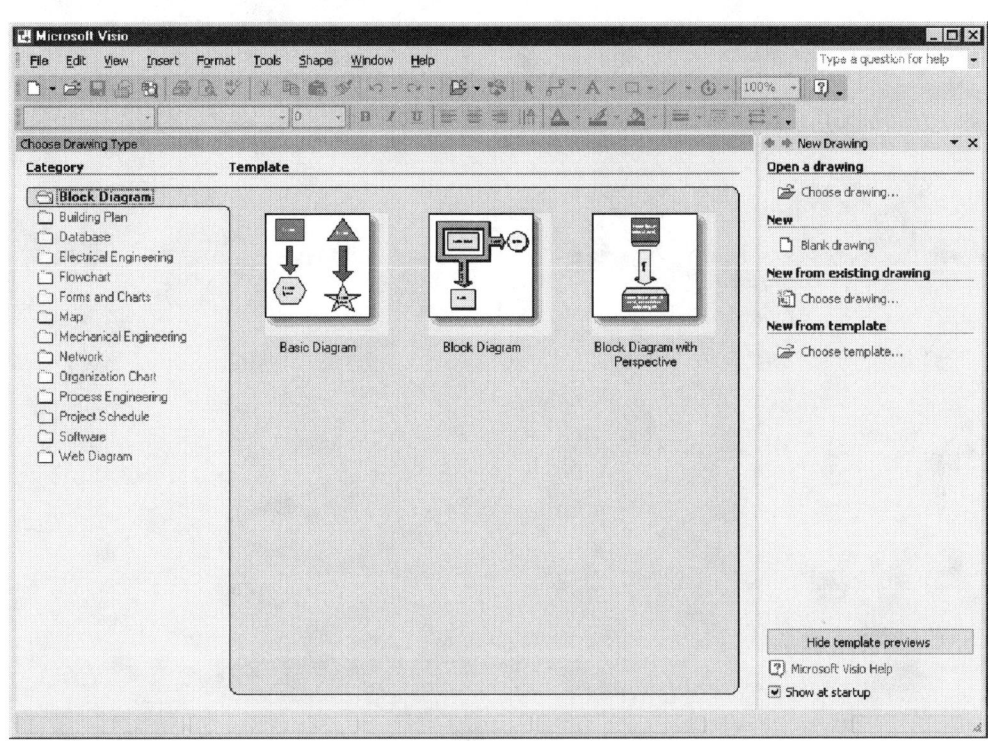

FIGURE 1-9   Choose Drawing Type window

Later, we'll discuss what each type of drawing listed in the window does; for now, simply select the Block Diagram from the list on the left, and then Basic Diagram from the Drawing Types window. When you select Basic Diagram, the main Visio window appears, as shown in Figure 1-10.

Take a moment to look at the main Visio window. Notice the drawing page in the center of the window. This is where you create a Visio diagram. The three most important parts of the main Visio window are:

■ The drawing page

■ The menus and toolbars

■ The stencils

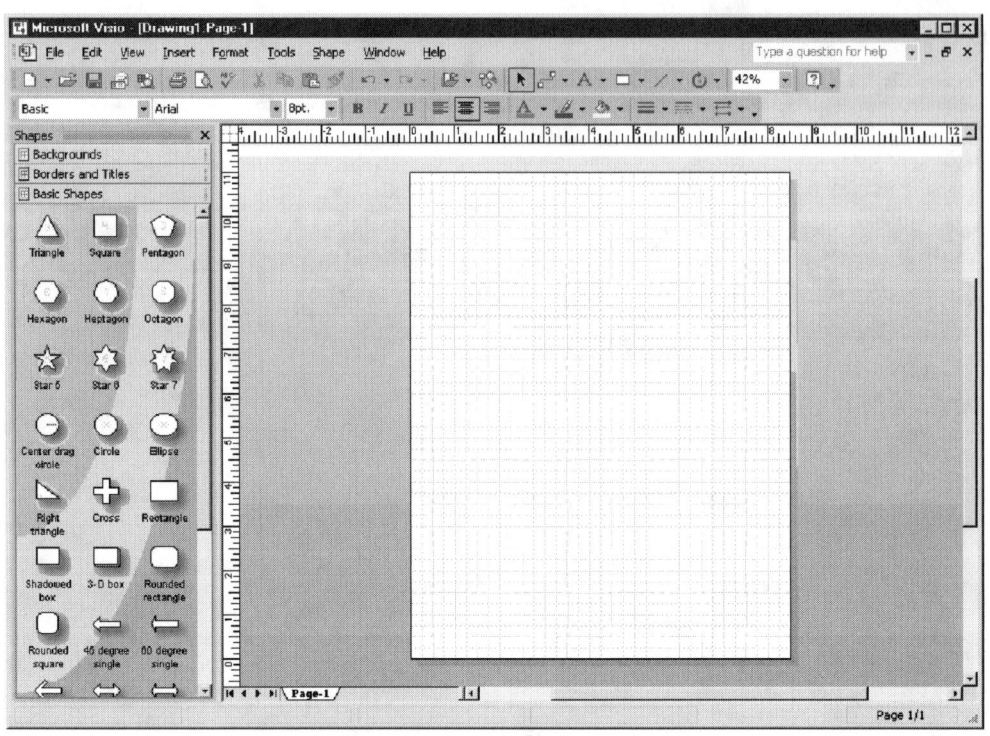

FIGURE 1-10   The Main Visio Window

Chapter 2, "Creating Your First Diagram," discusses stencils in more detail. For now, we'll focus on the other two parts—the drawing page and the toolbars and menus.

You create a drawing on the drawing page, which is contained in the drawing window. A blue background called the *pasteboard* surrounds the drawing page. The drawing page can display a grid, which consists of grid lines like those on traditional quadrille paper. The drawing page is where you'll arrange shapes as you create your diagram.

Drawing pages define the area that will appear on the paper when you print your diagram. You can think of the drawing page as a piece of paper you're working on. The pasteboard—the blue field around the drawing page—is your work surface. Any part of your diagram that is in this blue work surface won't print when you print the rest of your Visio diagram.

The drawing page title bar is located at the top of the drawing window and lists the page name and number. If you maximize the drawing window, the page name and number display in the title bar of the main Visio window, as in Figure 1-10.

> **TIP** *The pasteboard (the blue work surface) can be very handy when you have things you'd like to save with a diagram but don't wish to print, such as notes to others or extra pieces of the diagram.*

The menus in the main Visio window allow you to access all the commands you need to create Visio diagrams. The toolbars include buttons and tools you can use as shortcuts, instead of choosing menu commands.

Table 1-1 lists the various menus in the main Visio window and describes the commands they include.

We explain how to use these menus and commands in the following chapters.

> **NOTE** *Some drawing types add menus to the list in Table 1-1.*

Visio has two main toolbars, the *standard* toolbar and the *formatting* toolbar. Each has its own set of buttons. Visio's standard toolbar is much like the toolbars you find in many Microsoft Office products. However, you may not recognize several buttons. Table 1-2 describes the buttons on Visio's standard toolbar.

Menu	Description
File	Creates, opens, saves, deletes, and prints diagrams and opens stencils.
Edit	Cuts, copies, and pastes information. Also allows reordering and deletion of pages. Finds or replaces text during editing of diagrams.
View	Zooms in and out. Turns on and off toolbars, grids, rulers, and guides. Changes layer properties.
Insert	Inserts pages, graphics, Office documents, hyperlinks, and other objects.
Format	Formats text and shapes, as well as protects documents.
Tools	Checks spelling, changes the layering order of objects. Controls the snap, glue, and grid attributes of a diagram.
Shape	Controls the size, placement, order, and grouping of objects.
Window	Allows movement between open diagrams.
Help	Accesses both basic online and Web help sources.

TABLE 1-1   Visio 2000 Main Window Menus

Button	Name	Description
	New Drawing	If you click this once, it opens a new blank drawing. Through the drop-down list, you can select the drawing type from the list.
	Open	Displays the Open window, allowing you to open any -saved Visio 2000 diagram.
	Save	Saves the current diagram.
	E-mail	Opens your default email program with the current drawing as an attachment to a blank message.
	Search	Opens a search window allowing you to find any text in a drawing, or even find a file.
	Print	Prints the current diagram.
	Print Preview	Launches print preview mode.
	Spelling	Starts checking the spelling of the current diagram.
	Cut	Removes the selection to the Clipboard.
	Copy	Copies the selection to the Clipboard.
	Paste	Copies the Clipboard content to the drawing page.
	Format Painter	Allows you to use the painter tool to format and copy shapes..
	Undo	If you click this once, it removes the last action. You can use the drop down list to remove more actions.
	Redo	This enables once you have used Undo and allows you to add actions you have removed with Undo.
	Open Stencil	If you click this once, it displays the Open Stencil window. You can select the stencil from the drop-down list.
	Find Shape	Opens a window over the stencils to allow you to find any shape on the Visio stencils you have loaded on your computer.

TABLE 1-2   Visio Standard Toolbar Buttons

Button	Name	Description
	Pointer tool	Allows you to select and move shapes on the drawing page.
	Connector tool	The first of three tools in this drop-down list, all of which deal with shape functions. The Connector tool creates lines that connect shapes.
	Text tool	One of two tools that handle how text is added and looks on the page. The Text tool adds text to the page.
	Rectangle tool	One of two tools that allow you to create shapes. The Rectangle tool allows you to create freeform four-sided shapes.
	Line Tool	The first of four tools that handle adding lines to the drawing page. The Line tool allows you to create straight lines.
	Rotation tool	One of two tools that handle how shapes appear on the page. The Rotation tool handles the orientation of shapes.
42%	Zoom	Allows you to change the zoom level for your drawing.
	Help	Launches Visio 2000 help.

TABLE 1-2   Visio Standard Toolbar Buttons *(continued)*

The other main Visio toolbar, the formatting toolbar, is unique to Visio. Because Visio is a drawing program, it includes numerous graphics functions with corresponding tools. The formatting toolbar contains many of these functions, such as tools for changing colors of objects, changing font characteristics, and formatting lines. Table 1-3 describes all the tools on the formatting toolbar.

You'll learn more about the tools in Tables 1-2 and 1-3 throughout this book.

Understanding Diagrams

Before you create Visio diagrams, you need to understand some basic concepts. These concepts are the groundwork you'll use over and over as you create diagrams.

Visio diagrams are made up of shapes. These shapes can be almost anything—circles, squares, arrows, maps, clip art, and so on. You choose shapes from a *stencil*. Stencils are organized both by topic and by types of shapes. In order to choose a stencil, you should know what types of shapes you'll be using.

Button	Name	Description
Basic	All Styles	Lists all the shape styles in the current diagram.
Arial	Font	Lists all the fonts installed on your computer.
8pt.	Font Size	Allows you to change the size of your text.
B	Bold	Bolds the selected text.
I	Italics	Italicizes the selected text.
U	Underline	Underlines the current text.
≡	Align Left	Aligns the selected text block to the left.
≡	Align Center	Aligns the selected text block to the center.
≡	Align Right	Aligns the selected text block to the right.
A	Font Color	Click to change the selected text to the color displayed. Use the drop-down list to change the text to any color you like.
✎	Line Color	Click to change the outline of the selected shape to the color displayed. Use the drop-down list to change the outline to any color you like.
♦	Fill Color	Click to change the interior color of the selected shape to the color displayed. Use the drop-down list to change the interior to any color you like.
≡	Line Weight	Click to change the weight of the selected line to the last-selected weight (the default is 1). Use the drop-down list to change the line to any weight.
≡	Line Pattern	Click to change the pattern of the selected line to the last-selected pattern (the default is solid). Use the drop-down list to change the line to any pattern.
⇄	Line Ends	Click to change the ends of the selected line to the last-selected end (the default is none). Use the drop-down list to change the line to any ends.

TABLE 1-3   Visio 2000 Format Toolbar Buttons

(Note that some shapes appear on more than one stencil.) There are more than 1000 shapes in Visio Standard and Visio Professional has several hundred more shapes.

Templates contain the rules shapes use to relate to each other. They also control such things as the orientation of the drawing page and the stencils that open automatically when you create a new diagram. There are about a dozen templates in Visio Standard and several dozen more in Visio Professional. Templates are covered in detail in Chapter 4. For now, you can think of them as a helping hand that guides you as you create your drawings.

Planning Your Diagram

When you create a new drawing, you must choose a *drawing type*. The drawing type determines the stencils and template that open with the new drawing. Consequently, to select a drawing type, you need a conception of how your drawing will look. This means you must plan your diagram. Carefully planning your diagram parameters will save time and effort later.

The following questions will help you identify some of the necessary considerations before starting a drawing in Visio:

- What's the drawing about?

- What's the drawing for?

- How many different types of shapes are likely to be in the diagram?

- How are the shapes likely to be related?

- How will this diagram be viewed (i.e., printed on paper, viewed on the screen, embedded into another Windows program)?

- What size and resolution will the diagram be viewed at?

- How often will the diagram be updated? Daily? Weekly? Monthly? Never?

- Who will need to read the diagram? Will this diagram ever be passed outside your department or immediate working group?

- What will the diagram be called?

- Will the diagram be part of a larger presentation? How are you going to match the style of the diagram to the other documents?

- Is there a graphical style or look you should be adhering to, for instance a color scheme or design element you already own and want to use?

- Where will the diagram be saved? Who else will have access to see and to change the diagram?

- Will the diagram be used on a Web page?

- Will the diagram include more than one page?

- How many elements are likely to appear in the diagram?

- Will the diagram contain imported images and hyperlink tags?

- What fonts, formats, and colors will the diagram contain?

Perhaps the most important question to ask is, "What is the diagram supposed to convey to the viewer?" You should never start a diagram without the answer to that question firmly in mind. It's the most important question you can ask before you start a diagram. Visio is a great tool to help you graphically represent ideas to your readers, but to make the most of it you should always do some planning before you begin a new diagram.

Keep a list of all the Visio diagrams you've created and their content. Because the diagrams are reusable—and the shapes are easily rearranged—you can reuse parts of diagrams over and over. A list of your diagrams will help you reuse the work you've already done when creating a new diagram.

Saving a Visio Drawing

After you've created a Visio drawing, you need to save it. To save a drawing, choose Save from the File menu. The Save As dialog box appears, as shown in Figure 1-11. Replace "Drawing1" with the filename for your drawing (for example, "proposal"). Use the Save In drop-down list to navigate to the folder where you want your file to be saved. By default, Visio saves files in the My Documents folder.

If you want to change the default setting for where Visio saves drawings, select Options from the Tools menu. Click the File Paths tab and update the Drawings field with the name of the folder where drawings should be saved.

In the lower-right corner of the Save As dialog box, there is a drop down list next to the Save button. The list includes two entries: Workspace and Read Only. Workspace enables you to save the entire workspace; this box is checked by

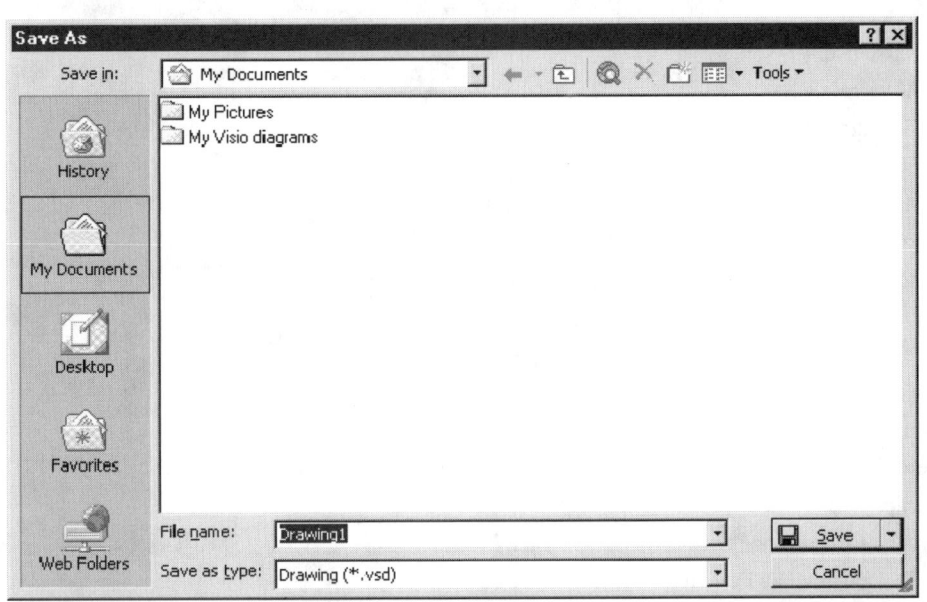

FIGURE 1-11   Save As window.

default. If you clear the check mark from Workspace, Visio doesn't save the open stencils with the drawing page. When you reopen the file, you'll need to open the stencils yourself. It's a good idea to keep the default setting unless there's some reason you don't want the stencils to open automatically with the file.

Read Only enables you to save the file as a read-only file; this is unchecked by default. If you select the read-only option, you won't be able to alter the file after you've saved it.

After you've provided the filename and adjusted the Save options as necessary, you need to choose the file type. With Visio, you can save your file in any of the formats listed here:

Format	File Extension
Visio drawing	.vsd
Visio stencil	.vss
Visio template	.vst
XML drawing	.vdx

Format	File Extension
XML stencil	.vss
XML template	.vtx
Visio 5 drawing	.vsd
Visio 5 stencil	.vss
Visio 5 template	.vst
AutoCAD Drawing	.dwg
AutoCAD Interchange	.dxf
Web Page	.htm, .html
Adobe Illustrator file	.ai
Microstation Drawing	.dgn
Computer Graphics Metafile	.cgm
Compressed Enhanced Metafile	.emz
Encapsulated PostScript file	.eps
Graphics Interchange Format	.gif
IGES Drawing File Format	.igs
JPEG Format	.jpg
Macintosh PICT Format	.pct
Portable Networks Graphics Format	.png
PostScript file	.ps
Tag Image File Format	.tif
Windows bitmap	.bmp, .dib
Windows metafile	.wmf
Zsoft PC Paintbrush bitmap	.pcx

After you've selected the file format from the "Save as type" drop-down list, click Save.

 *If you need to change the name of a file that has already been saved, choose Save As from the File menu.*

Printing a Visio Drawing

Because Visio is capable of creating many different types of diagrams, it includes many different printer settings. By default, when you print a diagram, Visio uses the printer settings for the default printer connected to your computer. These printer settings determine how Visio sizes the standard drawing page. In other words, your drawing page and your printer settings are linked, so the drawing page matches the size and shape of the paper you'll print on. However, you can change these settings to alter the size and orientation of the drawing page. To do this, you use the Page Setup dialog box.

Using the Page Setup Dialog Box

You access the Page Setup dialog box by choosing File | Page Setup. The Page Setup dialog box appears with the Print Setup tab displayed by default (see Figure 1-12). The Print Setup tab shows the printer paper size and orientation, along with the drawing page size and orientation. The picture on the right side of the dialog box shows the relative orientations of both, helping you make sure your diagram prints the way you want it to.

If you change the printer paper orientation, by default you also change the drawing page orientation. However, there are options on other tabs of the Page Setup dialog box that may affect page size and orientation. To make sure your

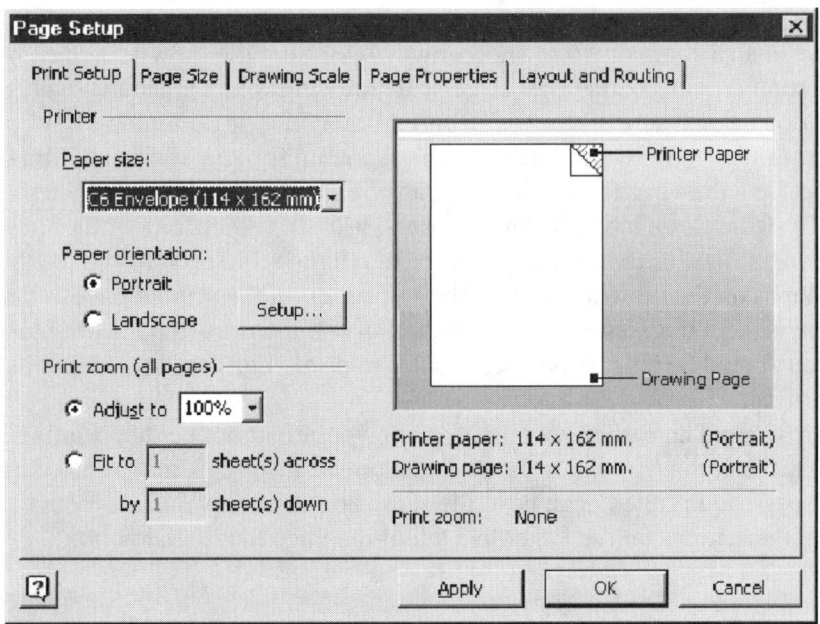

FIGURE 1-12   Print Setup window.

drawing prints correctly, verify that your paper orientation and your drawing page orientation are the same.

Troubleshooting Printing Problems

Sometimes Visio diagrams don't print the way you'd like them to because a page setting has been set incorrectly. Because your drawing page and your printer's paper settings are so dependent on one another, it's important to make sure both have been set correctly before you print a diagram.

To resolve a printing problem, view your diagram in Print Preview. This displays all the page breaks and margins in gray on top of your diagram, allowing you to see how your diagram breaks across pages.

The most common problem occurs when a large drawing prints across several pages by accident. To avoid this, make sure your drawing page and your printer page have the same orientation. If the diagram still prints across several pages (called *tiling*), try reducing the Print Zoom on the Page Size tab of the Page Setup dialog box. By default, this is set so the drawing page and the printed page have a one-to-one correspondence. If your drawing is large, its size may not allow you to print on one page. By reducing the print zoom, you can fit large drawings on one page.

You can also zoom down in another way by setting the drawing scale. Architectural drawings and other large-scale drawings use a standard scale so they print on one page. Many of the architectural or engineering templates have a drawing scale already set up, but you can set one up for yourself in any drawing.

To set up a drawing scale, open the Page Setup window from the File menu. On the Drawing Scale tab, you can choose to use a 1:1 scale, any of the standard engineering scales, or define your own scale. All the scale options reduce the size of the shapes on the drawing page so they fit better on the printed page.

If you've kept the drawing page orientation and the printed page orientation the same, you should be able to use these scales to print your drawing on one page and prevent tiling.

If you've used an earlier version of Visio, you might notice that printing has gotten a lot easier in Visio. For the simplest printing settings, make sure the drawing page and printed page have the same orientation by default by not changing the settings on the Page Size tab of the Page Setup dialog box.

1

Summary

In this chapter, you've seen how to install and start Visio and were introduced to the menus and toolbar buttons. You've also been introduced to the new features in Visio 2002. You've also learned the basics of creating Visio drawings—including how to start, save, and print them.

In the next chapter, you'll learn how to create a basic drawing.

Chapter 2

Creating Your First Diagram

How to…

- Create Your First Drawing
- Open a Stencil
- Drag Shapes
- Change Shapes
- Add Text
- Connect Shapes
- Use Visio Tools
- Save Your Diagram

The previous chapter showed you how to install and configure Visio and arrange the contents of the toolbar and menus.

This chapter will introduce you to creating Visio diagrams. You'll learn how to create a drawing using the standard tools such as stencils, connectors, and templates. You will also be shown how to use the text rotation, drawing, freehand, shapes, and pointer tools.

Understanding Shapes and Stencils

In other desktop publishing programs, you create the shapes and lines yourself, using a variety of tools. This can make the diagrams you produce look a little amateurish, and it certainly adds to the time and effort required to make a diagram. Visio makes creating diagrams easy by providing "smart" shapes that behave predictably when you move or resize them.

SmartShape symbols are shapes you would normally have to draw and refine yourself, like squares and circles. There are tens of thousands of predefined SmartShape symbols that come with Visio, allowing you to quickly add a wide variety of simple or complex shapes to drawings. Figure 2-1 shows examples of three common shapes: a circle, a square, and a five-pointed star. These are examples of SmartShape technology.

Visio shapes come with dimensions and other features that have been programmed into Visio. They have controls and dimensions that allow you to

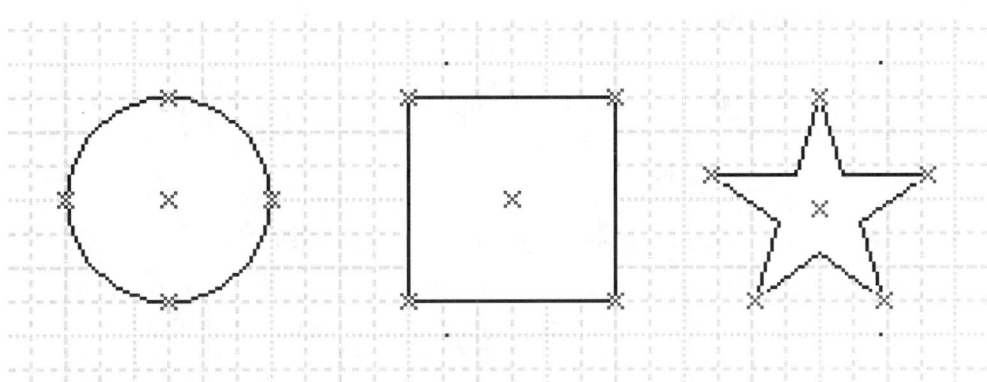

FIGURE 2-1   A SmartShape circle, square, and five-pointed star

customize them while still maintaining usable, professional-looking shapes. For example, in other desktop publishing programs, a circle drawn with a standard circle tool can be changed into an ellipse with the wrong click of a mouse. Visio's SmartShape circle, on the other hand, is controlled by a line from its center to its edge. That means the shape will always be a circle, no matter how you manipulate it with the mouse.

Visio groups shapes into *stencils* so you don't have to browse through all the shapes for every diagram you create. Stencils are collected in *folders*, so you can easily find the right stencil for the type of diagram you are creating. Visio ships with dozens of stencils packed with shapes ready for you to use. This means, for example, that you don't have to create a five-pointed star by drawing and assembling each line; instead, you simply choose the five-pointed SmartShape star from the stencil and drag it to your paper. Stencils save a lot of time. You don't have to know every shape in Visio; you just have to pick the right stencil. Stencils also ensure that all examples of one type of shape look exactly the same, because they all come from the same master shape. (Master shapes are explained in more detail in Chapter 4.) This consistency adds a level of professionalism to your drawings.

TIP   *You can also find a particular shape, and the stencil it resides on, by using the Find Shape button.*

Opening a Stencil

Most drawing types, called *templates*, have attached stencils that open when you select that drawing type. A basic drawing comes with three basic stencils. For many other drawings, you'll need to open another stencil. In this example, you'll open the Callouts stencil. Here's how:

1. Start Microsoft Visio selecting it from the Programs folder on the Start menu.

2. The Choose Drawing Type window appears, as shown in Figure 2-2.

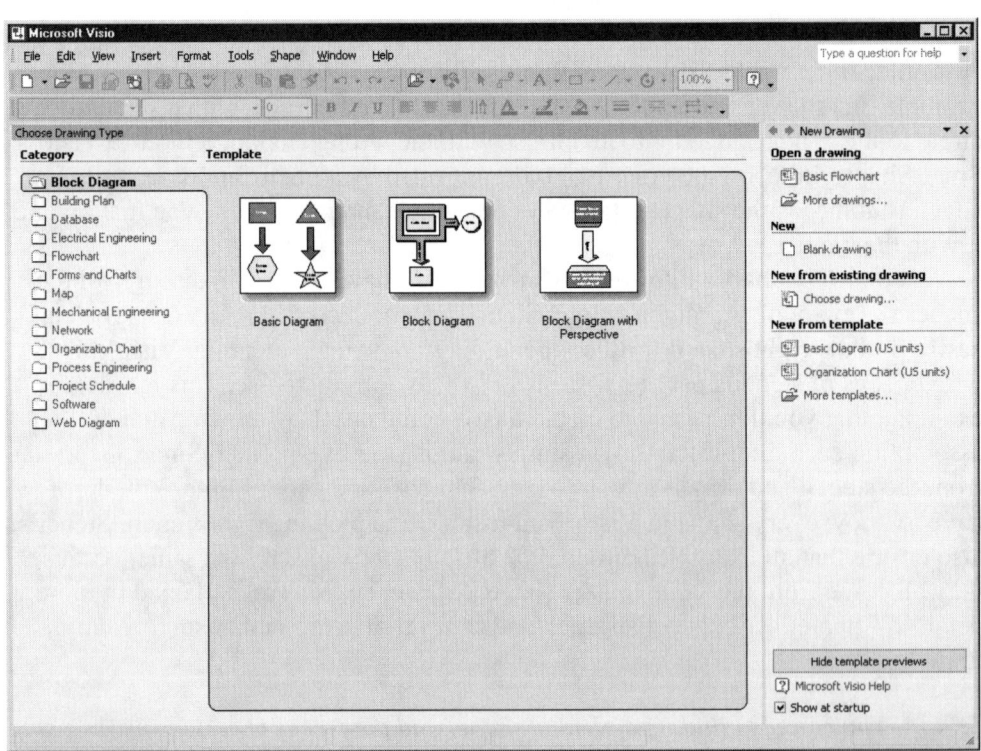

FIGURE 2-2   Choose Drawing Type

3. Open the basic drawing folder by selecting Block Diagram beneath Category.

4. Open a new drawing by selecting Basic Diagram beneath Template.

The main Visio window appears with a blank drawing, and three stencils.

5. Select Open Stencil by choosing Stencil from the File menu, or click the Open Stencil button on the toolbar.

The Open Stencil dialog box appears (shown in Figure 2-3) with a list of all the stencil folders.

6. Now open the Visio Extras folder by double-clicking it or by selecting it and clicking Open.

7. Open the Callouts stencil by double-clicking it or by selecting it and clicking Open.

The Callouts stencil appears on the left side of the window as shown in Figure 2-4.

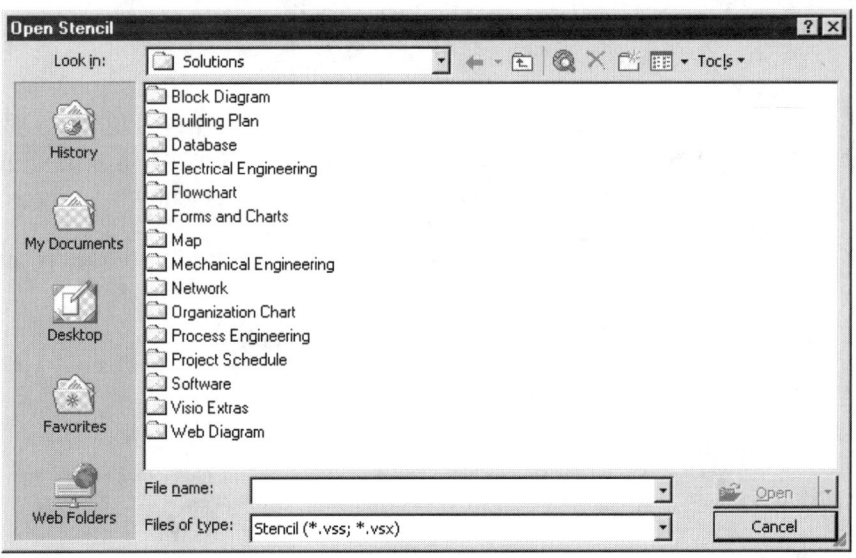

FIGURE 2-3   Open Stencil dialog box

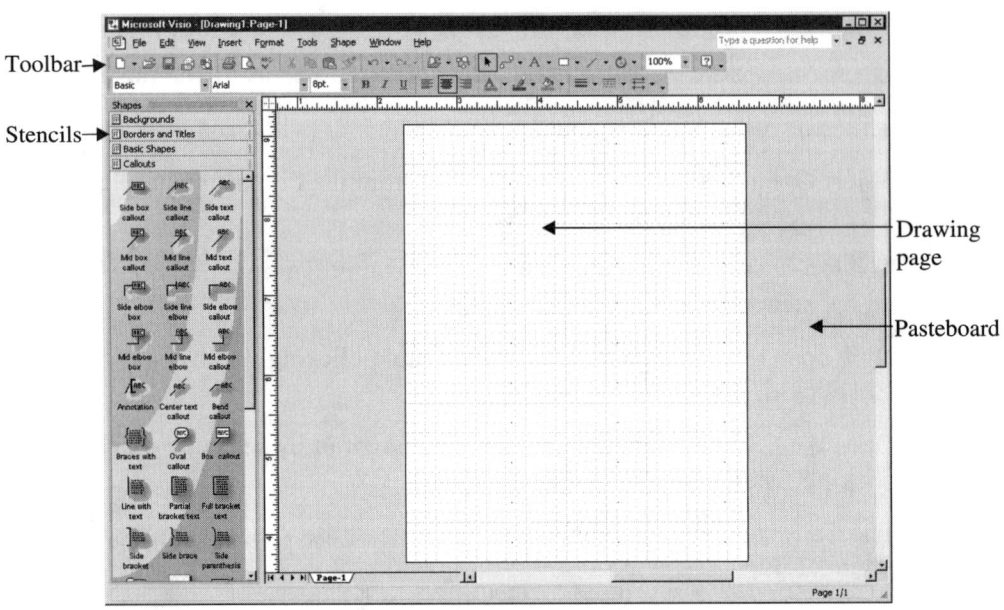

Toolbar➤

Stencils➤

Drawing page

Pasteboard

FIGURE 2-4   Main Visio window with Callouts stencil

Now that you have opened a stencil, your Visio window looks a little different than it did in Chapter 1. Take a moment to look at the screen shown in Figure 2-4. It shows you the names for each area in the Visio window.

There are five parts to the Visio window:

■ Drawing page

■ Toolbar

■ Pasteboard

■ Status bar

■ Stencil

Drawing Page   The drawing page indicates which part of your Visio diagram actually prints on paper. It is white with grid lines and has a slight shadow to indicate a 3-D page.

Toolbar   The toolbar in Visio is like the toolbar in most Microsoft Office programs. There are several drop-down buttons that give you access to other buttons. When you use a button, you launch a tool or function that you will use in creating your Visio diagrams.

Pasteboard   The pasteboard is the area on which the drawing page sits. It is indicated by the blue space around the page. You can place objects on the pasteboard; however, because they're not on the drawing page, they won't print.

Stencil   You drag shapes from the stencil to create your diagram. Figure 2-4 shows the Callouts stencil.

Status bar   The status bar gives information about the object you have selected. This is where Visio displays the width, height, and degree of rotation of the object. Figure 2-5 gives you a view of a sample status bar showing the width and height of a shape.

Dragging the Shapes

Now that you're familiar with the main Visio window, you can begin using shapes.

Visio shapes work on the "drag-and-drop principle." Simply click on a shape and, while holding down your mouse button, drag the shape onto the page and release the button. That's all there is to it! A standard-sized shape appears in the center of the page. It's a separate object you can then pick up and move around with your mouse. Later in this chapter you'll learn how to arrange and resize objects.

NOTE   *No matter how much they might look like buttons, shapes on stencils don't work like standard Windows buttons. You can't double-click to open them or move them to the drawing page; you need to drag them from the stencil to place them on the page.*

Practice dragging shapes onto the page until you get a feel for the way shapes and stencils work. It's important to be comfortable with this feature before you begin creating your first diagram—and it's kind of fun to drag the shapes onto the page.

Types of Shapes

On the Basic Shapes stencil you'll notice there are several different types of shapes. For instance, there is a standard square. Further down, in the sixth row, there's a 3-D box. These different types of squares work a little differently. There are three categories of shapes in Visio:

- 1-D shapes
- 2-D shapes
- 3-D shapes

You can use all three categories of shapes in your Visio diagrams.

1-D Shapes

1-D shapes are connector shapes and are very common in Visio diagrams. All lines and connectors in Visio are 1-D shapes, which mean they behave as if they just have endpoints, but no depth or height. Most 1-D shapes come off a stencil, but you can use the line-drawing tool to create them, too. Any single line is a 1-D shape. The Connector tool allows you to create lines very similar to the connector shapes you'll get from the stencils.

To see a 1-D shape, drag the Dynamic Connector shape from the last row of the Basic Shapes stencil. When you drop it onto your page, make sure that it doesn't touch any other shapes, or Visio tries to connect them. When you select a connector, Visio displays something like this:

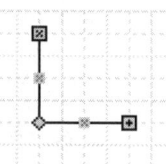

Connectors and all 1-D shapes have only two ends. One end has a green box with a plus, the other a green box with an "x". This allows you to place the 1-D shapes with an arrow at one end in the correct direction. This ensures the connectors know which object is the parent of the two objects you're connecting.

NOTE *Make sure the plus end of any 1-D object is on the primary object in your diagram, while the "x" end is on the secondary object.*

2-D Shapes

2-D shapes are the most common Visio shapes. The first three rows of the Basic Shapes stencil are all 2-D shapes, which include things like boxes, stars, and circles. You use 2-D shapes in almost every diagram you create, and they all behave the same way.

Try dragging the triangle from the Basic Shapes stencil onto the page. You'll see something that looks like this:

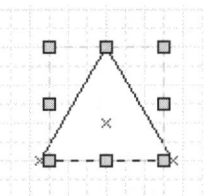

When you select the triangle, the green squares on the surrounding box are the *shape handles*. They allow you to change the size and shape of the object within certain parameters. For instance, you could make the triangle very tall and thin, but it would still have three sides. You can't change the basic parameters of any Visio SmartShape, and this is most obvious with 2-D shapes. There are some shapes that can change quite a bit and others that cannot. For example, a rectangle can look like a square, but a square can't look like a rectangle.

There are eight resizing boxes on the square surrounding a selected 2-D shape. If you pull on one of the corners, you resize the shape proportionally; in other words, the relative dimensions of the figure stay the same. The boxes on the sides of the surrounding square allow you to change the proportions of the 2-D shape; for example, pulling on the boxes on the left and right sides of a rectangle changes the width without changing the height.

3-D Shapes

3-D objects are the least common of Visio shapes. There's only one 3-D shape on the Basic Shapes stencil—a box. Drag the 3-D box from the sixth row of the Basic Shapes stencil to your page to see what it looks like. 3-D shapes are meant to represent the most lifelike objects in Visio, and they have an extra handle that allows you to control their depth. Your 3-D box should look like this:

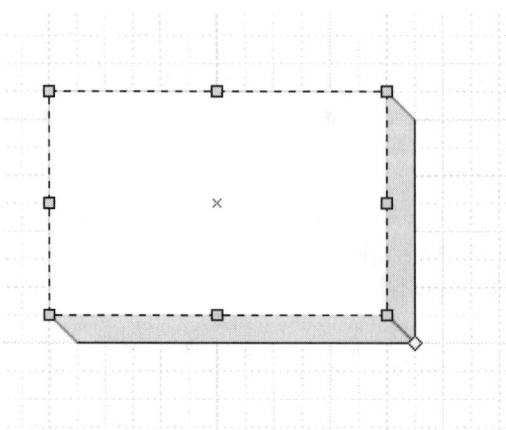

The tiny yellow diamond in the lower-right corner of the shape allows you to control the depth and angle of shadow for a 3-D object.

You'll rarely use 3-D objects; however, they can be very useful to indicate the top of a flowchart or some other important part of your diagram. Visio has two entire stencils dedicated to 3-D images, both in the Block Diagram folder, called Blocks Raised and Blocks with Perspective.

 *Make sure all the 3-D objects you use on one page have the same shadow depth. Otherwise, your drawing will look lopsided.*

Building Your First Diagram

Once you're comfortable with dragging shapes onto your page and you understand how the basic shapes work, you're ready to put the parts together into a Visio diagram. This section walks you though each step of the process.

Make sure you have the Basic Shapes stencil open to complete this drawing, and that you have a Visio window that looks like the one shown earlier in Figure 2-4. Creating your first drawing involves all the normal steps of diagram creation:

- Dragging and arranging
- Sizing
- Connecting
- Adding text

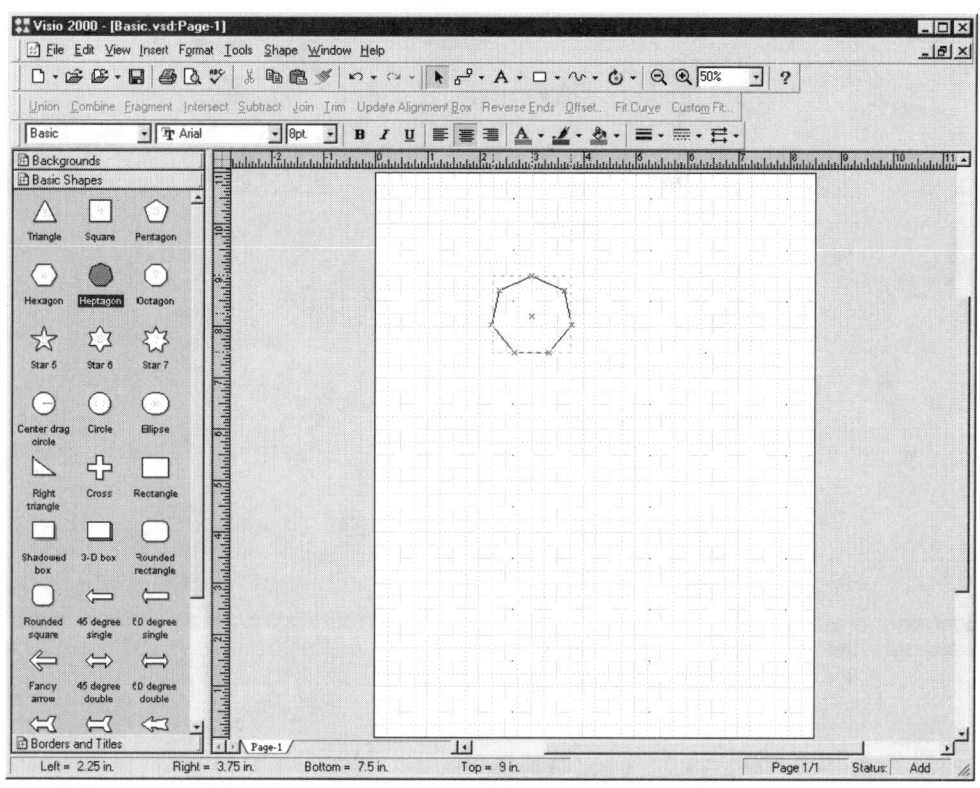

FIGURE 2-5   Dragging a shape to the drawing page?

Dragging and Arranging

You learned the basic techniques of dragging shapes earlier in this chapter. Now you'll need to drag the shapes for your diagram onto the page. Remember that the shapes on stencils don't work like buttons. Instead, you "pick them up" with the mouse, and "drop" them on the page by clicking and holding the mouse button as you drag the shape from the stencil.

Drag a square, a triangle, two arrows, and a circle to your blank page and place them so they're roughly in the arrangement shown in Figure 2-6.

Once all your shapes are on the page, you're ready to place them in the correct locations. Suppose you want to place all of the shapes in a straight line. You can

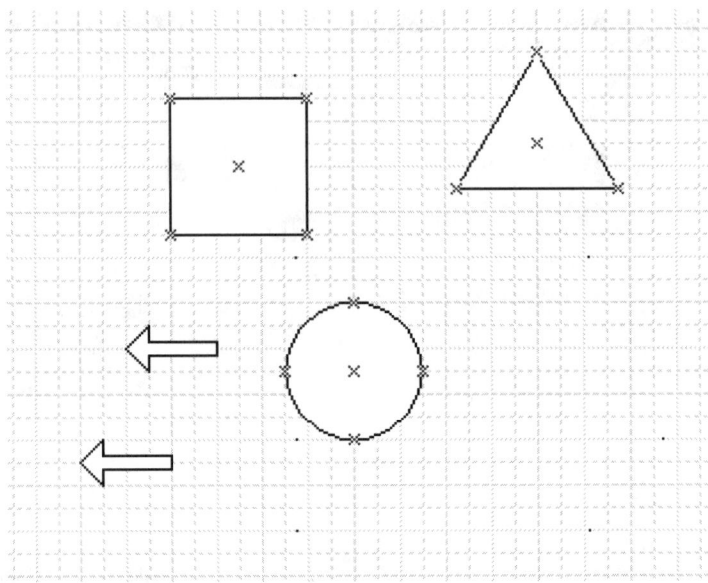

FIGURE 2-6 Add these shapes to your first drawing

easily line them up by using the grid to center the objects. Visio helps you with this by setting shapes to snap to the grid lines by default.

Sizing

Now that you have the shapes on your page, you'll notice that the standard circle looks smaller than the standard square. Both shapes have the standard dimensions, but because the circle has rounded corners, it looks a little smaller. This isn't a problem, because Visio allows you to quickly and easily change the size of a shape.

First, select the circle to resize it. You'll know it's selected, because a box with green squares at the vertices and in the middle of each side appears around it. These are the control handles. Next, click on one of the green control handles and drag it a short distance from the center of the circle. This resizes the circle. Now your drawing should look something like the one in Figure 2-7.

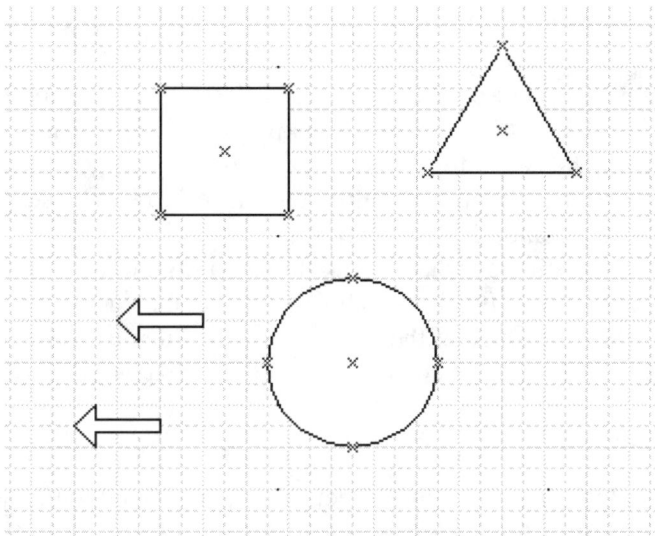

FIGURE 2-7   Resize the circle in your first drawing

 *These green control handles appear for any shape you've selected, allowing you to resize the shape. For any shape other than the circle or square, dragging on the green control handles on the sides of the control box also reshapes the object.*

Connecting

After your shapes have been arranged and resized, you're ready to make sure they're connected. Connecting shapes is one of the huge advantages of Visio: once a shape has been connected, it takes effort to disconnect it. Connections act like glue, holding your pieces together so you can't accidentally move them.

Connections can only happen at control points. Luckily, there are several control points around shapes, usually at every corner and in the middle of most sides. For shapes like the arrow, there is a control point at the tip and the end. For 1-D objects, there are control points at each end. For circles and round objects, there are four control points, one on each side of the selection box, except for circles or ellipses with the center drag feature, which only have one place where you can connect.

 *To make it easier to see them, control points are a green box with a small "X" in them.*

To make sure your shapes are connected, click on the control point of one arrow and move it until it touches the control point of another shape. You know the shapes have touched a control point when a small box appears between the two shapes over their contact point. If you drop the shape there, it loosely connects to the next shape and becomes difficult to move.

Connect the shapes in your diagram as shown in Figure 2-8 so that the arrows are connected to the circle. It is impossible to connect the end of the arrow to the side of the triangle, or the side of the square, because there are no control points there. Simply get the end of the arrow as close to the shapes as possible.

Adding Text

Once you have all the shapes in the correct places, connected with the arrows, you are ready to start adding text.

To add text, double-click on the shape, or just click once and start typing. When you're able to edit the text of a shape, a text box opens over the shape. Double-click the square, until looks like Figure 2-9.

Simply start typing, and the text appears in the box. For this example, type **Output** in the text box. Figure 2-10 shows the drawing with text added.

By default, text in Visio is set to center both horizontally and vertically within a shape. You can change that with the tools on the text-editing toolbar, or by

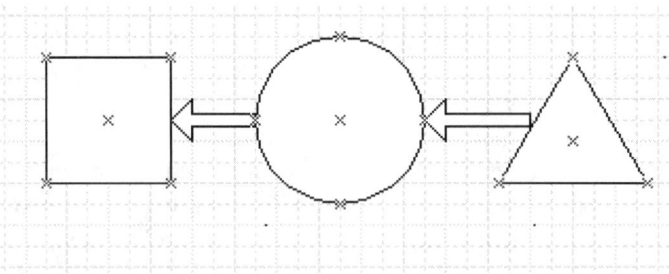

FIGURE 2-8   Connect the shapes in your first drawing.

2

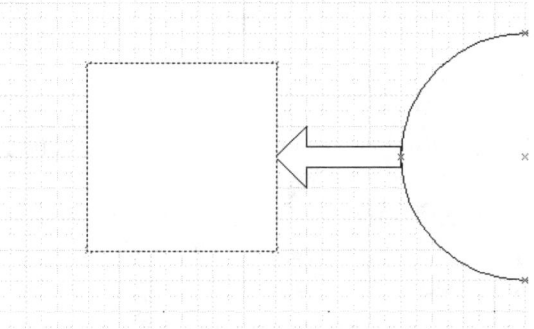

A text box

selecting Format | Text from the drop-down menu. All the text-editing features of Visio work like the text-editing features in your favorite word-processing program.

In Visio, the default text size is 8 pt, but you'll rarely want to use that size. Once you've added the text to your square, you can change the point size by selecting another size from the drop-down menu on the toolbar. For this example, the point size is 12 pt.

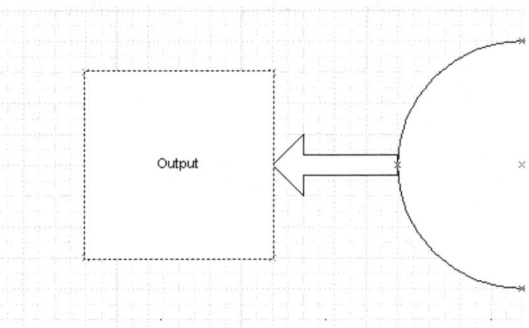

Add text to your first drawing

Now add text to the circle and the triangle in the same way. As you do, notice how the text is always centered in the middle of the objects.

Saving

Once you have added text to your drawing, you're finished creating your first Visio diagram. The last step is to save your diagram.

Go to File | Save As, and a standard Save dialog box appears. Select a place to save and a title for your diagram. Click OK. The Visio Details dialog box appears, prompting you for information about your new diagram. Enter as much information as you'd like, and click OK.

You have now created and saved your first complete Visio diagram. Congratulations!

Using the Tools

As you created your first diagram, you may have noticed that there are several tools on the toolbar to the right of the stencil and pointer buttons. These are the Visio tools.

Visio is packed full of useful and unique tools that help you create stunning, professional-looking diagrams. There are several different tools on the Visio main toolbar. In Chapter 1, you were given a brief outline of the use of each tool, but to make the most of these powerful tools you need more than a quick outline. The tools on the main toolbar are some of the most frequently accessed tools in Visio, and they fall into five main categories, based on their function:

- Connection and Replication

- Text

- Shape

- Drawing

- Alteration

NOTE   *You can have only one tool selected at a time, including the Pointer tool. The active tool is highlighted on the toolbar.*

Connection and Replications Tools

In the first set of buttons in Visio's mail toolbar are three tools dealing with connecting and replicating shapes.

The replication tool is called the Stamp tool and it helps you create the exact same shape over and over on your drawing page. The stamp tool is useful to give you unlimited copies of a shape you have altered or added to your Visio drawing page.

The connection tools are the connector tool and the connector point tool. Connection tools allow you to create connection lines between shapes quickly and easily and help you make sure that shapes connect exactly where you want them to. They also allow you to choose the location of connection points on an object. It's important to note that to make a solid connection with a line on any of the shapes that come with Visio, you'll need to make the two pieces meet at a connection point. Connection points have been set for all SmartShape symbols and are added to any clip art as you import it into Visio.

Connector Tool

The Connector tool creates 1-D connector lines between any two shapes you drag from a stencil. This is very useful when you're creating a flow chart or other diagram with many connections. The connector line is always the same, with the plus end attached to the first object and the "x" end attached to the second.

To use the Connector tool this way, simply select it from the toolbar before you drag the shapes from the stencil. As soon as the second shape has been placed on the page, Visio draws the connection line.

> NOTE   *Visio attaches the connector line to the closest points on the two shapes, regardless of the shapes between them. You can move the endpoints of the connection line with the Pointer tool.*

The Connector tool also allows you to create a connection line between any two legal connection points, even if they're on the same object. This means you can create a 1-D connection line between two points of the same object, if you wish, or between any two objects no matter when you dragged them to the drawing page.

To use the Connector tool this way, simply select it from the toolbar, click on a connection point and drag the cursor to any other connection point. Visio draws a 1-D connector between the two connection points.

 *You can tell you have the Connector tool selected because the cursor has a small 1-D connector line underneath and slightly to the right.*

Connection Point Tool

 The Connection Point tool allows you to add, move, and delete connection points on any shape in Visio. A connection point is a small point, usually at the corners and center point of a 2-D or 3-D shape, and at the ends of any 1-D object.

The ability to change connection points allows you to make sure your shapes connect exactly where you'd like them to and helps solve the sometimes difficult problem of connection lines behaving in ways you wouldn't like.

 *The Connection Point tool always works on the selected shape. It is best if, before using this tool, you use the Pointer tool to select the shape you wish to work with.*

To add a new connection point to the selected shape, hold down the CTRL key (the pointer displays a little × above it) and click the shape where you want to add the connection point. The new connection point is magenta while you have the shape selected so you'll be sure to see it.

To delete or move a connection point, you first need to select it. To select a connection point, position the mouse pointer over the connection point (the pointer is a four-headed arrow), and click. The connection point turns magenta when selected, just like it does when you add a connection point. Then, to delete a connection point, make sure it's selected and press the DELETE key.

 *You cannot delete a connection point that has something glued to it.*

To move a connection point, make sure the connection point is selected, then drag it to a new location. It stays highlighted in magenta until you select another connection point.

Stamp Tool

 The Stamp tool allows you, with one click, to make a copy of any object on your page or any object in any open stencil. These copies are called *instances* in Visio. You can create an infinite number of any shape you would like.

To create instances of a shape, first make sure you select the shape you want to copy. If the shape is on your drawing page, simply select it. If you'd like to copy a shape on a stencil, click on it, but don't drag it to your desktop. A dark-blue box appears around the shape on the stencil to show it has been selected. The selected shape becomes the master from which all your copies are made. Once the shape has been selected, then select the Stencil tool from the toolbar. The cursor changes to a shape similar to the one on the tool button. If you click anywhere in the drawing area, a replica, or instance, of the shape appears.

TIP   *This is a particularly great tool for when you need lots of copies of an object you've imported from another program. Instead of importing and reimporting, you can simply copy it.*

The Text Tools

Adding text to your Visio diagram is so important it's almost a requirement. The text tools allow you to add text to your shapes, and control how that text behaves. There are two text tools, the basic text tool that helps you add text to your shapes, and the text rotation tool that controls how the text displays in relation to the shape itself.

The Text tool

The Text tool is the tool you'll use the most after the Pointer tool. The Text tool, shown in the left-hand margin, works the same way as the Shape | Edit Text command you used in your first drawing. The Text tool allows you to add text to any shape, or to create a free-standing text block.

To add text to a shape, make sure the Text tool is selected on the toolbar, then select the shape. Visio zooms in on the shape, and a text-editing box appears with a text cursor blinking in the center. See Figure 2-10 for an example of a text box. Start typing to add text to the shape.

NOTE   *By default, all text in Visio is set to be 8 pt and centered, but 8 pt is usually too small to be readable on the printed page. Change the text size or justification using Format | Text.*

To create a free-standing text block, select the Text tool on the toolbar, then click anywhere on the drawing window that doesn't contain a shape. A text-editing box opens with a text cursor blinking in the center. Simply type to add text. You can resize free-standing text blocks once you have added text, just as you resize any other 2-D shape.

 *You can double-click on any shape at any time, and you'll automatically be taken into the text-editing box.*

Text Block Tool

 The Text Block tool allows you to control the orientation of your text block. All text that you attach to shapes is oriented to display at the default set for that shape. The default assumes the shape will be used with a certain orientation, and the text block is set to be read at that orientation. If you rotate a shape, the text rotates to stay in the same relationship to the shape and may become unreadable. For example, if you rotate a shape ninety degrees to the right, the text rotates with the shape and would now need to be read from the bottom on the page to the top. To solve this problem, Visio created the Text Block tool, which works in much the same way as the Rotation tool, except it rotates just the text on a shape.

To rotate a text block, first make sure the Text Block tool is selected from the toolbar. Select the text block, if it is a stand-alone block, or the shape that contains the text block. The same circular handles appear at the corners of the shape, but when you select one and begin to rotate, instead of the entire shape moving, only the text block rotates. For some rectangular and irregular shapes this is indicated by a lightly grayed version of the selection box, showing how much rotation you've given to the text block.

Just as with the standard Rotation tool, the degree of control you have with the Text Block Rotation tool is controlled by the distance from the rotation point for the text block, with the same set of defaults. The Text Block tool also controls the rotation point for the text block exactly as the Rotation tool controls it for shapes.

Shape Tools

Even though Visio has hundreds of pre-created shapes, there are times when making your own simple shapes is quicker and easier than altering one of Visio's shapes. The Shape tools allow you to create your own simple shapes for use on the drawing page. Each shape created by these tools acts like a standard Visio shape, with green boxes at its vertices, making it capable of standard resizing operations.

Rectangle Tool

 The Rectangle tool allows you to draw 2-D squares and rectangles. Although Visio comes with shapes for both squares and rectangles, this tool can be useful when you need to create a standard 2-D shape on your own. The shapes created by the Rectangle tool and the shapes you can drag off the Basic Shapes stencil behave identically after you complete the drawing process. For both rectangles and squares, Visio displays the size of the 2-D object you're creating in the status bar.

To draw a rectangle, first make sure you have the Rectangle tool selected on the toolbar. Then click and drag diagonally in any direction. A rectangle starts to appear between the cursor and the starting point, with the cursor at the corner diagonally away from the starting point.

To draw a square, hold down the SHIFT key as you drag. Instead of a rectangle appearing below the cursor as you drag, a square appears below and slightly to the right. Also, when you create a square your cursor will be on one of the sides adjacent to the corner of the starting point, and you'll define the square by one side alone.

To edit a square or rectangle you created using the Rectangle tool, first create the shape. Then, depending on what you wish, you may either use the standard Pointer tool or the Pencil tool to change the shape. If the shape simply needs to be resized, use the Pointer tool and the green shape handles to resize as you would any other shape. If the shape needs to be altered more fundamentally, use the Pencil tool on one of the control points to change the orientation of one of the sides. Remember that the Pencil tool creates lines if you pull directly away from the center, but it makes arcs if you pull in any other direction.

Ellipse Tool

The Ellipse tool allows you to draw 2-D circles and ellipses. Although Visio comes with shapes for both circles and ellipses, this tool can be useful when you need to create a standard 2-D shape on your own. The shapes created by the Ellipse tool and the shapes you can drag off the Basic Shapes stencil behave identically after you've completed the drawing process. As you draw circles and ellipses, the status bar displays the size of the rectangle that would encompass your 2-D object.

To draw an ellipse, make sure the Ellipse tool is selected on the toolbar. Then click and drag in any direction. An ellipse appears between the cursor and the starting point. As you draw, the cursor has a small ellipse below it and slightly to the right.

To draw a circle, hold down the SHIFT key as you move the cursor. The cursor has a small circle below and slightly to the right.

Both ellipses and circles are closed shapes made up of two arc segments. There are control points at four places on either shape, so you can change the way they look with the Pencil tool.

Like any 2-D shape, you can change the size by using the green handles and the Pointer tool.

 When you use the Pencil tool to reshape an object created by the Ellipse tool, the results can be surprising. Make sure you practice with this tool and these shapes before you attempt your final shape.

Any circle or ellipse you create with this tool allows you to change its shape, unlike the SmartShape circles.

Drawing Tools

Visio comes with hundreds of ready-made shapes, but there will be times when you want a shape or line of your own creation. To handle this situation, Visio comes with four drawing tools to create lines, arcs, and other shapes for your diagrams.

Line Tool

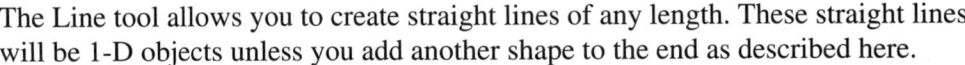

The Line tool allows you to create straight lines of any length. These straight lines will be 1-D objects unless you add another shape to the end as described here.

To draw straight line segments, make sure the Line tool is selected. Then click and drag the cursor in any direction and a line appears between the starting point and the cursor.

To draw a line at a 45-degree interval, hold down the SHIFT key as you click and move away in a straight line. Visio forces you to one of the 45-degree intervals on its grid.

Adding other line or arc segments creates a 2-D shape. After you've finished making the first part of your shape using the Line tool, use any other 1-D drawing tool and start the next part of the shape where the line ended. Continue adding 1-D shapes until you connect the end of the last shape to the head of the first. Visio creates a 2-D shape.

To change a line to an arc or to edit a line segment in a 2-D shape, use the Pencil tool. You can switch between the Arc tool, Line tool, Pencil tool, and Freeform tool to draw shapes consisting of several segments.

Arc Tool

The Arc tool allows you to create elliptical quarter-arc segments of any size. These arcs are different than the arc created by the Pencil tool, since they cannot bend back upon themselves and create almost-complete circles. The closest the arcs from the Arc tool can get is a quarter circle.

To draw an arc with the Arc tool, first make sure it has been selected from the toolbar. Then click and drag the cursor away from the starting point. The way you drag the mouse determines whether the arc has a horizontal axis (the endpoint is right or left of the beginning point) or vertical axis (the endpoint is above or below the beginning point). If the endpoint is exactly horizontal or vertical to the beginning point, the arc becomes a straight line.

To add other arc or line segments and create a 2-D shape, first draw an arc. After you've finished making the first part of your shape using the Arc tool, use any other 1-D drawing tool to start the next part of the shape where the line ended. Continue adding 1-D shapes until you connect the end of the last shape to the head of the first. Visio creates a 2-D shape.

Freeform Tool

The Freeform tool allows you to create a 1-D line of any shape. Visio simply evens out some of the curves while you move the cursor across the page. These smooth curves are sometimes called *splines*, which allow you to create a very specialized shape for your diagram.

To create a spline, make sure the Freeform tool has been selected from the toolbar. Then click on the page and start drawing. While you hold down the mouse button, Visio creates one continuous line. The line has control points at every Visio ruler mark and can be edited further with the Pencil tool.

You can also create a 2-D shape with the Freeform tool, an ability that allows you to create a shape to fit any need. Simply start and end your freeform drawing in the same place. Visio makes the figure into a 2-D shape.

Pencil Tool

The Pencil tool is one of the most powerful tools in Visio. It allows you to draw line and arc segments to whatever length or arc you might need, singly or in groups. It also allows you to edit any shape in Visio no matter how it was created. The ability to edit shapes, as well as to create lines and arcs, makes this one of the tools you're likely to use often.

To edit existing shapes, make sure the shape you'd like to edit is on the drawing page. Make sure the part of the shape you wish to edit has an endpoint, a control point, or a vertex. Select the Pencil tool from the toolbar then simply move the Pencil tool over the control point. The cursor turns into a cross with arrows at the tips. Click on the control point and move it where you'd like it to be. If you pull the control point directly away from the center of the shape, Visio creates straight lines on the sides that are connected to the control point. If you pull in any other direction than straight from the center, Visio creates an arc on the sides that are connected to the control point.

 *When editing shapes with the Pencil tool, it's best to play with it for a while to get used to it. The tool is powerful, but it can be difficult to use well at first.*

To create lines and arcs with the Pencil tool, you need to understand that the tool works on gesture recognition and creates lines or arcs depending on how you move the cursor once you start drawing. There are also several options you can access with the CTRL and SHIFT keys that give you even greater control over how the drawing looks.

To draw a line segment, click on a blank spot on the drawing page and move the cursor straight in any direction. A line starts to appear between the cursor and your starting point.

To draw an arc, click on a blank spot on the drawing page and move the cursor in a circular motion in any direction. If you loop the cursor back toward the starting point, you can create an arc that is almost a full circle. However, if you try to complete the circle, the arc collapses.

NOTE *Visio looks for the slightest motion away from a straight line to draw an arc, so it's easy to end up with an arc when you intended a line.*

To draw a line at 45-degree intervals, hold down the SHIFT key as you click and move away in a straight line. Visio forces you to one of the 45-degree intervals on its grid.

To draw a perfect half arc, hold down CTRL as you click and move away in a circular motion. Visio lets you go only halfway around and creates a perfect arc. You can control the size and depth of the arc by going closer or farther from the starting point.

To draw a group of lines or arcs, start drawing a line or arc, and then hold down both SHIFT and CTRL. Make sure you start a shape first, or you'll end up zooming in on the page instead. As long as you hold down both keys as you draw, every line and arc you create becomes part of a group. You may need to make a wider gesture to create arcs and the lines can only be at 45-degree angles. This grouping can also be done using the Freeform, Line, and Arc tools, as long as all the shapes in the group are made at one time.

You can also create a closed shape by linking several lines or arcs head to tail by starting the next shape at the exact endpoint of the old one. Once you've completed enough parts, and the end of the last one reaches the head of the first, Visio creates a completed shape out of the drawing, which then acts like any other 2-D shape.

Alteration Tools

Visio diagrams often need their shapes to be a different than they were when you added them to the drawing page, and the alteration tools help you do that. The two alteration tools (the rotate shape tool and the crop tool) change the look of a shape once it is on your Visio drawing page. The rotation tool changes the orientation of shapes, and the crop tool changes the look of a shape you've imported as clip art.

Rotate Shape

This rotation tool allows you to rotate any shape to any degree. Both 1-D and 2-D objects rotate exactly the same way, and everything listed here applies to both types of shapes. 3-D shapes rotate similarly, but they take their shadow with them as they move, so it can look very odd to rotate them very far. You want to make sure all 3-D shapes in a diagram have been rotated similarly, or you'll lose the effect of their three-dimensional shape.

To rotate a shape, select the Rotation tool from the toolbar, then select the shape you wish to rotate. The green handles at each corner of the square selection box changes from boxes to circles. Grab one of the circles and rotate the shape. As you do, the degree of rotation appears on the status bar as well as the snap to degree. This is the amount of control you have over the rotation—a smaller number indicates a finer control over the rotation angle. To get finer control over the rotation angle, move the cursor farther from the point of rotation.

NOTE   *In the full-page view, Visio sets the default minimum and maximum degree control at 15 degrees at the point of rotation and .1 degrees at the largest point away from the center of rotation. The more you zoom into the page, the finer is the degree of control.*

You can resize while using the Rotation tool, but only in one of the stretching directions using the square handles on the side of the selection box.

The shape rotates around the default rotation point, usually set as the center for Visio shapes and all the shapes you create yourself. The rotation point looks like the green rotation handles with a dot in the center. You can change the shape's center of rotation by making sure you have the Rotation tool selected, and then clicking on and moving the rotation point. When you pick up the rotation point, the cursor turns into a small circle with a dot in the middle. The shape rotates around wherever you set as the new rotation point.

Crop Tool

The Crop tool allows you to change the visible amount of any object you have imported or of any of the clip art that comes with Visio. With the Crop tool, you can resize the border that surrounds each shape. When you do this with clip art, it reduces the amount you can see on the page, thereby cropping the piece. You can also move the shape within its border, changing how much of it is visible on the page but leaving the border the same size.

> **NOTE** *You can't use this tool with any of Visio's shapes. It's only for use with clip art and objects imported from other sources.*

To crop a shape, first make sure the Crop tool is selected from the toolbar. Then select the shape, and the green control handles appear. Simply move the control handles until they have cropped the part of the shape you wish to have obscured.

To move an imported image within its border, select the Crop tool from the toolbar, and then select the image to be moved. When you move the cursor inside the border, it changes to a hand shape. Click and drag the image inside the border until the part you wish to have obscured is no longer visible. Visio dynamically redraws your image while you do this, so you are able to see what's happening.

Summary

This chapter introduced you to the basics of creating Visio diagrams. You saw how to create a drawing using SmartShapes, stencils, and connectors. You also saw how to use tools to rotate text, draw freehand shapes, edit, and copy objects on the page.

In the next chapter you will see how to take your basic knowledge of Visio even further by learning to use layout tools, adding pages and backgrounds, and including graphics in your Visio diagrams.

Chapter 3

Adding Groups, Layers, Pages, and Graphics

How to...

- ■ Use Rulers
- ■ Use Grids
- ■ Snap and Glue
- ■ Group Shapes
- ■ Add Pages
- ■ Add Layers
- ■ Use Backgrounds
- ■ Import Graphics
- ■ Alter Graphics

In the last chapter, you created your first Visio diagram, toured the main Visio window, and learned about the basic Visio tools.

In this chapter, you will see how to take your basic knowledge of Visio even further by learning to use layout tools, adding pages and backgrounds, and including graphics in your Visio diagrams.

Understanding Layout Tools

You've learned about all the basic tools that Visio offers; however, as you create more drawings, layout tools help you take your diagrams to a new level. Layout tools allow you to precisely place your shapes using rules, grid lines, and guides, as well as giving you control over how the shapes in your diagrams stack and group together.

Exploring Rulers

The rulers are the most commonly used tools in Visio. You may not have realized it, but the rulers were probably a huge help when you created your first drawing, allowing you to align the shapes and helping you see their relative sizes.

By default, the rulers are visible in Visio, and, in the U.S. version, are set to measure the pasteboard and drawing page in inches. For the international version of Visio, the default units are metric. Figure 3-1 shows the default rulers for the U.S. version.

As you zoom in on a page, the ruler changes scale. If you need a finer ruler, just zoom in. Visio also zooms in the grid lines.

Shape Shadows

Rulers also help you place shapes, by showing you exactly where the selected shape is at any given time. Visio does this by placing a *shape shadow* on the ruler for the selected shape. The shape shadow is a series of faint lines on each ruler showing the outer edges of the shape you have selected. For 1-D shapes, these lines correspond to the endpoints. For 2-D shapes, these lines correspond to the outer edges of the shapes, with another line corresponding to the center point.

Shape shadows help you know exactly where a shape is, enabling you to line it up with other shapes on the page, even if those shapes are very far apart. Figure 3-1 shows shape shadows for a heptagon.

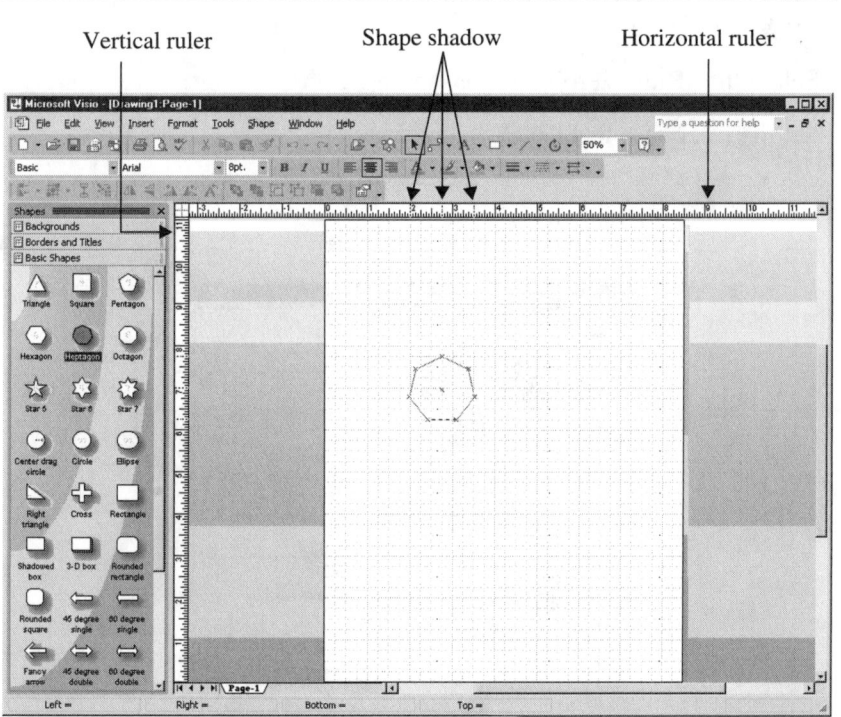

FIGURE 3-1   Visio 2000 rulers with shape shadow

Zero Point

The zero point for your ruler defines where the ruler counts from and is set by Visio for both rulers. The horizontal ruler's zero point is the left edge of your drawing page; the vertical ruler's zero point is the lower edge of your drawing page. This makes the 0,0 point for the drawing page in the lower left-hand corner, known as the *origin*.

For some people this origin can be a little counterintuitive, since they think the page should have an origin in the upper left-hand corner. To move the origin to the upper left-hand corner, you leave the horizontal ruler the same as the default setting and flip the vertical ruler so it starts with zero at the top of the page. Here's how to change your ruler's zero point settings so they start at zero in the upper-left corner:

1. Start Visio.

2. Open a new drawing.

3. Select Tools | Ruler & Grid. The Ruler & Grid dialog box appears, as shown in Figure 3-2.

4. Select the "Ruler zero" box for the vertical ruler.

5. Set the ruler zero to 11 inches and click OK.

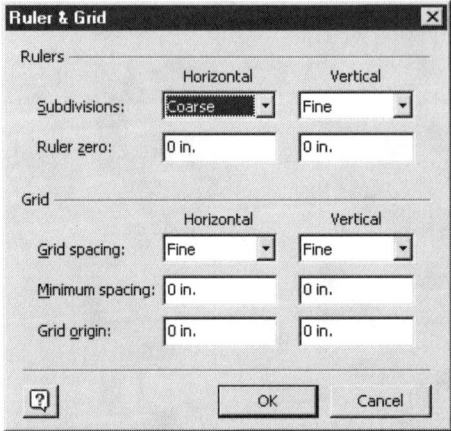

FIGURE 3-2   Ruler & Grid dialog box

NOTE *Changing your zero point to this setting causes the vertical ruler to show negative numbers, but at least you'll have a better orientation, because the zero will be in the upper left-hand corner of the drawing page.*

You might also want to change the ruler's zero point to help you find the end of the printed page as you lay out diagrams. Just as you changed your zero point to the upper-left corner of the page, you can set the zero points on either ruler to reflect the actual printing edges of your page. Most printers can't print within half an inch of the edge of a piece of paper, so you may find it useful to set your rulers so their zero points are half an inch from the edge of the drawing page.

Ruler Units

Ruler units give you a lot of control over how you place shapes with Visio. Ruler units can have a large impact on how your diagrams look because you use the ruler with all the shape placement and creation tools. Subdivisions are the most common settings to change on your rulers. By default, Visio sets your ruler to open with inch units in 1/4-inch subdivisions. To get finer control over shape placement, you may want to increase the subdivisions.

NOTE *The number of subdivisions within an inch increases as you zoom in on the drawing page.*

Here's how to change your ruler units:

1. Open a new drawing.

2. Select Tools | Ruler & Grid. The Ruler & Grid dialog box appears as shown in Figure 3-2.

3. Select the drop-down list for subdivisions on the horizontal ruler.

4. Select Fine from the list.

5. Select the drop-down list for subdivisions on the vertical ruler.

6. Select Fine from the list, and click OK.

TIP *Make sure your grid and ruler subdivisions work well together. For example, set them both to fine, instead of one to fine and one to coarse. It can be confusing to work with them set too far apart.*

Understanding Grid Lines

Grid lines are the small gray lines that cover the Visio drawing page, and they are a powerful tool for arranging shapes in your diagram. They form a grid that follows the ruler subdivisions, much like the grid lines on a page of graph paper. Here's what grid lines look like on the drawing page:

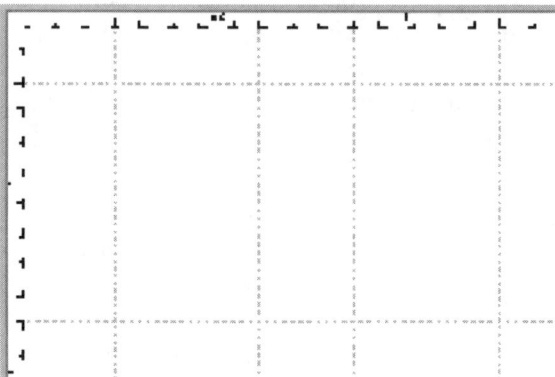

Grid lines are visible by default in Visio, so every new drawing includes them. However, by default, grid lines do not print with the rest of your diagram.

In Chapter 2, you used grid lines when you created your first diagram. They helped you arrange the shapes in a straight line. Grid lines are vital to making your diagrams look well organized and carefully laid out. They also help you create great-looking diagrams quickly and easily.

 *Grid options are easy to change and can help you create diagrams much easier. It's worth your time to change these options, since the right settings save you time later.*

Changing the Grid Options

You can change many of the grid options. From the Tools menu, choose Ruler & Grid. The Ruler & Grid dialog box opens, as shown in Figure 3-2. Here's what each of the options controls:

Grid Spacing   This option sets the distance between the grid lines on the drawing page. You can choose Fine, Normal, Coarse, or Fixed. Fine, Normal, and Coarse allow the grid to resize as you zoom in and out. Use Fixed to force the grid to maintain the same spacing as you zoom in and out.

Fixed grids can get in the way when you need to zoom in. It's best to choose one of the variable grids if you'll be working at several sizes. However, fixed grids can be invaluable for placing objects in line, or for measuring a fixed distance between shapes as you place them. The distance between the grid lines for fixed spacing is set in the minimum spacing box.

> **NOTE**   *The intervals of the grid correspond to the units of measure set in the Options dialog box.*

Minimum Spacing   This option sets how close the grid lines can get no matter how far zoomed in you are. Grid spacing of Fine, Normal, or Coarse gives the minimum possible distance between grid lines. A grid spacing of Fixed gives the exact distance between the grid lines.

Grid Origin   This option sets the grid's zero point. The default is set to start in the lower-left corner. Grid Origin works very much like ruler origin from the previous section. You only need to set this if your ruler and grid increments are different.

Understanding Snapping

Snapping is the action that forces any shape you drag to the Visio drawing page to attach to the nearest grid line, connection point, guide, or ruler subdivision. This feature helps you create diagrams with shapes in straight lines with a minimum of effort.

Snapping also affects how you use the drawing tools, which are also set to snap to the nearest grid line. This makes it easier for you to draw shapes of the same size as well as helps you create straight lines.

By default, all shapes you drag or create on the Visio page snap to the closest grid lines in both horizontal and vertical directions. Since the snapping function is closely tied to the ruler and its settings, as well as the grid lines, make sure you choose the ruler options first.

Understanding Gluing

Gluing is what holds shapes together once they have snapped into place. Only shapes glue together firmly, but you can set Visio to glue to any shape-part that you can snap to.

Gluing is important because it makes sure your shapes stay where you put them and together in the way you placed them. This is most obvious when you glue a 1-D shape to a 2-D shape, for example a line to a connection point on a square. Gluing insures the line stays with the square when you move them.

You can tell when Visio has glued shapes together because it draws a red square around the connection point where the two shapes touch.

Using the Snap & Glue Options

As you work with your diagram, you may want to turn some of the snap and glue options on and off. You can control how the different screen objects snap and glue to the grid lines, connection points, guides, and ruler subdivisions, and you can change these settings at any time without affecting shapes already positioned or glued.

To change your snap and glue settings, choose Snap & Glue from the Tools menu. The Snap & Glue dialog box appears, as shown in Figure 3-3.

 *For placing shapes, the most useful Snap & Glue options are Ruler subdivisions, Grid, and Guides. The other options are useful when gluing shapes.*

"Snap to" and "Glue to"   The "Snap to" and "Glue to" areas of the General tab list the various selectable screen elements.

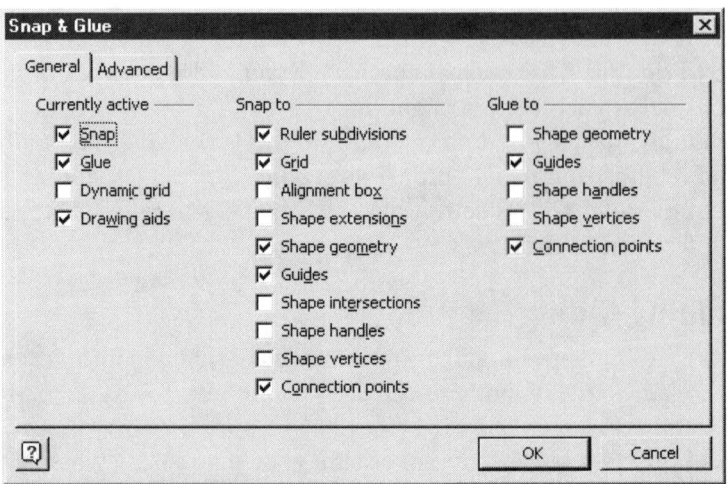

FIGURE 3-3   General tab of the Snap & Glue dialog box

> **TIP** *If you want to both snap to and glue to a particular screen element, you need to have that element checked in both lists. For convenience in placing objects, it is possible to snap to something but not glue to it, and vice versa.*

When an element is checked in the "Snap to" and "Glue to" lists, Visio automatically snaps and glues to that element when you create a new shape or drag an existing shape onto the page. Table 3-1 lists the elements to which you can snap and glue shapes, and it describes how the settings affect objects on the page. The table also shows the default settings for the screen elements.

Currently Active   These checkboxes allow you to turn on and off the snapping and gluing actions without changing the selections in the "Snap to" and "Glue to" lists. When you select the Snap or Glue checkbox, all the checked elements in the respective list become active. When you clear the Snap or Glue checkbox, all the elements in the respective list become inactive.

The Currently Active checkboxes allow you to turn off all snapping or gluing with one click, without having to reselect all the elements when you want to turn them back on. For example, if you're working on placing a shape you'd like to move slightly, snapping can sometimes get in the way. You can clear the Snap checkbox, place the shape, and then reselect the Snap checkbox without changing the individual selections in the "Snap to" list. You can turn both Snap and Glue off to get complete control of shape placement or turn both on to use the grid lines and other screen elements to help with placing shapes.

Element	Effect	Default
Ruler subdivisions	Shapes stick to the nearest ruler subdivisions.	On
Grid	Shapes stick to the nearest grid line.	On
Alignment box	Shapes stick to another shape's alignment box.	Off
Shape geometry	Shapes stick to any part of the nearest shape, no matter which part of the shape that is.	Off
Guides	Shapes stick and/or glue to guides.	On
Shape handles	Shapes stick and/or glue to any handle of the nearest shape's selection box.	Off
Shape vertices	Shapes stick and/or glue to any vertices of the nearest shape.	Off
Connection points	Shapes stick and/or glue to any connection point of the nearest shape.	On

TABLE 3-1   Snap and Glue elements

 *Unlike early versions of Visio, Visio 2002 has a nudge function you can use by selecting the shape and using the arrow keys to move it slightly.*

The Snap & Glue dialog box has another tab, Advanced, which is shown in Figure 3-4.

Snap Strength   The sliding bars in this section set the distance (in pixels) that screen elements pull when snapping is active. The strength of the grid, guides, rulers, or points (connection points, vertices, or handles) is set here. The higher the number, the farther away shapes can be when pulled to the element.

For most Visio diagrams, guides should be set to about 5; rulers, grids, and points should be set to about 2.

Shape Extension Options   These options control how the *drawing aids* function in Visio. They help you place shapes, but only if set correctly. By default, none of these options are checked. If you want very fine control of how your shapes snap and glue, you may want to review these thirteen options and select some to help you create drawings that are more precise.

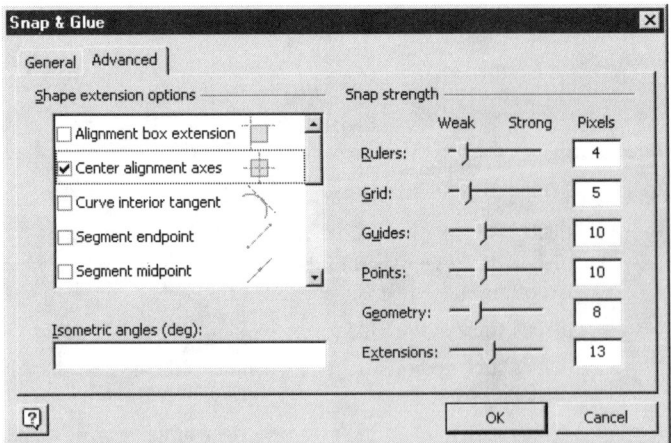

FIGURE 3-4   Advanced tab of the Snap & Glue dialog box

Isometric Angles   By holding down the SHIFT key as you rotate a shape, Visio constrains your angles to 30, 45, and 60 degrees. You can change the rotation angles by adding new values to the Isometric Angle field. Separate the angles with commas. Visio will cycle through the list.

Using Guides

When you create diagrams, you often need to line up several shapes. *Guides* can help you do this with precision to give your diagrams a professional look. Although grid lines can be very useful for aligning objects, the grid lines are all over the page. That can make it confusing when you're trying to get perfect alignment. Guides, however, act like straight edges you can place *anywhere* on your page and use to align objects consistently. In addition, guides are easier to see on the drawing page than grid lines. With guides, you can be assured you're placing objects precisely.

There are two types of guides in Visio: guide points and guide lines. *Guide points* give a single point to which you can affix the connection point of any shape. *Guide lines* provide a solid line you can use to connect two or more connection points. Both are useful in placing your objects on the page precisely.

NOTE   *Gluing and snapping for guides can be set in the Snap & Glue dialog box (refer to Figure 3-3), as explained earlier in this chapter.*

Making Guide Lines and Guide Points

Guide lines and guide points are created using the standard rulers in Visio. All Visio drawing pages come with rulers turned on by default, so you should be able to create guides without changing any default settings.

You start using guide lines and guide points by placing them on the page, then you can snap and glue shapes to them. Then, when you move the guide line or guide point, the shape or shapes glued to them move where you move the guide. It's a powerful way to keep a tightly organized drawing while still being able to move shapes on the page.

TIP   *If you've turned off the rulers in Visio, you can turn them back on by selecting View | Rulers.*

To create a guide line, place your cursor over one of the rulers, and then click and drag the cursor onto the drawing page. A blue line appears under the cursor.

Move it to the drawing page and then release the mouse button. This blue line is a guide. When you release the guide, it turns green.

To create a guide point, place your cursor where the two rulers meet. The intersection has two crossed blue lines. Click on the intersection and drag the cursor onto the drawing page. A blue crosshair appears, centered on your cursor. This is your guide point. As you drag the guide point to the drawing page the cursor turns into a four-headed arrow. Figure 3-5 shows examples of guide lines and guide points.

NOTE *Both guide lines and guide points lightly snap and glue to grid lines. You can use this to make sure you have properly placed the guide.*

Gluing and Snapping

Once you have your guides on the page, you need to know how to use them. Snapping and gluing to guides is similar to snapping and gluing to grid lines. By default, the strength is set stronger for snap and glue to guides than for grid lines. These features can be turned on and off for guides in the same way they are with grid lines, by using the Snap & Glue dialog box, shown earlier in Figure 3-3.

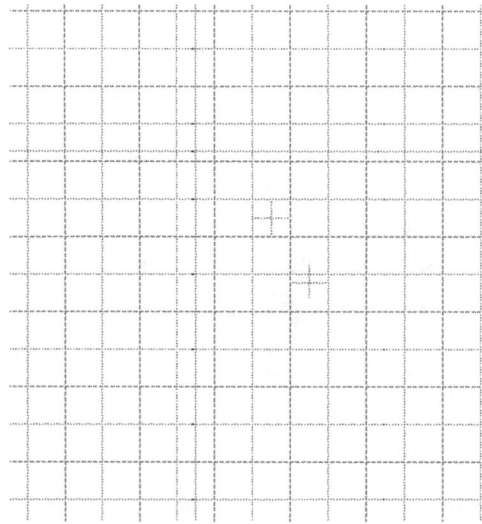

FIGURE 3-5   Guide lines and guide points

TIP *Snapping and gluing are the best features of guides. They help with shape placement and don't get in the way of creating your drawing. Leaving them on is usually for the best.*

When an object snaps to a guide, Visio brings at least two of the shape's connection points in contact with the guide. For guide lines, Visio tries to get two connection points in contact with the guide; for guide points, Visio snaps two adjacent sides of a shape's selection box to the guide points.

Gluing allows you to move attached shapes with the guide. If you glue a shape to a guide, the connection points of the shape turn red when you move them over the guide. Figure 3-6 shows a square with one side glued to a guide. By gluing several shapes to one guide you can make sure that all the shapes always line up, no matter where you move the guide.

To get a shape to snap or glue to a new guide, move the guide near the shape, and then drag the shape onto the guide. Snapping and gluing should happen automatically. If a shape doesn't snap or glue where you want it, try moving the shape a little and then put it back in place.

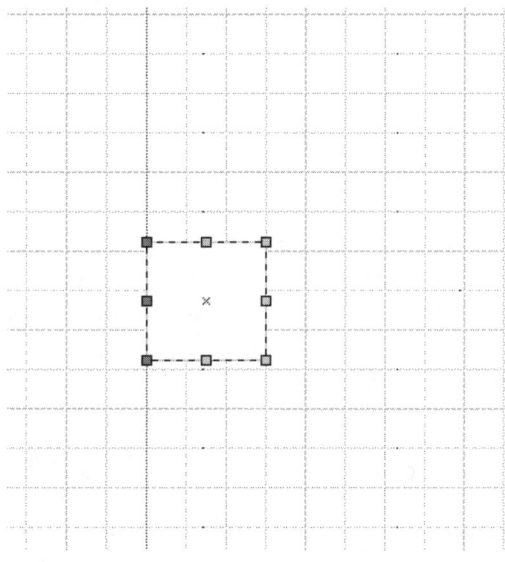

FIGURE 3-6   A square glued to a guide

 *For precise placement of a shape, right-click on the shape and select View | Size and Position window. The Size and Position window lets you set the numerical value coordinates for a shape.*

Moving Guides

Guide lines and guide points are great for shape placement, especially when they are snapped and glued to shapes. When you move the guide, you also move all the shapes that are glued to it. This gluing action allows you to quickly rearrange your diagram to incorporate new ideas or a new layout without picking up each piece individually and replacing it. To take advantage of this feature you need to move the guides.

To move a guide, place the cursor over the guide away from any shape. The cursor turns into a double-headed arrow for a guide line and gets a four way arrow under the normal white cursor for a guide point. Click the guide and it turns green. Once a guide is green, you have selected it and can move it. Click and hold on a guide and move it to the new location. All the shapes glued to the guide move with it.

Guides have the same shadow on the ruler that lines and points do. Use the shadow to help you place guides as you move them. Guides also attempt to snap to the grid by default. This can make it difficult to get the precise placement you need as you move your guides. You can turn off snapping to the grid in the Snap & Glue dialog box, explained earlier in this chapter.

 *To remove a guide, select it and press* DELETE.

Grouping

Grouping shapes allows you to place shapes in relation to each other and then make sure that relationship always stays the same. Grouping in Visio helps you manage shapes by helping you collect them into sets that work together.

Creating and Dissolving Groups

To create a group of shapes, select each shape individually while holding down SHIFT. The shapes you've selected will have a blue dotted line around them. When you are happy with the shapes in your group, go to the Shape menu, select Grouping, and then select Group from the submenu, as shown in Figure 3-7. The Shape | Grouping menu commands give you several submenu commands for grouping shapes.

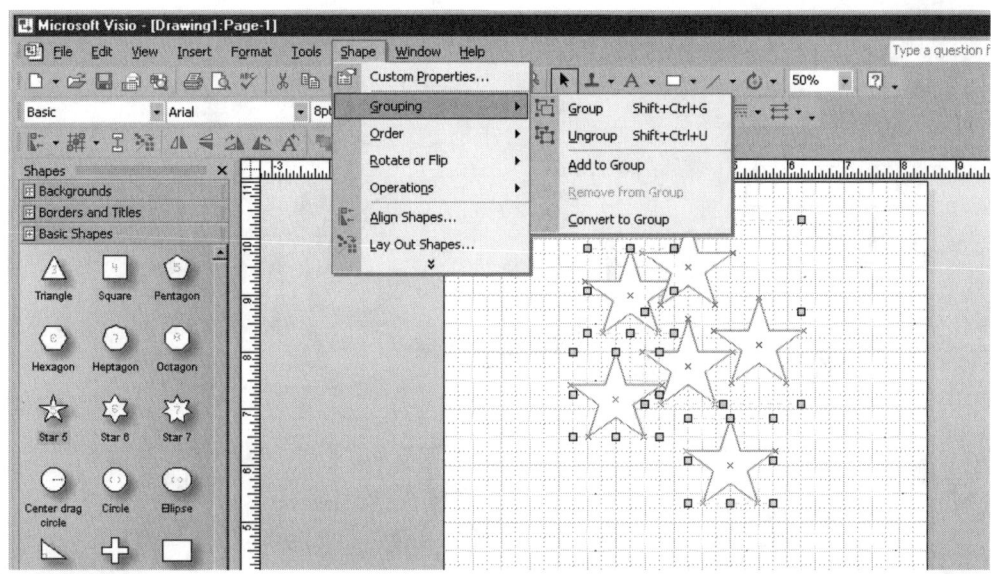

FIGURE 3-7   Shape | Grouping submenu

Formatting, Adding, and Removing Shapes in Groups

Once you create a group, you may want to format, add, or subtract member shapes within the group structure. Groups of shapes behave like a single shape, so dealing with a shape in a group often requires more steps than simply dealing with a single shape on your drawing page. Formatting a shape that has been grouped requires selecting the individual shape without selecting the entire group.

To format a shape in a group:

1. Deselect everything by clicking on an unoccupied part of the drawing page.

2. Select the group containing the shape you wish to format.

3. Select the shape within the group. You might notice the shape handles are slightly different from normal ones. They have small X's inside them to indicate that the shape is part of a group, as shown in Figure 3-8.

4. Format the shape.

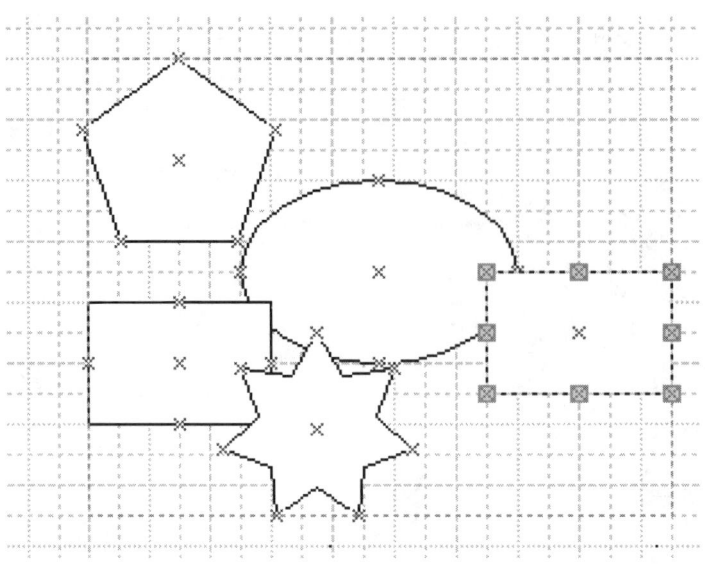

FIGURE 3-8   A selected shape within a group

Formatting a shape can change the group size, making the group smaller or larger than the group window. To adjust this, right-click on the group and select Format | Behavior.

Adding or removing shapes is best accomplished by using the Shape | Grouping menu commands.

To add a shape to a group:

1. Deselect everything by clicking on an unoccupied part of the drawing page.

2. Select the group to which you wish to add the shape.

3. Hold down SHIFT and select the shape to be added. The shape has a selection box with blue control points.

4. Select Shape | Group | Add to Group. A box appears containing the original group and the new shape.

Add to Group adds the new shape to the group without affecting the original group or the new shape in any way other than expanding the group. The added shape remains in its place, and Visio repositions the group's selection rectangle to encompass it. You can also add a group to another group.

To remove a shape from a group:

1. Deselect everything by pressing ESC or by clicking on an unoccupied part of the drawing page.

2. Select the shape you wish to remove from the group. The shape has a selection box with green control handles with crosses inside them.

3. Select Shape | Group | Remove from Group, or press the DELETE key.

Remove from Group takes the selected shape out of the group without changing the group or the shape in any other way. Both the selected shape and the remaining shapes in the group stay where they were. Once you remove a shape from a group, you're free to place it as you would any other shape.

Changing the Behavior of a Group

Once you have a group, the Behavior window determines how that group behaves. To see the behavior window, right click on a group and choose behavior from the list. The Behavior window opens as shown in Figure 3-9.

The group behavior dialog box has three tabs, and controls what happens when you click on, change, delete, or in any way affect a group. Each type of action is handled on one of the three tabs: Behavior, Double Click, and Placement.

The behavior tab deals with what happens when you change or select a group. It allows you to treat groups as a 1-D or 2-D shape, controls how the shape handles appear in a group, and what happens when you resize the group or any part of it. It also controls the printing settings for the group, and how other shapes on the page handle the group.

The Double Click tab handles only what happens when a group is double-clicked. A double-clicked group can have any of almost a dozen actions, including running a macro or opening another page. Some options have settings that you can alter; others are as basic as setting a double-click to perform no action or simply the default action for the shapes. The default setting is for a double-click to perform the default action of the shapes in the group.

The Placement tab handles how the group behaves in automatic layout. If, on the behavior tab, you left the default Box (2-D) designation unaltered, or you set your shape to be 2-D, you can use the placement tab to change how it behaves. In automatic layout, Visio determines the best possible way to lay out the shapes. If

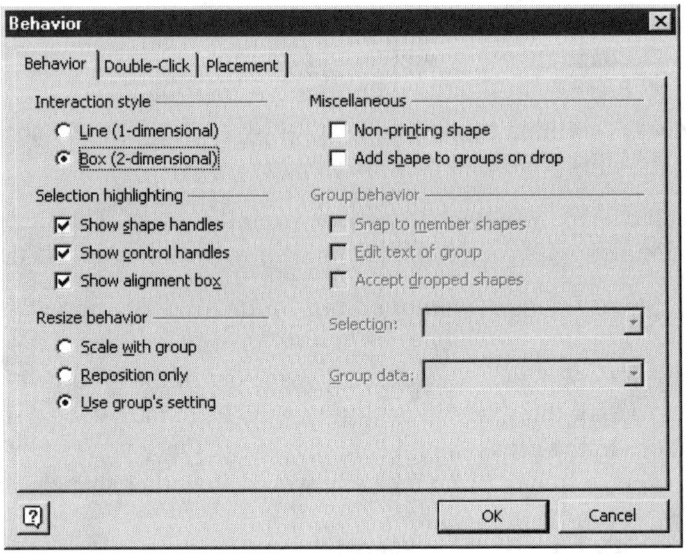

FIGURE 3-9   Behavior window

you want to change how this group acts under automatic layout, select to layout and route around, which enables the rest of the tab so you can alter how layout happens. You can tell Visio to simply route shapes around this group, or you can have shapes lay on top of the group. You can also effect how connectors and other shapes attach to the group, or let Visio move the shape but control how the shapes are dropped back onto the page.

After you are finishing setting the behavior options for your group, click Ok on the Behavior window.

NOTE   *All of the behavior window options are also available to standard shapes by right clicking on them and selecting behavior.*

Convert to Group

When you import Windows metafiles or linked objects from other programs into Visio, they don't automatically come in as a Visio shape. Instead, when you import these into Visio, they're placed as one single shape and act very differently from Visio shapes.

Convert to Group allows you to change these imported shapes into groups that act more like you expect shapes to act. Usually, the conversion allows you to ungroup and manipulate parts of the imported shape.

To convert an imported object into a group, first you need to import the object. Select the correct type of object (usually Picture) from the Insert menu and proceed with the insertion. Once the object is inserted, select the new shape and nothing else. Select Shape | Grouping | Convert to Group. The shape should now be a group and you can format, add, or remove shapes from the group using the other Shape | Grouping options. Not all objects can become Visio groups, so test this before relying on your object being able to do it.

If you use this feature on a linked object that has been embedded or linked in another program, you'll be unable to edit it in any program other than Visio.

Stacking Order

Stacking order determines how shapes overlap other shapes on the page and the order in which shapes are selected. You can change the stacking order by using the Bring to Front, Bring Forward, Send to Back, and Send Backward commands on the Shape menu.

Shapes on a background always appear behind shapes on a foreground. Layers, however, have no effect on stacking order.

The selection order is important when you select multiple shapes by dragging a selection net around them. The shape at the front of the stacking order becomes the primary shape, displaying green handles. When you select multiple shapes by holding SHIFT and clicking, the stacking order doesn't affect the selection order. The first shape you click becomes the primary shape.

Adding Pages, Layers, and Backgrounds

Visio diagrams can have hundreds of shapes and cover topics that require dozens of pages of diagrams. Sometimes a diagram has shapes in a complicated arrangement, or there can be different diagrams on separate pages that need to look like part of a set. Visio has created three ways for you to manage these issues: pages, layers, and backgrounds.

Pages, layers, and backgrounds allow you to create diagrams that are more than just what you see on the drawing page. Pages allow you to create diagrams that have more than one page. Layers allow you to work with shapes in a complicated diagram without worrying about moving shapes you've already placed. Backgrounds make it easy to create several different diagrams that have a similar look.

Working with Pages

Visio diagrams are divided into two parts: foreground pages and background pages. So far, you've just dealt with foreground pages, and only one page at a time.

Visio diagrams can contain several foreground and background pages, allowing you to create multipage diagrams that have the same look throughout, as well as allowing you to get the most mileage out of using the same complicated diagram in several different page layouts. When you decide to create a multipage diagram, you need to make sure you know what the page will look like. Good planning is essential when working with multipage diagrams, since you won't be able to see the complete diagram at once, making it easy to become confused about where shapes are located. Planning helps reduce confusion and increases the effectiveness of pages.

NOTE *Visio windows can only display one page at a time.*

The distinction between the drawing page and a page in Visio can get confusing, especially because as you add pages they look just like the drawing page you have dealt with so far. It may help to keep the following distinctions in mind: The page you see on the screen is the *drawing page.* When you print the diagram you do so on the *printed page.* When you add a page to your Visio diagram, you're adding a whole new Visio document that is linked to the one you have open, with its own desktop and possibly its own stencils.

Using pages allows you to keep related diagrams together and gives you the option of using backgrounds.

TIP *Save all the different versions of diagram showing steps as different pages. That way, you can keep the progression of the diagram together for later reference, and you can still print each page separately.*

Pages also let you present a series of diagrams like a slide show. Using full screen view, you can navigate through a series of pages to see how they would look when presented in that manner. You can also place links between pages that are saved together and then navigate through them like a Web site.

You can also rotate pages individually. If you have part of a diagram that needs to be set differently on the printed page, you can add another Visio page and rotate it to make it easier to edit the material.

   *Most Visio templates are set up with the drawing page, printed page, and printed drawing sizes all the same, so you don't have to change any settings or sizes to get the printed drawing you expect.*

Adding Pages

If your plan calls for layers, backgrounds, or multiple pages, the first step is to add a new page.

NOTE   *To move between pages, use the page tabs at the bottom of the Visio window.*

To create a new page, make sure you're on the page that directly precedes the new page. New pages inherit their properties from the page displayed when they are added. Choose Insert | New Page. The Page Setup dialog box opens, as shown in Figure 3-10. This dialog box allows you to change the size, scale, and other settings for a drawing page by using four tabs: Page Size, Drawing Scale, Page Properties, and Layout and Routing.

- ■ **Page Properties**   Specifies the type of page and the name of the page. This portion of the tab also lists the assigned background page and the unit of measure set for the rulers. The type of page, background page settings, and ruler settings are inherited from the page that was displayed when you added the new page.

NOTE   *Either give your pages very meaningful names, or leave them to be named by Visio. If Visio names the pages they renumber automatically when you add more pages.*

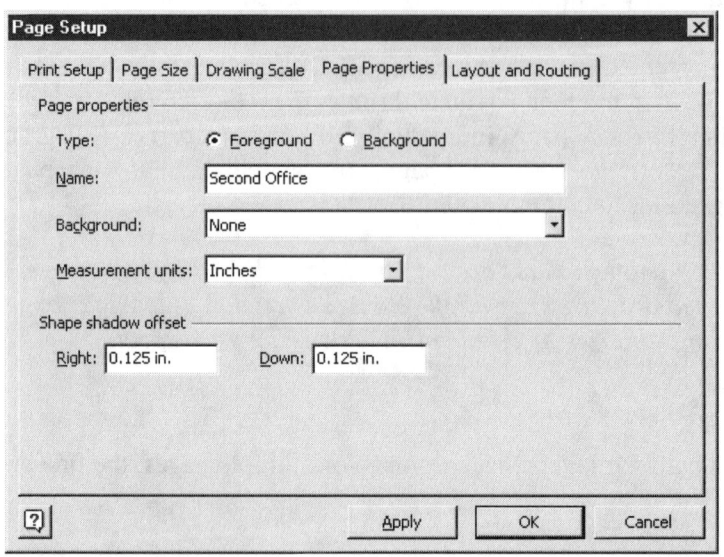

FIGURE 3-10 Page Setup dialog box

- **Shape Shadow Offset** Specifies the location of shadows in relation to shapes. All shadows on a page have the same offset. By default, shadows appear 0.125 inches down and to the right of the shape. For shadows above or to the left of a shape, type negative numbers.

- **Layout and Routing** Add line jumps to a page. A *line jump* is a small, uneditable arc that Visio draws on one of two crossed lines, showing the lines are crossed, not connected. Add line jumps to specify which line of the two has the small arc. Jumps can be set for horizontal or vertical lines only or set to happen on the last line that was created or adjusted. If you choose Last Routed Line, jumps occur on both horizontal and vertical lines.

- **Page Size** Displays the page size settings for Visio. By default, the page size is set to match the paper size set for the printer.

- **Drawing Scale** Displays the current scale set for the drawing, which is 1:1 by default. You can edit the scale here, but remember that the page size and printer settings directly affect how this looks on the printed page.

Once you're satisfied with the information in the Page Setup dialog box, click OK, and Visio adds the new page. Visio takes you to the new page, which is blank, ready for you to start another part of your diagram.

Deleting Pages

You can delete pages when you no longer need them. All information on a page will be lost when you remove it. Be very sure that you don't need any information on the page when you delete it.

 *Always save your diagram before you remove pages. That way, if you need to go back, you can use your saved file.*

To delete a page, right-click on the tab for the drawing page and select Delete Page. After the page is deleted, Visio renumbers your pages if you haven't named them.

Sizing and Reordering Pages

After you've added pages, you often need to reorder or resize them. This ability to customize pages can be useful; however, make sure you verify that the printed page settings are correct so the diagram prints the way you expect. (Printing settings can be accessed by selecting File | Print.)

If you print a diagram that's larger than the printed page, the drawing prints across several pages. This is called *tiling*. You can verify whether and where your drawing breaks across pages by choosing View | Page Breaks. Gray lines appear to show the page breaks.

TIP *You may resize pages by placing the mouse over an edge of the drawing page, holding down* CTRL*, then clicking and dragging. The page dynamically resizes as you do this. You can also alter the page size by choosing File | Page Setup and selecting the Page Size tab.*

Since new pages inherit the attributes of the page that was displayed when they were added, it usually works best to add the page next to a very similar page and then reorder it so it appears in the right place in your page flow.

To reorder pages, right-click on any page tab and select Reorder Pages. The Reorder Pages dialog box appears, as shown in Figure 3-11. Move the pages around by selecting them and using the Move Up and Move Down buttons. Once they're in the order you need, click OK.

Visio automatically renumbers or renames pages if you select the "Update page names" checkbox and didn't rename the pages yourself.

Using Layers

Layers give you control over how you edit a diagram. With layers, you can work with or display some parts of your diagram without the other parts being visible or movable. Layers also allow you to print part or all of a diagram at a time. For example, if you have diagrammed your office and you have all the different types of building parts on different layers, then you can move the furniture without worrying about mistakenly moving a wall or electrical socket.

Layers are there to help facilitate the diagram-creation process. They allow you to look at a set of shapes at once, possibly even making them all one color so you can see where they are. They help you lock down shapes you've already placed so they aren't accidentally moved as you edit other shapes. Layers also help you

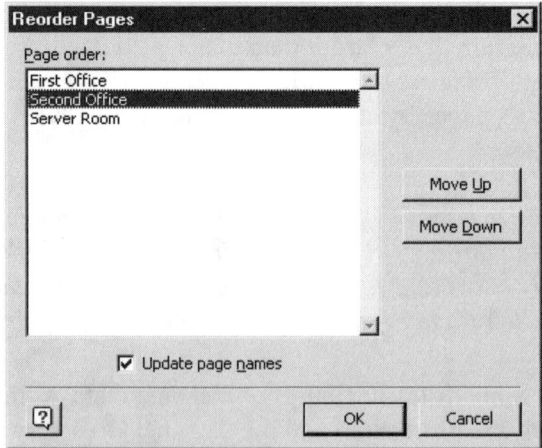

FIGURE 3-11   Reorder Pages dialog box

control the snapping and gluing action of shapes in your diagram, since snapping and gluing can be set differently for each layer. You can even print reports listing the shapes in each layer, a feature that is particularly useful when doing office diagrams or floor plans.

Layers are so useful in building floor plans that templates for office diagrams and floor plans come with shapes already assigned to the layers. For example, you can lay out the walls and computer networks and assign them to one layer. Then, when you start to place furniture and cubicles, the walls and network wiring won't be accidentally moved. If the furniture is on its own layer, you could then run a report of all the furniture shapes, greatly helping you plan your purchases and organize your office needs.

For more information about using reports in Visio, see Chapter 5, "Creating Flowcharts."

Adding Layers

In Visio, a *layer* is a named category of shapes. Any single shape can be assigned to multiple layers or no layer, and every page in a drawing can have a different set of layers. To add a layer to a diagram, select View | Layer Properties. The Layer Properties window appears, as shown in Figure 3-12.

You can also get to the Layer Properties window from the View menu on the Preview screen.

- ■ **New**   Allows you to create a new layer. A dialog box asking for the name of the new layer appears when you click this button.

- ■ **Remove**   Deletes the selected layer.

- ■ **Rename**   Changes the name of the selected layer. A dialog box asking for the new name appears when you click Rename.

- ■ **Name**   Lists the names of the layers. Clicking the Name button opens the Rename Layer window for the currently selected layer. You can also use the Rename button to rename the selected layer in place.

- ■ **#**   Lists the number of shapes in each layer.

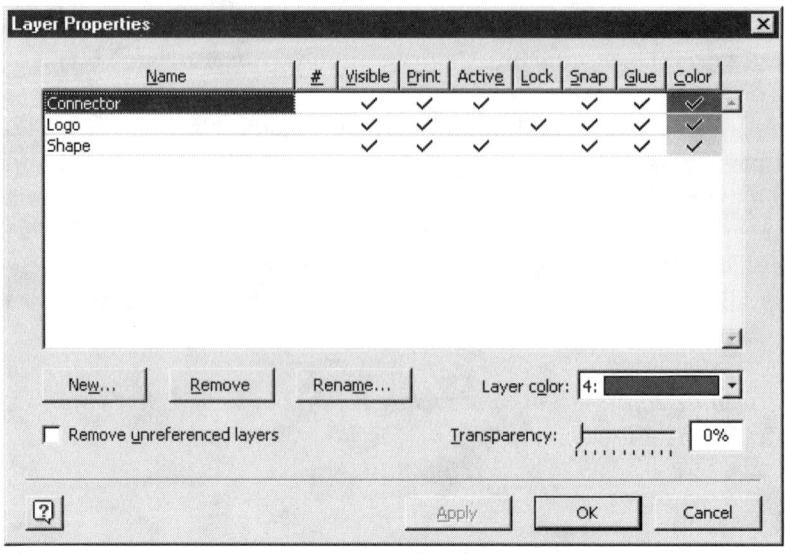

FIGURE 3-12 Layer Properties window

NOTE   *The numbers in the # column only tell you how many shapes are on each layer; they don't provide an accurate count of how many shapes are in the entire drawing. A single shape may be assigned to two or more layers.*

■ **Visible**   Allows you to set whether the shapes on a given layer are visible or hidden. Place a check mark in the column to show the layer; clear the check mark to hide the layer.

■ **Print**   Allows you to set whether the shapes on a given layer print. Place a check mark in this column to have the layer print; clear the check mark to have the layer not print.

■ **Active**   Specifies the default layer to which shapes are assigned. More than one layer can be active at a time, so any shape added belongs to all active layers if you don't assign it a specific layer. You may find it useful to change your active layer or layers as you progress through your diagram, making sure that the shapes you add attach to the correct layer.

> NOTE   *Active layers cannot be locked.*

- **Lock**   Prevents shapes on a given layer from being selected or changed. An active layer cannot be locked, and a locked layer cannot have any of its Visible, Print, Snap, Glue, or Color properties changed. You are not able to move any shapes on a locked layer.

- **Snap**   Specifies whether any other shapes can snap to shapes assigned to this layer. A shape on a layer that has Snap unchecked can still snap to other shapes, no matter what their layer, but other shapes cannot snap to it.

- **Glue**   Specifies whether any other shape can glue to shapes assigned to the layer. A shape on a layer that has Glue unchecked can still glue to other shapes, no matter what their layer, but other shapes cannot glue to it.

- **Color**   Specifies the color for all shapes on that layer. Use this option to identify all the shapes assigned to a color, or to help move shapes on different layers within a complicated diagram. This option doesn't permanently change the color of the shapes; it simply overrides the shape's color in favor of the layer color. To return a shape to its original color, uncheck this option

> NOTE   *Layers do not determine how shapes appear on the page, so layer order has very little effect on the page. The way shapes overlap on the drawing page is determined by their stacking order and background settings.*

Once you have added all the layers you need and selected their options, click OK.

Removing or Renaming Layers

When you have created a drawing with many layers, you may find that you have more layers than you need, or that layers you added and named earlier now need to be renamed. You can accomplish both of these tasks in the Layer Properties window, shown in Figure 3-12

> CAUTION   *If you select the checkbox for Remove Unreferenced Layers, Visio automatically deletes any layers that don't contain shapes. Only do this if you want to remove Layers you've added.*

To remove a layer, first make sure that you don't need any shape on the layer; shapes on removed layers are deleted. Once you are sure, select the layer and click Remove. A window appears asking you to confirm the removal, warning you that the shapes on that layer will be deleted. Click OK.

To rename a layer, select it from the list, and click Rename. The Rename dialog box appears. Once you enter the new name, click OK.

Understanding Backgrounds

Visio's pages and layers tools help you create complicated diagrams; however, they aren't the best tools to allow you to create a seamless look for all the pages in a diagram. A special type of page, called a *background*, can be added to every drawing page to help your diagrams look the same for a whole set of pages.

Backgrounds are added like pages and behave somewhat like layers. Like layers, they allow you to have shapes in your diagram that cannot be edited as you place other shapes on the drawing page. Unlike layers, backgrounds hold shapes completely static and won't allow you to snap or glue any shape on the drawing page to the background.

Add a background when you want the same shape in the same place to show on more than one page. Backgrounds allow you to place a common graphic element and use it to create a seamless look from page to page. For example, you can place your company logo in the lower-left corner of the background and then assign that background to all your pages. The element appears exactly the same size, shape, and placement on each page you assign that background to, significantly adding to the professional look of your diagrams.

Backgrounds act like the company logo on an office letterhead: they're visible on the page, but not editable. Backgrounds are also inherited as you add new pages. You can edit the background itself separately, as a page on its own, and the changes update on all the pages that reference that background.

Visio diagrams can have several backgrounds, just as they can have several pages; however, each page can have only one assigned background. Fortunately, backgrounds can have backgrounds, allowing you to make a multilayered page with several backgrounds working together. For example, you could place your company logo on one background and a border on another, allowing you to move them separately.

 *When adding a background page to a background page it's easy to get confused about which shapes you can edit on which page. A good planning document that lists where each shape is going to be from can make this a lot easier.*

Adding Backgrounds

You can create a new page as a background or convert a foreground page to a background. When you create a background, Visio automatically adds it to the list of available backgrounds for other pages in the Insert Page and Properties windows.

 *The Page Layout Wizard creates a background for your diagram and puts in placeholders for elements such as title blocks, borders, and logos. To edit these placeholders you must display the background page.*

To create a background, add a page by choosing Insert | Page. The Page Setup dialog box appears, as shown earlier in Figure 3-10. Add the page as you would any other, but make sure to select Background for the Type. The background inherits the page size and drawing scale from the page on the screen when you added it, but you can change that just as you would for any other page. Click OK when you're done.

To convert an existing foreground page into a background page, display the foreground page you wish to convert in the Visio window. You can move between pages by using the page tabs at the bottom of the Visio Page.

Select File | Page Setup. The Page Setup dialog box appears. Click the Page Properties tab. The dialog box should look like the one shown earlier in Figure 3-10. Change the Type option from Foreground to Background and then click OK.

Assigning a Background Page

Once you've created a background page that didn't exist before (either by creating a new page or by converting a foreground page) you need to set a foreground page to use it. This is called *attaching a background*.

To attach a background, select the page tab to go to the foreground page you'd like to attach a background page to, then go to File | Page Setup. The Page Setup dialog box opens, as shown earlier in Figure 3-10. On the Page Properties tab, set the Background for the new background page. Its name should be in the drop-down list of backgrounds.

The background appears behind the foreground. Remember to save your diagram after you do this to make sure you have all the changes saved.

Editing Backgrounds

Since a background's main purpose is to remain unchanged as you edit the foreground, you need to go through some extra steps to edit a background. To edit a background, you must first open the background by selecting Edit | Go To and going to the page. If the background is attached to the page currently displayed, you can simply open the background by choosing Background. If the background isn't attached to the current page, you need to select it by name from the list. It may be easier to open the background in a new window. That way, you can have both the page and its background open simultaneously, allowing you to edit both at once. To display a background in a new window, choose Edit | Go To | Page, select Open Page In New Window, and then click OK. To see both pages at once, choose Window | Tile.

Once a background is open, you can edit it as you would any other page. The edits you make are reflected on all the pages with that background attached. Those pages are updated as soon as you finish editing the background and move to another page.

 *If you'd just like to view, edit, print, or lock shapes down individually on one page, use layers. Backgrounds are for forming a cohesive look across pages.*

Once you've finished editing the background, you need to return to the foreground page to continue constructing your diagram by selecting the Page tab from the bottom of the Visio window.

Deleting Backgrounds

Backgrounds are special types of pages, so deleting them works similarly to deleting pages, with one small difference. As in other pages, everything on a background page will be deleted when you remove the page. However, any background page that is still attached to a foreground page cannot be removed. You need to remove all the attachments to a background before you delete it.

NOTE *If you try to delete a background page while it is still assigned, Visio warns you to remove it from the foreground page and takes you to that page in order to use the Page Setup window.*

To cancel a page's background assignment, display the foreground page it's attached to. Choose File | Page Setup. The Page Setup dialog box appears, as shown earlier in Figure 3-10. On the Page Properties tab, select None from the Background drop-down list and then click OK.

Once the background page is detached from all foreground pages, you can delete it by right-clicking on the Page tab and selecting Delete from the list.

Adding Graphics

Graphics in your Visio diagrams add personalization and panache to the finished product. There are two ways to add images to your Visio diagrams: you can import images or embed them. Imported images such as bitmaps and JPGs are supported by Visio and work best when you plan to integrate them into your diagram as shapes, annotate an image, or when file size is a concern. This section discusses imported images.

NOTE *Embedded images usually come from Object Linking and Embedding (OLE) programs, such as other applications in the Microsoft Office Suite. For information on OLE functions with Visio, see Chapter 6.*

When you import an image created in another program into Visio, it only exists as a picture in Visio and has none of the properties of Visio shapes. You can only reposition, resize, or crop imported images in Visio, so you should make sure the image editing that needs to be done is finished in the image's original creation program.

You cannot edit imported pictures in Visio because the images go though a filter that translates the image, stripping away the information added by the original creation program so it can be displayed by Visio. You also need to make sure that you save the image in a format Visio can read. A list of all importable formats is in the next section.

Images you import into Visio go though two translations—one when they are saved from the creation program and one when they are imported into Visio—so they may not look the same in Visio as they did in the original program. Make sure you have verified, by both viewing it on the screen and by printing the imported image, that the translated image works for your purposes.

TIP   *Bitmaps and JPGs undergo the least conversion when imported into Visio.*

Importable Image Formats

Visio has translators for many graphics file formats, which are listed in Table 3-2.

File Extension	Creation Program or Interchange Formats
.ai	Adobe Illustrator
.emz	Compressed Enhanced Metafile
.cgm	Computer Graphics Metafile
.cmx	Corel Clipart
.cdr	CorelDRAW Drawing, versions 3.0, 4.0, 5.0, 6.0, and 7.0
.eps	Encapsulated Postscript File
.emf	Enhanced Metafile
.gif	Graphics Interchange Format
.igs	IGES Drawing File Format
.jpg	Joint Photographic Experts Group Format
.pct	Macintosh Picture
.drw	Micrografx Designer Version 3.1
.dsf	Micrografx Designer Version 6.0
.png	Portable Network Graphics
.ps	Postscript File
.tif	Tag Image
.bmp and .dib	Windows Bitmap
.wmf	Windows Metafile
.pcx	ZSoft PC PaintBrush Bitmap

TABLE 3-2   Graphics import formats

Most files you import into Visio as graphic images are translated into metafiles. However, bitmap files (such as .dib, .bmp, and .pcx files) remain bitmaps in the Visio drawing.

Vector-based graphic programs or formats, such as Adobe Illustrator (.ai), CorelDraw (.cdr), Encapsulated PostScript (.eps), and Micrografx Designer (.drw) files, occasionally do not import as smoothly as metafile formats like bitmaps. Their lines sometimes appear jagged when the images are imported into a Visio drawing. You'll usually get better results if you save these types of files in a metafile format before importing them into Visio.

Metafiles are the best type of images to import into Visio, since the Convert to Group command allows you to deconstruct them into groups and then edit the pieces individually.

Importing Images

Visio adds imported images to your diagram as simple shapes with a rectangular selection box and control handles. It's best to add images early in the diagram process to make sure the translation worked well, that way you can take a look at them in Visio and if they didn't work well you still have time to change them.

Importing images into Visio is a simple process. First, make sure you're on the page where the image is to be placed, then choose Insert | Picture | From File. The Picture window appears, as shown in Figure 3-13.

Locate the image file. Once you have selected it, click Open. Depending on the image's file type, Visio may display an Import dialog box like the one shown here:

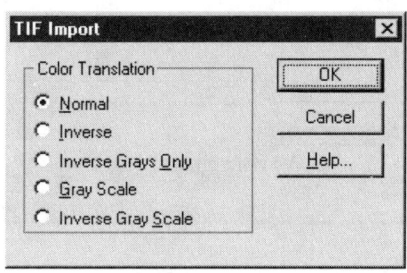

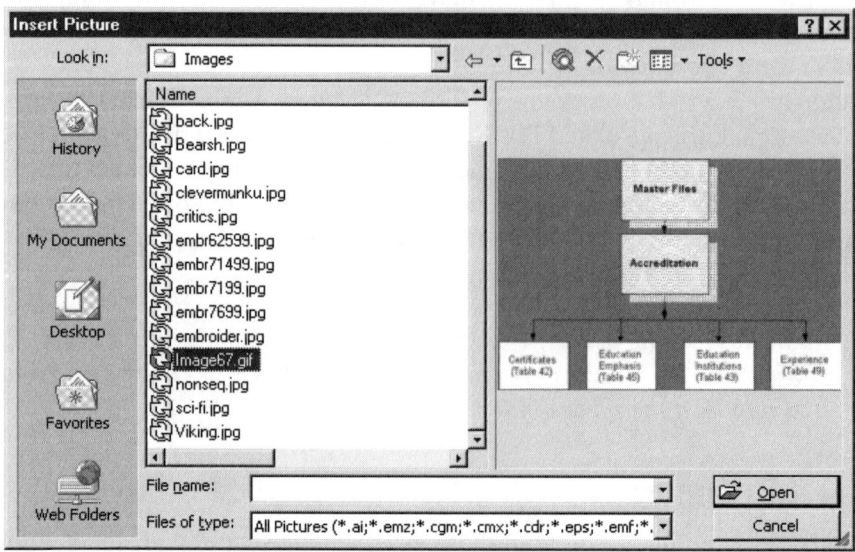

FIGURE 3-13 Insert Picture dialog box

The Import dialog box allows you to set the color and gradient for some image formats. Select the import settings, and click OK. An importing progress bar may appear, like the one shown here:

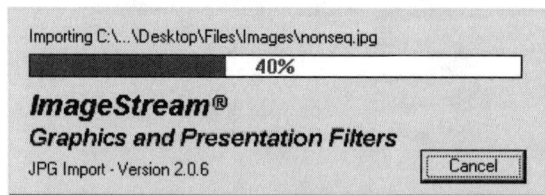

Once the image has been imported, it appears centered on the drawing page you selected. You can now place and resize the image as you would a Visio SmartShape image. However, the imported image will not resize in a way that retains its dimensions or image clarity.

Cropping

Imported images are a special type of shape in Visio. They don't work like SmartShape images, so Visio created a special tool to help you edit imported images: the Crop tool. The Crop tool doesn't work on Visio images, only on imported ones, and is the only tool you have to edit images that don't use the Convert to Group or Fit to Curve functions.

The Crop tool allows you to edit imported images in two ways: you can remove a portion of the image by *cropping* or you can move the image within its selection box by *panning*. To learn how the Crop tool works, see Chapter 2.

You should try to keep cropping to a minimum. Although the cropping tool hides a piece of a graphic, the entire graphic is still stored in the drawing and sent to the printer, causing a lot of unnecessary data pushing. It's best to do major cropping in another application so that the copy stored in the Visio drawing is as small as possible.

Summary

In this chapter, you learned how to use the many Visio layout tools, how to add graphics to your Visio diagrams, and how to take advantage of pages, layers, and backgrounds. In the next chapter, you'll learn how to choose, use, and create stencils and templates.

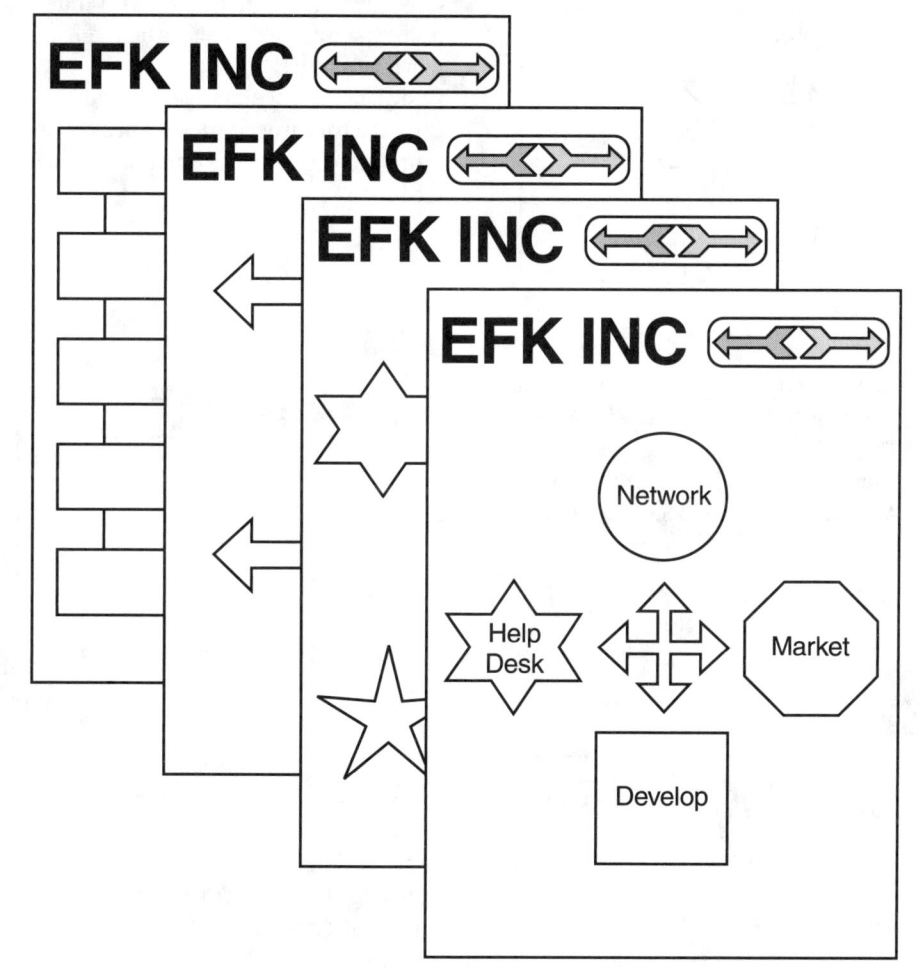

Creating Letterheads or Adding Logos Using Backgrounds

This example shows you how to achieve a coherent look across several pages of your diagram by adding letterhead information or a logo to each page. For more information about how to use backgrounds to achieve this affect, see Backgrounds previously in this chapter.

1

EFK INC

There are several beginning steps to using backgrounds to create a coherent look.
- Open the Visio diagram that has several pages you want to look more uniform.
- Add a new page.
- Designate that page as a background. Once the background page is open on your Visio page, start dragging shapes onto the page..

Create the Logo, or import the logo graphic, and layout how the letterhead will look.
- Think about how your dagrams will interact with your logo or letterhead.
- Also, don't forget to spellcheck any text you've added.

2

EFK INC

3

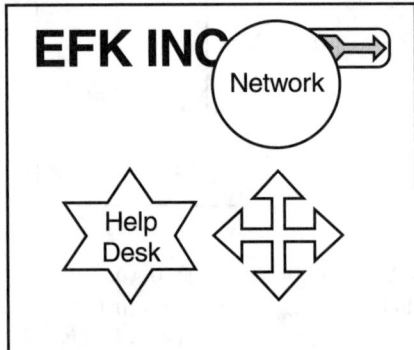

Once you are pleased with your logo and the position of your letterhead, Save your diagram. Then go to one of the pages where you want the letterhead. Select File/Page Setup. On the Page Properties tab, choose your new background page from the list. Click OK and take a look at how the letterhead looks with the diagram already on the page.

4

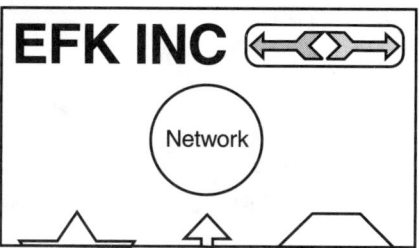

Rearrange the shapes already on the page so the letterhead and logo are clearly visible. **Note**: The letterhead and logo do not move when you move the other shapes, they are locked down from this page and can only be moved on the background page you created. If you need to move them, you'll need to do it from there.

3

Continue to add this background to all the other pages in your diagram, rearranging as necessary to achieve the coherence you need.

5

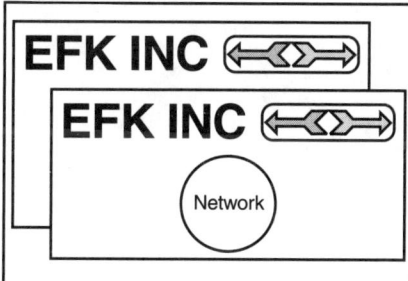

6

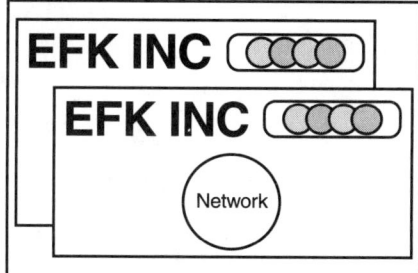

If you ever need to alter the letterhead, or if your logo changes, go back to the background page and make the alterations necessary. All the diagrams that use that background page will automatically update to include the changes.

Chapter 4

Using Stencils and Templates

How to...

- Open and create stencils
- Open and create templates
- Create shapes

In the last chapter, you learned how to use the Visio layout tools, backgrounds, layers and how to add graphics to your diagrams.

In this chapter you'll learn how to find, use, modify, and create stencils. You'll also learn how to create your own master shapes and how to include them in your stencils, and how to find, use, modify, and create templates.

Introducing Master Shapes, Stencils, and Templates

When you began your first diagram in Chapter 2, you may not have realized it but the combination of shapes, stencils, and templates helped you as you drew your first shapes to the page. In Visio these three tools are three interrelated operators. Shapes on your drawing page are created by master shapes. Master shapes are collected into groups and saved for later retrieval on stencils. Stencils and Macros, as well as page options such as orientation and background settings, are collected into templates.

Each of these pieces of a Visio drawing make your creation process quicker and easier. Understanding how stencils and templates work helps you understand how to make your drawings happen quicker and more easily. Understanding even the most basic information about master shapes helps you create your own shapes. Knowing how stencils operate helps you use them more effectively. Templates have great power to collect your most used functions, not only saving you time, but ensuring that similar drawings look the same no matter who did them or when.

To start to understand how all three (shapes, stencils, and templates) interrelate, think back to your first basic diagram. You chose Basic Drawing from the opening window. This is a template. The Basic Drawing template opens, and on the far left-hand side of the Visio window is a green field that contains names and symbols. In the Basic Drawing there are three of these collections, which are your stencils. The Basic Drawing template contains information that opens these three stencils, as well as sets the orientation of the drawing page, the drawing

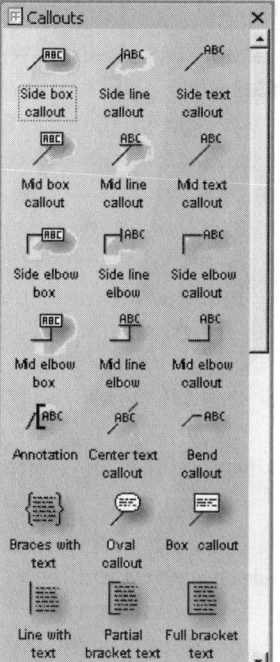

FIGURE 4-1   Callouts stencil

scale, and the default font and colors. The stencils that open (basic shapes, borders and tiles, and backgrounds) all have several shapes with titles on them. These are master shapes. They tell Visio to create a version of themselves when they are moved to the drawing page. This means they create an instance of themsel·es which is the shape you manipulate and use on the drawing page.

You can create your own master shapes and move them to stencils. You can even move master shapes from one stencil to another, or collect master shapes you use often to a stencil you create. You can then collect several stencils into a drawing that has settings that you tend to set over and over into your own new template. This chapter tells you how to accomplish all of these steps.

NOTE   *To learn much more about creating shapes from scratch or about how to significantly alter already existing master shapes, see also Chapter 9 "Creating Shapes."*

Getting to Know Stencils

We'll start this chapter talking about stencils since you are already comfortable using them in your diagrams. Stencils are the workhorses of Visio. They allow you to add shapes to your diagrams with minimal effort, and they ensure that the shapes in your diagrams have a consistent appearance. This ease of creation and uniformity sets Visio apart from other graphics programs.

Stencils are collections of shapes that are related in some way. The Callouts stencil, for example, has all the shapes you need to create callouts in diagrams—including lines, callout bubbles, and brackets. These shapes are included on one stencil to help you complete your diagrams quickly and easily. To use the shapes in a diagram, you simply open the Callouts stencil and drag the shapes from the stencil to your drawing page. Figure 4-1 shows the Callouts stencil.

NOTE   *A shape can appear on many different stencils. For example, some of the shapes on the Callouts stencil appear on other stencils as well.*

Stencil files contain information about the shapes contained on the stencil; they have a .vss file extension and are usually kept in the same folder as the Visio program files. The shapes on a stencil are *master shapes,* which become individual shapes when you drag them off the stencil onto the drawing page. The information that determines a shape's attributes and behavior is contained in the master shape. You can create your own master shapes, or you can move a master shape on to another stencil so you have it when you need it.

Choosing the Right Stencil

When you start a new diagram, you should have a plan for it. This gives you some idea of the types of shapes you'll need and helps you identify the stencils you'll need to finish the project. If you know what shapes you'll be using, you can determine which stencils to open.

TIP   *You can open as many stencils as you like while working on a diagram.*

Choosing the right stencils for the job may seem a bit confusing at first, because Visio includes a tremendous number of stencils. But the people at Visio have worked very hard to make the process as painless as possible. Stencils have been grouped into folders by topic to help you locate the ones you need.

In addition, Visio includes a search engine—the Find Shape window—to help you find stencils containing particular shapes. Visio also includes many templates that open certain stencils automatically. For now, though, we'll only discuss opening stencils using the folders and the Shape Explorer.

Navigating Stencil Folders

Stencils can be added to any diagram. But first you need to know how to choose the right stencils from the large selection included in Visio.

Visio Standard has nine folders containing stencils. Table 4-1 lists these folders and describes the types of stencils they contain.

Appendix A of this book lists all of Visio's stencils, the folders where they're located, and the shapes they contain.

Using Find Shape

Sometimes, you'll want to use a particular shape or set of shapes, but you won't know which stencil you need. Visio has included Find Shape to help you find the right stencil. You can use Find Shape to search for shapes by entering keywords. Find Shape tells you the stencils on which a particular shape appears and the folders where the stencils are located, as well as giving you some basic information about the intended use for that particular master shape.

To use Find Shape to find a shape, open the Find Shape window by clicking the Find Shape button on the toolbar, or by selecting File | Find Shape. The Find

Folder	Description of Stencils
Block Diagram	Basic diagrams and simple connections, usually used in conjunction with more complicated stencils.
Flowchart	Complete flowcharting tools with hundreds of different shapes.
Forms and Charts	Simple charts and graphs, basic forms, and marketing-support diagrams.
Map	Tools for creating directional maps of any location and for integrating maps into diagrams.
Network	Computer and network shapes for basic network outlines and other related diagrams.
Organizational Chart	Shapes for creating organizational charts.
Project Schedule	Calendar, process-mapping, and timeline shapes.
Visio Extras	Miscellaneous stencils, including clip art and callout stencils.

TABLE 4-1   Stencil folders in Visio

Shape window opens over the stencils on the left-hand side of your screen, as shown in Figure 4-2.

To see Find Shape in action, type **diamond** in the "Search for" box and click Go. Find Shape searches Visio for the keyword and returns a list of shapes, as shown in Figure 4-3.

The entirety of each portion of Find Shape is replaced by the results of your search. Use the scroll bar on the side of the Find Shape window to see all the results your search generated and for more options. When you perform a search, Find Shape tells you how many matches your keywords found. For example, if you search for the keyword "diamond," Find Shape comes up with six matches for shapes.

Find Shape, by default, also gives you information about each occurrence of the shape it found. This information is meant to help you decide which of its many matches are the diamond shape you looking for. You also receive information

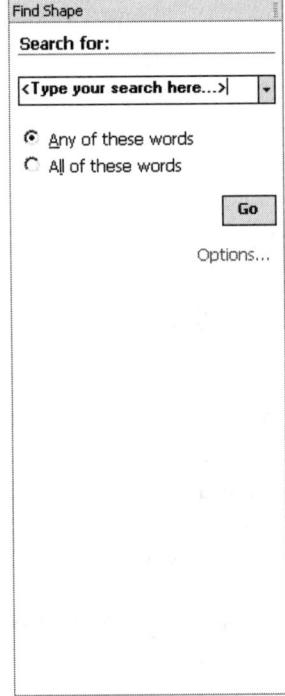

FIGURE 4-2   Find Shape

FIGURE 4-3   Find Shape with results

about the stencil the shape is on. the way (Visio collects the shapes that meet your search criteria into green folder shapes that list the stencil that contains them).

Setting Options for Find Shape

To make Find Shape more versatile and to help you find the shapes you are looking for, Visio has included an Options window.

First, there is a right-click menu available once you have found the shapes that allows you to turn on and off the information you receive about the shapes. You can choose to remove the green folders around the shapes by deselecting group from the right-click menu. You can also alter the view of the shapes by using the View menu. There are four options on the View menu in Find Shape, listed with their actions in Table 4-2.

View menu options	Effect
Icons and Name	Removes the descriptive text from the shape and gives you just the name and shortcut icon.
Icons and Details	The default, gives you names, details, and the shortcut icon for each shape found.
Names Only	Displays just the name of the shape with no image or text.
Icons Only	Shows the shortcut icon with no text of any kind.

TABLE 4-1 View options for the right-click menu in Find Shape

NOTE *All of the View options work with the group option turned on or off.*

There are still more options you can set in the Find Shape window using the Options… link at the bottom of the Find Shape window. The Options window, shown in Figure 4-4, opens when you click Options… and has two tabs.

The General tab of the Options window lets you set where Visio looks for the shape. By default Visio looks on the Visio Internet site for shapes as well in the program files you have on your system. You can turn off this option by selecting the drop-down list for Where: under Search. Deselect both The Internet and Visio Web Shape, and Visio will only look on your system for shapes you ask it to find.

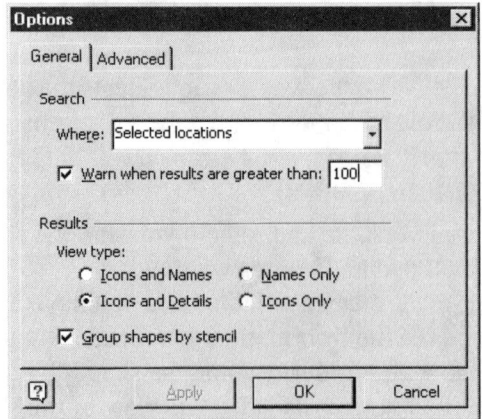

FIGURE 4-4 Find Shape Options

NOTE *Searching for shapes over the Internet can cause shape files to be copied to your hard drive, which may be a security problem. Talk to your system administrator about this issue before searching for shapes over the Internet.*

You can also ask Visio to warn you when there are more than a certain number of shapes found. This can be any number of shapes, but the default is 100. To enable this option, check the box next to Warn when results are greater than: and make sure to set the number. Since it appears that nothing is happening when you hit Go on the Find Shape window until shapes appear on the list, set this number fairly low.

NOTE *The last set of options in the General tab are the same View and Group options you can set via the right-click menu in the Find Shape window itself.*

The Advanced tab of the Options window has two parts.

The first part lets you delete any temporary shape files that were created when you searched for shapes over the Internet. The files take up quite a bit of hard drive space, and once you no longer need these shapes you should delete them using the button provided.

The second part of the Advanced tab allows you to update your index of shapes on your own computer. If you have created shapes of your own, or if you have added shapes from some external source, make sure to click the button provided so you can find these shapes with Find Shape.

NOTE *Once you have found the shape you are looking for you can simply drag it to your drawing page or you can right-click on the stencil name and open the stencil.*

Working with Stencils

Stencils are essential for creating professional-looking Visio diagrams. To get the most out of Visio's stencils you need to know how to open them and how to reposition them onscreen. As you'll see, it can be very handy to have multiple stencils open and accessible at the same time.

Opening Stencils

In addition to using Find Shape to open stencils, you can open a new stencil using Visio's menus. To open a stencil, in the main Visio window, select File | Stencils | Open Stencil. The Open Stencil window appears, as shown in Figure 4-5.

NOTE   *You can also display the Open Stencil window by clicking the Open Stencil button on the toolbar.*

The Open Stencil window allows you to choose from several dozen stencils. Double-click a folder in the window to see a list of the stencils it contains. Each stencil contains a different set of shapes. (Remember, however, that a particular shape may appear on more than one stencil.) Visio helps you choose among stencils by providing a description of each stencil in the lower left-hand corner of the Open Stencil dialog box. Select a stencil (without opening it) to view its description.

Once you've found the stencil you need, select it and click Open. The Open Stencil dialog box closes and the stencil appears in the main Visio window.

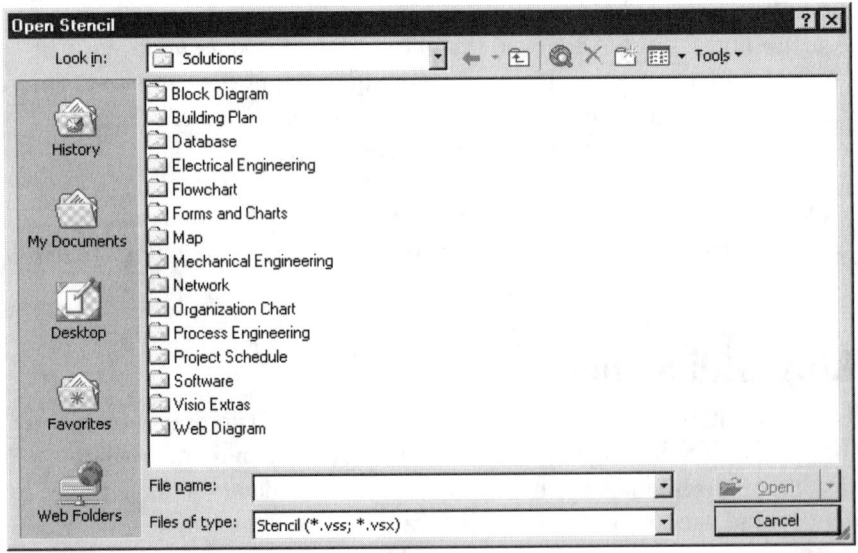

FIGURE 4-5   Open Stencil window

 *You can have more than one stencil open at a time. To view an open stencil that's hidden behind another stencil, click the stencil's title bar to bring it to the front.*

Moving Stencils

When you open new stencils, they automatically appear on the left-hand side of the main Visio window. If you've rotated the drawing page and zoomed in, having all your stencils on the left side of the window can be inconvenient. Once you've altered the page orientation the stencils can get in your way. Visio gives you several ways around this problem. You can move stencils to the outside of the sides of the window, you can stick them to the edge of the pasteboard, and you can "undock" them.

When a stencil appears on the left side of the window, as you've seen so far, it is considered *docked,* or locked to the pasteboard. A docked stencil is locked in place and can't be dragged from its location. Although by default, stencils are docked on the left side of the main Visio window, you can dock them on any side of the window. To dock a stencil on a different side, click on the stencil's title bar and drag the stencil to another side of the window.

In addition to docking stencils on different sides of the window, you can undock stencils so they can be moved around freely within the main Visio window. You can move undocked an stencil, which is called a *floating stencil,* by click on its titlebar and dragging it on to the pasteboard. This makes it much easier to move out of the way than a docked stencil.

Floating stencils are totally unattached to the Visio window and will float anywhere on your desktop.

Floating stencils are also handy because they can be attached to the sides of the pasteboard and then you can use Autohide to roll up the stencil. When you roll up a floating stencil, only its title bar is visible until you place your mouse on the titlebar and then the whole stencil is visible. This enables you to keep many stencils open without using up a lot of valuable screen real estate. Figure 4-6 shows three floating stencils, two of which are rolled up.

To make a docked stencil become a floating stencil, click on its titlebar and drag it to the pasteboard. To use the Autohide feature, move the stencil until it is near the side of your pasteboard. You'll know it's attached to the side of the pasteboard when the titlebar for the stencil moves so it is between the stencil shapes and the drawing pages instead of at the top of the stencil.

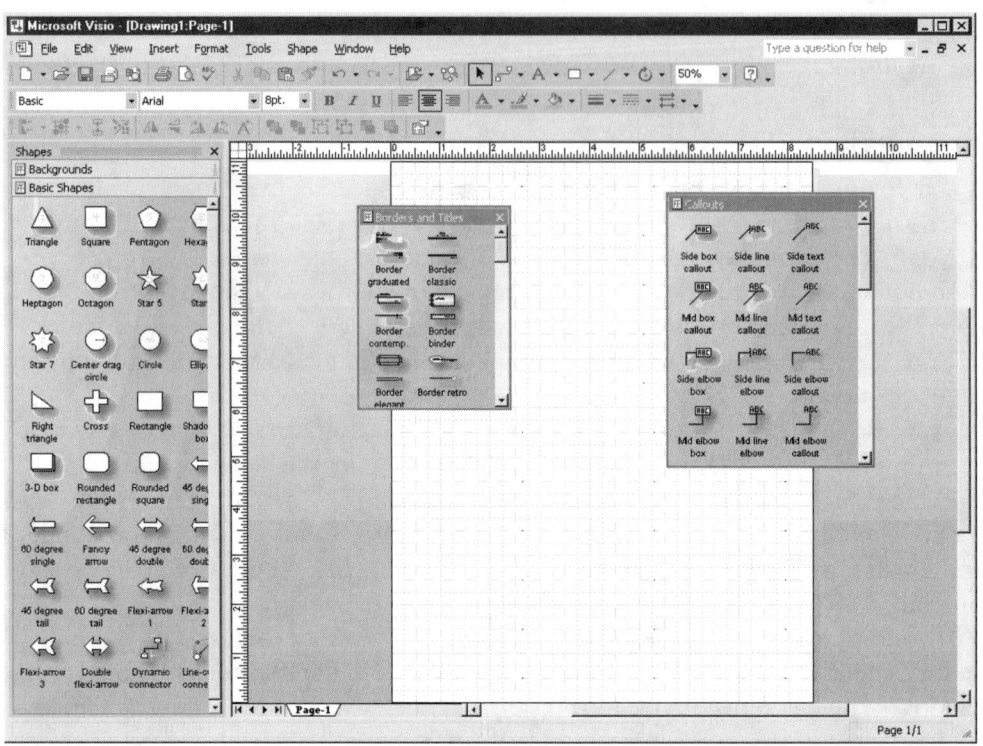

FIGURE 4-6   Floating stencils

To autohide the stencil, right-click and choose Autohide from the right-click menu. Now only the stencil's titlebar is visible until you place your mouse cursor over the stencil's titlebar.

TIP   *You can also enable Autohide by using the push-pin icon on the titlebar of the stencil. When the push-pin icon is down, Autohide is off and the stencil won't move. When the push-pin is up, Autohide is on and the stencil rolls up to show only the titlebar.*

The stencil can be redocked by clicking on the title bar and dragging it back to the upper-left or upper-right corner of the pasteboard.

Closing Stencils

To close a stencil, right-click on the stencil's title bar and choose Close from the stencil's shortcut menu. Alternatively, you can click the Close button, the small X in the upper-right corner of the stencil. This removes the stencil from your diagram.

Understanding Master Shapes and Changing Stencils

Having mastered choosing, opening, moving, and closing stencils, you're ready to tackle the slightly more complicated processes of modifying stencils and creating new stencils. However, before you can do this, you need to understand the concept of *master shapes,* which comprise stencils.

Master Shapes and ShapeSheets

Master shapes are the shapes on the stencils. To modify or create new stencils, you'll be dealing with master shapes. Master shapes contain all the information that goes into making Visio's shapes smart. This includes not only the number of sides and the color of the shape, but also how it's resized, how it behaves under rotation, and how added text behaves, as well as all the custom properties that come with some shapes.

All information for master shapes is stored in *ShapeSheets,* which are databases that contain the programming information for the master shapes. The basics of ShapeSheets are discussed here and they are addressed in more detail in Chapter 9, "Creating Shapes."

To modify an existing stencil or create a new one, you change master shapes. There are hundreds of master shapes that come with Visio, and there's also a way to make master shapes of your own.

Modifying a Stencil

Modifying a stencil means changing the order, arrangement, content, or number of master shapes on it. The most common type of stencil modification is the addition of shapes to a stencil by including their master shapes.

No matter what kind of change you're making to a stencil, the first step should always be to open the stencil so you can change it. This means you need to open the stencil in *read/write mode.* Normally, when you open a stencil, you open it as *read-only,* meaning you can't make any changes to the original stencil. All changes you attempt to make are blocked.

NOTE
If you try to make changes to a read-only stencil, Visio asks if you'd like to open the stencil in read/write mode.

To open a stencil so you can change it, select File | Stencil | Open Stencil. Select the stencil you'd like to modify. Then, on the lower right-hand side of the Open Stencil window (shown earlier in Figure 4-5), select the drop-down list activated by the arrow just to the right of the Open button. Select the option to open a Copy of the stencil file. Once you've done that, click Open to open a copy of the stencil in read/write mode.

CAUTION
Never open the original file for a stencil unless you intend to destroy the original configuration or the only access you may have to some of the master shapes on that stencil. Always open a copy instead.

You can also convert an open stencil you've already created from read-only mode to read/write mode by selecting Edit from the Stencil menu.

Copying Existing Master Shapes

To copy an existing master shape from one stencil to another, make sure both stencils are open, and then drag the master shape from the original stencil to the stencil you're modifying. The new master shape appears on the modified stencil along with the other shapes, which automatically move aside to make room for the new shape.

NOTE
When you close a modified stencil by clicking the Close button, Visio asks if you'd like to save the stencil.

When you're satisfied with the arrangement of the master shapes on the stencil, select Save from the File menu. The Save As dialog box appears, as shown in Figure 4-7. Make sure to save the stencil in a place where you can find it again. The best place to save a modified stencil is where Visio keeps its stencils: in the Visio directory, under Solutions.

TIP
If you create several stencils, you may want to group them in a folder of their own (under Solutions).

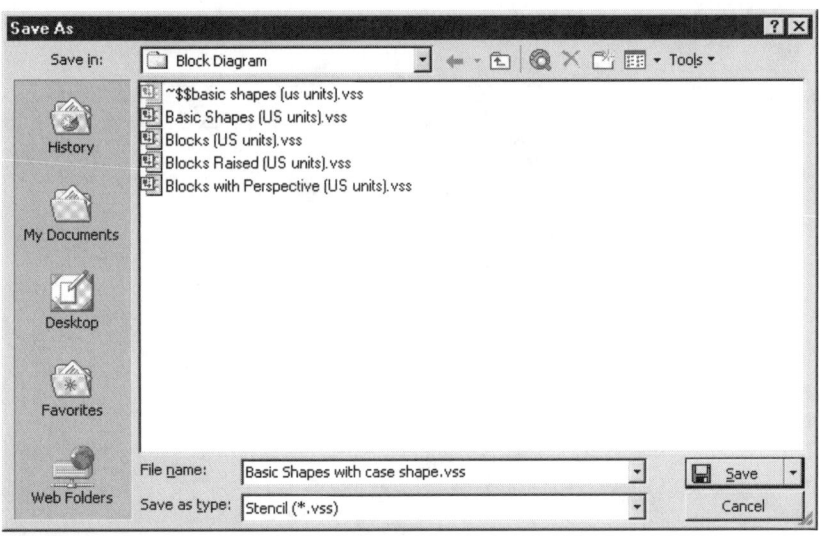

FIGURE 4-7   Saving a stencil

Removing Master Shapes

To remove a master shape from a stencil, open the stencil in read/write mode and right-click on the master. Choose Delete from the menu. This removes the shape from the stencil. The other shapes automatically rearrange themselves to fill in the gap. Make sure to save the modified stencil by selecting the stencil and choosing Save from the File menu.

Never remove a shape from a stencil that came with Visio. This may be your only access to this shape.

Changing How Master Shapes Appear

To change how master shapes appear on a stencil, first open the stencil in read/write mode. Then right-click the master shape and choose Master Properties. The Master Properties window opens as shown in Figure 4-8. This window allows you to change the name and other display properties for the master shape.

For more information about using the options in the Master Properties window, see Creating New Master Shapes later in this chapter.

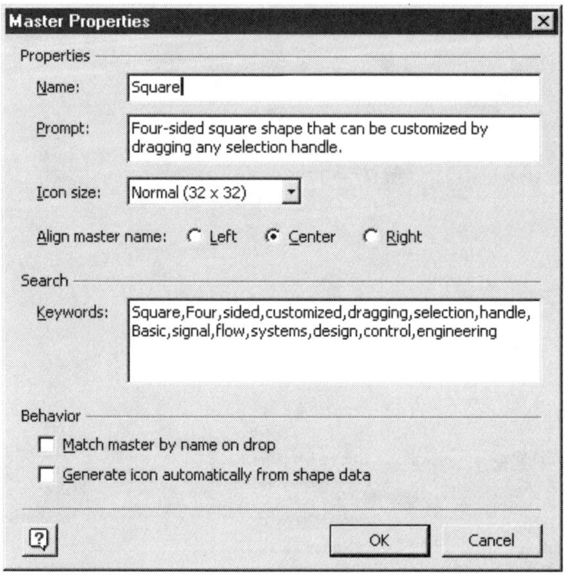

FIGURE 4-8   Master Properties window for a square

If you'd like to change the icon for a master shape, right-click on the shape and choose Edit Icon. This opens a dialog box for editing the icon. Make sure to save the stencil after any modifications.

NOTE   *For more information on editing how a master shape appears on a stencil, see Chapter 9 "Making Shapes"*

To reorder the master shapes on a stencil, first open the stencil in read/write mode. You can then reposition the master shapes by dragging them. When they are arranged in the proper order, save the stencil.

TIP   *Visio automatically arranges the masters on a stencil so they are in neat rows. When you move shapes around on a stencil, the alignment is all done for you.*

Introducing ShapeSheets

Visio keeps track of all shapes using ShapeSheets. Whenever you create a new shape, Visio uses a ShapeSheet to keep track of it. Likewise, Visio uses ShapeSheets to keep track of changes to all of the original shapes on the stencils that come with the program. ShapeSheets are how Visio knows how to draw and move a shape when you drag it to the drawing page.

ShapeSheets are a series of tables that contain all the settings for a shape. Figure 4-9 shows the ShapeSheet for a standard square.

ShapeSheets are generally used by developers when creating new shapes or modifying the behavior of existing shapes. You can view the ShapeSheet for a shape by selecting it on the drawing page and then choosing Window | Show ShapeSheet.

ShapeSheets are made up of tables that describe the shape. For example, the ShapeSheet for a square, shown in Figure 4-9, starts with a Shape Transform table, listing the width and height of the square as well as its current location and the

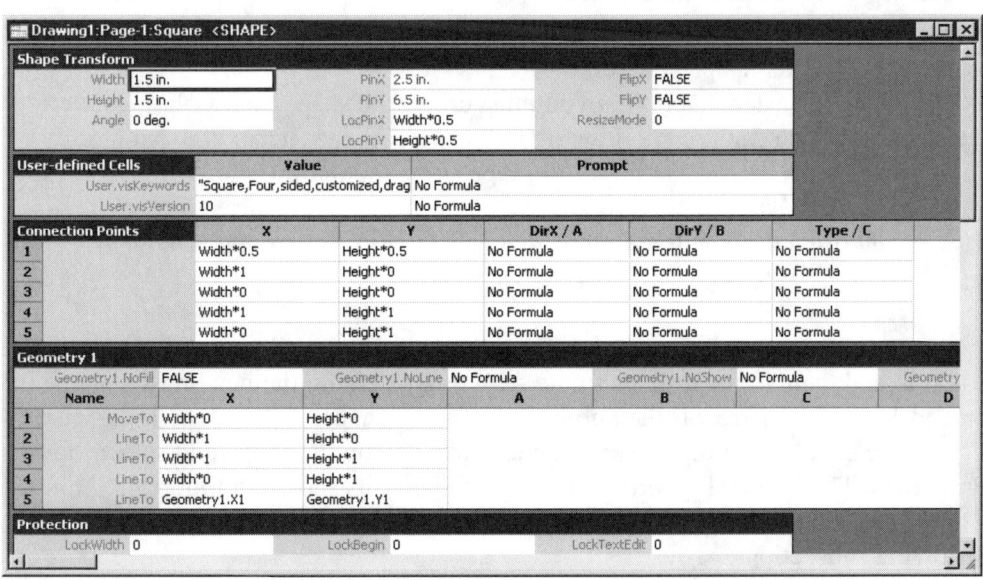

FIGURE 4-9   ShapeSheet for a square

degrees it's been rotated. Then there is a Connection Points table listing all the connection points set for the square, and so on until the end of the ShapeSheet. There is a total of 15 tables on the ShapeSheet describing a basic square. ShapeSheets for more complicated shapes have many more tables.

Inside the cells of some of the tables in a ShapeSheet are formulas. It's often more accurate to describe the movement and relationship of a shape with formulas rather than simply with numbers or text. The formulas are what makes Visio's shapes "smart," because formulas can handle complex motions and changes and still keep the shape looking the way you expect. ShapeSheet information can be viewed as current values instead of the formula by choosing View | Values.

ShapeSheets are a very advanced topic for most Visio users. If you need more information about Visio ShapeSheets go to Chapter 9, "Making Shapes," and you should install and read the developer's documentation that comes with Visio.

> **NOTE**   *To close a ShapeSheet, click on the Close button in the upper-right corner of the ShapeSheet window.*

Creating New Master Shapes

If the shape you'd like to add to a stencil doesn't already exist in Visio, you need to create the master shape yourself.

To create a master shape, first you must create the shape you wish to convert into a master. You can use the drawing tools to create the shape, you can modify an existing shape, or you can import a shape from another program.

> **NOTE**   *Imported objects are often turned into clip art master shapes, not Visio SmartShape objects.*

Once you've created the shape, open a copy of the stencil you would like to add it to and then drag the shape to the stencil. By default, the new master shape is named Master.x, where x is the number of existing shapes in the stencil plus one. To change the name of the master shape, right-click on the shape and select Master Properties. The Master Properties dialog box opens, as shown in Figure 4-8. Enter a new name for the master shape, and set other options as described in the following subsections.

- ■ **Name**   Sets the name that appears beneath the master shape's icon in the stencil window. Master shape names can be up to 31 characters.

■ **Prompt**   Specifies the text that appears when you hover the mouse pointer over the master shape's icon in the stencil window.

Keep your icon names and prompts short.

■ **Icon Size**   Sets the size of the master shape icon. The default setting for an icon's size is Normal. The Tall setting is the same width as Normal, but twice the height. The Wide setting is the same height, but twice the width. The Double setting is twice as wide and twice as tall as Normal.

■ **Align Master Name**   Sets how the name appears in relation to the icon for the master shape on the stencil.

■ **Keywords**   Lists the names and words that cause this master shape to come up when Find Shape is used. Visio search all the keywords for all master shapes when you click the Go button in Find Shape. Separate your keywords with a comma.

■ **Match master by name on drop**   When checked, allows you to make sure that no matter which stencil a shape comes from, it will always be formatted the way you have it formatted. When this box is checked and a shape is dragged from the stencil, Visio automatically checks to make sure that no other versions of that shape are on open stencils. If there is another version of the shape on an open customized stencil, Visio makes sure the new formatting is carried over to the shape you just added, even if it was dragged from a standard stencil.

■ **Generate icon automatically from shape data**   When checked, Visio automatically creates the master shape's icon from the shape.

You can also edit an icon so it displays better at a different size by right-clicking on the master shape on the stencil and choosing Edit. This opens a dialog box for editing the icon.

For more information about editing icons or about the Master Properties window, see Chapter 9 "Making Shapes."

Once you've chosen all the options needed for the new master shape, click OK, and the Master Properties window closes. Complete your changes to the stencil and save it.

Remember that all the master shapes supplied by Visio are copyrighted. You may not sell or distribute original or modified Visio masters. Feel free to copy, reorganize, and modify them for your own use, though. You may also distribute drawings that contain them.

Creating a New Stencil

Creating a new stencil allows you the flexibility of collecting the shapes you use most often together on one stencil without the bother of deleting shapes from an already existing stencil. New stencils, like all Visio stencils, can contain any master shapes that come with Visio or new master shapes you've created.

To create a new stencil, select File | Stencil | New Stencil. A new blank stencil opens, as shown in Figure 4-10.

Once the blank stencil is open, add shapes to it as you would any stencil you're modifying. Remember to save the stencil in a place where you can find it again. It's best to save stencils where Visio stores its stencils, in the Solutions folder in

FIGURE 4-10   New stencil

the Visio directory. You may even want to create another folder in the Solutions directory to hold your new custom stencils.

Understanding Templates

Stencils allow you to create shapes quickly and uniformly. However, a Visio diagram consists of more than just shapes; page dimensions, shape colors, and backgrounds are all important features of professional looking diagrams. To help you with these other features, Visio includes a variety of drawing types, called *templates,* with preformatted layout and page information. Templates handle the formatting for you when you create standard types of diagrams.

A template is a Visio file that opens one or more stencils and contains styles and settings for a particular kind of drawing. You can create a new drawing with a template's styles and settings by opening that template. When you open Visio and choose a drawing type (other than Basic Drawing), you automatically open a template.

When you start a drawing with a template, a Visio file opens containing:

■ One or more stencils containing related shapes.

■ A blank drawing page using a grid and measurement system that's appropriate for the type of drawing you're creating.

■ A drawing page set up with the correct scale and page size, if appropriate.

■ Styles for text, lines, and shape colors appropriate to the type of drawing you're creating, saving you the time it takes to define your own styles.

NOTE   *Some templates also include preformatted text blocks where you can add your own text, backgrounds, and even shapes.*

Using templates ensures consistency in your diagrams. The templates in the Solutions folders were created to help you with many common tasks. These templates save you time and energy by automatically setting formatting and other options. They let you get right to the task at hand.

Choosing the Right Template

When you open a new diagram, Visio asks you to choose a drawing type. At that point, it helps to know which template is likely to be the most useful. Like stencils,

Visio makes the job of choosing the right template easy by grouping templates into folders. Both templates and stencils have been organized into a simple structure. Table 4-3 lists the template folders for Visio Standard.

 *Appendix A includes a complete list of all the templates that come with Visio Standard and Professional and describes what each template contains.*

Working with Templates

When you opened your first diagram, you opened a template, but you may not have known that. To get the most out of templates, you need to not only know how to open a template, but you should understand how a template differs from a blank drawing. This section walks you though the use of a basic template.

Opening a Template

A template can be opened with a new diagram, or it can be added to a diagram that already exists.

You can open a new template at any time by selecting Open on the toolbar. If you click Open, Visio opens Basic Diagram. If you choose the list accessed by the arrow just to the right of the button you'll see the list of all templates organized by their folders. You can open one by selecting from that list. A new diagram opens on a new blank page, in a separate window.

Folder	Description of Templates
Block Diagram	Three templates for basic diagrams, both 2-D and 3-D.
Flowchart	Complete flowcharting tools with ten templates.
Forms and Charts	Templates for graphs and charts, including pie charts, form designs, and marketing charts.
Map	Templates for creating 2-D and 3-D directional maps.
Network	Templates for creating diagrams of networks, including specialized templates for specific manufacturers.
Organizational Chart	Templates for creating charts of a company or organization and the Organizational Chart wizard.
Project Schedule	Templates for calendar, process-mapping, and timeline shapes.

TABLE 4-2 Templates in Visio Standard

> **TIP**   *You can also open a template by selecting File | New and then choosing a template from the list.*

The new diagram has all the formatting and stencils included in the template. Figure 4-11 shows a new diagram with the Basic Flowchart template attached. As you can see, diagrams with templates attached look just like normal Visio diagrams, but they have stencils and styles already included.

> **NOTE**   *You can open more than one diagram at a time in Visio, allowing you to have several templates open at once, each in their own window.*

You can also alter any diagram currently being created by attaching a different template to it. Attaching a template to an already existing drawing will have

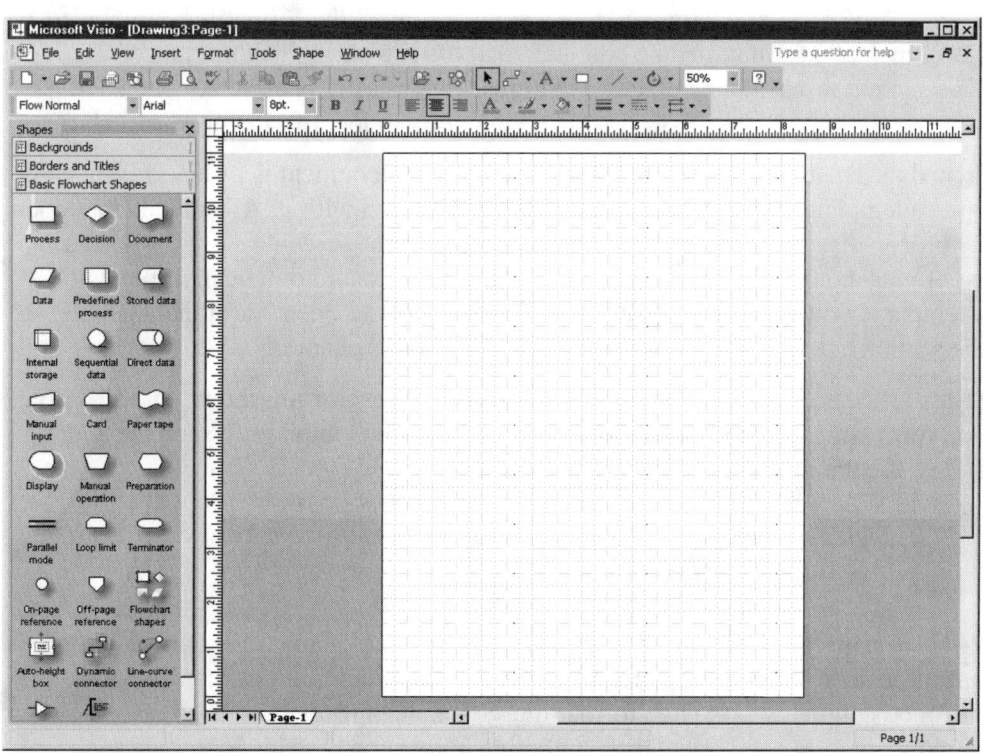

FIGURE 4-11   Basic Flowchart template

a dramatic effect on the drawing since all the formatting and other settings from the new template overwrite all the settings in the original template. However, this can be a useful approach when you realize you need other settings for your drawing halfway though creation.

To attach a template to an existing diagram, first make sure the diagram is open in the main Visio window, and then select File | Open. Navigate to your Visio directory (usually in the Program Files folder) and then to the Solutions folder. Find the template you want, and click Open. The template attaches to the open diagram, overwriting all conflicting formatting.

 *Because templates contain formatting to help you create diagrams, they can overwrite your own formatting when you add them to existing diagrams.*

Identifying Included Formats

To make the most of a template, you need to know all the formatting it includes. The template's formatting acts like defaults, often working behind the scenes. This section discusses the diagram features that are usually affected when you attach a template. You'll also learn where to look to identify the new settings.

Stencils   The most noticeable addition to a blank document is a stencil. When you open a template, at least one stencil will usually open with it. All stencils that open with templates are docked on the left-hand side of the screen.

If you should need stencils other than the ones that automatically open with a template, you are free to open more. To learn how to open additional stencils, see the section entitled "Opening Stencils" earlier in this chapter.

Styles   A template often includes many styles. Styles for lines, text, and fills give you formatting options and are an important part of a template. To see the added styles, use the drop-down lists on the toolbars.

 *Styles only work for you if you use them. Be sure to take advantage of the styles in your templates.*

Page Formatting   Units, page size, layer settings, and many other formatting options can be set in a template. To make creating diagrams easier, Visio has included templates with page formatting. Some page formatting changes are obvious, such as page orientation. Other page formatting is less obvious, such as layer settings.

To find the page formatting settings, you may need to look in a couple of places. The File | Page Setup menu is one place. So is the Ruler & Grid dialog box, which you access from the Tools menu. Page formatting changes vary widely from one template to another, so it's best to check for these changes whenever you open a template for the first time.

Altering and Creating Templates

Now that you understand the basics of template use, you're ready to move on to modifying templates and creating templates of your own. Templates, like stencils, always need to be opened in read/write mode before any alteration can take place.

To open a template so you can alter it, select File | Open. Navigate to the Visio folder where the templates are stored (usually in your root directory under Program Files|Microsoft Office|Visio|1033|Solutions). Navigate though the template folders, identifiable by their .vst extension, and select the template you'd like to modify. Then, on the lower right-hand side of the Open window, shown in Figure 4-12, select the drop-down list activated by the arrow just to the right of the Open button. Select the option to open a Copy of the template file. Once you've done that, click Open to open a copy of the template in read/write mode.

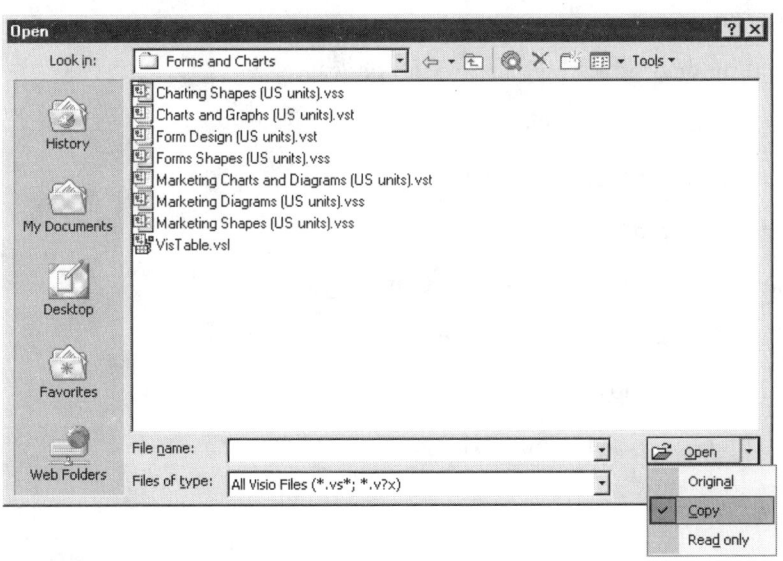

FIGURE 4-12   Opening a template in read/rite mode

 *Don't open the original file for a template unless you intend to delete it. Open a copy of the template instead.*

Modifying a Template

If you're creating several diagrams that need to look the same, modifying one of Visio's templates will save you time and ensure that no matter who creates the diagrams they will look the same. Modifying an existing template allows you to include your own style and page formatting settings and the stencils you're likely to use. Modifying a template saves you the repetitive steps required to open the appropriate stencils, create styles, and establish page settings for each drawing, and guarantees that you won't forget a step or setting that could make your drawing turn out differently than you had envisioned.

To modify a template, first open a copy of the template in read/write mode, as explained in the previous section. Then make all the setting changes you need to create the new template. The most common setting changes are:

- Adding or subtracting stencils
- Creating new stencils with special master shapes
- Changing page formatting options
- Altering the size of the page
- Adding or subtracting background pages
- Changing printing options
- Changing connector options
- Adding or removing macros
- Changing the View or Snap & Glue options
- Changing backgrounds or layers
- Adding or removing styles
- Adding or removing buttons from the toolbars

Adding Styles

New styles save you the effort of repeatedly making the same changes to text or shapes. Adding a style to a template that already exists saves you even more effort because each time you open the new template, you'll have the style there waiting for you. Before you can add a new style to a template, you need to create the style.

To define a new style, choose Define Styles from the Format menu. The Define Styles dialog box appears, as shown in Figure 4-13.

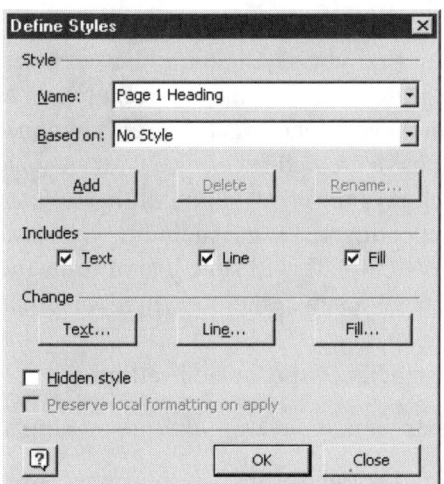

NOTE   *Defining styles assumes you're creating a new style and not simply modifying an old one.*

- **Style**   Shows all the current styles in the document. If a shape is selected, the style for that shape is highlighted in the list. If you're naming a new style, type the name here.

- **Based on**   Selects the parent style for your newly created style. If you don't want to base your new style on an existing style, choose No Style in this box.

- **Includes Text, Line, Fill**   Specifies whether the style includes attributes for lines, fills, or text.

- **Change Text, Line, Fill**   Allows you to change the styles for text, line, and fill. The buttons open the Font, Line, and Fill dialog boxes so you can change attributes for the style. By default, these dialog boxes show the

FIGURE 4-13   Define Styles

attributes for the style listed in the Style box. If the style is listed as New Style, they show the Visio default styles. Choosing OK in the Line, Fill, or Text dialog box returns you to the Define Styles dialog box.

- **Hidden style**   Makes the style unprintable (and possibly unseen on screen). All shapes with this formatting are hidden.

- **Preserve local formatting on apply**   If checked, prevents the style's attributes from replacing formatting you have applied directly to the shape. Uncheck the "Preserve local formatting on apply" checkbox if you want the style to replace all previous formatting.

> **NOTE**   *If you try to close a modified template by clicking on the Close button, Visio asks if you'd like to save the template.*

Once satisfied that you've made all the setting changes you need, you're ready to save the template. Select Save As from the File menu. It's vital that you save the file with a .vst extension, since the difference for Visio between a template and a diagram is the extension. Also, make sure you save the new template somewhere you can find it again. It's best to save the template where Visio has its templates, under the Visio directory in the Solutions folder. This location guarantees the template will be available to you in both the File | New and Open menus.

Creating a New Template

There are times when you find you're changing the same settings over and over again as you work on new diagrams; or maybe you always open the same stencils when you create a certain diagram, stencils that aren't included in an already existing template. Or maybe you have created several of your own stencils and want them collected in one place for easy retrieval. If any of these statements are true for you, or if you find yourself repeating tasks and including the same information over and over, making a brand new template will save lots of time and energy.

You might want to create a new template when you create drawings that:

- Use specialized stencils or specialized settings.

- Need new styles as well as several other formatting settings.

- Require customized layout settings such as page size or scale, window size and position, or even something as simple as page orientation.

■ Often use a particular background or set of layers. For example, if you place your company logo in every drawing, you can create a template with that background or set of layers in place.

Another bonus of new templates is that a new template allows you to start from scratch. You don't need to find out what settings have been modified in an existing template. This will help assure that your diagrams look uniform and are exactly the way you want them without any formatting or layout surprises.

Creating a template completely from scratch is almost exactly like modifying a template with one small difference. Instead of opening a template's read/write mode to start the process, all you need to do is open a plain blank new document.

To open a blank Visio template with no stencils or formatting set, choose Blank Drawing from the list on the right-hand side of the Select Template window that opens when you launch Visio. The Blank Drawing can be difficult to find, it's listed under New, but is worth the search since it has no formatting of any kind set.

Make all the alterations you want to the blank diagram, then save it. It is vital to make sure your template gets saved with a .vst extension, since it becomes a document if you do not. Also make sure to check the workspace is saved by selecting the drop-down list activated by the arrow just to the right of the Save button. Select the option to save the Workspace of the template file. Once you've done that, and verified you're saving it as a .vst file, click Save.

 *If you don't save the workspace, the changes you've made to the blank diagram won't be saved and you'll have to re-create your new template.*

Summary

In this chapter you've learned how to find, use, and create stencils, how to create master shapes and include them in your stencils, and how to find, use, and modify templates.

In the next chapter, you'll learn the how to create and use flowcharts. You'll also learn how to use databases to create flowcharts, as well as how to use flowcharts to create databases.

Personalizing Diagrams by Adding Your Shapes to Stencils

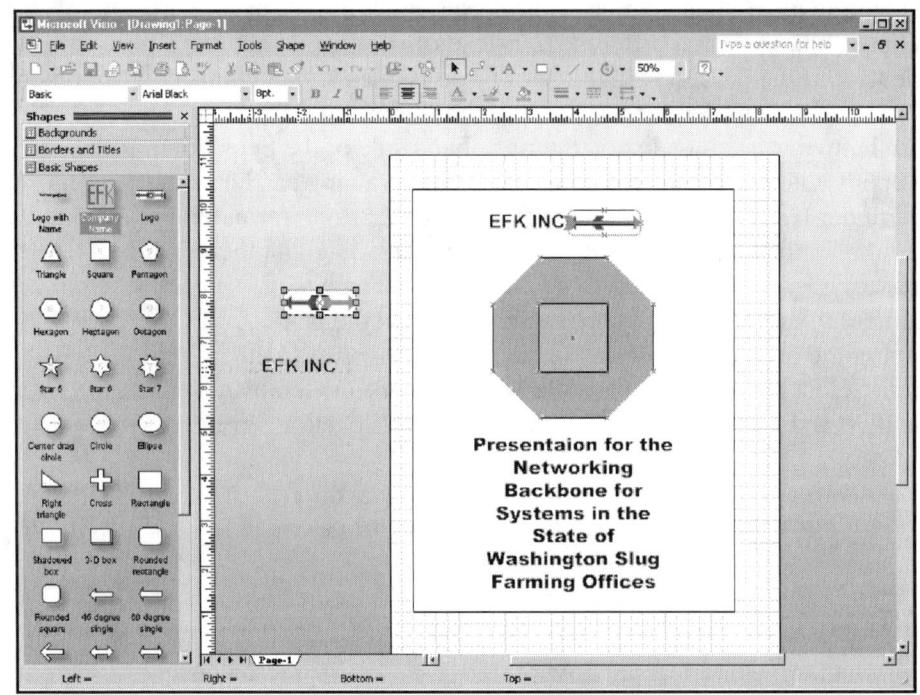

This example shows you how to add your own shapes to stencils, allowing you to quickly and easily personalize all your diagrams with your company logo or any other shape. For more information about altering stencils, see Understanding Stencils previously in this chapter.

1

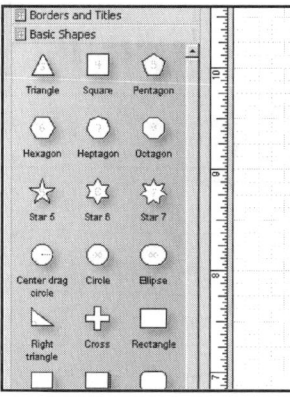

Creating stencils that contain not only standard Visio shapes but shapes of your own as well gives you the option to use your shapes to personalize your diagrams. Personal shapes can be anything, but here are a few ideas to get you started:

- Company Logos or Names
- Personally Important Symbols
- Initials in a particular font or style
- Images for awards or affiliations
- Degrees or other certification information.

Once you have decided what your personalized shapes will be, open the stencil you want to place them on. This should be a stencil you almost always use.

2

Get the stencil ready for adding your shapes by opening it for editing. Right click on the stencil icon on the toolbar and choose to edit. Immediately choose to save the stencil under a different name, which guarantees that you will not accidentally save over the stencil. You'll know your stencil is ready when you see a small orange star over the stencil icon.

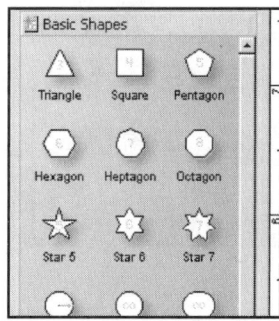

3

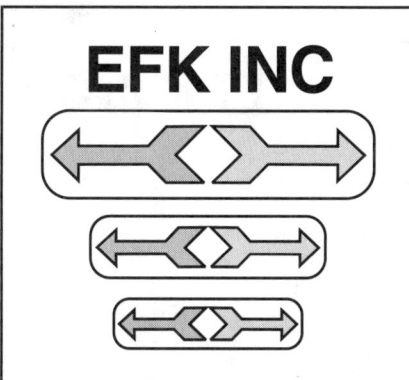

Once your stencil is open and ready, you can create your logo, titles, or other text in Visio. If you already have an electronic image of the shapes you want to add, you need to import them into Visio as graphics. Make sure your personalized shape is the right size, shape, color, and verify that all the spelling is correct. Don't forget that this shape could be used in many different circumstances. You may even want to copy the shape several times and resize it so you have several ready made shapes for all uses.

4

4

Once you have your shapes how you want them, and you have your stencil open and ready to edit, start moving your shapes over onto the stencil. As you move them you'll see they automatically move to the bottom of the stencil.

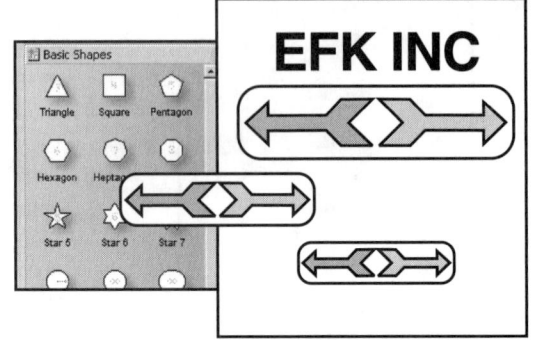

5

Once your personalized shapes are on the stencil, use the right click menu on them and reset their titles using the Master Properties window. Pick the shapes up and rearrange them so they are on the stencil where you want them. To make your shapes easier to use you may want to:

- Alter their icon
- Change their properties
- Move them around on the stencil.

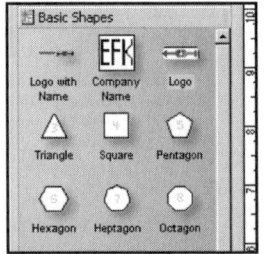

6

When you are happy with your personalized shapes and where they are on the stencil, save the stencil. Then, close the stencil and reopen it. Now your personalized shapes are ready to be used in any diagram where you think they may add effect. When ever you feel like you need them, simply open the stencil into any diagram in which you are working.

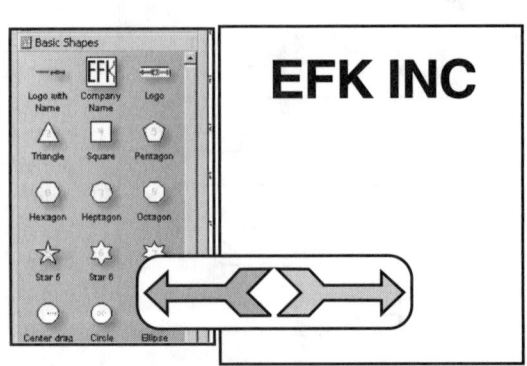

Create Uniform Diagrams Quickly with Your Own Templates

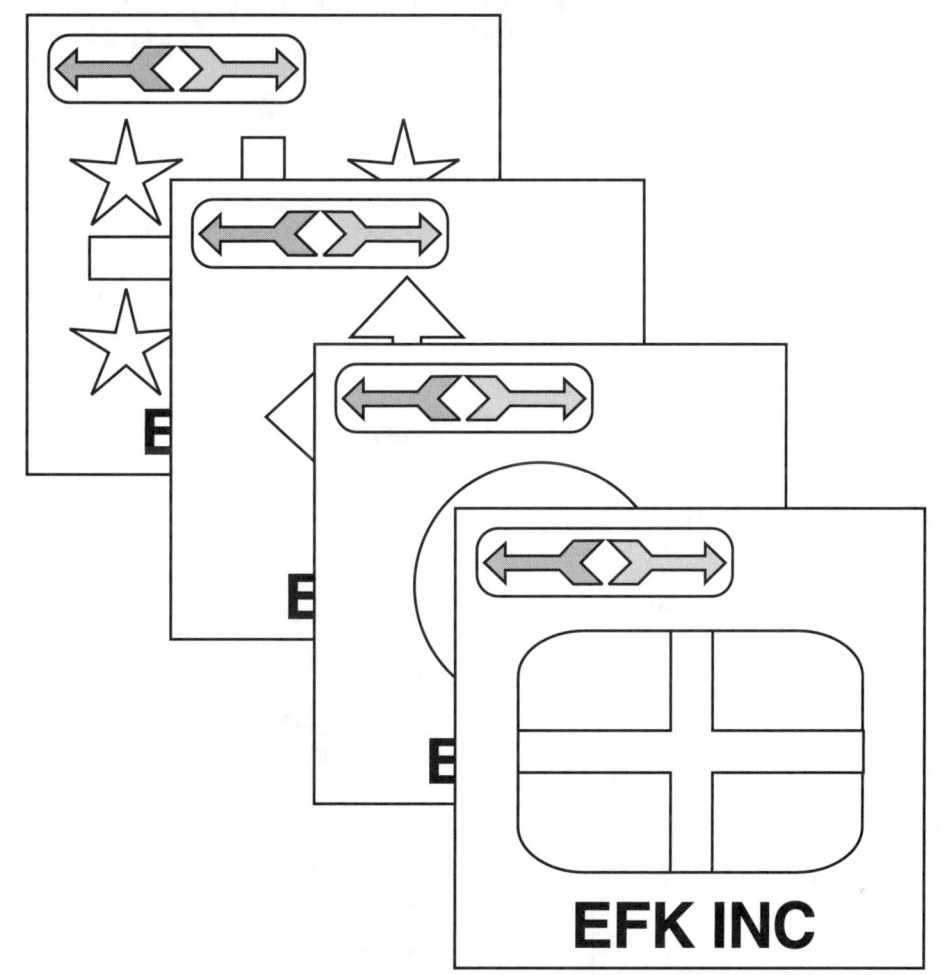

This examples shows you how to create uniform diagrams quickly and easily using templates. For similar diagrams you make over and over, especially if they non-standard page layout or size, templates will not only save you time, but they guarantee that every time you create the same type of drawing it look the same.

1

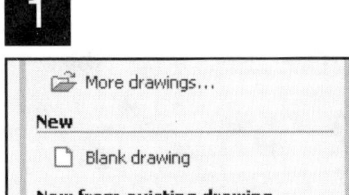

To create a template of your own, make a list of all the types of changes you tend to make over and over. For example, every time you start a type of diagram, do you:

- Alter the page setup
- Change the orientation of the page
- Add a style
- Open a particular stencil, maybe one with personalized shapes
- Add header and footer information
- Add a background or layer
- Insert a logo
- Add a Macro

If any of these happen more than occasionally when you open a new template, then creating a template of your won will save you time and energy. To create a template from scratch, open a blank diagram. To open a blank diagram, choose Blank Drawing when you start Visio.

2

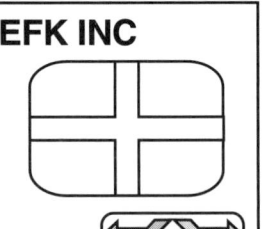

Start adding stencils you use often to your blank diagram, including more basic stencils you may not have thought of such as the callouts stencil or the basic shapes stencil. Keep adding stencils until your template has all the stencils you use often. You might even do a small practice diagram to make sure you have everything you'll need. Do the same for styles and macros.

3

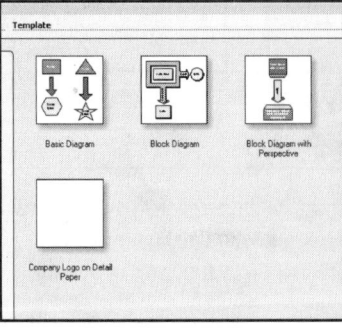

Now edit the page layout and orientation, including adding background and layers where you use them most often. When you have finished editing the blank diagram, you'll need to save it. Don't forget to use Save As a .vst file and to make sure the workspace is saved with you save the template. Now any time you need your customized template, it will be there for you, and the diagrams it creates will always look the same, no matter who creates them, or when. If you save your template in the same place Visio saves it's templates you'll even be able to open it from the Choose a Template screen that starts Visio.

Chapter 5

Creating Flowcharts

How to...

- Create flow charts
- Create organization charts
- Modify organizational charts
- Import organizational chart data
- Export chart data
- Compare organization charts
- Create reports

In the last chapter, you learned how to use stencils and templates, how to create your own shapes, and how to add master shapes to stencils.

In this chapter, you'll learn about flowcharting in Visio and how to create several types of flowcharts. You'll also learn how to use databases to create flowcharts, and how to use flowcharts to create databases.

Understanding Visio Flowchart Diagrams

With Visio, flowcharting is easy. Flowcharts are diagrams you can use to represent a business's organization and processes. Flowcharts make it easy for people to visualize a business or process in action. With a variety of simple ways to create many different kinds of flowcharts, Visio may well be the best product on the market for flowcharting.

> **TIP** *To get the most out of Visio's flowcharts, make sure you always plan your diagram before you start creating it on the drawing page.*

The word *flowchart* generally refers to a diagram outlining a process of data-flow; however, it can also refer to any type of diagram with shapes and connections. One of the simplest types of flowcharts is an organization chart. Organization charts illustrate how people in a business (or other organization) work together. Organization charts show who reports to whom, how pay structures and management structures operate, and how departments are linked. They're a powerful tool for creating better-organized and more dynamic business structures.

In this chapter, we explain organization charts in detail to introduce you to the general format of flowcharts.

Getting to Know Visio Flowcharting

Flowcharts are composed of shapes and lines. The shapes usually represent people or steps in a process. Lines indicate the exchanges between these people or steps, and they indicate relationships and hierarchies. In Visio, there are hundreds of shapes specifically for flowcharts, but you can use any shape you wish. One important tool, the Connection tool, has been designed specifically to create flowchart lines. Figure 5-1 shows a Visio flowchart. It is an organization chart that depicts the business structure of a small company.

A good flowchart is like a house. The foundation is the flowchart's shapes, the walls are the connections, and the roof is the text. Without all these parts, a flowchart cannot stand. The following subsections provide some guidelines for effectively using the various parts of a flowchart.

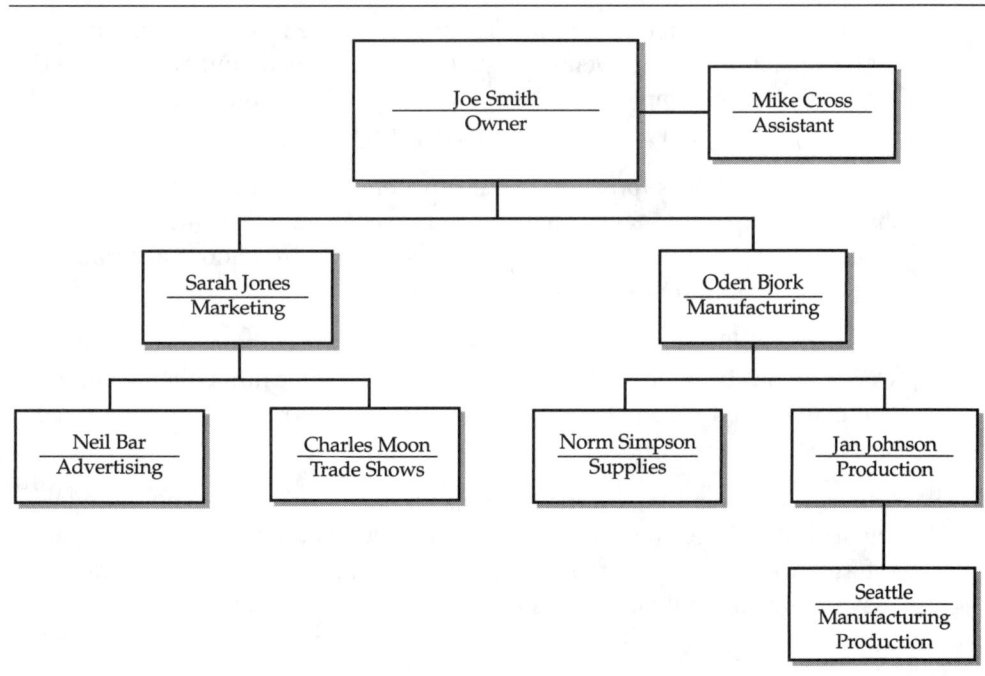

FIGURE 5-1   Basic flowchart

Using Shapes

Shapes in flowcharts are information containers. They represent the people in a business or the steps in a process. In the organization chart shown in Figure 5-1, there are three different types of boxes. These boxes are standard Visio flowchart shapes, and their differences convey information about the different positions held by the people represented in the diagram.

While the placement and connection of shapes are important features of a flowchart, the most important feature is its shapes. People can tell a lot about a flowchart simply by looking at its shapes. The shapes in a flowchart provide basic information, beyond what you can learn by reading the text and looking at the connections.

> TIP   *The shapes you select affect the way Visio builds reports based on your flowcharts. Choose your shapes carefully to make the reports informative.*

Here are some things to consider as you choose shapes for a flowchart:

- The most complicated shape should always represent the top level or highest position on a flowchart page. People who read your flowchart will equate the more complicated shapes with higher positions, and they may be confused if the chart isn't organized accordingly.

- The bottom or lowest position in the flowchart should be a simple shape that can be repeated many times. Flowcharts can get very cluttered if you repeat a complicated shape many times, so it's best to choose a simple shape for low-level positions.

- Use shapes with light or dotted borders for temporary positions—or for work that has been out-sourced. The different border immediately conveys that the position is somehow different from other positions with the same shape on the same level.

- Use no more than five different shapes on one page, and use no more than ten different shapes for an entire flowchart. Although you can convey more information by using more shapes, your flowcharts may be confusing if they include more than ten different shapes.

Using Connections

When used correctly, flowchart connections can give people a clear picture of how a business operates.

There are two main types of connections: with arrows and without arrows. For most flowcharts, use simple 1-D connection lines without arrows. Simple connection lines are usually sufficient to indicate relationships, and they help you avoid cluttering diagrams that have a lot of shapes and text. Simple connection lines are especially useful in complicated flowchart diagrams.

If necessary, you can use connection lines with arrows to show information flowing in a particular direction. Don't overuse connections with arrows; they can make your diagrams more complicated than they need to be.

Using Text

Text in flowcharts gives the reader information about the shapes. The text may be the first thing readers grasp consciously, so make sure you've made careful choices about what you include in the text.

Text in flowcharts should be simple and easy to read. The font should be uniform throughout. Sometimes it can be helpful to use boldface text for the position at the top of each page. Using a larger font size for some high-level positions can also be useful. It's important to remember, though, that no matter how you format the text at the top of the tree, the text at the bottom also needs to be legible. Also, no matter which fonts you choose, never exceed three fonts on one page. This maximum of three fonts includes both the title font and the font you use to label the shapes.

Using the Organization Chart Template

There are two ways to create an organization chart in Visio: using the Organization Chart template and using the Organization Chart Wizard. This section deals with the template; for most simple organization charts, the template is the best way to start. For charts based on databases, text files, or spreadsheets, you'll want to use the Organization Chart Wizard, as described later in this chapter.

NOTE   *You can also convert old Organizational charts with old Visio shapes into current Organizational charts using the Organizational Chart converter. See Converting Older Organizational Charts later in this chapter.*

The Organization Chart template can be used to diagram the personnel structure of a business. Positions, job descriptions, and even managerial styles all affect the way a business works, and organization charts help you to understand them better. The diagram in Figure 5-1 is an organization chart that depicts a small

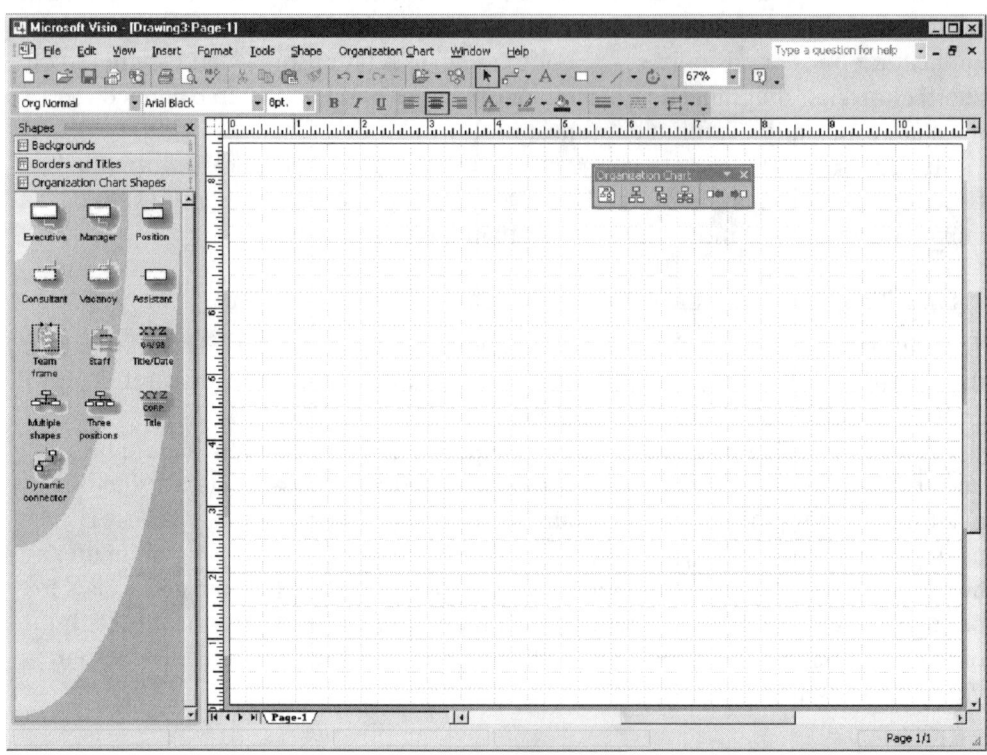

The Organization Chart template

computer company; it illustrates how reports and managerial duties flow through the company.

To create your own organization chart, first you need a list of positions and employees. When you've collected all the information you need, you're ready to open the Organization Chart template. Open the template as you would any other Visio template. When the Organization Chart template opens, it changes the orientation of the drawing page to landscape, opens the Organization Chart Shapes stencil, and opens a floating Organization Chart toolbar. A newly opened Organization Chart template is shown in Figure 5-2.

The Organization Chart toolbar has five buttons, which are explained in Table 5-1. The first three buttons are drop-down buttons.

To help you to create organization charts, the template has additional features beyond its own toolbar and stencil that help you create and organize the shapes.

Button	Function
	Autoarranges shapes
	Allows horizontal arrangements of subordinates
	Allows vertical arrangements of subordinates
	Allows side by side arrangement of subordinates
	Moves the selected shape to the left
	Moves the selected shape to the right

TABLE 5-1   Organization Chart Toolbar Buttons

Understanding Organizational Chart Position Shapes

When you create an organizational chart, you are creating a visual representation of the positions in your organization. Each of these positions has a level. For example, a Vice President is usually some sort of manager or executive. A secretary is usually an assistant.

Visio includes a set of position shapes that represent this hierarchical organization structure. These shapes start with an Executive shape, and include Manager, Assistant, Consultant, Vacancy and Position shapes. The Executive shape is considered to be the top of any organizational structure, with the Manager shape directly below that. The Assistant, Consultant, Vacancy, and Position shapes are all meant to be below the other two in hierarchy. This means that Executive and Manager shapes are superior, and other shapes are subordinate.

Understanding the order of shape hierarchy that programmed into Visio helps you use the template more effectively. Below is a list of the intended order of hierarchy for the position shapes in the Visio Organization template.

1. Executive

2. Manager

3. Position

4. Consultant

5. Vacancy

6. Assistant

So, all shapes are subordinate to an executive shape, and all shapes are superior to an assistant shape.

 *Even if your organization doesn't use the terms used in the Visio template, just remember the Executive shape is on top and use it first, with either managers or position shapes second.*

Dragging Positions to the Page with Automatic Connection

Organization charts use lines to indicate a business relationship between positions. These lines are usually 1-D connection lines that are glued to both the position and its superior. Creating all the lines in an organization chart manually would take a great deal of time and effort, so Visio has an automatic connection feature for shapes in the Organization Chart Shape stencil.

 *For the automatic connection feature to work, shapes need to be added from the top of the structure down. To use this feature, you need to have a plan for your diagram before you start.*

To connect shapes from the Organization Chart Shape stencil, first drag a superior shape to the drawing page. The first time you use this option, Visio displays a window telling you it will arrange the shapes automatically and that you can drag a shape onto the superior, as shown in Figure 5-3.

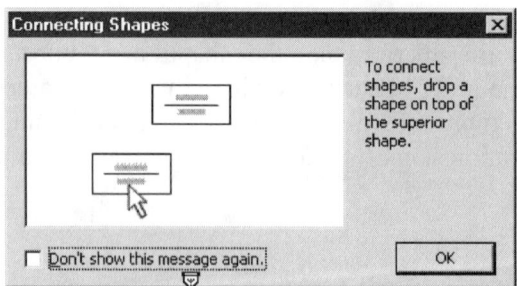

FIGURE 5-3   Automatic arrangement notification

Once you've placed the superior shape, drag one if its subordinates to the drawing page and drop it on top of the superior shape. Visio places the subordinate and connects it to the superior with a 1-D connection line.

To add another subordinate to a superior, drag it from the stencil and drop it on the superior. Any subordinates that already exist for the superior rearrange themselves to make room for new subordinates. This reorganization occurs because of the "dynamic glue" that Visio uses when it connects shapes in this way.

Adding Text

The default text style for the Organization Chart template is 8-point Arial. In addition, by default a divider line appears between the names of people represented on the chart and their titles. The default divider line helps keep the diagrams neat by separating text that might otherwise be confusing.

As you add text to your organization chart, remember to be brief. Textual information tends to be secondary to the shapes and their connections.

When you're satisfied with the placement of the shapes and the text, you're done with your organization chart. Remember to print the chart at least once during the final stages to make sure you like the way it looks on the printed page and then save the diagram.

Moving with Dynamic Connectors

Dynamic glue, which is discussed in more detail later in this chapter, allows shapes to stay glued together even though one of them moves. Dynamically glued connectors act slightly differently than you are used to with standard connectors. Not only do they stay connected even if the shape moves, but dynamically glued connectors change shape and orientation automatically as you move the shapes they connect.

TIP   *You can break a connection by moving the connector instead of one of the connected shapes.*

Dynamic connectors route themselves around shapes that lie between the shapes they connect. Because dynamic connectors have this capability, you can maintain connections when you move the shapes around the page. Your diagram stays neat and tidy as you rearrange shapes. Dynamic glue is the default setting for all shapes in the Organization Chart template, so you can add as many positions as you like, and the shapes always stay neatly connected to their superiors.

 *Connector shapes are added automatically when you drop a subordinate shape on top of a superior shape.*

Arranging Subordinates and Superiors

By default, dropped subordinates arrange themselves horizontally underneath their superior. However, if your diagram has three levels or more, this arrangement can be cumbersome—using the width of the page without making use of the height. You can alter the arrangement of subordinates by using the arrangement buttons on the Organization Chart toolbar. If you have too many positions arranged horizontally beneath a superior, select the superior, click the second button on the Organization Chart toolbar, and then choose a vertical orientation for the subordinates.

The superior now uses a new organizational scheme, and all new subordinates dropped on it arrange themselves according to the new scheme.

You can also access the layout options for subordinates by right clicking on any superior shape and choosing Arrange Subordinates. This gives you a window, shown in Figure 5-4, showing all the possible auto-arrange options for subordinate shapes. Select an arrangement and that becomes the default for that superior.

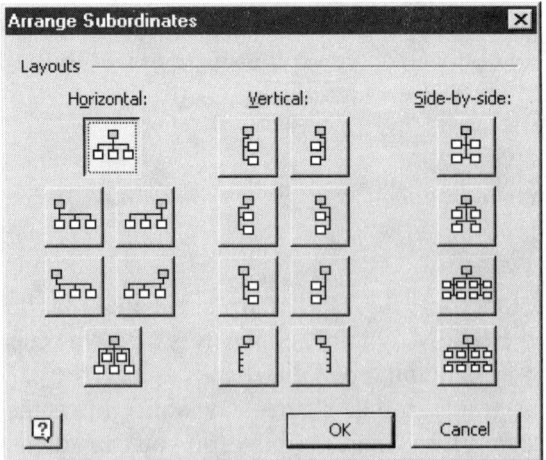

FIGURE 5-4 Arrange Subordinate

Placing Multiple Positions at Once

There are times when it's useful to add multiple positions to an organization chart simultaneously. The Organization Chart Shapes stencil includes two special master shapes for those cases: the Three Positions master shape and the Multiple Shapes master shape. Both of these master shapes allow you to drag and drop several subordinates at once.

 *To quickly convert a shape into a different type, for example an Executive shape into a Manager shape, right-click the shape, then choose Change Position Type and select the type you want.*

5

The Three Positions master shape creates a set of three position shapes, exactly like the position shape in the second row of the stencil. When you drag it onto a superior, it adds three position shapes arranged by the method set as the default for the superior.

The Multiple Shapes master shape adds a designated number of organization chart shapes to your diagram. When you drag the Multiple Shapes to the drawing page and drop it on a superior, an Add Multiple Shapes window opens, like the one shown here, where you can choose the type of shape and the number of shapes to drop:

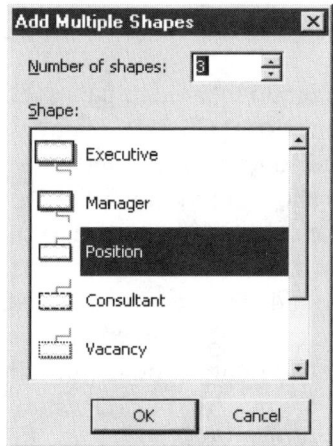

 *To show or hide subordinate positions in organization charts, select the shape representing the top-level position, and then choose Organization Chart | Hide Subordinates.*

Select the shape type and number, and click OK. Visio automatically arranges and connects the shapes.

Converting Older Organizational Charts

Older versions of Visio were not as sophisticated in their use of Organizational shapes. Visio includes a Macro that allows you to convert these old diagrams so they use the new shapes. This allows you to take advantage of the improvements in Visio, and the wizard that walks you though this process is quick and easy.

To convert a Visio 5.0 or earlier Organizational chart to the new format, select Tools | Macros | Organizational Chart | Organizational Chart Converter. The Organizational Chart Converter wizard opens and walks you though the process of updating your old Visio diagrams.

Using Synchronized Copies

Often when you are creating Organizational charts for large to medium organizations, there is too much information to display well on one page. Moving whole departments, or even just small subgroups of the organization to new pages, can make your pages cleaner and easier to read and work with.

Synchronized copy allows you to move groups of personnel to other pages with their superior. A synchronized copy is a copy of a superior and all their direct reports that Visio places on another page. You can choose to hide the subordinates of the superior on their original page, and then they only take up page space on the new page.

To copy a part of your diagram to another page, select the superior you want to move, and then select Organizational Chart | Create Synchronized Copy. Visio verifies you've chosen a valid superior shape and then displays the Create Synchronized Copy window shown in Figure 5-5.

You can select to have the subordinate moved to an already existing page or you can choose to have Visio create a new page when it moves the shapes. This is also where you can choose to hide the subordinates so they no longer show on the original page. Once you have chosen how to create your synchronized copy, click OK. Visio creates the copies and returns you to your diagram.

NOTE   *To make sure all parts of your diagram stay in sync, choose Organizational Chart | Synchronize Relationships for every page in your diagram before you exit your diagram. This allows you to synchronize the relationships of all shapes on the page to the original page of the diagram.*

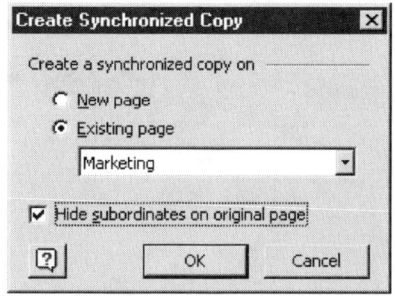

FIGURE 5-5   Create Synchronized Copy window

Understanding Organizational Chart Options

Organizational Charts can become complicated with lots of information and it is common to have many pages for even a small organization. Visio has tried to set up the Organizational Chart template to take into account all of these needs, however sometimes the defaults Visio set up for the display and layout of shapes needs altered to fulfill your needs. The Organizational Chart Options allows you to change the display and layout options for your chart.

You change the Organizational Chart Options by selecting Organizational Chart | Options. The Options window displays as shown in Figure 5-6.

Using the Options window, you can alter your Organizational Chart in several ways:

- **Shape Size and Theme** Allows you to set the options for the default size of your Organizational shape. All Organizational Shapes have the same size defaults of 1 in by .5 in. You can also alter the look of the shapes you bring to the page by changing their theme to one of the default Visio themes.

NOTE *You can alter the spacing between the shapes by choosing Organizational Chart | Change Spacing. This allows you to change the default space between shapes and to select which shapes change their spacing.*

- **Automatically Moving Shapes** Allows you choose how your shapes are arranged as you bring them to the page. By default, Visio automatically arranges shapes.

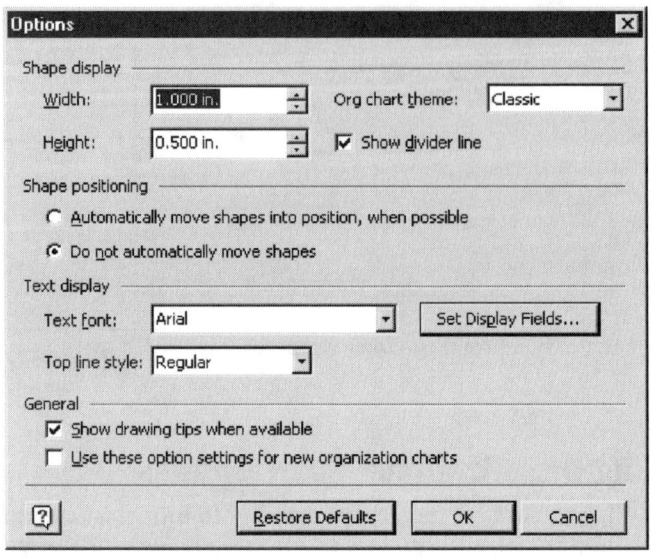

FIGURE 5-6   Organizational Chart Options

- **Text Display** Allows you to alter the default text font and style for each Organizational Shape. You can also alter the default for the custom property text Visio displays on each shape.

- **General** Turns on and off the drawing tips. If you do not want Visio to give you hints on how to create your diagram, deselect this box. You can also choose to use all of these options in every Organizational Chart you create by selecting the "Use these options settings for new organizational charts" box.

TIP   *Many of the options and settings discussed in this section are also available using the right click menu on your Organizational shape or on the Organizational Chart drawing page.*

Using the Organization Chart Wizard

The Organization Chart Wizard helps you create organization chart diagrams based on databases. Since most companies keep their human resource information in some sort of database, Visio includes an easy way to turn that database information into organization charts. When you choose the Organizational Chart Wizard from the template types, Visio opens up the Organizational Chart template discussed earlier in this chapter and a Wizard to walk you though the process of adding information from a database.

The Organization Chart Wizard asks you for the location and name of a data source. Although the wizard allows you to create a new database on the fly, usually the database will already exist in a format the wizard can import.

Visio can import data from the following formats:

- Text files (.txt), or Org Plus files exported to text files.

- Microsoft Excel spreadsheets (.xls)

- Microsoft Exchange Server directories

- ODBC-compliant database applications

Most often, organization charts are built from text files or Excel files, but the other two formats can be useful if your organization already has this information in its database software.

Formatting Text and Excel Data Files

In text files and Excel files, the source data needs to be formatted in a way that Visio can use.

For text files, the data in each line needs to be separated by commas, with hard returns inserted at the end of each line. Also, when you use a text file as the data source, it needs to have the following first line, which specifies the headings for the data:

```
Name,Reports_To,Position,Department,Telephone,Master_Shape
```

CAUTION *The heading line needs to appear in the exact format shown here. There should be no spaces before or after the commas.*

Every line in the text file becomes its own shape, and must include *at least* the Name and the Reports_To fields. All other fields need to be represented by commas, even if there's no corresponding text between the commas. Each line must include a unique name; otherwise, Visio won't accept the file. The Master_Shape data is not required and is used only if you want to control which

Organization Chart Shapes are applied to specific positions. If you choose not to define a master shape for each line, leave the Master_Shape field out of the heading line.

For Excel files, the data needs organized into columns and rows. The Excel file should have the following headings in the first row of cells:

```
Name Reports_To Position Department Telephone Master_Shape
```

You should have a total of six columns. Each row of the spreadsheet then becomes a shape in the organization chart.

> **NOTE**   *You may have more than six columns if there are "custom properties" for the shapes. Custom properties are explained later in this chapter in the section "Creating Reports from Flowcharts."*

The fields in text and Excel files are as follows:

- **Name**   Defines the name that appears on the corresponding shape in the organization chart. Capitalization and spacing carry over into the diagram.

- **Reports_To**   Defines the shape's superior. The data must exactly match the Name field of another line in the text file or another row in the Excel file. This field should only be blank for the shape at the top of the chart.

- **Position**   Defines the title that appears on the corresponding shape in the organization chart. Remember, the title appears below the divider line that separates the name and title.

- **Department**   Specifies the department for the position. This information appears as part of the custom properties for the shape.

- **Telephone**   Specifies the telephone number for the position. This information appears as part of the custom properties for the shape.

- **Master_Shape**   Defines the shape assigned to a position. Visio assigns shapes based on the total number of lines in the file and the number of Reports_To relationships. This optional field allows you to select a shape for each line or row. Entries in this field should match shape names that appear in the Organization Chart Shapes stencil.

Using Other Data Files

Open Database Connectivity (ODBC) is a Microsoft standard that allows applications to access, view, and modify data from a variety of databases. Examples of ODBC-compliant database applications include Microsoft Access, Microsoft SQL Server, and Oracle SQL Server. For example, Visio's interpretation of a Microsoft Exchange Server directory creates an organization chart based on information set up in the address book. It is a fast and easy way to translate your e-mail information into graphical form.

Importing the Data

When you have a database with the source data in the proper format, you're ready to use the Organization Chart Wizard to import the data. Open the Organization Chart Wizard as you would a template. The opening screen of the wizard appears, as shown here:

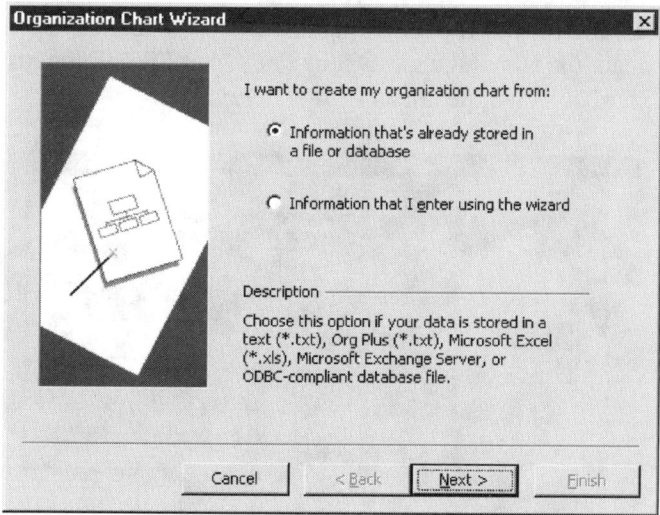

Choose to create your chart from information already stored in a file and click Next.

The second wizard screen appears, as shown here:

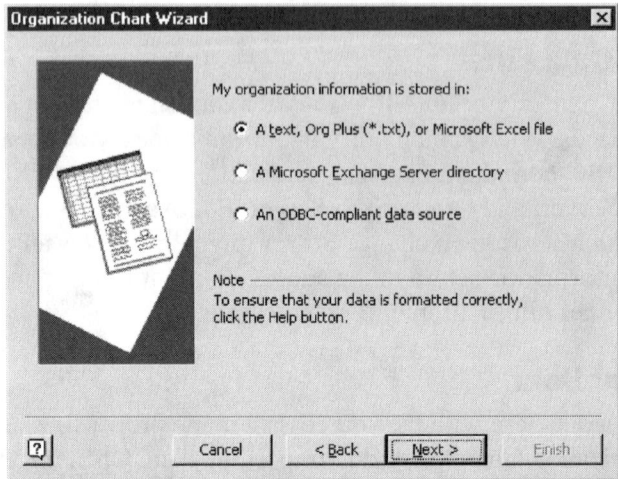

This screen lists all the types of files Visio can use to create organization charts. Choose the correct file type for your data file and click Next. The next screen appears asking for the file location. Click Browse and an Open File dialog box appears. Locate the file and click Open. The Open File dialog box closes.

The next wizard screen appears, as shown here:

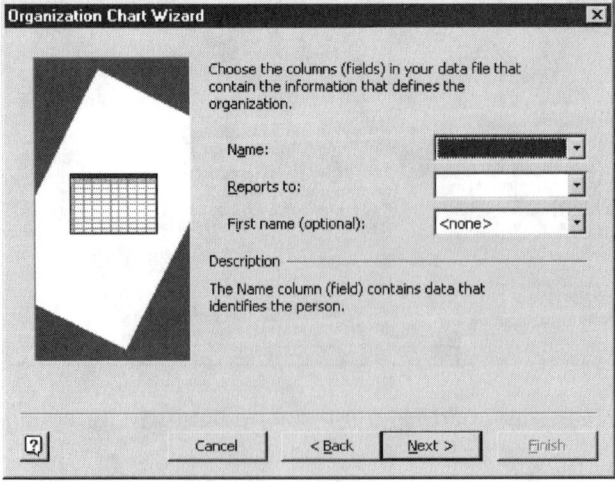

This screen allows you to identify which of the fields define the relationships between the shapes in your organization chart. For most charts, leave the fields as they are listed. Then click Next. Another screen appears, allowing you to define the text that displays in the shapes for your organization chart. As with the previous screen, it's best to leave the drop-down menus with their default and click Next.

The following wizard screen appears:

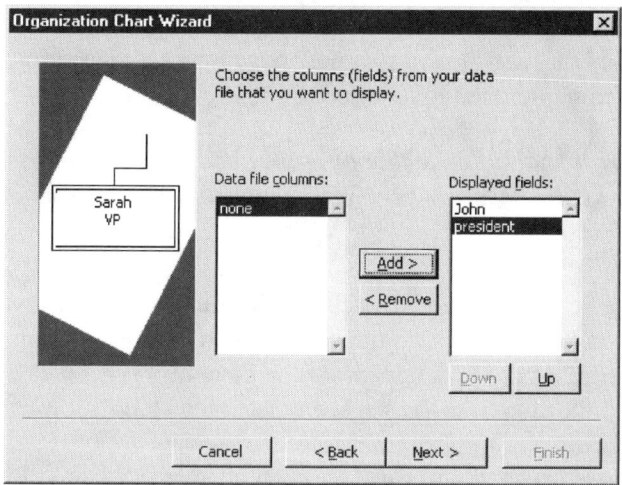

This screen asks if you want to add information to the Custom Properties field for your chart. Select all the data fields in the left-hand box, then click Add. They appear in the right-hand box. Click Next.

The next wizard screen appears, as shown here:

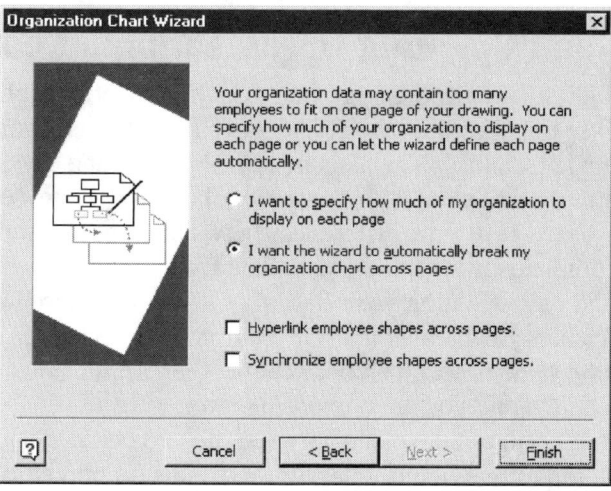

This screen allows you to decide how your organization chart breaks across pages. You can choose how the chart breaks, or you can let Visio decide automatically. For most cases, Visio does a nice job of deciding how your charts should be laid out, so that has been set as the default. Visio calculates the number of shapes that would appear on a page and breaks across levels when including all of a level would mean more than 50 shapes on a page. You can also choose to have any superiors that are moved to a new page synchronize across the pages, or even hyperlink from one page to another.

Choosing to manually decide how your chart breaks across pages opens another wizard screen where Visio prompts you to make additional page layout decisions.

When you've determined how the chart will break across pages, the wizard has all the information it needs. Click Finish, and Visio begins creating your organization chart. Process bars appear on the page as Visio reads and uses your data file to create the chart. As the wizard creates the chart, it may need to add pages to the diagram.

When Visio has finished your organization chart, the wizard closes, and the chart appears on the drawing page. The Organization Chart template should be open, allowing you to make any changes as necessary.

Remember to save your new organization chart before closing the drawing.

Comparing and Updating Organizational Charts

Once you've put all the time and energy into your organizational charts, it can be disheartening to see that they are out of date, or to find out that someone else has a more correct or update chart. Visio takes this into account and gives you two options to create the most complete organizational chart you can. You can simply compare the two charts to see the differences between them, or you can choose to update the less complete chart with the new data from the more complete chart.

Comparing and then updating your Organizational chart starts with the same process. Both the chart you created and the chart you use to update it need to be open in Visio at the same time. Open both charts, then decide what you want to do with your chart and the one you are comparing it to.

No matter what changes take place between the two charts during the process, Visio gives you a report that you can save as text. This report can be useful in its own way—you now have a detailed outline of the changes that have taken place in your organization.

TIP

Always save your new organizational charts with a new name. This allows you to compare new charts to old ones and get the report of changes without needing to hand create it.

Identifying the Changes Between Two Organizational Charts.

On the Organizational chart menu, Visio offers you the option of comparing data. To compare the data on two different Organizational charts, select Organization Chart | Compare Organization Data. This opens the Compare Organization Data window shown in Figure 5-7

NOTE

If you don't have both charts opened, you can do so by selecting one of the Browse buttons and navigating to it.

To identify the changes between two charts, select one in each of the two drop-down windows in the upper half of the Compare window. Make sure you have two different files selected in these two boxes. Then tell Visio which file is the older, or less complete, chart by selecting one of the radio buttons in the lower half of the window. The first radio button tells Visio the file in the uppermost of the two boxes is the oldest. The second radio button tells Visio the file in the second of the two boxes is the oldest.

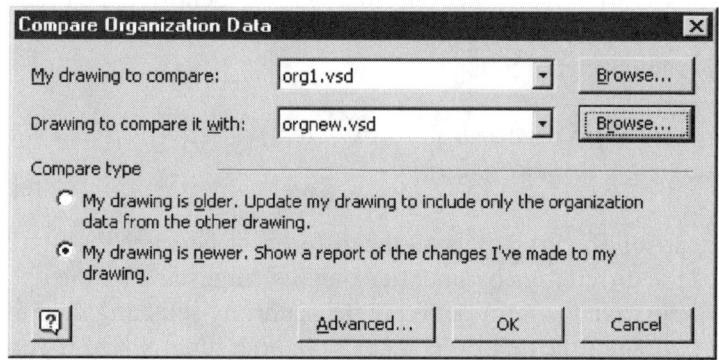

FIGURE 5-7   Compare Organization Data window

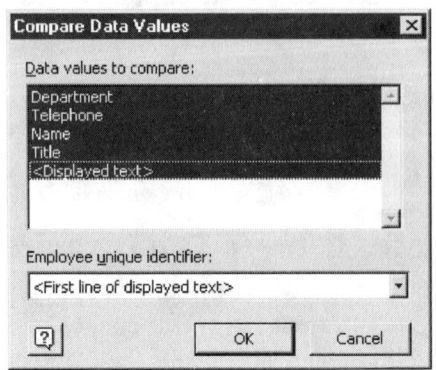

FIGURE 5-8   Compare Data Values window

You can select advanced options in the Compare window and choose which information to compare, shown in Figure 5-8.

Using the Compare Data Values window, you can choose to compare only parts of the information, or you can choose to distinguish individual by their position instead of their name. These options are helpful if you want to see how your organization has changed over time, beyond how personnel have moved around. Or you can simply see who has been added or removed from your corporation by choosing to compare only the names of people and not their positions. Select the information you are looking for from the list on the Compare Data Values window and then click OK. Visio takes you back to the Compare window shown in Figure 5-7.

Once you have all the settings selected and have identified the older drawing, click OK. Visio compares the two drawings and displays a report of the changes, an example is shown Figure 5-9.

NOTE   *If you told Visio your drawing was older, the report will also include an option to update your diagram.*

The Comparison Report details all the differences between the two charts. Visio outlines the differences by both personnel changes and by the operation of changes. You can save the information in the report by selecting the Save As Text button at the bottom of the report. You can save both reports, and if you want to do so, you need to use the Save as Text button for each tab.

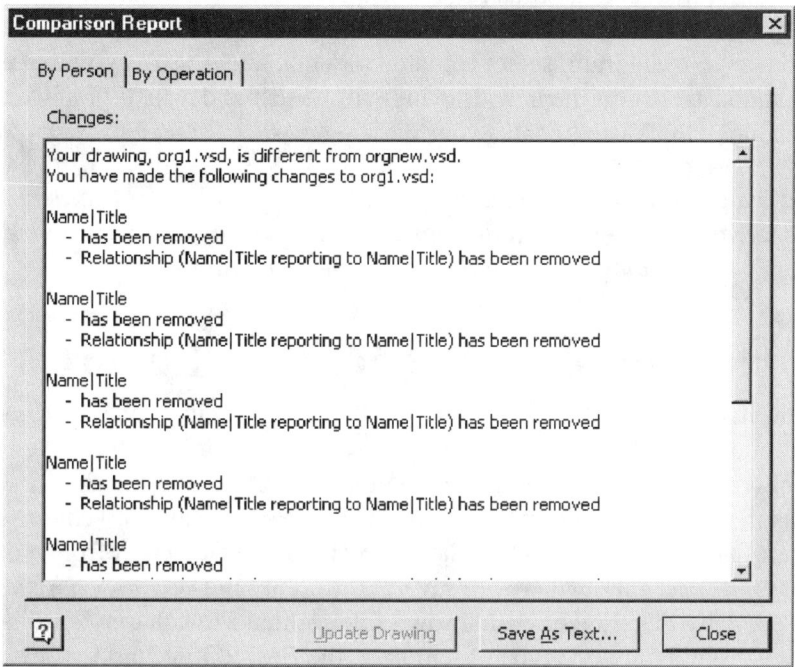

FIGURE 5-9   Example Comparison Report

When you are finished with the Report, use the Close button to return to your diagram.

Updating Your Old Organizational Chart

Visio offers you the option of updating your organizational chart if you want to do more than simply see the differences between the two charts. Updating your organizational chart proceeds much like comparing.

To update an old organizational chart to with data from a new chart, first open both charts in Visio. Then select Organization Chart | Compare Organizational Data. This opens the Compare window shown in Figure 5-7.

To make sure you update the correct chart, the older chart needs listed in the uppermost box for the two charts. Then select the first of the radio buttons, the one that says "My drawing is older". When you have set up the comparison, click OK. Visio compares the two diagrams and generates a report like the one shown in

Figure 5-9 with an added tab illustrating the steps Visio would take to update the older diagram.

To update your diagram, select Update Drawing. Visio warns you that all the shapes that don't exist on the new drawing will be lost and asks if you want to continue. Click OK. Visio updates your drawing.

It's a good idea to keep old records, especially old organizational diagrams. Once you update your diagram, save it with a new name and keep the old diagram should you ever need it again.

Creating Flowcharts and Generating Reports

Visio flowcharts are like the big brothers of Visio organization charts. They're more complicated and often require more steps to complete; however, the basic concept of connections and shapes conveying information is the same.

Just as in organization charts, Visio has two ways to create flowcharts: creating a flowchart from scratch with a template, and creating a flowchart from a data file. Unlike organization charts, there are several different kinds of flowcharts. In fact, there are so many that they have their own folder titled Flowcharts. For this section, we discuss only one type of template: the Basic Flowchart template.

To understand how to use the other templates in the Flowchart folder, see Appendix A. Every template is listed there with information about when to use it.

Using the Basic Flowchart Template

When you select the Basic Flowchart template from the Open dialog box, Visio opens a new blank page and the Basic Flowchart stencil.

The shapes on the stencil work the same as the shapes on the Basic Shapes stencil; simply drag and drop them onto the page to create shapes based on the master shape. However, connections don't work the same way as for the shapes on the Organization Chart Shapes stencil. You'll need to create the connections between shapes yourself by using the Connection tool.

Using the Connection Tool

The Connection tool helps you create flowcharts in two ways: by giving you a quick way to connect shapes that are already on the drawing page and by connecting two shapes as you drop them. As a rule, it is easier to connect shapes that are already on the drawing. However, using automatic connections as you drag shapes from stencils may be more efficient and has, by default, the added advantage of a special Connection tool feature: dynamic glue.

Dynamic glue is a type of connection that allows the endpoints of a connector line or shape to move around the object it's glued to as the shape and those around it move. Like Visio's normal gluing action, dynamic glue can only be removed by clicking on the attachment point and moving the connector away. However, unlike normal gluing, connectors that have dynamic glue never overlap other shapes on the page. The jumping action as dynamically glued connectors move around the page is triggered by moving the shape or the connector.

To connect shapes that are already on the drawing page with the Connection tool, select the Connection tool from the toolbar, click on a connection point of the first shape, and drag to a connection point on the second shape. Visio creates the connector and handles the gluing of the shapes.

You can get the benefit of dynamic glue with shapes already on the drawing page if you hold down CTRL as you join the shape. While holding CTRL, click on a connection point for the first shape, and then drag to the next shape, creating a connector that is dynamically glued to each shape.

> **TIP** *You can also connect a shape to itself with the Connection tool by selecting it from the toolbar, then clicking on one of the shape's connection points, and then dragging to another of the shape's connection points.*

When you've successfully connected two shapes, the endpoints of the connector turn red when the connection is selected. The shade of red varies according to the type of glue: dark red is static, bright red is dynamic.

To connect shapes as you drag them from a stencil:

1. Choose the Connection tool from the toolbar. The cursor now has a connector with an arrow below it.

2. Choose any 2-D shape from the Flowchart or Flowchart (Additional) stencil and drag and drop it on the page. 2-D shapes are indicated by a gray background on the stencil.

3. With the first 2-D shape selected, drag and drop a second 2-D shape. Visio connects the shapes using dynamic glue.

4. Drag and drop enough shapes to complete your flowchart. As long as you have the tool selected, each new shape you drop connects to the shape selected on the drawing page.

5. When you're done with the Connection tool, choose the Pointer tool from the toolbar.

The shapes are connected with an instance of the Connector master shape selected in the stencil. If no master shape is selected, Visio creates an instance of the dynamic connector to connect the shapes.

 *Don't forget that you can add additional information to your shapes by including custom properties. Right-click on the shape and select Properties to open a dialog box where you can add custom properties.*

Creating Reports from Flowcharts

Creating reports for flowcharts you've made in Visio can be an important part of your business process. For example, if you've done a lot of fact-finding about your company's supply process and kept the data as a Visio flowchart. You can retrieve that data by creating a report, and you can choose to either have the report as a separate Visio shape, or as a database file. You can also use the reporting feature of Visio to create a printed report that you can hand out during presentations in which you use the flowchart as a visual aid.

The ability to create reports from flowcharts is based on the "custom properties" of shapes. The custom property fields of shapes populate the fields, or columns, in the database table.

A *custom property* is a Visio database field that holds specific information about a shape. Many Visio master shapes come with property fields already assigned. You can always add custom property fields of your own to a shape by right-clicking and selecting Properties. If the shape doesn't have any custom properties assigned, you're asked if you'd like to add them.

By default, every 2-D flowchart shape has three property fields: Cost, Duration, and Resources. You can enter data into the fields by right-clicking the shape, and then choosing Properties from the shortcut menu.

Using Existing Reports

To create a report in Visio, open the diagram you want the report created from and then choose Tools | Reports. The Report window opens as shown in Figure 5-10.

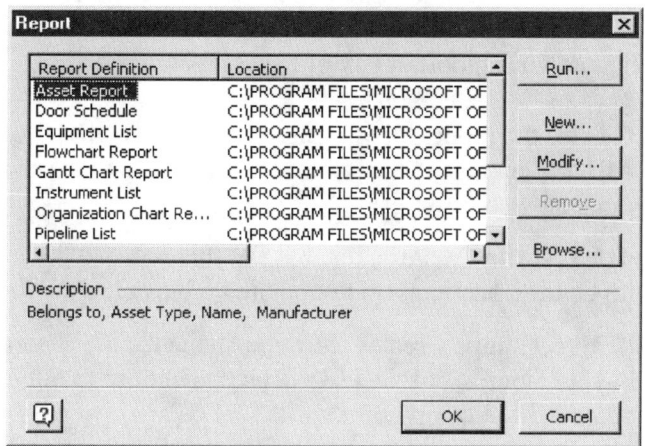

FIGURE 5-10   Report window

There are 5 reports that come with Visio Standard and an additional 7 reports that come with Visio Professional, and even Visio. Table 5-2 lists all the reports that come will Visio and the use their intended uses.

NOTE   *Visio Professional Reports are discussed in detail in Chapter 10.*

Report Name	Intended Purpose
Flowchart Report	Meant for all types of flowcharts. Lists each shape and the text it includes. Also lists the duration and type of shape.
Gantt Chart Report	Meant for Gantt planning diagrams. Lists the time functions of each shape as well the percent to which it's been completed.
Organizational Chart Report	Meant for diagrams created on the Organizational Chart template. Lists the positions, reports to, and other important organizational information. Also groups the shapes by like position.
Shape Inventory	Meant for any type of Visio drawing. Lists each shape's position and size. Also groups like shapes so you know how many of each shape is in the diagram.

TABLE 5-2   Reports in Visio Standard

To run a report, select it from the list and click Run. Visio displays a window asking you what kind of report you'd like to generate, shown in Figure 5-11.

Visio can generate your report in any of these ways:

- **HTML** Creates the report for your diagram in an HTML file complete with HTML display tags that can be uploaded directly to the internet and viewed using an web browser.

- **Microsoft Excel file** Creates a database in that you can open in Microsoft Excel with column headings and populated table cells.

- **Microsoft Excel shape** Creates a drop in shape for the report that you can include in your Microsoft Excel file. You can choose to either link to the report or create a static copy of it.

- **Visio Table Shape** Creates a shape like any other Visio shape with the report data. You can choose to either link to the report of create a static copy of it.

- **XML** Creates the report in XML format to inclusion in any program that can read XML files.

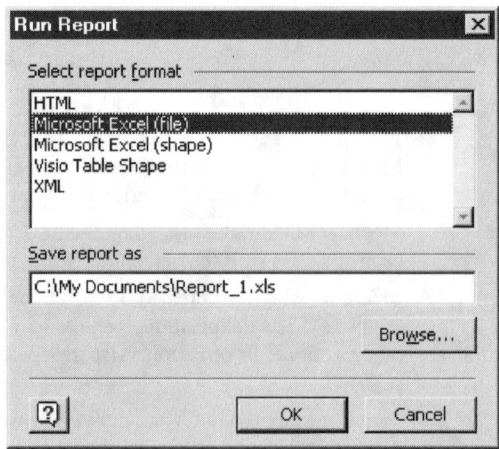

FIGURE 5-11   Run Report window

 *Any report that generates a file asks you where you want that file saved. The Browse button works like most others in Visio and helps you navigate to the location you want to save your report.*

If you try to run a report that doesn't apply to the current diagram, or if you don't have shapes selected and the reports needs selected shapes to run, Visio tells you the report cannot finish to due lack of shapes and takes you back to the report window.

Creating New Reports

Even the 12 reports that come with Visio Professional may not be enough to generate the type of report you need. This section walks you though the creation of a basic new report.

 *For a further discussion of the options you can set when creating reports, see Chapter 10, "Using Visio Professional with Engineering Diagrams."*

You can create a customized report for any diagram by clicking New on the Report window and Visio walks you though a wizard.

The Wizard starts by asking you which shapes you'd like to use in the report, as shown here.

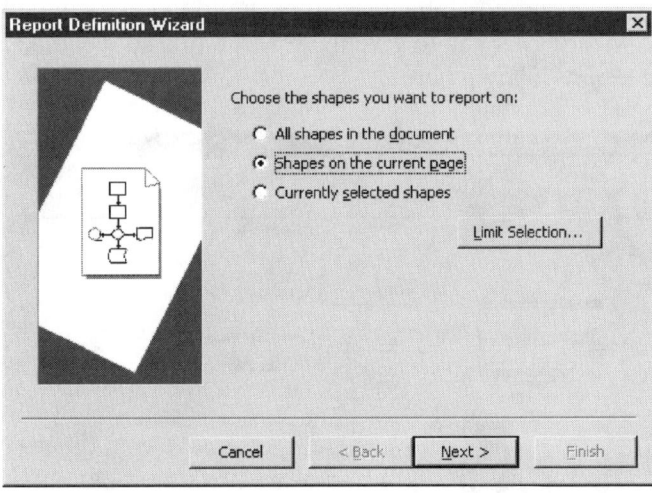

Your options are: the shapes you currently have selected, all the shapes on the current page, or all the shapes in the document. If you haven't selected shapes before you begin to create a new report, you can always exit the wizard and select the shapes and then run the wizard again. Once you have decided which shapes you need, click Next. This displays the next screen, asking you which custom properties you'd like to use in your new report, shown here.

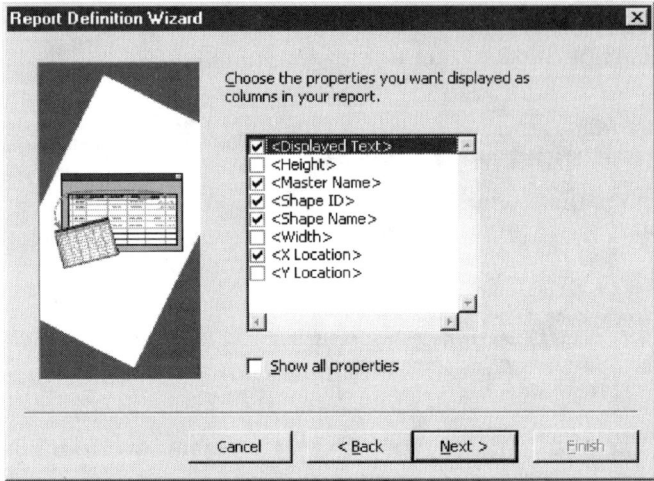

Scroll down the list and check the properties you'd like in the report. You can also select to show all properties so you can select properties that aren't listed by default. When you've chosen all the properties you'd like to include in the report, click Next. The wizard asks you to give the report a title so it can be added to the list of available reports, shown here.

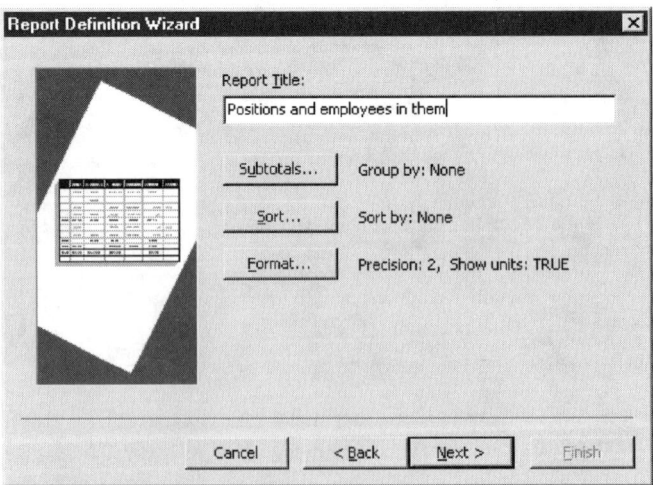

The title of your report should be clear and useful since it will be the display name in the Report window shown in Figure 5-10. Type the name of your report, and then click next. The wizard asks you to save the report definition file, shown here.

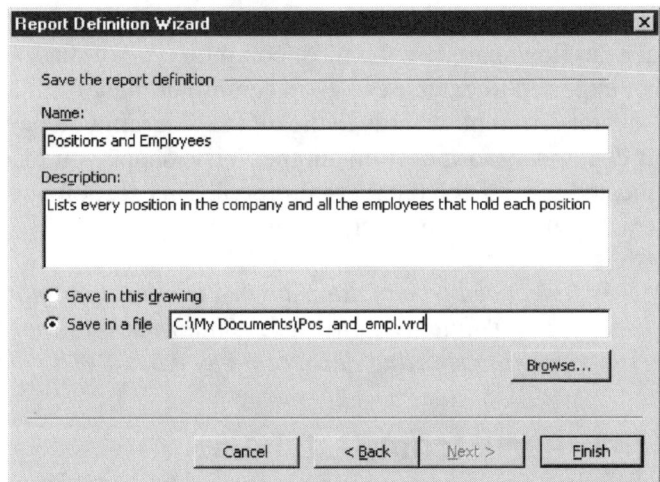

The wizard also asks you to give the report a definition. The Report window shown in Figure 5-10 has a definition section where information about what the report displays when you select the report from the list. Entering a description for your report file means that not only will you remember what your new report does, but that others who use the report have that information as well. You also need to select where the report is saved on this part of the wizard. You can choose to save the report information as part of the current diagram, or as a separate file.

> **TIP** *Saving your report with your diagram means you can't access it from other diagrams. To get the most out of your new report, save it as a separate file where Visio keeps all of its reports.*

Once you have told Visio where to save the report file, you are ready to finish the report. Click Finish and Visio saves the report and takes you back to the report window shown in Figure 5-10 with your new report now on the list of available reports.

To run your new report, select it from the list and click Run.

Using Databases with Flowcharts

All types of Visio diagrams display information that you may not have collected in any other way. Or you may have data in a database that you want to graphically illustrate. Visio both exports to and imports from databases to make this process as useful and painless as possible.

As a general rule, flowcharts are the most common type of diagrams that need to be imported or exported to databases. Visio can import data from a number of sources, using several different wizards to create the diagram you need. Visio can also export your data to any format from another Visio shape you place on the page to a complicated specialized database protocol. This section outlines all they ways Visio interacts with database for flowcharts.

 *Almost every advanced type of diagram in Visio has information that would be useful in a database. Most of the information given later in this chapter can apply to exporting data from any type of Visio diagram.*

Creating Flowcharts from Databases

Often when you wish to create a flowchart of a process, you already have some or all of the data for the flowchart in a file or program somewhere on your computer system. Visio has macro that allows you to turn that data quickly and easily into a flowchart: the Import Flowchart Data Wizard.

 *Always create the data file before you start the macro. You can do it the other way around, but it wastes time and doesn't work as smoothly.*

The first step to creating a flowchart from a data file it to make sure your data file is complete and in the correct format. Visio can import data from these formats:

■ Text files (.txt)

■ Microsoft Excel spreadsheets (.xls)

■ Microsoft Project Exchange files (.mpx)

■ Microsoft Exchange Server directories

■ ODBC-compliant database applications

NOTE   *ODBC stands for Open Database Connectivity, a Microsoft standard that allows applications to access, view, and modify data from a variety of databases.*

For most flowcharts, you'll work with a text file (.txt) or Microsoft Excel spreadsheet (.xls). The macro requires the data file to include specific column headings, so it's best if you use one of the data file templates that come with Visio, located in the Flowchart folder in the Solutions folder under the Visio program directory.

If you plan to use an ODBC database application, the database must be set up as an ODBC data source. You can set up a database as a data source using the ODBC Database Administrator, which you can run from the Windows Control Panel.

Whichever type of database you choose, you need to make sure to attribute a shape to each entry in the database. The shape should correspond to the proper name of one of the hundreds of shapes in Visio. The Shape ID field in the database should list the name of the shape to be used for the information in that row. It's very important to make sure the name is an exact match for the shape or Visio may reject your data file.

When you have the data source set up correctly, you're ready to run the macro.

Using the Import Flowchart Data Wizard

The Import Flowchart Data Wizard is the quickest and easiest way to create a flowchart using data. This macro launches a wizard that helps you create a standard data flowchart using a data file you have already created.

To create a flowchart using the wizard, select Tools | Macros | Import Flowchart Data Wizard. The first screen of the Import Data Flowchart Wizard opens, as shown here:

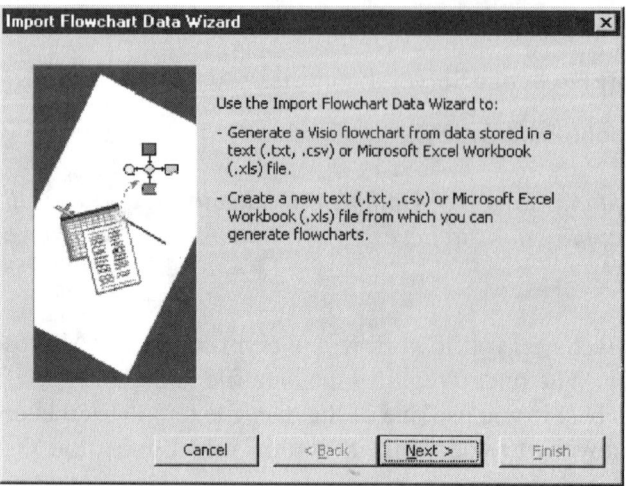

Behind the first wizard screen, a new blank drawing opens using the Basic Flowchart template. Click Next.

The next window opens, asking for the data source, as shown here:

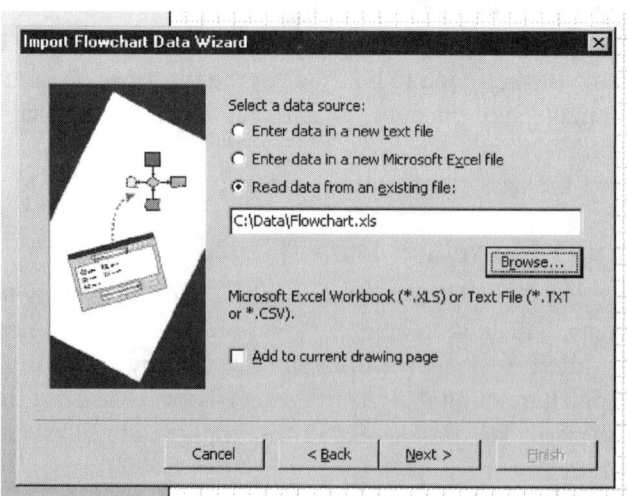

You can create flowcharts using this wizard that have several different data sources or no data source at all. The options on the second wizard screen are as follows:

- ■ **Enter Data in New Text File**   If you select this option, you'll need to create a text file with the data in tab-delimited format. This option is most useful when data has been exported from some other program, because most database and accounting programs can export data as text.

- ■ **Enter Data in New Microsoft Excel Workbook**   If you select this option, you'll need to enter data in a new Excel workbook or spreadsheet, with the data organized in simple columns. This option is only useful if you've already stored a record of all the data in Microsoft Excel.

- ■ **Read Data from Existing File**   If you select this option, the wizard uses an existing file, such as an Excel workbook or plain text. Visio can import data from only certain kinds of files, Microsoft formats chief among them. See the discussion earlier in this section for more information about the types of files from which Visio can import data.

- ■ **Add to current drawing page** Allows you to add not only the data as flowchart shapes, but includes the Microsoft Excel or text file as part of the diagram as an embedded object.

> **NOTE**   *It's best to create a data file before running the wizard. (The previous section details the requirements for Visio data source files.) If you choose to create the data file from within the wizard, Visio walks you through the creation process and then drops you out of the wizard, forcing you to start over again. To save time, create the data file first, and then start the wizard.*

Select Read Data from Existing File, and click Next. The third wizard screen appears, telling you the wizard is ready to create your flowchart. Click Finish. A progress bar appears, letting you know Visio is attempting to read your data file. Once it has verified your file works, a screen appears, indicating that Visio is converting your file.

The File Converter asks which character has been used in the data file to indicate columns, as well as the characters used as "text delimiters" and "comment separators." The *text delimiter* is the character you put around anything you want Visio to display as is, be it standard ANSI text or extended characters (such as the end-of-line character). The text delimiters should surround the text, one at the beginning and one at the end. The *comment separator* is the character you use to add comments to your data file that you don't want Visio to use in the flowchart. They go at the very front of the field with the comment. Once you've set all the conversion parameters, click OK.

Visio creates the flowchart on the drawing page, and the Import Flowchart Data Wizard closes. You can now alter your flowchart using the techniques outlined in the section "Using the Basic Flowchart Template" earlier in this chapter.

 *You can include number shapes in your flowchart by selecting Tools | Macros | Visio Extras | Number Shapes.*

Exporting Flowchart Data

Not only does Visio interface with databases to create new flowcharts, but you can also export your flowchart data into a format a database will read. Much like exporting your Organizational flowchart data into reports you can use in your business, exporting flowchart data allows you to use your diagram to create other types of information.

There are several ways to turn your Visio diagram into data. First and foremost for the basic types of flowcharts is the Database Export wizard. Visio specifically created this wizard to make creating database information from your Visio diagram as quick and painless as possible.

For more complicated or specialized database requirements, or for flowcharts that are especially complicated, you can use the fully featured Export to Database feature. You can use Export to Database in any and all Visio diagrams. This section discusses both of these options. Chapter 10 explores database interaction more in-depth for those that need to program interfaces or that want to create automatically updating databases from Visio information.

 *For the simplest type of database information, reports create a simple set of data that you can save in Microsoft Excel or text formats. See the "Creating Reports from Flowcharts" section previously in this chapter.*

Using the Database Export Wizard

If you need a report in some format other than a Visio report, or if you need to create a database from flowchart data, you can export the data from a flowchart into standard ODBC-compliant format using the Database Export Wizard. The Database Export Wizard can be used with a few templates that may incorporate frequently-used data into your databases, such as flowcharts, office layouts, and organization charts.

You can create an entirely new database or insert new tables into an existing database. To run the Flowchart Database Wizard, you must have the database program you wish to use to read the data installed on your computer.

NOTE *It's best to run through this wizard at least once before attempting to create or modify a functional data source file.*

To run the wizard, choose Tools | Macros | Visio Extras | Database Export Wizard. This launches the wizard.

The Database Export Wizard has almost a dozen screens. As you follow along with the Database Export Wizard, you are asked to make the following choices and specifications in the order listed here:

1. A filename to export to.

2. The shapes you would like to export (every shape or selected layers of shapes).

3. The information from those shapes that you would like to export.

4. The Data Source File to export to.

5. If the data source file doesn't already exist, you're asked to create one. At the very least you are asked to browse and locate the file.

6. Database export details, including the Table Name.

7. The way each piece of information will be represented in the table.

8. A right-mouse option for exporting the data from the drawing page.

9. Verification of the data to be exported.

When the Database Export Wizard to used for exporting shape data, the wizard stores export-related information with the drawing page. If you make changes to the shapes and want to re-export the data, you can right-click the drawing page and choose Database Table Export.

NOTE *The exact information asked for in each Data Export Wizard Screen depends a great deal on the type of data source you're exporting to.*

When you've completed all the information for the export, the Data Export Wizard informs you it's ready to finish and create the report. When you click Finish, Visio creates or updates the data source as a background process and then tells you when it's completed.

Using Export to Database

Export to Database is a highly advanced feature of Visio that allows you to create very specialized database information from you Visio diagrams. If the Database Export wizard doesn't have enough options for you, or if your database requirements are very stringent, they you may need to use the Export to Database option to get the most out of your Visio diagrams.

To use Export to Database, choose Tool | Export to Database, which opens the Export to Database window shown in Figure 5-12.

There are about a dozen different options to set in the Export to Database window, and several that require an in-depth knowledge of the type of database that will use the exported data. Here's a rough overview of the types of information and settings available to you in the Export Database window.

■ **ODBC Datasource** Choose the type of database you want to use. You can browse directly to your database file, or create a new one if Visio

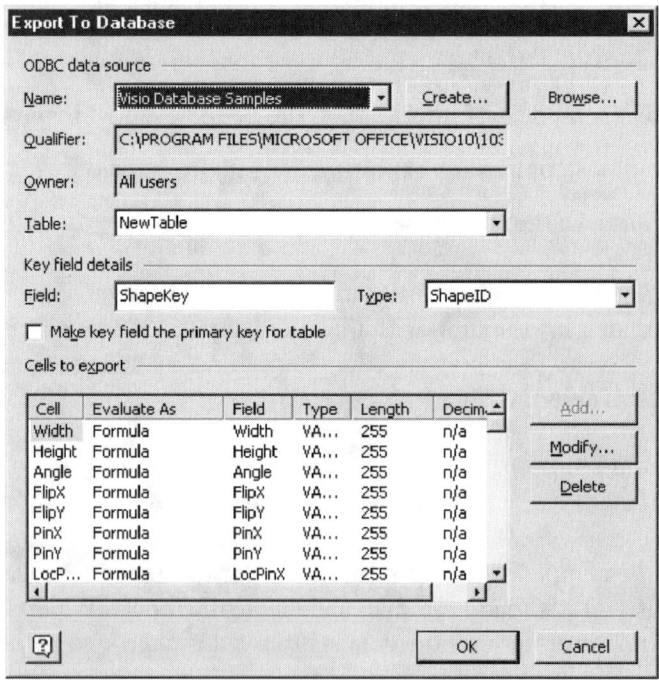

FIGURE 5-12   Export to Database window

doesn't have the database filter by default. If you choose to create a new database, a wizard launches to walk you though the process. Remember to choose the table and owner information, as well as qualifier settings if they apply to your database type.

■ **Key Field Details** Sets how each shape represents itself in the database. The uniqueness of each shape is defined here, as well as the information that the database uses to identify each shape in the table.

■ **Cells to Export** Sets the information to export. You can select all or part of the default data by using the delete key to remove any data you don't want to export. You can also create new fields to export by using Modify.

When you are ready to export your information, click OK. Visio creates the ODBC database table in the database you indicated.

Summary

In this chapter, you learned how to create organization charts and flowcharts by hand and with an imported data file. You also learned how to export data from flowcharts into reports or into their own data sources.

In the next chapter, you'll learn how to create more types of Visio diagrams to help your business get its point across graphically.

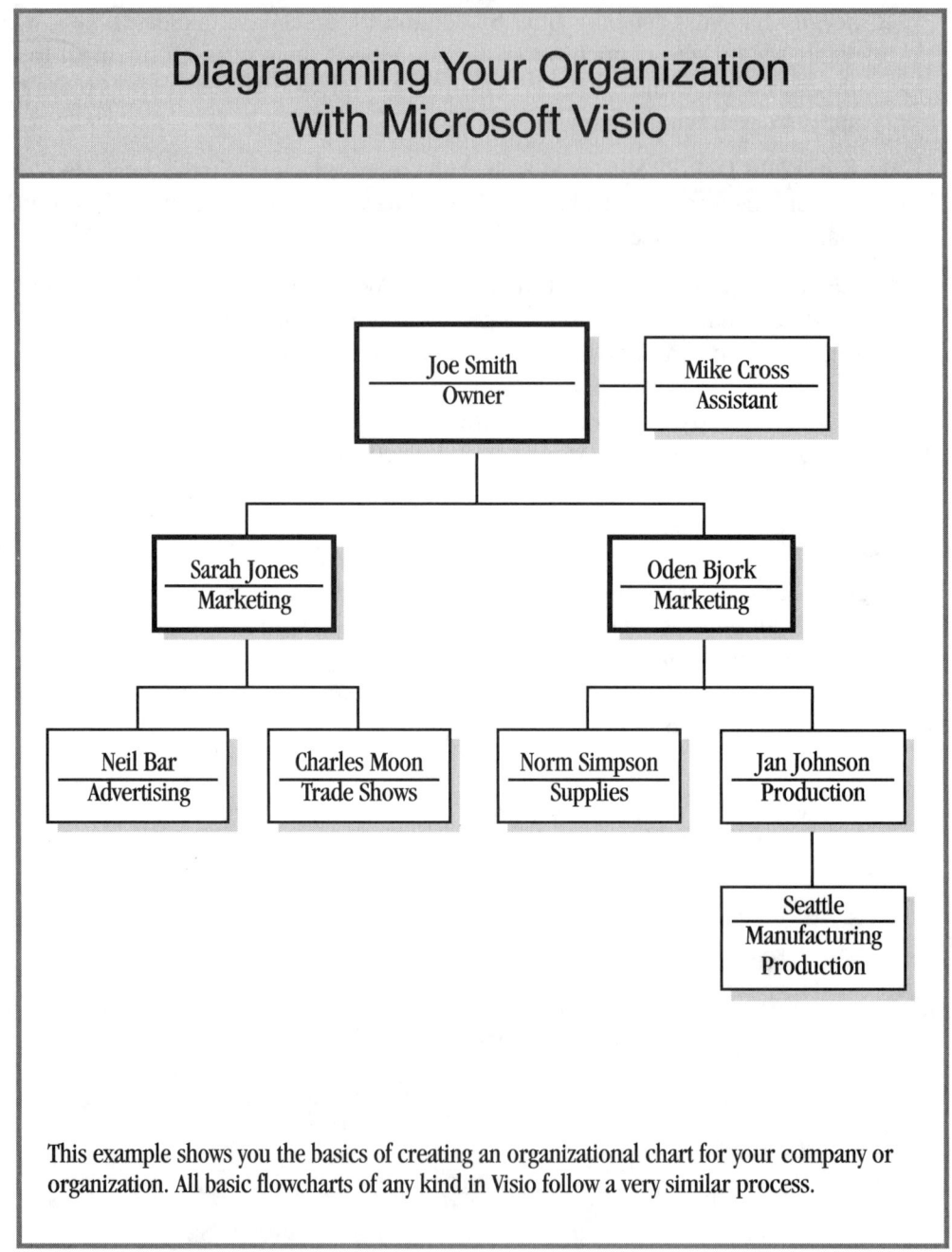

Diagramming Your Organization with Microsoft Visio

This example shows you the basics of creating an organizational chart for your company or organization. All basic flowcharts of any kind in Visio follow a very similar process.

Creating an Office Flowchart
from Scratch

1

Collect information on the whole company or the part you are diagramming. Having this information to start will make the diagramming go quicker and easier.
List all the direct reports to one manager at once, and then the secondary reports under those managers. This will make it easier to construct the diagram in Visio.

2

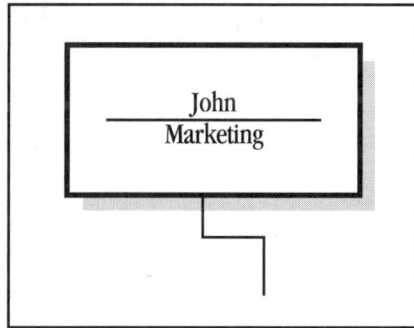

Open Visio, choose the Orgainizational Chart. Once Visio is open, drag the Executive shape onto the page for the highest level manager on your list. Enter the Name of the Manager and their department.

3

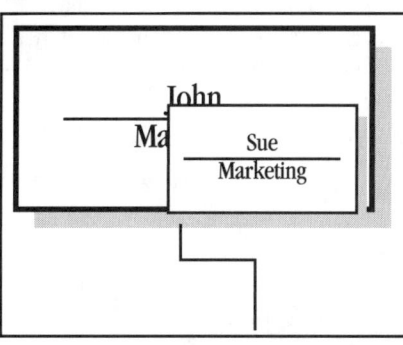

Pick up either a Position or Manager shape for each of the people that report to your first manager. Drop the reporting shape directly onto the executive shape. Visio automatically connects the shapes correctly.

5

4

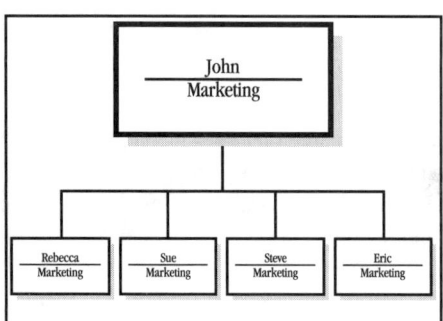

Drop all the direct reports onto the Executive shapes. Make sure that anyone who has reports of their own gets a manager shape.

Visio Automatically arranges the shapes horizontally. Select the Executive shape and then choose a layout from the Organization Chart Toolbar.

5

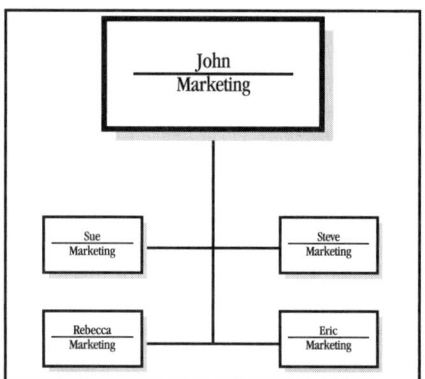

Repeat steps 1-5 with all the other managers in this department. When you finish make sure your chart can be printed, or save it in a format you can use later to include in documents.

6

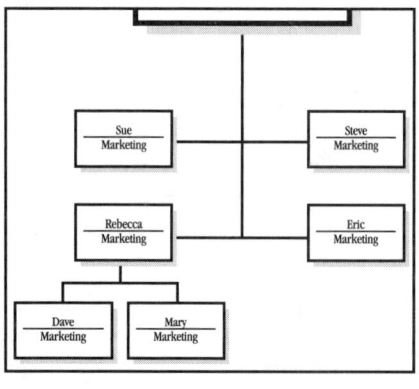

Chapter 6

Getting Your Point Across Graphically

How to...

- Schedule with Visio
- Create PRT and Gantt charts
- Create an office diagram
- Create forms
- Generate charts
- Create a slide show
- Create a map
- Add comments

In the last chapter, you learned how to create and use flowcharts in Visio.

In this chapter, you'll learn how to use Visio to convey information graphically in presentations and on paper. You'll learn how to use the project scheduling templates in Visio, as well as how to work with these templates to manage your business. You'll also learn how to work with the Office Layout template, using it to create office diagrams and to generate inventory and ownership reports. You'll learn how to create charts, forms, and graphs, as well as how to add maps to your diagrams. You'll also learn how to create a slide show in Visio, how to use color schemes, and how to add comments to shapes.

Scheduling with Visio

Schedules are an integral part of any business. Visio has made scheduling easy with four different ways to create and display schedules using Visio templates. All four of the Visio scheduling solutions are stored in the Project Scheduling folder. They are:

- Calendar template
- Timeline template
- PERT template
- Gantt template

Using the Calendar Template

Of the project scheduling solutions, the Calendar template is the easiest to use. It creates complete one-month and one-year calendars on which you can note important dates and project information. The calendars produced by this template are meant to look like most standard commercial calendars. Each day of the week has its own box. Figure 6-1 shows an example of a monthly calendar created by the Calendar template.

To create a calendar with the Calendar template, first open the template by clicking Project Schedule | Calendar when you open a new Visio document. The Calendar template appears with the Calendar Shapes stencil open and the drawing page set to landscape, as shown in Figure 6-2.

There are three kinds of calendar shapes on the Calendar Shapes stencil. The Large Month shape is the most commonly used one. However, the Yearly shape and the Small Month shape are also very useful. The following sections discuss each type of calendar shape in more detail.

6

NOTE   *All the calendar shapes on the stencil can be resized proportionally, so you can make them as large or as small as you like.*

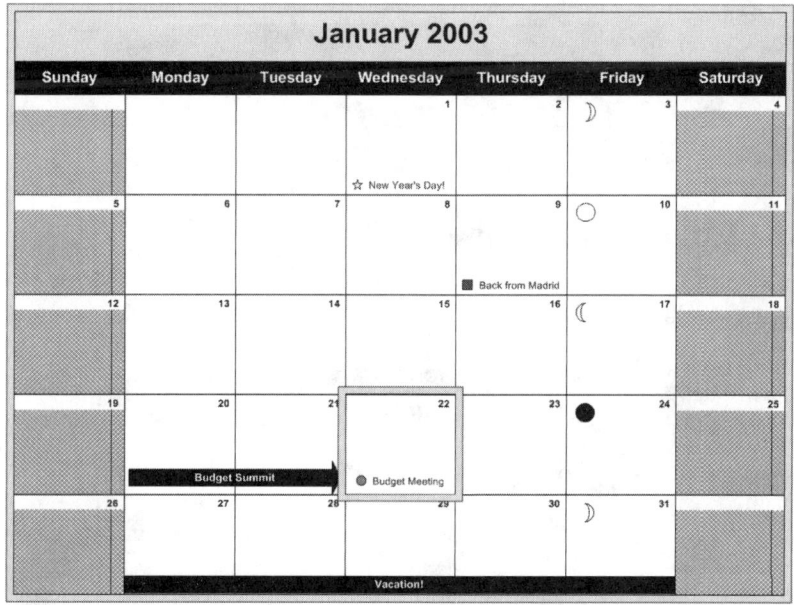

FIGURE 6-1   A monthly calendar created with Visio

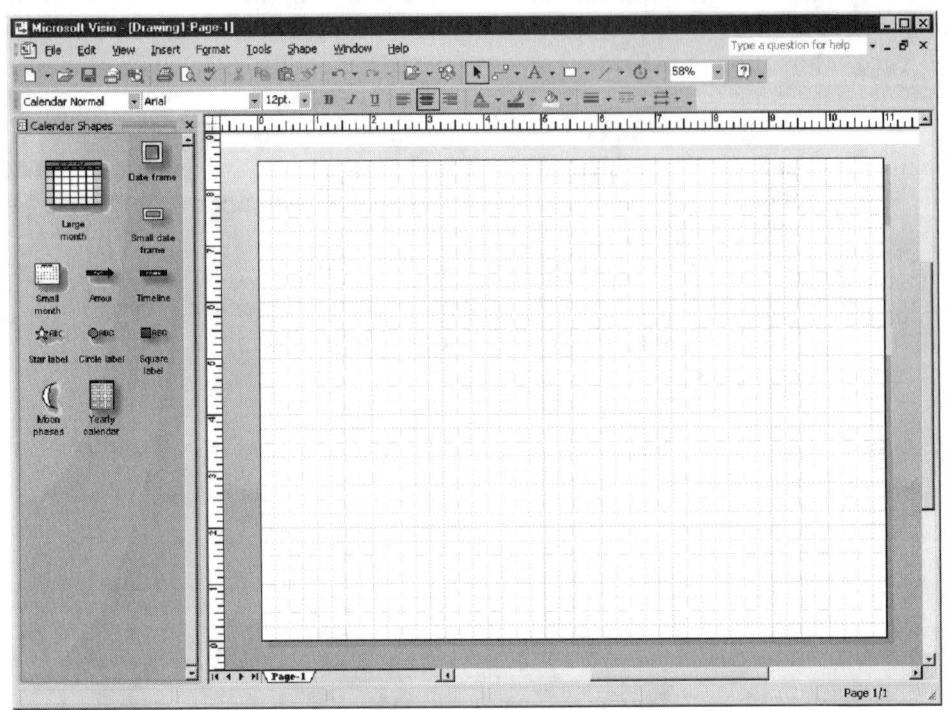

FIGURE 6-2   The Calendar template

Using the Large Month Shape

To create a single, large monthly calendar, drag the Large Month shape to the drawing page. A Custom Properties dialog box automatically appears, as shown here:

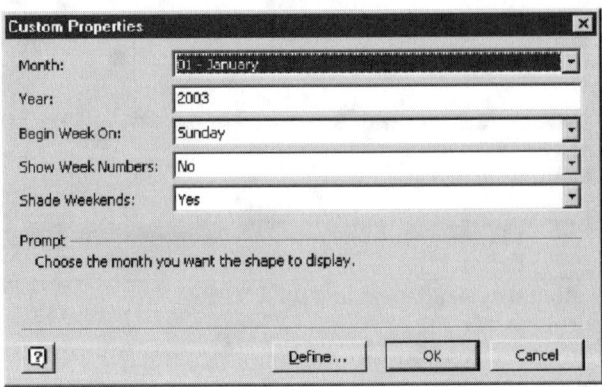

- **Month**   Lists all the months in the year, with the current month set as the default. To set the month for your calendar, select it from the list.

- **Year**   Lists the current year. If you need to create a calendar for another year, fill in the year (using all four digits).

- **Begin Week On**   Allows you to choose to start your week on either Monday or Sunday. (Sunday is the default.) If you need your week to start on a different day, click the Define button and change the options.

- **Show Week Numbers**   Toggles week numbering on and off. The default is No.

- **Shade Weekends**   Controls whether the boxes for the weekend days (Saturday and Sunday) are shaded. The default is Yes.

If the Custom Properties dialog box contains all the options you need, set those options and then click OK.

Occasionally, you will find that the options in the Custom Properties dialog box are not exactly what you need. To modify the fields in the Custom Properties dialog box, click the Define button. When you click Define, you'll see the Define Custom Properties dialog box, shown here:

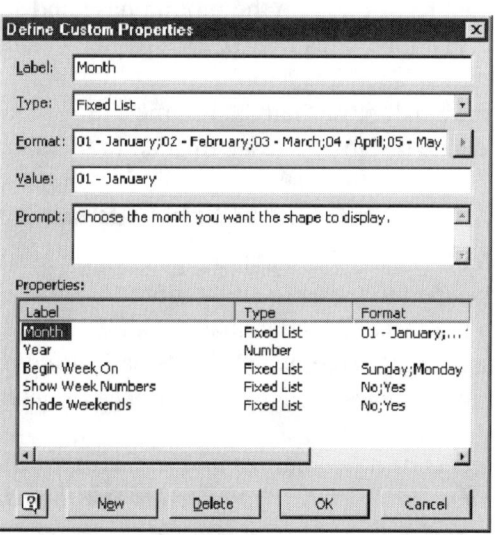

The custom properties fields are listed at the bottom. To modify a custom property field, select that field in the Properties area of the Define Custom

Properties dialog box. Then update the field's label, type, format, value, or prompt, as needed. After you've made the necessary changes, click OK. For more information about defining custom properties, see Chapter 11, "Using Advanced Visio Features."

 *For all calendar shapes, the drawing page has a landscape orientation by default. Check the printer settings to make sure your printer is ready to print pages with landscape orientation.*

Modifying a Monthly Calendar

After you drag the Large Month shape to the drawing page, you may want to make some modifications to the calendar.

To add text to the calendar's squares, click on a square where you'd like to add text and start typing. Visio zooms the view to 100 percent as you enter the text. When you're finished, click the Pointer tool.

To add arrows or timelines, drag them from the stencil and add them to the calendar. Using the green control handles, resize the shapes until they cover the number of days you need. Be sure to snap them in place.

To add labels, drag them from the stencil, and then type the text to create the label.

To add moon phases, drag the Moon Phases shape from the stencil and place it on the correct date. Then right-click on the moon phase and select the correct phase from the menu. Visio includes four phases for the calendar moon: First Quarter, Full, Last Quarter, and New Moon.

To include either the small or normal data frames, drag them from the stencil and place them around the date or label. They will snap to the date box or label shape.

Using the Small Month and the Yearly Calendar Shapes

The Small Month and the Yearly Calendar shapes can be used individually on a page or they can be grouped together to show more than one month or year per page. For example, two Yearly Calendar shapes can be grouped so that two years appear on one landscape legal-sized page. Five Small Month calendar shapes fit side-by-side on the drawing page when the printer page orientation is set to portrait.

 *None of the labels or other shapes on the Calendar Shapes stencil fit on the smaller calendar shapes. If you need to use labels, frames, and so forth, you can resize them, or you can simply use the Large Month calendar shape, group it, and size it down when you're done.*

When you drag the Small Month shape or the Yearly Calendar shape from the stencil to the drawing page, you'll see a dialog box asking for the dates to use. This dialog box looks much like the Custom Properties dialog box shown earlier; however, for these shapes, the dialog box has fewer fields. For the Small Month calendar, it asks for the month. For the Yearly Calendar shape, it asks for the year and the first day of the week.

Timelines

Timelines are a good way to visually convey information about scheduling. They can provide a lot of information in a way that is both interesting to look at and easy to grasp. Figure 6-3 shows an example of a timeline diagram.

To create a timeline, open the Timeline template as you would any other of the Visio templates. The Timeline template is located in Project Schedule. When you open the template, the main Visio window appears with three stencils open, as shown in Figure 6-4. The three stencils are the Backgrounds stencil, the Borders and Titles stencil, and the Timeline Shapes stencil. Both the Backgrounds and Borders and Titles stencil are standard business stencils. The Timeline Shapes stencil holds all the shapes needed to make timelines.

Using Timeline Backbones

There are six timeline shapes to use as the backbone of your timeline. The first part of making a timeline is deciding which of these shapes you'll use, since all the markers you later drag to the timeline depend on the type of backbone you choose. The six backbones are:

- **Block timeline** A simple rectangle with start and end dates. All added dates display outside the rectangle.

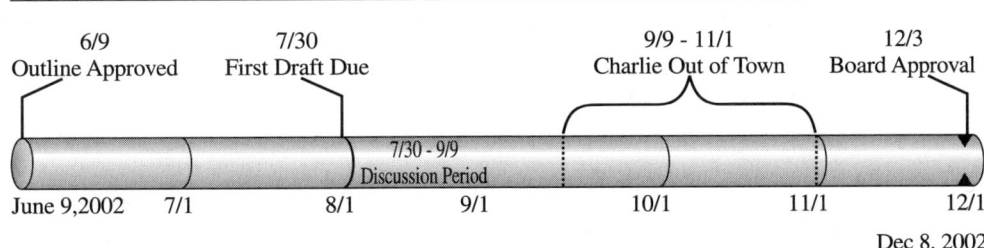

FIGURE 6-3 A timeline diagram

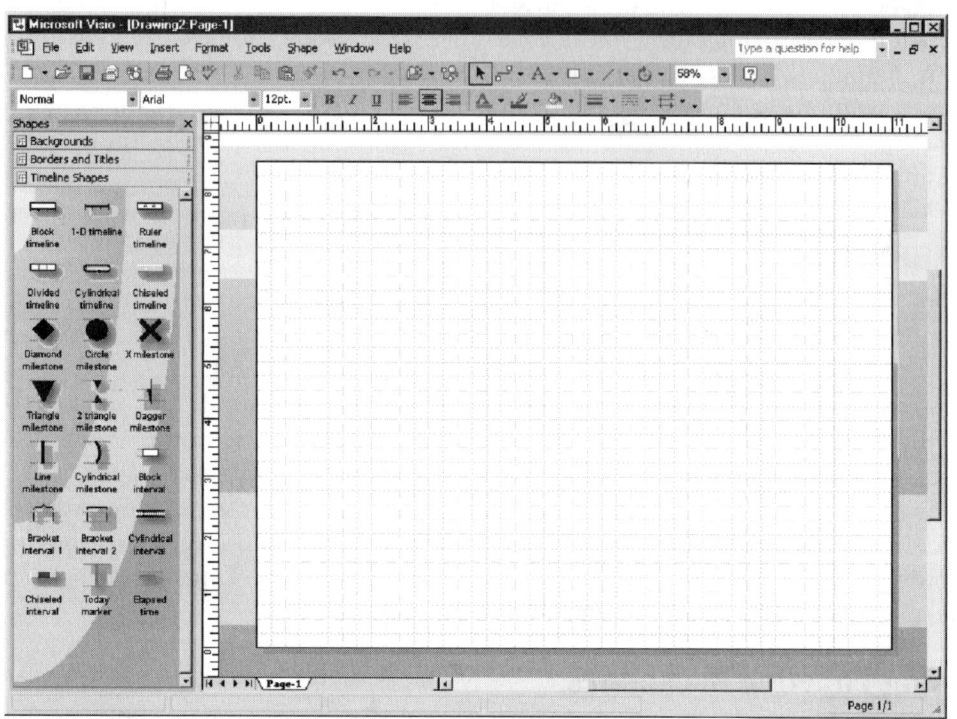

FIGURE 6-4   The timeline template

- ■ **1-D timeline**   A line with start and end dates, including several date markers or "ticks" in the middle of the timeline.

- ■ **Ruler timeline**   A rectangle with several date markers or "ticks" in the center, and all dates listed inside the rectangle.

- ■ **Divided timeline**   A rectangle with several separate sections created by lines that go from one side to the other. This is a good timeline backbone for projects with very distinct parts.

- ■ **Cylindrical timeline**   A three-dimensional cylinder with all dates placed either above or below the line. This is a very useful shape for multimedia.

- ■ **Chiseled timeline**   A three-dimensional rectangle that has divided sections. This backbone is best used on a colored background so you can see the chiseled effect.

 *You may want to use different timeline backbones for your printed and projected versions.*

When you've decided which of the timeline backbones to use, drag it to the drawing page. The Configure Timeline dialog box opens, as shown here:

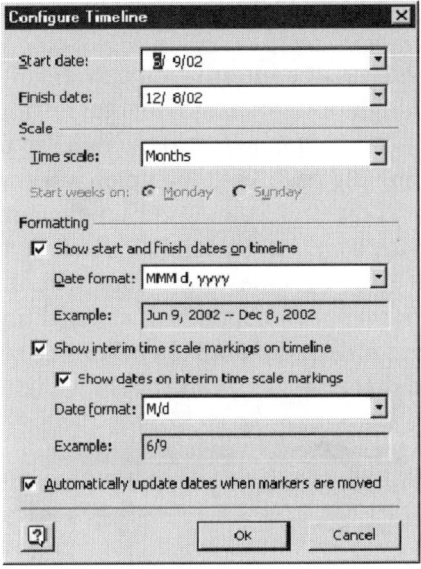

- **Start date**   Specifies the start date for the timeline backbone. This date displays by default on the far left below the backbone. The default is the current date.

- **Finish date**   Specifies the end date for the timeline backbone. This date displays by default on the far right below the backbone. The default is six months from the current date.

- **Scale**   Sets the timescale as well as the date a week begins on (if week is selected). Months is the default.

- **Formatting – Show start and finish dates on timeline**   Specifies how the beginning and ending dates are displayed and allows you to select if they are shown on the timeline at all.

- **Formatting – Show interim time scale markings on timeline**   Specifies the date format for all the dates listed on the timeline, as well as whether any date scale markings are shown on the timeline backbone.

■ **Automatically update dates when markers are moved** Specifies if and when Visio automatically updates the dates you set on the timeline as you move the marker shapes. There's very little reason to uncheck this box.

Adding Milestones and Intervals

When you've configured and set the timeline backbone, you're ready to place milestones and intervals.

Milestones and intervals are the information carriers of your timeline. All timelines should have enough milestone and interval information to make them worth the reader's time, but not so much as to overwhelm them with information. If you find you're crowding the page with too much information, use the arrow at the end of the timeline backbone to separate your timeline into more than one page.

To add milestones to the timeline, select the milestone that matches your timeline backbone. Eight different milestones come with the Timeline Shapes stencil, each different in shape, meaning, and associated timeline backbone. Once you've selected the correct milestone, drag the milestone to the timeline backbone. The Configure Milestone dialog box appears, as shown here:

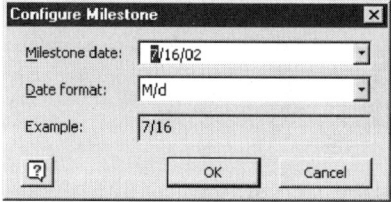

This dialog box sets the date for the milestone as well as the display format for the date. The down arrow to the right of the date displays a small calendar from which you can choose a date for the milestone. Once you're satisfied with the date information, click OK.

 *To access the Configure Milestone dialog box again, right-click on the milestone and choose Configure Milestone.*

To add an interval, pick one of the five interval shapes, making sure it coordinates with the timeline backbone you chose, then move the interval to the timeline backbone on the page. The Configure Interval dialog box appears, much like the Configure Milestone dialog box. The dialog box specifies beginning and ending dates, set by default when you dropped the interval on to the backbone. The dialog box also displays the default format for displaying the date. You can also access the Configure Interval dialog box by right-clicking on the interval and selecting Configure Interval.

To change, expand, or move an interval, select the interval with the Pointer tool and move it along the timeline backbone or use the green control handles to change the shape of the interval. As long as the "Automatically update dates when markers are moved" box is checked on the Configure Timeline dialog box, Visio revises the dates to reflect the new length and location of the interval.

To add text to intervals or milestones, click on the shape and type in the new text.

> **NOTE**   *If you change the width or length of the timeline backbone, the milestone and interval shapes may not fit and will need to be resized.*

When you're pleased with the look of your timeline, save it to the format you need to display. Make sure, if you are printing the timeline, that it fits on your drawing page and looks good with the page orientation.

PERT Diagrams

PERT diagrams were developed by the U.S. Department of Defense to help manage large and complex military projects. PERT stands for "Program Evaluation and Review Technique." This graphical way of organizing and managing projects became very popular with research and educational organizations and is now in use wherever large projects are managed.

PERT diagrams are used to create a high-level project management chart—usually at the start of the project at the brainstorming stage—to help everyone involved understand the project's timetable and dependencies. The planning and brainstorming advantages afforded by PERT diagrams makes them invaluable when managing large projects.

Each rectangular shape in a PERT diagram represents a task, and each arrow represents a dependency. The dates are shown in sets of beginning and ending dates. The use of dependency arrows in PERT diagrams is especially handy for showing which steps must precede others. Figure 6-5 shows an example PERT diagram.

Visio makes it easy to create these powerful charts by including PERT shapes, which can be dragged onto the drawing page. PERT charts are usually created during meetings where brainstorming about a new project is taking place. You can use Visio to convert meeting notes into a form that can be used in documentation and presentations.

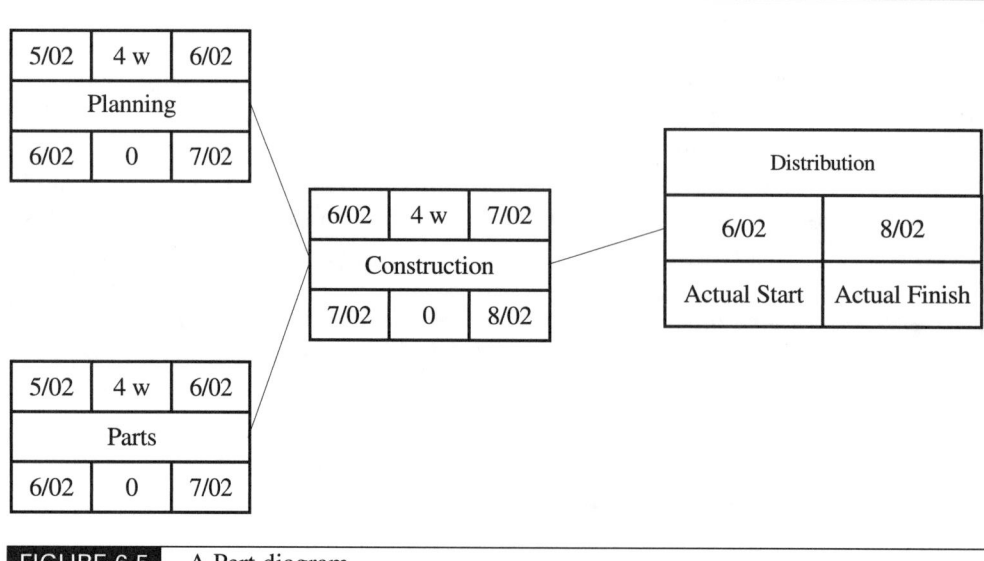

FIGURE 6-5   A Pert diagram

To create a PERT chart with Visio, first you need to open the PERT Chart template by choosing that template when you open a new document. The PERT Chart template opens three stencils: PERT Chart Shapes, Borders and Titles, and Backgrounds. The PERT Chart Shapes stencil has nine shapes, including two types of PERT task boxes. To start your diagram, drag one of the PERT task box shapes to the drawing page. Usually, PERT diagrams start with either a PERT 1 or PERT 2 shape, as shown in Figure 6-6.

PERT 1 shapes are task boxes that include not only the name of the task, but its duration, projected start and end dates, possible late start and end dates, and the difference between the projected and late dates. PERT 2 shapes are task boxes that only track start and end dates, both projected and actual. For most projects, the information in the Task Name box is the first to be filled in. Then duration is filled in. The start and end dates are added after the place the task holds in the project is free. For PERT 2 shapes the bottom row of boxes, those pertaining to the actual start and end dates, are left blank until the project is actually underway.

Once you've added all the PERT 1 and 2 shapes you need for your diagram, you're ready to start adding connections between the tasks. Connections between tasks in PERT diagrams indicate a dependency. The dependency can be due to supply issues, human resource issues, or even simply timing issues. It's best to

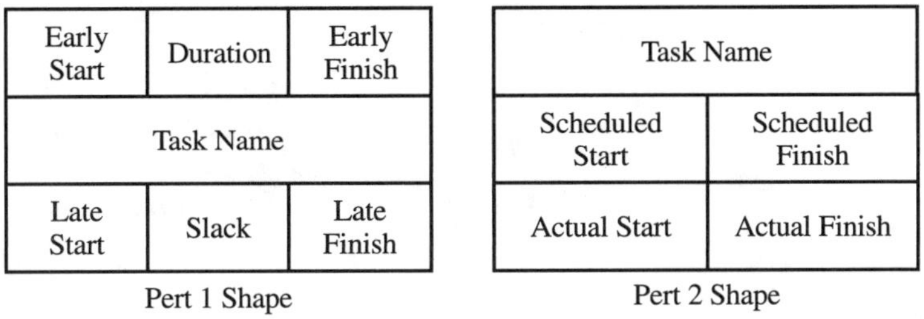

Early Start	Duration	Early Finish
Task Name		
Late Start	Slack	Late Finish

Pert 1 Shape

Task Name	
Scheduled Start	Scheduled Finish
Actual Start	Actual Finish

Pert 2 Shape

FIGURE 6-6   PERT 1 and PERT 2 shapes

make sure you have some understanding of the likely dependencies before you begin to connect your PERT 1 and PERT 2 shapes.

After all your connections have been made, you may wish to add callouts to your shapes to explain the dependencies or to give more information about the tasks. You may also find you need one of the "summarization structures." Summarization structures give information about a shape. They have a special gluing function: by pulling the extra control handle in the middle of the Summarization Structures shape to the control point of any other shape, Visio automatically connects the two shapes with a dynamic connector.

After all the shapes and connections have been completed, drag the Legend shape to the drawing page and fill in the information with the Text tool. When you've labeled the diagram with a Legend shape, you've completed your PERT diagram. Remember to save your diagram before you exit Visio.

Gantt Diagrams and Microsoft Project

You may recognize Gantt charts if you've used project management software such as Microsoft Project. Gantt charts illustrate the time each part of a project takes and where in the project flow each step happens, giving everyone in a project a visual cue to how the flow from step to step takes place. Powerful visual reminders are an important part of helping a project succeed, making these charts among the most popular charts in business. Figure 6-7 shows an example of a Gantt chart.

Visio includes a template to help you quickly and easily create Gantt charts on your own. Visio also includes a set of filters allowing you to import and export data for Gantt charts to and from Microsoft Project.

ID	Task Name	Start	End	Duration	Jul 1999														
					7	8	9	10	11	12	13	14	15	16	17	18	19	20	
1	Planning	7/7/02	7/11/02	3d 4h															
2	**Completion**	**7/8/99**	**7/18/02**	**7d**															
3	Outlining	7/8/02	7/10/02	3d															
4	Construction	7/9/02	7/12/02	3d 4h															
5	Documenting	7/14/02	7/18/02	3d 4h															

FIGURE 6-7   A Gantt chart

Making Gantt Chart Diagrams

Typically, the first step in creating Gantt charts is to create a PERT diagram. Often the brainstorming that goes into a PERT diagram is too valuable to lose, so the tasks and dependencies that make up a PERT diagram are reworked into the more visually powerful Gantt charts. However, even if you haven't created a PERT diagram, brainstorming about the ways your project might proceed is a vital first step before you begin a Gantt chart.

After you've conceptualized your project, open the Gantt Chart template as you would any other—by opening a new document and selecting the Gantt Chart template. After Visio loads the template, a dialog box asking for information about your Gantt chart pops us, as shown here:

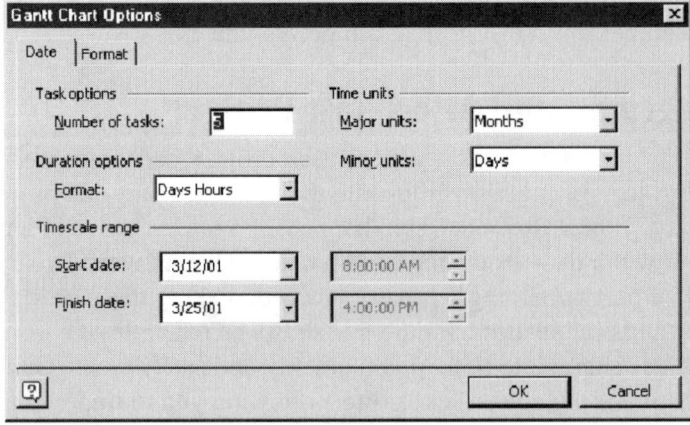

NOTE   *The Gantt Chart Options dialog box also opens when you select Options from the Gantt Chart menu.*

- **Number of Tasks**   The number or rows in your Gantt chart. This cannot be altered from this dialog box later. However, you can add and remove rows as you need them with other tools.

- **Duration Options, Format**   Sets the default timescale for the chart. Task bars display with units set here.

- **Start and Finish Dates**   Sets the start and end dates for the project. All tasks are set by default to start on the start date.

- **Time Units**   Sets the upper (major) and lower (minor) labels for the column holding the task timeline bars

6

TIP   *Don't worry about setting these options perfectly the first time. You can easily change them later.*

The Format tab of this dialog box contains information about the shapes Visio uses to indicate the start, end, and milestone dates for the project. Typically, you won't need to change the defaults. However, you may wish to if the project becomes very complicated. The Format tab is also where information about the default titles for the columns can be changed. Again, you need not do that because you're able to manually change these labels after you've finished setting the options.

When you've completed setting the Gantt chart options, click OK. Visio automatically creates a Gantt chart in the drawing page based on the options. The basic chart Visio creates with the option information is almost blank, formatted only by the number of tasks you specified and the start and end dates. All project-specific information needs to be set by changing the Gantt chart information.

Changing Gantt Charts

Whether you've just created a new chart or you need to alter an existing chart, most of the work with these charts falls under the category of changing Gantt chart information. There are four basic types of information to change on your Gantt charts: task length and labels, text formatting, column labels and formatting, and overall chart options.

Tasks   The rows of your Gantt chart represent the individual parts of your project. To add a task, select the task preceding the new task and choose Insert Task. To remove a task, select it and then choose Delete Task. There can be more than one level of tasks in Visio Gantt charts, allowing for tasks to have subtasks to help you refine your planning. To create a subtask, first make sure it's directly under the task that will be its superior, then select the subtask and choose Demote Task. To remove a task's place as a subtask but keep it as part of the chart, select it and choose Promote Task.

Columns   The columns of your Gantt chart hold individual information about each task in your chart. Adding columns means adding information about each task. To add a column, select the preceding column and choose Insert Column. The Insert Column dialog box appears, asking for the column title. Choose a name from the drop-down list and click OK. To label a column, select the rectangle containing the title text with the Text tool and edit the text. To delete a column, select it and choose Delete Column.

Links   Tasks can also be linked together to show a dependency in a project. To link tasks, select both tasks, and then choose Link Task. To remove a dependency relationship, select either task and choose Unlink Task.

Chart Settings   These options are important not only to the look of your chart but to the calculations needed to plan your project. Some of the chart settings are decided as you open the Gantt chart; others can only be changed once you start your Gantt chart. Settings for your entire chart are set in either the Gantt Chart Options dialog box, or the Configure Working Times dialog box. The Configure Working Times dialog box allows you to set the days and times your team is likely to work, assisting Visio in calculating the number of days a project or task will probably to take.

NOTE   *With all this information to sort out, planning your Gantt chart before you start is very important.*

With all these different types of information to change, Visio provides four ways to modify the content and appearance of a Gantt chart.

Right-Click   Most information on your Gantt chart can be reached by right-clicking on the relevant area and choosing a selection from the menu. This is the quickest and easiest way to access the basic information about your Gantt chart.

Gantt Chart Menu   The Gantt Chart template includes an addition to your standard menu bar: the Gantt Chart menu. Inside this menu you can access the configuration for the tasks and columns in your chart, as well as the Gantt Chart Options menu and all of the other dialog boxes needed to change your Gantt chart.

Gantt Chart Shapes Stencil   The Gantt Chart Shapes stencil opens automatically with the Gantt Chart template. It allows you to drag and drop columns, rows, labels, links, titles, and other chart tools into your Gantt chart, or have them float on the page outside your chart.

Gantt Chart Toolbar   The Gantt Chart template comes with its own toolbar allowing you access to several content-altering processes with the click of a button. Table 6-1 describes the function of each button in the Gantt toolbar.

Using Microsoft Project and Visio

After you've finished creating your Gantt chart, you may wish to export the information into a Microsoft Project file. Or, instead of creating a Gantt chart from scratch, you may want to create the chart from a Microsoft Project file where the project has already been planned.

Visio makes it easy to exchange data between Gantt chart diagrams and Microsoft Project. See Chapter 8, "Using Visio with Microsoft Office," for more information

Visio provides import and export commands so you can exchange data with Microsoft Project and other project management tools that use the MPX file format. You can also enter project information into an Excel workbook or text file, as explained in Chapter 8.

Designing an Office with Visio

Visio has a powerful tool for businesses to plan their facilities: the Office Layout template. All businesses go through stages where they need to rearrange facilities, either to move to another building or simply expand. The Office Layout template enables you to create floor plans effortlessly, so the moving or expansion process goes smoothly. The template includes shapes for walls, furniture, computers, even electrical outlets, allowing you to generate a very detailed representation of the office space.

Open the Office Layout template like any template, as a new document. However, before you start your office layout diagram, make sure you:

■ Measure the room you want to diagram.

Button	Name	Function
	Go to Start	Scrolls the task timelines to the start date for the project.
	Go to Previous	Takes you to the previous linked task.
	Go to Next	Takes you to the next linked task.
	Go to Finish	Scrolls the task timelines to the end date for the project.
	Scroll to Task	Displays a dialog box that allows you to locate a task based on text you input.
	New Task	Inserts a blank row without an attached task.
	Delete Task	Removes a row without an assigned task.
	Outdent	Turns a subtask into a full task.
	Indent	Turns a full task into a subtask.
	Link Tasks	Creates a new link between tasks.
	Unlink Tasks	Breaks an already-established link between tasks

TABLE 6-1   Gantt Chart Toolbar Buttons

- Measure the objects you want in the office you're planning, and make a complete list.

- Measure the windows, doors, and any other structural members in the room. Remember to note which direction the doors open.

- Make sure you know who might occupy the space and which items of furniture belong to that employee.

Creating an Office Diagram

A Visio office diagram includes several different parts, from the page size and scale to placing the walls, to including the furniture. These steps need to be done in a systematic way, otherwise you may need to completely redo your diagram to take into account a new page size or other fundamental change.

Setting the Scale and Page Size

Before you add any shapes to the page, make sure your drawing is set up correctly. By default, the Office Layout template opens with a drawing scale of 1/4 inch = 1 foot, and a page size of 8.5 × 11 inches with the page orientated to landscape. This allows you to draw a room of up to 30 × 45 feet.

If you need to change any of the drawing settings, you can do so on the Drawing Scale tab in the Page Settings dialog box by choosing File | Page Setup.

When you're determining a drawing scale for an office layout, remember:

- In Visio, drawing units are sizes in the real world. Page units are sizes on the printed page. The ratio of page units to drawing units is the drawing scale.

- The smaller the drawing scale, the larger the area you can represent. A scale such as 1/8 inch = 1 foot allows you to draw an entire floor on one page. A scale such as 1 inch = 1 foot allows you to focus on one cubicle.

- When you drop shapes onto a scaled drawing page, they adjust to the scale you've set. Shapes dynamically resize themselves as you change the drawing scale.

Creating the Walls

When you're satisfied with the size of your drawing page and the size of the room you can create, you're ready to place the walls. There are three ways to place walls on your Visio drawing page: dropping a whole room, placing each wall individually, and converting a line drawing to walls.

Dropping Rooms   Dropping whole rooms allows you to quickly create the basic outline of your space and Visio has included three room shapes to make it easier. The "T" room, the "L" room, and the square room shapes are all basic outlines for most room shapes and are meant to be dropped onto your drawing page and resized to match the actual dimensions of your room. To use the complete rooms, drag them to the blank drawing page and then resize them to the dimensions of your actual room.

Placing Individual Walls   For some room shapes, the only option is to place the walls individually. This is usually the case when one wall in a room is at an angle or has a curved shape, or when the room is of a very unique shape. Individual wall shapes allow you to create a room to the exact specifications of your space.

To create a room with individual walls:

1. Drag guides from the horizontal and vertical rulers to indicate the dimensions of the room on the drawing page. This gives the walls something to glue to.

2. Force the zero point of the drawing to be at the corner of your room by holding down the CTRL key and dragging the zero point from the intersection of the two rulers to one of the corners of the room. Moving the zero point allows you to have a scale that starts at the corner of your room, helping you place other shapes by having a more useful ruler setting.

3. Place a wall shape on one side so the wall thickness is outside the room's perimeter. If necessary, choose an option from the Shape menu to flip or rotate the shape.

4. Repeat Step 3 until you have as many walls as you need for the room. Make sure to snap and glue the walls together. The selection handles turn red when the shapes are glued.

Convert Space Shapes into Walls   The Convert Shape function allows you to drag space shapes onto the drawing page, merge them together, and then have Visio place the walls based on the shape. Here's how:

1. Drag space shapes onto the drawing page.

2. Overlap the space shapes to approximate the floor plan shape you want, then select all the space shapes.

3. Right-click the selected shapes, and then choose Union from the right-click shortcut menu.

4. Right-click one of the selected shapes, and then choose Convert to Walls from the right-click shortcut menu.

5. Under Settings, specify the actions you want—Add Dimensions and/or Add Guides.

6. Under Original Geometry, choose an option—Delete, Retain, or Convert to Space Shape.

7. Click OK.

On the drawing page, Visio creates walls to fit your shapes.

Placing Structural Details

After you've created the walls of your drawing, you're ready to start placing the doors, windows, switches, and electrical outlets.

First, align the window and door shapes on top of the walls. If necessary, flip or rotate window shapes so their endpoints snap to the guides on the inside of the walls and flip or rotate door shapes so the doors open in the correct direction. Both window and door shapes have control handles to help you change their angles and sizes to fit your needs.

Then attach the outlets and switches to the wall, being careful to make sure to glue the wall in place. You may want to group the wall with the outlets once you've have placed them to make sure they aren't accidentally moved out of place.

NOTE   *You can also place cubicles in your office space using the shapes on the Cubicles stencil.*

Placing Furniture

After you've placed the walls and all the pieces that go on them, you're ready to start placing furniture in the room.

All the furniture shapes on the Office Layout Shapes stencil are set to be the same physical size regardless of the drawing scale; the dimensions are based on standard office furniture measurements. The shapes dynamically resize when you use the control handles. However, it's best to resize them only if you're sure your office furniture isn't a standard size.

The shapes on the Office Layout Shapes stencil include just about everything you might need in an office floor-plan: chairs, tables, computers, files, even a sofa has been included. Most of these shapes behave like standard Visio shapes. However, a few of them have some special properties allowing you to make the most of them when you use them in your office layout. Table 6-2 describes the most common office layout shapes.

6

Shape	Name	Special Function
	Chair	Extra control handles allow you to rotate the chair.
	Conference table	The chairs can be moved in the group by clicking on them. They behave like standard chairs.
	File	The extra control handle allows you to open the file drawers.
	Bookcase	These have openings on one side. Make sure to place them in the correct direction in relation to the wall.
	Control Dimension	Glues to any shape allowing you to change the dimension size it shows and consequently dynamically resizes the shape it's attached to.

TABLE 6-2   Special Functions of Office Layout Shapes

Creating Office Layout Reports

The beauty of creating your office layout diagrams with Visio is that not only do you have a neatly drawn page to use as a layout chart, but you can also create reports based on the furniture and floor space. The reports that come with Visio allow you to glean this information from your Office Layout diagram by reading the information from the shapes on the page.

Information resident in the master shape is data that Visio keeps with the master shape in the ShapeSheet, including the name and the dimensions of the shape. Master shape information is useful if, for example, you'd like to know how many tables you have in your office. The Shape Inventory Report can help you retrieve this information.

Information you enter for the shape is data you manually include on each shape in the Custom Properties fields. Custom property information is useful if, for example, you'd like to know how many pieces of furniture belong to one person, or if you'd like to generate a list of every piece of furniture on a diagram by its inventory number. The Asset Report can help you retrieve this information.

For more information about using reports, see "Creating Reports from Flowcharts" in Chapter 5.

Creating Charts and Forms

When you give a presentation, it's often useful to present information graphically. Charts, forms, and graphs are the most common visual aids. Visio is first and foremost a program to help you create business diagrams, including graphical ways to display business information.

There are three templates designed specifically for creating charts, forms, and graphs. These templates are collected in the Forms and Charts solutions folder. The templates are:

- Charts and Graphs
- Form Design
- Marketing Charts and Diagrams

Understanding the Charts and Graphs Template

The Charts and Graphs template contains shapes for several types of reports and presentations. The chart tools in this template can be used in many types of reports such as financial reports and market projections—and even in complex documents like annual reports. Figure 6-8 shows the main Visio window with the Charts and Graphs template open and an example of a chart.

The Charts and Graphs template includes two standard Visio stencils (the Borders and Titles stencil and the Backgrounds stencil) as well as the Charting Shapes stencil. The Charting Shapes stencil has all the shapes you need to create many types of business charts, including 2-D and 3-D bar graphs, pie charts, process charts, and line graphs. Although this section describes how to create 2-D and 3-D bar graphs, the procedure for creating other types of charts is very similar. All charts created with the Charting Shapes stencil follow the same basic pattern.

Creating 2-D Bar Graphs

2-D bar graphs are the simplest type of business chart. Visio has two different kinds of 2-D bar graph shapes. Bar Graph 1 formats the bars based on numerical values; Bar Graph 2 formats the bars based on percentage values.

To create a 2-D bar graph:

1. Open the Charts and Graphs template.
2. Drag either the Bar Graph 1 or Bar Graph 2 shape from the Charting Shapes stencil. The Custom Properties window appears, as shown in Figure 6-9.

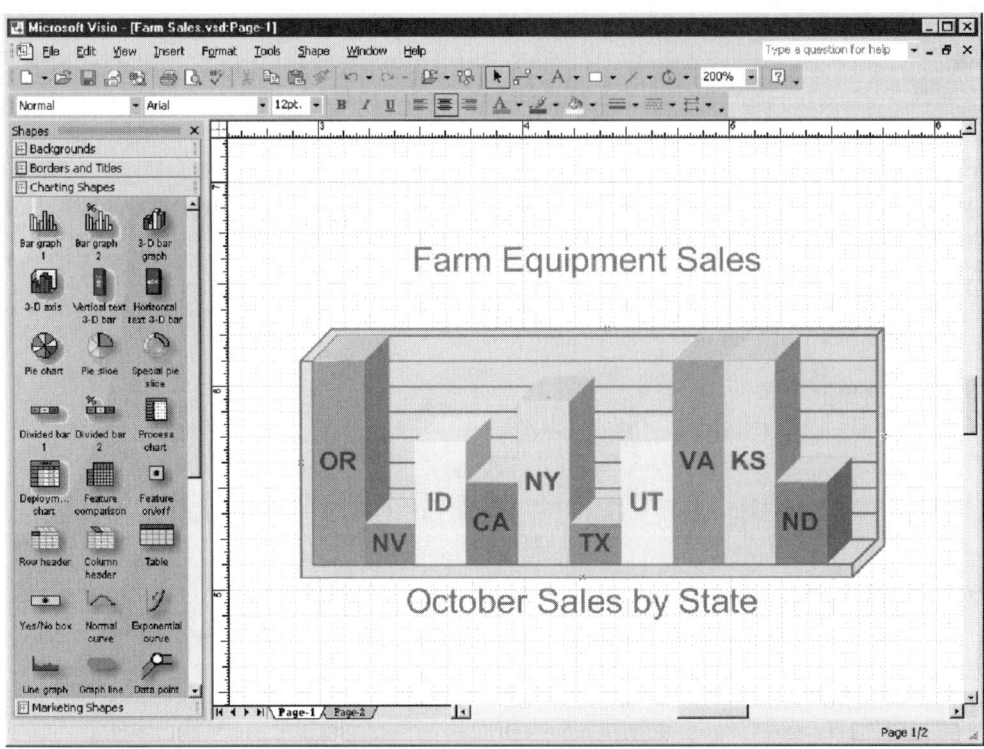

A bar chart created in Visio

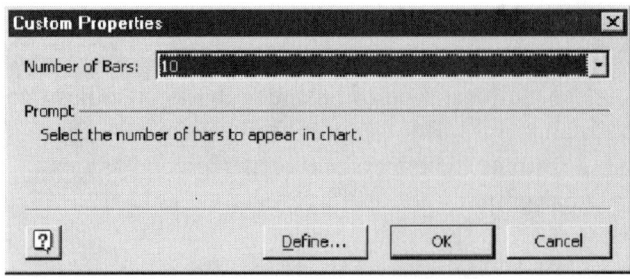

Custom Properties window for a 2-D bar graph

3. In the Custom Properties window, select the number of bars you would like in your graph, and then click OK.

> **TIP** *If you need to add another bar later you can access the Custom Properties dialog box by right-clicking on the bars and choosing Custom Properties, or by selecting the bars and choosing Shape | Action | Set Number of Bars.*

4. Set the size to ten segments (Bar Graph 1) or 100 percent (Bar Graph 2) by resizing the "phantom" bar just to the left of the locked group of bars. The height of the locked group is set at 100 units.

5. Change the text in each bar of the graph. Visio adjusts the size of the bars based on the text in them.

> **NOTE** *Make sure to add the percent sign (%) after the number for Bar Graph 2; otherwise, the bars will be formatted incorrectly.*

6. Change the colors of each bar by selecting it and using the Fill button to choose a new color.

7. Add a Graph Scale shape to provide a sense of scale. When you drag the Graph Scale shape to the drawing page, a Custom Properties dialog box appears (similar to the one shown in Figure 6-9), asking you to set the number of divisions for the graph's scale.

8. Finally, add a title to the graph by selecting the entire graph and starting to type, or by using the Text tool.

When you have finished creating the bar graph, remember to save it.

Creating 3-D Bar Graphs

The procedure for creating 3-D bar graphs is slightly more complicated than for 2-D bar graphs, but 3-D bar graphs can provide a more interesting graphic representation—making the extra work worth the effort.

To create a 3-D bar graph:

1. Open the Charts and Graphs template.

2. Drag one of the 3-D Bar Graph shapes from the Charting Shapes stencil. The Custom Properties dialog box appears, as shown in Figure 6-10.

6

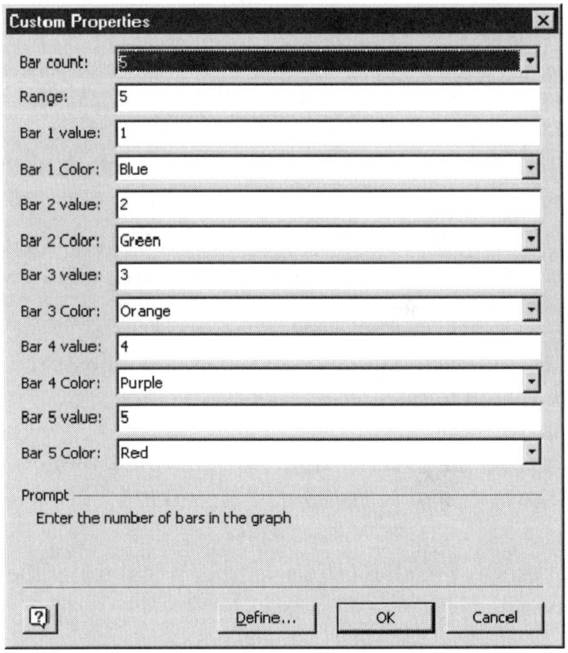

FIGURE 6-10 Custom Properties window for a 3-D bar graph

3. In the Custom Properties dialog box, set the number of bars, the color of each bar, and the value of each bar.

NOTE *The Range field sets the total height of the graph. This should be what you expect the largest number in the graph to be. Visio resizes all the bars in the graph based on the range.*

4. When you've set the custom properties for each bar, click OK. If you must change the value or other settings for a bar, you need to do so in the Custom Properties dialog box. 3-D bars don't dynamically resize based on their text the way 2-D bars do.

5. Choose Shape | Action to hide or reveal the numbers and lines for the bars. You can also use menu commands to change the number of bars, the value of bars, and the color of bars.

6. Add a 3-D axis shape to provide a sense of scale. When you drag a 3-D axis shape to the drawing page it may appear on top of the bar graph. If so, select the axis shape and then choose Shape | Send to Back.

7. Add titles for the axes of your graph by selecting the graph or the axis shape and starting to type, or by selecting the shape and then choosing the Text tool.

When you've finished creating the 3-D bar graph, remember to save it.

Getting to Know the Form Design Template

Sometimes, it's useful to provide a handout with your presentation, such as a form for the audience to fill out or use later. Visio includes the Form Design template for just this purpose. The template can be used to create forms of all kinds, including order forms, invoices, fax coversheets, certificates, and even rosters—as well as several dozen other types of forms. Figure 6-11 shows the main Visio window with the Form Design template open and an example of a fax coversheet created using the template.

To make creating forms quick and simple, Visio includes many types of ready-made form shapes on the Form Shapes stencil, which opens with the Form Design template.

To create a form, the first step is to design the form on a piece of paper. There are so many form shapes on the stencil that it's easy to go a little overboard if you don't have a clear idea of how your form should look before you start.

After you've created a basic concept for the form, drag the appropriate shape from the stencil onto the drawing page. Visio comes with Fax Cover and Business Card shapes to create these common forms, but there are many other standard form shapes to choose from as well. Table 6-3 gives a quick overview of some of the more popular shapes on the Form Shapes stencil and their behaviors.

When you've finished creating a form, be sure to save it.

Exploring the Marketing Charts and Diagrams Template

Selling a product or service requires a certain flair. Graphics and charts can help, but a sales pitch also needs to be visually impressive. To meet this demand, Visio includes a special template, the Marketing Charts and Diagrams template, which has everything you need to create eye-popping marketing materials. Figure 6-12 shows the main Visio window with the Marketing Charts and Diagrams template open and an example of a marketing diagram.

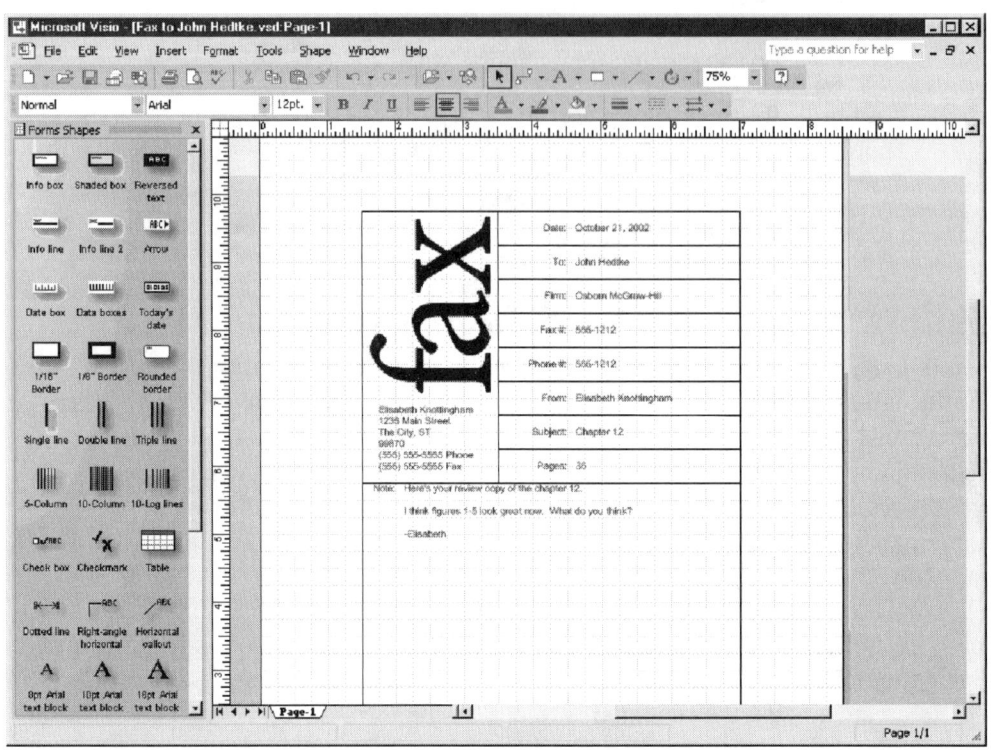

A fax cover sheet created with the Form Design template

Shape	Use	Behavior
Info Box, Shaded Box, Reversed Text	Fill-in boxes for building forms	Creates a standard size rectangle for adding text.
Info Line, Info Line 2	Labels for sections of a form	Creates a text box with a line underneath for labels.
Data Boxes	Fill-in box for one-character-at-a-time data	Creates a series of small boxes; increasing the width of the shape adds more boxes.
Check Box	Small checkbox with text	Creates a small box and accompanying text; to uncheck the box, right-click and choose Uncheck Box.

TABLE 6-3 Shapes on the Form Shapes Stencil

Shape	Use	Behavior
Lines—including Single, Double, 5-Column, 10-Column, Triple, and 10-Log	Borders for columns or rows in a form	Creates a fixed number of lines. The number of lines in the shape cannot be altered, and the width of the shape determines the distance between each line. However, you can overlap several column or line shapes to show more columns. You can also rotate the line shapes to create rows instead of columns.
Grid	Borders for lists of options, names, and so forth; can include checkboxes	Has control handles to change the size of the box and lines. Changing the size of the shape adds more lines or boxes.
Date, Time, Page, and Filename	File information that can be added to a form	Inserts information about the Visio 2000 file. The file information is updated automatically.

TABLE 6-3   Shapes on the Form Shapes Stencil *(continued)*

6

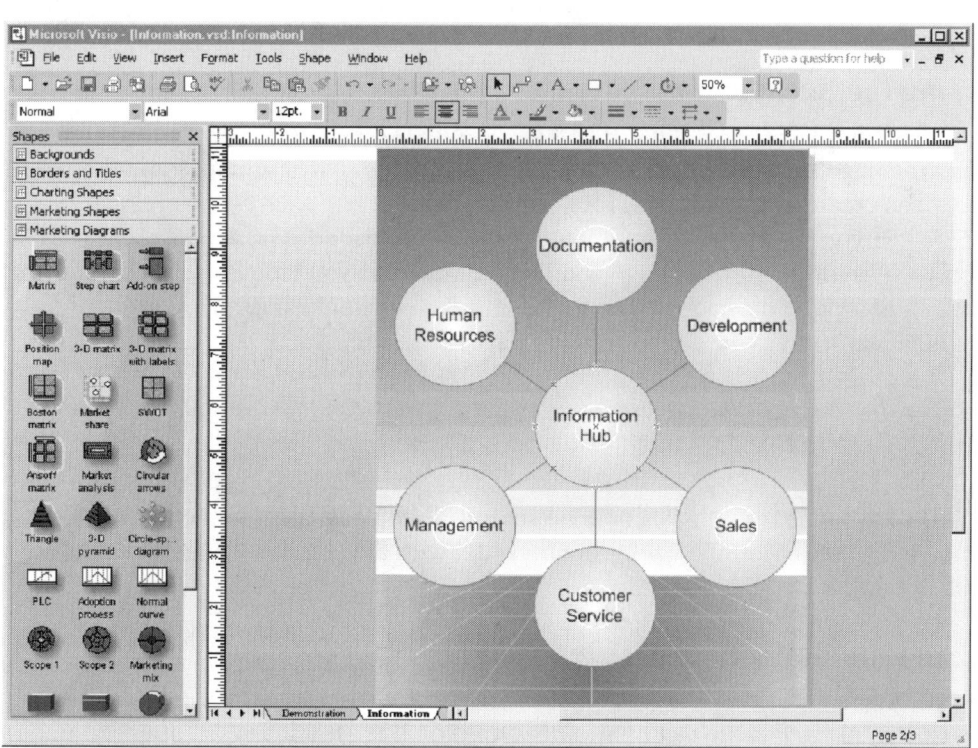

FIGURE 6-12   A marketing diagram created with Visio

Five stencils open up automatically with the Marketing Charts and Diagrams template:

- Backgrounds stencil
- Borders and Titles stencil
- Marketing Clip Art stencil
- Marketing Diagrams stencil
- Charting Shapes stencil

The Charting Shapes stencil is described earlier in this chapter in the section "Understanding the Charts and Graphs Template." The other four templates are explained here.

> TIP *To add color to your marketing diagrams, see the section "Using Color Schemes" later in this chapter.*

Using the Backgrounds Stencil

The Backgrounds stencil includes 18 backgrounds meant to fit any of the standard drawing page sizes. The backgrounds coordinate with color schemes and themes to help you create an overall look for your diagrams.

When you drag a background onto the drawing page, Visio automatically rotates it to fit the drawing page and locks it down. If you later rotate or change the size of your page, the background rotates or resizes with the page. Backgrounds also automatically cover the entire drawing page, no matter where you drop the shape.

> TIP *If a background covers other shapes, select it and choose Shape | Order | Send to Back.*

Backgrounds from this stencil are set to fill with any color you choose. When you change the color of a background, it fills with the color in a way that suits the background's image.

Using the Borders and Titles Stencil

The Borders and Titles stencil contains dozens of shapes to enhance the look of Visio diagrams. For the most part, the shapes on this stencil are not intended to be used as stand-alone diagram elements, but instead are designed to accent text and other shapes.

Included in the Borders and Titles stencil are fifteen border shapes that resize and change orientation to fit the drawing page. The stencil also includes 14 title shapes that resize to fit the text inside. There are also six note box shapes on the stencil. In addition, there are three hyperlink shapes for use on HTML pages created in Visio.

Using the Marketing Clip Art Stencil

Marketing Clip Art is a special subset of Visio clip art. This clip art has been specially formatted to enhance marketing diagrams. Included in this stencil are stretchable shapes that replicate themselves instead of resizing. For example, the stretchable dollars shape adds more dollar icons as you increase the width of the shape.

Also included in this stencil are shapes with special control handles and special resizing capabilities. For example, the Variable Stack and Variable Smoke Factory shapes allow you to increase the size of the three-stack or smoke shapes without altering the rest of the image. If you hover the cursor over one of the shapes on the drawing page, a tool tip appears explaining how the shape behaves.

NOTE   *Shapes on this stencil often have special functions when you resize them. If you're not sure how a shape will behave, save your diagram before you start resizing marketing clip art.*

The Marketing Clip Art stencil also includes useful shapes for reports and other marketing projects. Shapes like standard credit card images, global currency shapes, and award shapes allow you to convey information with professional-looking graphics.

Using the Marketing Diagrams Stencil

Marketing diagrams often include shapes for illustrating processes, path-routing, and cost projections. The Marketing Diagrams stencil includes shapes that look stunning and convey information clearly. Most of the shapes on the Marketing Diagrams stencil are colored, and many are three-dimensional.

TIP   *You may find it useful to open the Blocks Raised stencil when you're are creating a marketing diagram. The Blocks Raised stencil includes many more three-dimensional shapes. It's located in the Block Diagram folder.*

When you drag some shapes from the Marketing Diagrams stencil to the drawing page, a dialog box asking for information appears. Use the Custom Properties dialog box to set the number of shapes in the group or the number of subdivisions. If you need to change these properties after you've set them, you can access the dialog box again by selecting the shape and choosing Shape | Action.

Making and Using a Slide Show

Slide shows allow you to view multiple-page diagrams as a succession of full page images. You can also use a slide show to preview how your diagrams will look when you add them to a document in another program. Figure 6-13 shows an example of one screen of a Visio slide show.

NOTE *Other programs can be used to create slide shows on the computer, such as Microsoft PowerPoint.*

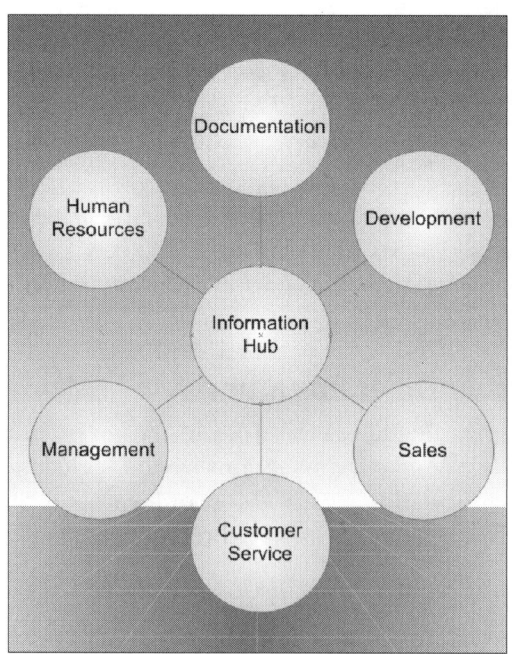

FIGURE 6-13   A Visio slide show screen

You should use slide shows *after* you have completed your diagrams. When you create a slide show, you can't change the shapes on the drawing page. The slide show is simply a way to view the diagrams.

The first step to using a slide show is to display the diagram in Full Screen view. To see a diagram in Full Screen view, choose View | Full Screen. To leave Full Screen view, right-click and choose Close from the shortcut menu. You can also press ESC to leave Full Screen view.

TIP   *The slide show starts on the page currently displayed in the Visio main window.*

6

Navigating Between Images in a Slide Show

When you have your multiple-page diagram in Full Screen view, you need to navigate between the pages differently than you do in the main Visio window. To go forward in the page order, use the RIGHT ARROW key. To go backward in the page order, use the LEFT ARROW key.

You can also use more sophisticated navigation by right-clicking and using the shortcut menu. Right-click anywhere on the page and a shortcut menu appears, as shown here:

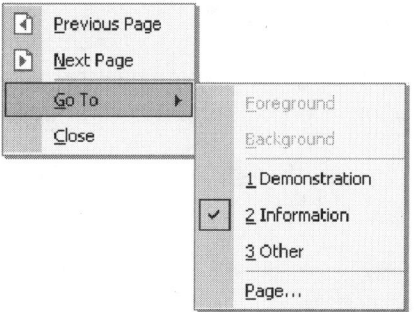

The options are as follows:

- **Previous Page**   Takes you to the page preceding the displayed page. This option disappears on the first page of the slide show.

- **Next Page**   Takes you to the page following the displayed page. This option disappears on the last page of the slide show.

■ **Go To**   Displays a list of pages, the option to open a window with a list of pages (Page...), and the option to view the foreground or background of the displayed page.

■ **Close**   Ends the slide show and takes you back to the main Visio window.

 *Page order is set in the Visio main window and cannot be changed in Full Screen view.*

Using Hyperlinks in a Slide Show

Hyperlinks set in a diagram work in Visio's slide show. You can tell where a hyperlink has been set because the mouse pointer changes from an arrow to a pointing finger when you move the pointer over the link. Activate a hyperlink by clicking on it. Then Visio opens up the hyperlinked document. If there's more than one link on a particular shape, a drop-down menu appears, and you can choose the link from the list.

 *Visio is unable to open other documents (including other Visio documents) in Full Page view. Instead, they are opened in the native program and are displayed in the same view they had when they were last saved.*

In order to not interrupt your slide show, documents you link to are opened up in a new program window. Even Visio documents operate this way, creating the situation where two copies of Visio are running at the same time.

 *Comments do not display in Full Screen view.*

Using Color Schemes

Creating an overall set of colors for your presentation can be difficult and time-consuming. Visio includes *color schemes* to make the process of choosing colors faster. This allows you to add an extra touch to your documents without taking time away from working on the content.

 *Color schemes in Visio are almost identical to color schemes in many Microsoft Office programs—for example, Microsoft PowerPoint. To learn more, see Chapter 8, "Using Visio with Microsoft Office XP."*

Color schemes can be added at any time during the creation of your Visio diagram. To set a color scheme for your document, choose Tools | Macros and then select a color scheme from the Visio Extras folder. The Color Schemes window appears, as shown in Figure 6-14.

The options in the Color Schemes dialog box are as follows:

- **Choose a Color Scheme**   Lists the 17 color schemes that come with Visio as well as any schemes you've created.

- **New**   Allows you to add a new color scheme based on settings you choose. Clicking this button displays a dialog box like the one shown in Figure 6-15.

- **Edit**   Allows you to edit the selected existing scheme. Clicking this button displays a dialog box like the one shown in Figure 6-15.

- **Delete**   Removes the currently selected scheme.

- **Preserve my shape color changes**   Makes sure any color changes you have made to shapes are not overwritten by the color scheme you choose.

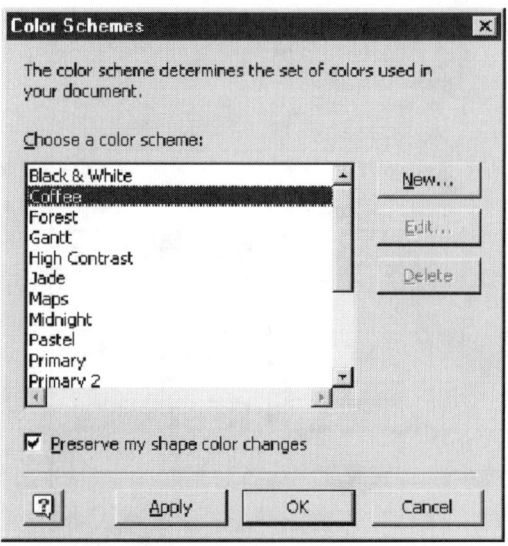

FIGURE 6-14   Color Schemes window

 *You cannot edit or delete one of the standard schemes. Only schemes you create can be edited or deleted.*

When you add a new color scheme by clicking on the New button shown in Figure 6-14, the Color Scheme Details window appears, as shown in Figure 6-15. The Color Scheme Details dialog box also appears when you edit a color scheme you've created previously.

The options in the Color Scheme Details dialog box are:

- **Name**   Sets the name for the color scheme.

- **Style**   Sets the style for the color scheme.

- **Color-setting buttons**   These five buttons set the colors for the foreground, background, shadow, line, and text. The boxes directly to their right show the currently set color. Click on the button for the setting you want to change to display in the Color Selection window.

- **Use Current Document Style Colors**   Uses the settings for the current document to create a new color scheme. Styles and colors are taken from

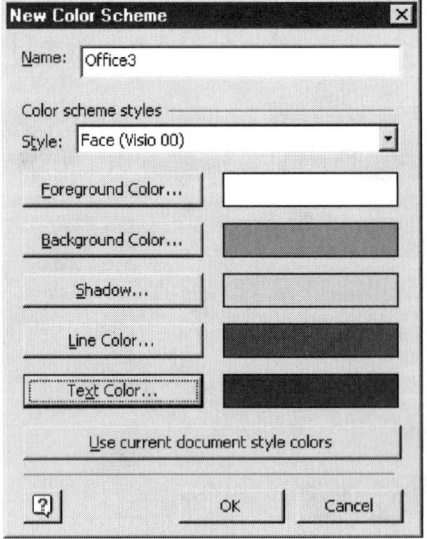

FIGURE 6-15   Color Scheme Details window

the settings in the displayed window of the current document. This is the fastest way to create a new scheme.

NOTE   *You cannot undo applying a color scheme you've already applied. To return to the default black-and-white color scheme, choose Black & White in the Color Schemes window and click Apply.*

Adding Maps

Certain projects may require a detailed map—complete with roads, bodies of water, and landmarks. Visio has the Maps templates for presentations and projects that require these special types of supporting materials.

Sometimes merely providing directions to a meeting or event isn't enough—you need a map. Visio includes the Directional Maps template for creating maps that can be used to give directions. Not only can directional maps be used to show how to get somewhere, they can also be used to list resources in a particular area. Figure 6-16 shows the main Visio window with the Directional Maps template open and an example directional map.

The Directional Maps template includes shapes for highways, parkways, traffic, road and street signs, routes, railroad tracks, transit terminals, rivers, and interstates. They also have added styles and layers to help you create and print the part of the map you need. These shapes are on the five stencils that come with the template. Here's a quick overview of each stencil:

- **Transportation Shapes stencil**   Contains street signs, traffic signals, transportation shapes, and direction signs.

- **Road Shapes stencil**   Contains roads, bridges, interstate and other highway signs.

- **Recreation Shapes stencil**   Contains informational signs for recreation centers.

- **Metro Shapes stencil**   Contains mass transportation shapes for metros, including transfer and station shapes.

- **Landmark Shapes stencil**   Contains buildings, and other physical shapes, as well as compass, text callout, and city shapes.

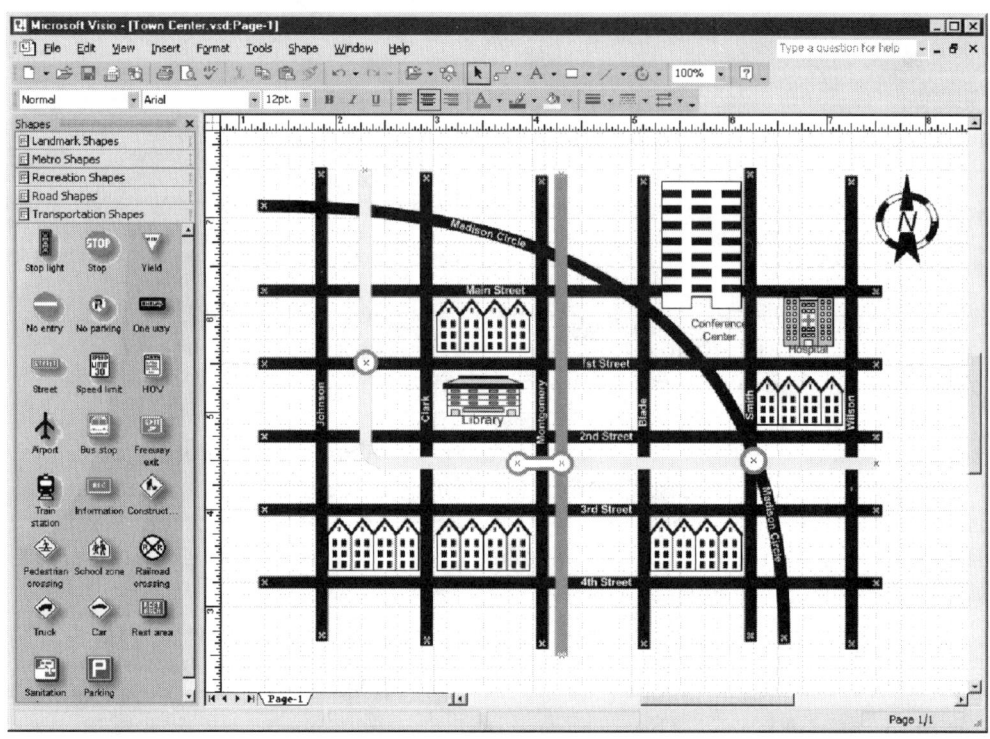

FIGURE 6-16   A directional map

TIP   *For a complete list of the shape on each stencil, see Appendix A, "Stencils and Templates."*

Many of the shapes included in the Directional Maps template have special control handles. They also have other special functions you can access by right-clicking and choosing options from the shortcut menu. Here's an overview of some of the special functions:

■ All the shapes in the Recreation Shapes stencil, and some of the shapes on the Transportation Shapes stencil, have an extra control handle you can use by right-clicking and choosing Show Control Handle from the shortcut menu. The extra control handle sets where text added to the shape appears in relation to the shape.

■ The tree shape, on the Landmark Shapes stencil, has a right-click option
that turns the tree from Deciduous to Coniferous and back again.

■ Roads and metro lines can be any of three default widths, or you can
choose to make them a custom thickness. If you choose to make a road or
metro line a custom thickness, an extra control handle appears in the lower
left-hand corner of the shape, allowing you to dynamically change the
thickness of the line.

Adding Comments

Comments are small text references you can place in documents as notes that
won't appear in the finished diagram. Adding comments helps in the creation
process by allowing you and others who work on a document to annotate the
actual diagram. Figure 6-17 shows an example of a comment.

Comments are viewed by placing the mouse pointer over the shape. Visio
displays the comment in a text box, as shown in Figure 6-17. Comments are only
displayed in the Normal view and are not available in Full Screen view or to print out.

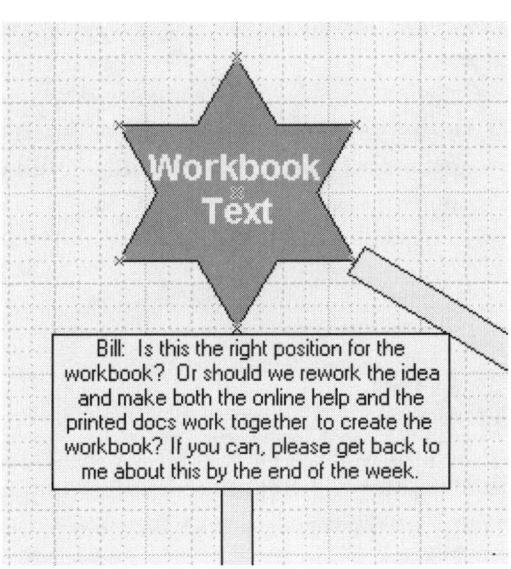

Bill: Is this the right position for the
workbook? Or should we rework the idea
and make both the online help and the
printed docs work together to create the
workbook? If you can, please get back to
me about this by the end of the week.

FIGURE 6-17   A comment

To insert a comment, you need to first place the shape. Comments, like hyperlinks, are added to already-existing shapes. With the shape on the drawing page, select it and make sure nothing else is selected. Then choose Insert | Comment. The Comment window opens, as shown here:

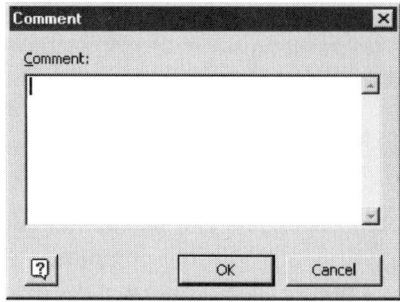

Fill in the text you want displayed in the comment. The text can only be in plain text and can have no formatting at all. Click OK to close the window. Visio adds the comment to the shape. Make sure to test the comment by hovering the mouse pointer over the shape and waiting for the comment to appear.

NOTE   *Only the first five or six lines of your comment display on the screen when you hover the pointer over the shape. The rest of the text can be seen when you edit the comment.*

To edit a comment, select the shape and then choose Insert | Edit Comment. The Comment window appears, as shown earlier, with the full text of the comment. Change the comment text and then click OK.

When you've finished inserting or editing a comment, remember to save the Visio document.

Summary

In this chapter, you learned how to use Visio to convey information graphically in meetings or on paper. You learned how to create charts, forms, and graphs, as well as how to add maps to your diagrams. You learned about the Project Scheduling templates in Visio, as well as how to work with the Office Layout template You also learned how to create a slide show in Visio and how to add comments to shapes.

In the next chapter, you will learn how to make the most of using Visio with the Internet.

6

Diagramming Your Home Using Visio

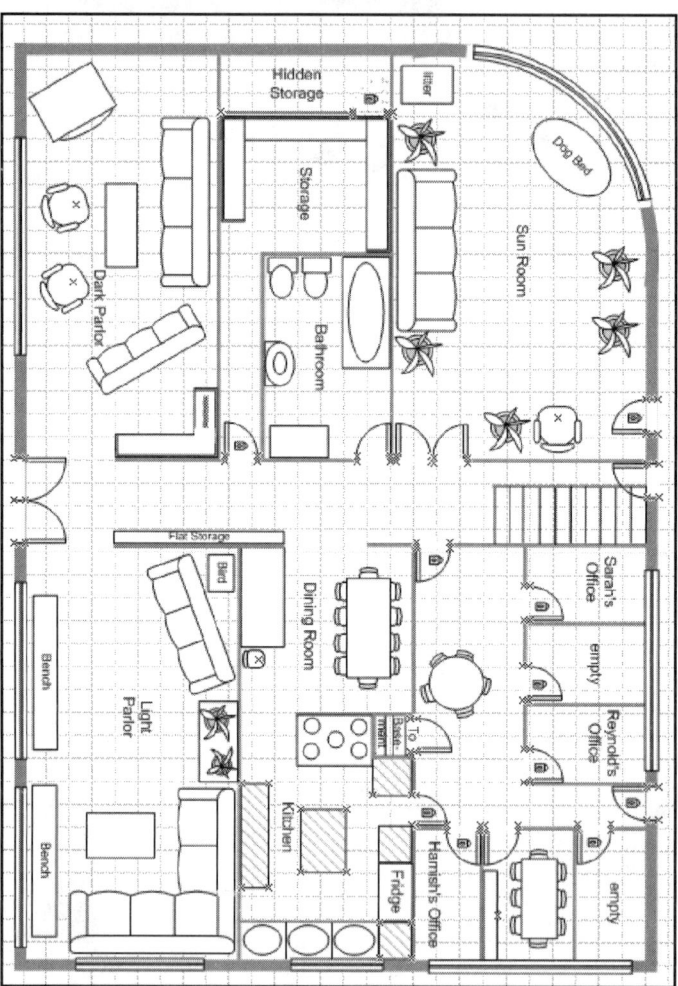

This example shows you how to diagram all or part of your home in Visio. Once you have a completed diagram of your home you can use it as a guideline to help with renovations or alterations. You can even use it as an aid to decorating since you can see how layouts and arrangements will look without having to move furniture first.

1

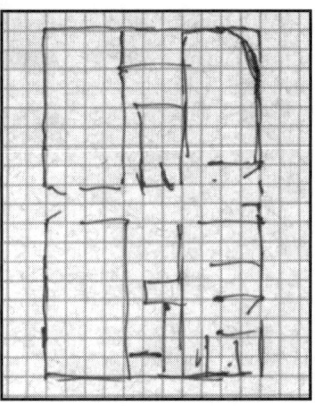

Before you start diagramming your home with Visio, make sure you have this information:

- A rough sketch of the outline of your home and its interior rooms.
- Measurements for all the appropriate rooms.
- A list of furnishings and their measurements.

Once you have the information you need, you are ready to start diagramming your home.

Open the Office Layout template, and move on wall shapes, starting with the largest walls in the area you're diagramming. If you are diagramming a whole house, these would be the exterior walls. If you are doing one room, start with the longest continuous wall. Stretch the wall until the measurement guide tells you it is the correct length.

2

3

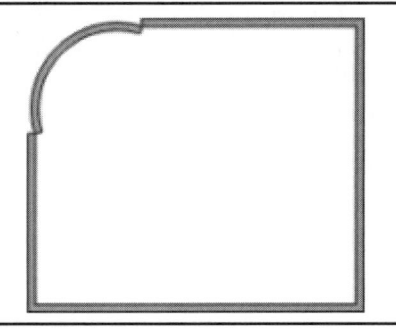

Add other walls, including curved walls, making sure to connect the walls by gluing their connection points together. Build the entire outer shell of your structure, making sure all the measurements are correct and that you have completely connected the walls together.

6

4

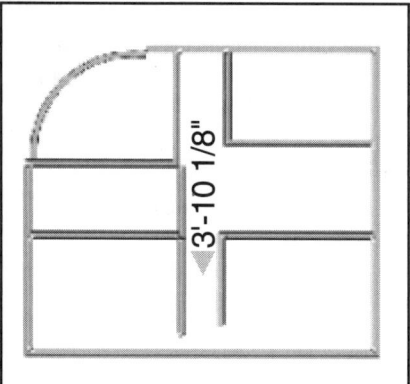

3'-10 1/8"

Now place the inner walls, and any windows, doors, or other structural concerns in your space. Make sure all the inner walls are glued to the outer walls, and use the automatic measurements as a guide to verify that your walls are the correct shape. You can also flip the orientation of any structural shape by using the right-click menu.

Now zoom in on a room or part of a room, and make sure all the structural parts of your space are correct. Once you are sure your measurements are right, start to drag on shapes for furniture and other room parts. Use the Action toolbar to rotate and flip pieces until they are correctly oriented in your room.

5

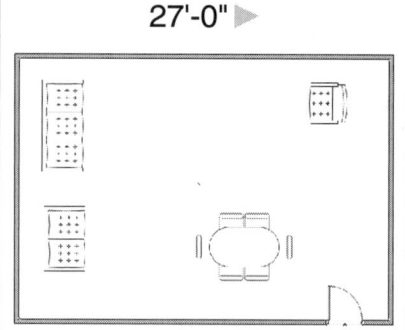

27'-0"

6

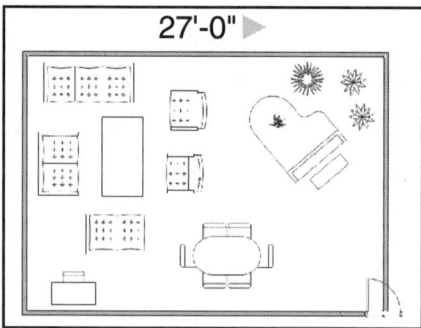

27'-0"

Now you can rearrange all or part of your room, or even your whole structure to help create the home you want. Make sure you save your diagram at several intervals as you rearrange the parts, using different names for each saved version. This way you can later compare the different layouts your rearranging came up with. Repeat this process for each room in your home.

Chapter 7

Hyperlinking, HTML and XML

How to...

- Link to other Visio drawings
- Link to Web Pages from Visio drawings
- Save Visio drawings as Web Pages
- Create XML with Visio

In the last chapter, you saw all the different kinds of basic diagrams Visio can create. In this chapter, you'll learn how to add hyperlinks to your Visio diagrams. You'll learn how you can create internal links within Visio diagrams and external links to other documents. You'll also learn how to save Visio diagrams so they can be viewed on the World Wide Web.

The Web and Visio

Thousands of new technologies have become part of our daily lives in the last few decades, but none more so than the World Wide Web, better known as the Internet. The Internet is one of the most popular new inventions in 50 years, and has become a staple in most of our homes. The popularity of the Internet has meant an immense growth in the ways to use it, and the linking and remote viewing of information that has made the Internet so popular has encouraged many people to include its ease of use in the new technologies they develop. Visio is no different, and has integrated linking into its most current version. This means you can add links in your Visio documents, both to other Visio documents or to any type of document you can have access to on your local system, in your internal network, or even over the Internet itself.

Visio also can create documents meant for the World Wide Web. Visio has two different pathways for creating Internet ready documents. You can save your whole Visio diagram as a Web page, or you can save your diagram in XML for use in any of hundreds of ways. Saving your diagram as a Web page generally means you are exporting all or part of it as HTML. Using XML is a more complete way to save your image, and then you can use it in any of the many programs that are able to read XML.

This chapter walks you through each of Visio's new Internet ready features. Linking is first, since it is the simplest, then we'll discuss HTML and saving your diagrams as Web pages, and lastly we'll walk through saving as XML.

Linking in Visio

With the prevalence of the Web, hyperlinks have become a part of everyday life for many people. As you may already know, hyperlinks typically appear as underlined text on Web pages. When you click a hyperlink, you jump from one page to another (or from one part of a page to another part). Likewise, in Visio, you can use hyperlinks to jump from one diagram to another, or to different parts of the same diagram. You can also use hyperlinks to jump from a Visio diagram to a completely different type of document.

Hyperlinks are links between a *host document*—the place where you click—and a *linked document*—the place where you are taken. Hyperlinks can be included in any Visio diagram and can be especially helpful when you have large diagrams that span several pages. For example, if you have an organization chart that spans many pages, you could link the managers' shapes to pages that discuss the performance of the departments they oversee. Each manager shape would be a host, and the departmental pages would be the linked pages. If you clicked the link on a manager's shape, Visio would automatically display the departmental page.

> NOTE *Microsoft Visio 2002 includes advanced hyperlinking features that are not available in earlier versions of Visio.*

Understanding Visio Hyperlinks

Visio hyperlinks fall into two categories: internal and external. These two types of hyperlinks have much in common. Both kinds of links can open other documents when clicked, and both are set using the same dialog boxes. They differ, however, in the types of documents they link, so the process for setting internal and external links is slightly different—and the results can be dramatically different depending on the type of link you create.

Internal Links

An *internal link* is a link to a Visio drawing. Often, internal links are links to different pages within the same Visio drawing. Linking within a single drawing can provide easy access to information when the drawing spans many pages. Linking within the same drawing can also add new meaning; the link between two objects can indicate a relationship that may be difficult to illustrate in any other way.

External Links

An *external link* is a link to any file other than a Visio drawing. With Visio, you can create hyperlinks to virtually any kind of document or file. When someone clicks the link in a Visio drawing, Visio opens the linked file using the default program set to open that file type.

 *To find out which program opens a particular file type, open any Windows folder and select View | Folder Options | File Types. On the File Types tab, select a file type to see the program that opens it.*

Setting Links

Setting Visio links involves several steps. First, create the drawing to contain the links, or open an existing drawing. To create hyperlinks, you need to already have shapes on the page. Second, make sure to always save the document that will host the links before you start adding hyperlinks. (This only takes a few moments and can save a lot of grief later.) Third, open the Web toolbar by going to the View menu of the main Visio window and selecting Toolbars | Web. The Web toolbar makes accessing hyperlink features quick and easy. Table 7-1 describes the buttons on the Web toolbar. Once you have taken these three steps, you're ready to add hyperlinks.

Adding Hyperlinks

With Visio, you can add links to any shape or group of shapes, as well as to backgrounds and text. You can also add a hyperlink to an entire page. When you add a link to a single shape, the link only exists on that shape. The ramifications of linking to groups, backgrounds, and pages are not as intuitive. For example, if you

Button	Name	Function
	Insert Hyperlink	Creates a hyperlink on the selected shape or shapes.
	Back	Takes you back to the last hyperlink you clicked. Enabled only after you have clicked a link.
	Forward	Takes you forward to the next link. Enabled only after you have gone back to a link.
	Visio on the Web	Opens the default Web browser to the Visio home page.

TABLE 7-1   Hyperlink Toolbar

add a link to an entire page (by displaying a page without selecting any shapes), the link exists wherever there's no shape on the drawing page. Or, if you add a link to a group of shapes, all the shapes in the group have that link; however, if you add a link to one of the individual shapes in the group, the new link takes precedence, even though the group link still exists. Also, links to backgrounds affect all pages that use the background.

Once you've selected the object (that is, the shape, group, background, or page) to which you want to add a hyperlink, click the Insert Hyperlink button, or select Hyperlink from the Insert menu. The Hyperlinks window opens, as shown in Figure 7-1. The following paragraphs explain the different parts of the Hyperlinks window.

- **Address**   Shows the location of the linked document. Links to documents on the local hard drive are listed as file paths. Links to documents on the World Wide Web are listed as URLs. The next section, "Browsing for Addresses and Sub-addresses," explains how to add a file path or URL to this field.

- **Sub-address**   Specifies an exact place within the linked document. Sub-addresses can only be used for internal hyperlinks (that is, links to Visio documents). Often, the sub-address creates a link to a particular page in the linked document, but it can also be used to create a link to an individual shape.

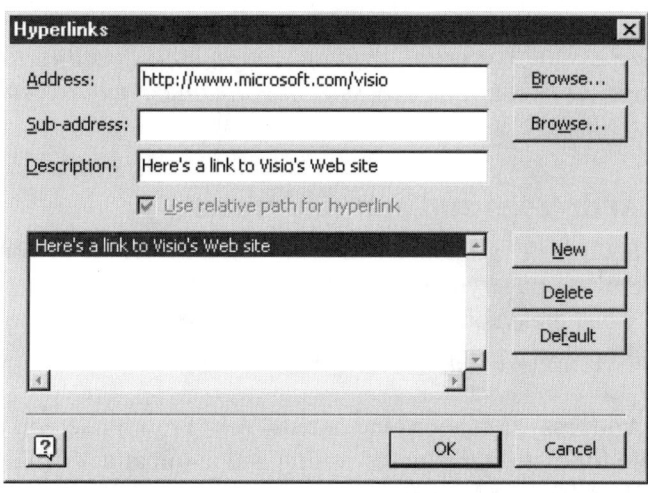

FIGURE 7-1   Hyperlink window

- **Browse**   Allows you to browse through files to locate the address and sub-address of the linked document. These buttons are explained in more detail in the following section, "Browsing for Addresses and Sub-addresses.

- **Description**   Shows the text that displays for the link. The default is the filename for the document. The description also displays as pop-up text when the mouse pointer is hovered over the link in an HTML file.

- **Use relative path for hyperlink**   Defines how the link is saved to the system. When the box is checked, Visio lists the link in relation to the location of the current Visio document or the "hyperlink base." The *hyperlink base* is a custom file path you can set by selecting File | Properties | Summary and entering a path in the Hyperlink Base field. When the "Use relative path for hyperlink" checkbox is unchecked, Visio lists the complete address for the link. For local links this is the complete path name. For Web links, this is the complete URL.

- **Link list**   The Link list shows all the links that have been set for the selected object. The first link in the list is the *default link*; this may be the only active link if the host document is saved in HTML format.

- **New**   Allows you to add a new hyperlink after one has already been set.

- **Delete**   Removes the link selected in the Link list.

- **Default**   Sets the selected link as the default link. That link moves to the top of the Link list.

 *You can access the Hyperlinks window for an object (that is, for a shape, group, page, or background) by selecting the object and clicking the Insert Hyperlink button.*

Browsing for Addresses and Sub-addresses

When you set an address or sub-address in the Hyperlinks window, you can browse to find the file or page you need.

To browse to the address for a link, click the Browse button next to the Address field. A drop-down menu appears, as shown in Figure 7-2.

- **Internet Address**   Launches the default Web browser so you can find the URL. Visio follows your Web-browsing and automatically places the current URL in the Address field.

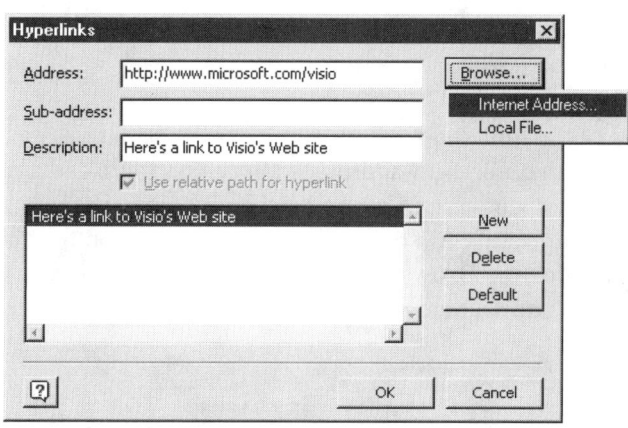

FIGURE 7-2   The Browse button's drop-down menu

■ **Local File**   Opens the Link to File dialog box, which is shown in
Figure 7-3. Browse to the file, select it, and then click Open. The Link to
File dialog box closes, and the Address box is updated with the file path.

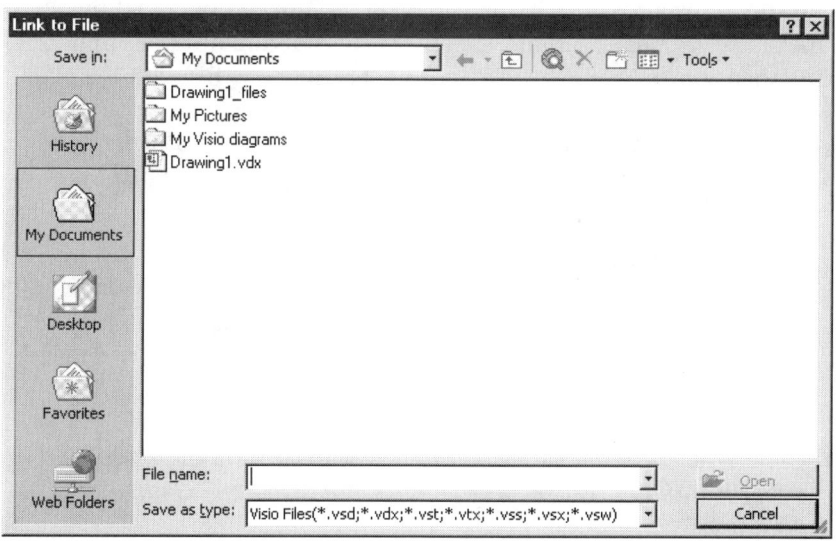

FIGURE 7-3   Link to File dialog box

 *Before clicking the Browse button for the Address field, make sure you're connected to the Internet or to the server that holds the file to which you're creating a link.*

If the address of the linked document is a local file path to a Visio file, you can set a sub-address for the link. Sub-addresses allow you to link to a particular page or shape in the linked document. You can do this by manually entering text in the Sub-address field, but usually it's easier to use the Browse button for the Sub-address field. Click the Browse button next to the Sub-address field to open a Hyperlink dialog box shown here:

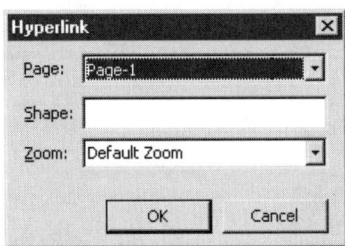

- **Page** Specifies a particular page in the linked document. By default, the first page of the document appears in this field.

- **Shape** Specifies a particular shape in the linked document by entering the shape's name. To find the name of an individual shape, right-click on the shape and select Format | Special. The name is listed in the Name field.

 *If you set the Shape field incorrectly for a sub-address, when you select the link, Visio takes you to the end of the document and displays an error message.*

- **Zoom** Sets the page view used when Visio opens the linked document. By default, this is set as the default zoom for the page. You may set it for any of the standard page views available in Visio, but not to a custom zoom setting.

CAUTION *If you select a shape as the sub-address, make sure the Page field in the Hyperlink dialog box shows the page that the shape is on.*

When you're finished setting the sub-address for the link, click OK. The Hyperlink dialog box closes, but the Hyperlinks window remains open. Click OK again to close the Hyperlinks window.

Accessing Links

Once you've set a link for a shape, you can view its hyperlinks by right-clicking on the shape. If there's more than one hyperlink, the default hyperlink is listed at the top. When you select a hyperlink from the list, Visio automatically jumps to the link's destination, centering on the sub-link if one has been set.

> **NOTE** *If a hyperlink has been set for a shape, the mouse pointer displays a hyperlink symbol when you move the pointer over the shape.*

You can also access links if you are in full-screen view by simply clicking the shape or page to activate the hyperlink. Visio opens the document using its native program. To move between hyperlinks in full-screen view, use the right and left arrows on the Web toolbar or left-click with the mouse. This takes you backward and forward through the links.

> **NOTE** *When you click a link in full-screen view, Visio doesn't open the new document in full-screen view. Instead, Visio opens the document in a normal window for the program.*

As you move back and forth between your Visio diagram and linked documents, remember that you'll need to have the native program loaded on your computer to see the linked documents. Also, there are some limitations on how you can move between documents. You can only move back and forth between Visio drawings and Microsoft Office documents (Office 97 or later). Other programs don't have the capacity to switch back and forth with Visio. If you want to go to and from other document types, such as text files, you must host the files in Internet Explorer (version 3.01 or later).

Adding Special Hyperlink Shapes

Visio includes several shapes as hyperlinking shapes that can be used as buttons on finished Visio HTML pages. They are located at the bottom of the Borders and Tiles stencil, which opens with Visio's Basic Drawing template. If you use another template, you can open the Borders and Tiles stencil by clicking on the Open

Stencil button and choosing the Borders and Tiles stencil from the Visio extras folder.

There are three hyperlinking master shapes on the stencil: Hyperlink Button, Hyperlink Circle 1, and Hyperlink Circle 2. Each of these is actually a set of shapes, and you must choose a specific shape after you drag the master shape to the drawing. When you drag one of these master shapes to the drawing page, Visio opens the Address dialog box, asking you what you'd like the address of your hyperlink to be for these pages.

Right click on these hyperlink shapes, and then choose Change Icon, to see a custom properties window that allows you to change the type of icon, shown here:

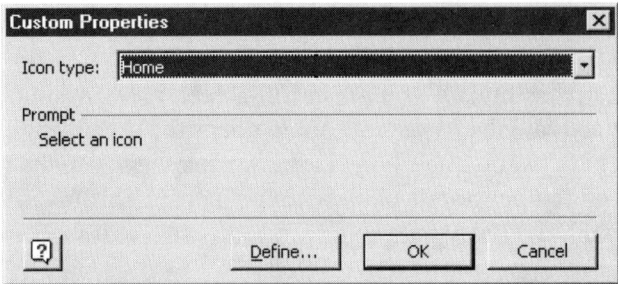

- ■ **Icon Type**   Sets the icon that appears on the page. Choose between Back, Directory, Down, Forward, Help, Home, Info, Mail, None, Photo, Search, and Up. Each choice creates a different shape on the drawing page. You can change the shape at any time by right-clicking on it and selecting Change Icon. This opens the Custom Properties dialog box.

Once you've selected the type of shape, Visio displays the Hyperlinks window, shown earlier in Figure 7-1. Fill in the data for the link, and then click OK.

 *Before you use these shapes, it's best to plan your Web site so you can set the right links.*

Changing Hyperlinks

There are many reasons you may need to change a hyperlink after it has been set. For example, you may need to add more than one link to a shape, or you may wish to remove links you previously added. You may also need to change the path or filenames for links when the documents they reference have moved or changed. Also, if during the process of creating your Visio diagram, you added links simply for your own use (ones that won't be part of the finished document), you'll need to delete all those links.

Whatever your reason for needing to alter a link, make sure you always save your Visio document before you begin this process.

Adding More Than One Link to a Shape

To add another hyperlink to an object that already has one, simply follow the procedures for adding the first hyperlink, with one small difference:

1. Select the shape, group, or page.

2. Click the Insert Hyperlink button. This opens the Hyperlinks window.

3. Click the New button to access the fields where you enter information for the new link.

4. Fill in the Address and Sub-address fields.

5. Add a description.

6. Click OK when done.

When you add more than one hyperlink to a shape, the first hyperlink added is set as the default.

Changing the Default Link

To change the default link:

1. Select the shape, group, or page.

2. Click the Insert Hyperlink button. This opens the Hyperlinks window.

3. Select the link you want as the default link from the Link list.

4. Click Default.

5. Click OK when done.

The default link is sometimes the only link recognized when you save files as HTML. For more information about HTML files, see the section "Saving as HTML" later in this chapter.

Changing Hyperlink Information

To change any information other than the default link, proceed as if adding or deleting a link:

1. Select the shape, group, or page.

2. Click the Insert Hyperlink button. This opens the Hyperlinks window, shown earlier in Figure 7-1.

3. Select the link you need to change.

4. Change the information, including address, sub-address, and description.

5. Click OK when done.

Deleting Hyperlinks

To remove a hyperlink from any Visio object, first select the object. If the link is on the page, select the page by deselecting everything else, so that no green control squares appear anywhere on the page. If the link is on a shape, select the shape. Then click the Insert Hyperlink button on the Web toolbar. The Hyperlinks window opens. In the Link list, select the hyperlink you want to remove and click Delete. When you've deleted all the hyperlinks you want to remove, click OK to close the Hyperlinks window.

Creating Web Pages in Visio

The Internet has become a cornerstone of business and is quickly becoming a part of our everyday lives. Web pages have become vital to a company's operation and communication. Intranet sites have become primary distribution points for company information. Both of these modes of communication require HTML and graphics to get the point across, and Visio is a powerful tool for creating graphical Web content.

 *Microsoft Visio 2002 was developed with Microsoft's Internet Explorer 5.0. All HTML content is optimized for this, or later, versions of the browser.*

Visio has ways to help you integrate your diagrams into both intranet and Internet sites. You can save your files in any of a number of Web-friendly formats, or you can create individual pages for your diagrams with the HTML code already included.

This section assumes you know something about how HTML works and how to create Web sites. If you need information about using the Web for business, or a primer on how to create Web pages, see Appendix B, "Resources," for more information.

Designing Your Site

The first step in any Web-page creation process must always be to plan out your pages. Since links between pages require an idea of what directory the file is located in, you must have a clear idea of what files you need and how they interrelate before you start.

If you're creating Web pages that are to fit inside a design framework already in place, you need to know the file-naming conventions, the folder structure, and the computer where the pages will eventually reside. If you're creating a completely new site, you need to plan out beforehand how it'll look and what your file structure will be. Make sure you have all this information before you begin to save your diagrams as HTML.

> **TIP** *Visio is a great tool for Web site design. Use the shapes and connections to create a visual representation of your Web site before you begin. Later, you can use the design diagram on a Web page as a site map.*

Using Visio Images on the World Wide Web

Once you've created your diagrams, including hyperlinks, you're ready to start thinking about using your images on the Web. Visio includes an option called Save As Web Page. However, there are several issues about using your Visio diagrams on Web pages you must consider before making your final choices.

Web Issues

When it comes to the Web, there are often as many issues as there are options. The ability for infinite information distribution and the flexibility for clients and servers leads to lots of choices you need to make up front.

Browser Versions Most content on the Web is viewed using a Web browser (for example, Netscape Navigator or Microsoft Internet Explorer), and each browser has several different versions. Consequently, the first thing to consider is how users will view your pages. Because the different versions, let alone the different products, all have unique sets of standards, it can be quite difficult to plan a site that looks good in all browsers.

Fortunately, the entire browser issue gets much less complicated if you know who'll be looking at the pages you create. It's easier to make decisions regarding browser-compliance if your Web pages will be used in a limited context—for example at a company meeting or on an intranet where everyone uses the same browser.

Visio was developed with the Internet Explorer version 5.0 standards in mind, meaning that HTML files produced in Visio are optimized for that browser. Some of the newer features available for exporting to HTML may not be usable on earlier versions of the browser, and some may not work at all.

> **TIP** *Always test your HTML files in a few different versions of both the Netscape and Microsoft browsers if you plan to put the files on the Web.*

Image Types No matter which browser you choose, in the end, when you save your drawings as Web pages, Visio exports your diagrams as images. These images can have special properties—such as different links for different parts of the image and the ability to zoom in—or they can just be flat images you place inside other HTML documents. The choice of which type of image you need is partially based on the browser version you think is mostly likely to be used to view your pages. Newer browsers are capable of more sophisticated image-handling than older browsers.

But the choice of browser is not the only consideration when you decide on image types. The more complex the image, the larger the file will be. Since the size of the file determines how long it takes to load, large image files might hinder people from visiting your site. This is especially important if you plan to have your images up on the Web, where bandwidth and download times are major issues.

There are two basic kinds of images for Web pages: flat images and image maps. *Flat images* are simply pictures that have no special features. Like any image, however, flat images can have links if you create the links in the Web page's HTML code. *Image maps* are graphics with different links or features in different regions. They have attached HTML files that give the browser all the information it needs to process the different regions.

Flat images can be small and are often added to pages with text to give them a nicer look and feel. Visio can save images in both of the standard Web image formats: Graphic Interchange Format (.gif) and JPEG format (.jpg). Images saved in one of these formats can be included in any Web page and can be displayed by any browser. As long as they are a reasonable size, they pose no problems with download time or bandwidth.

Image maps are more complicated. They come in two types: client-side image maps and server-side image maps. *Client-side image maps* are the most common and are more widely accepted. They allow different regions of one image to have different "hot spots" or links, and they also allow different parts of the image to behave independently from other parts. Client-side image maps are supported in most browsers. By default, when you save drawings with links as HTML pages, the drawing is converted into a client-side image map. *Server-side image maps* require a program on the Web server to examine map data to make the different regions of the image work independently. Server-side image maps also require that you move all your images and HTML code to the server before they work. Since client-side image maps are the default in Visio, they're the only type of image map covered in this book.

7

> **NOTE**   *For more information about server-side image maps, see Appendix B, "Resources."*

Visio's HTML Template   After you choose the browser you'll design for and make decisions about the types of images you'll include, the next consideration is how your pages will look.

Visio includes a template for formatting HTML files. All diagrams saved as Web pages use this formatting by default. If you choose to create pages yourself, creating a template of your own gives you more control over where your images belong and what general size they need to be.

If you export your pages as images, you can, of course, bypass the template issue entirely and simply create your own pages with their own links to the images you exported out of Visio.

> **NOTE**   *For more information about using and changing the Visio template, see "Altering and Creating Visio HTML Templates" later in this chapter.*

Visio's HTML Export Feature vs. Standard Web Image Formats

Deciding whether to use Visio's HTML export feature or to use your own HTML and save diagrams as standard Web images can be confusing. Here's a quick reference for when it's best to use each type of solution.

It's best to Visio's Save As Web Page for your drawings when:

■ You want to create a Web-ready version using several pages of a multiple-page drawing.

■ Your drawing includes shapes with links you'd like to preserve by creating an image map.

■ You have several linked Visio diagrams you'd like to stay linked after exporting.

■ You have a very complicated Visio diagram that clients may need to zoom in on.

It's best to save drawings in standard Web image formats when:

■ You know clients with older browsers may look at your Web pages.

■ You already have an HTML-coded page in which you want to insert a Visio drawing.

■ You want to export only a portion of a Visio diagram.

Creating a File System

No matter how you decide to export your pages, you must have some sort of file system framework created before you begin creating HTML pages or Web-ready images. If you don't create a file system first, you'll be forced to rename all your files and may lose functional links. Therefore, you need to make sure you know how files will be stored; in other words, you need a file system before you begin setting links.

Creating a file system also means deciding how your files will link together. There are two types of links in HTML: relative and absolute.

A *relative link* lists the location of the linked file in relation to the host file. These links are useful because you don't need to know where the entire Web site will eventually reside to create them. However, you must move the entire site together, or else you'll break the links.

Absolute links list the location of the linked file with a complete file path. If done correctly, it's impossible to break these links, since they give a global reference to a file. However, they require that you know the absolute path to your files before you begin adding links.

Relative links are often the safest for small Web sites that have few outside links or dependencies. Absolute links can be more time-consuming to create, but they're impossible to break once they've been set up.

 *To set the absolute path for relative links, go to the File menu of the main Visio window and select Properties. In the Properties dialog box, set the Hyperlink Base field on the Summary tab.*

Saving as a Web Page

Once you've created diagrams and dealt with all the issues surrounding Web page creation, you're ready to start saving your diagrams for use on Web pages. This section details how to use Visio's Save As Web Page feature. Saving diagrams as images is covered in the next section.

CAUTION   *Always save your diagram in standard Visio format (.vsd) before you save it as HTML. If there's a problem with the conversion and you haven't saved a Visio version of the diagram, you may lose your data.*

Visio has the option to save your drawings as Web pages as part of the File menu. There are two ways to use this option. First, and easiest, you can simply export your pages using the defaults; this is a quick way to get Web pages from your diagrams and view them in your browser. Second, you can change the options and create custom looking pages using the Save As Web Page window. This section walks you through both options.

TIP   *No matter what options or types you choose in save your diagram as a Web page, Visio creates pages that include Java script. If you don't want to use Java-scripted pages, you'll need to save your pages individually as images, a process described later in this chapter.*

Quickly Saving as Web Page

To save your file as a web page, select Save As Web Page from the File menu. The Save As window opens, shown in Figure 7-4, with Web Page (*.htm, *.html) listed as the file type. Enter the name and location you want Visio to save to and then click Save. A progress bar opens and when Visio has finished saving the pages as HTML, it opens them up in your default Web browser.

Changing Options in Save As Web Page

The quick and simple way of exporting your diagrams as Web pages can be powerful if you just want Web pages of your diagrams and aren't too concerned about what they look like. However, if you have specific requirements for your

7

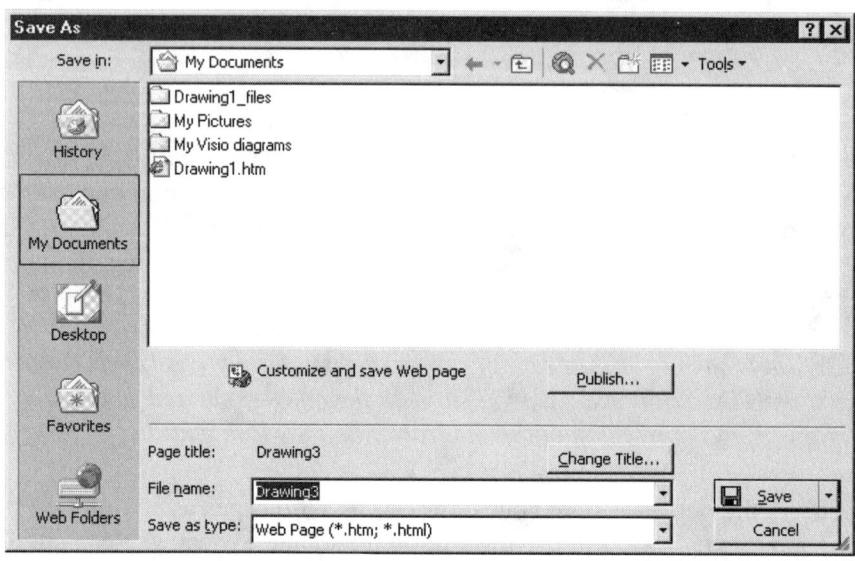

FIGURE 7-4 Save As window, with Web page file extension

pages, for example, you want to save only part of the diagram as a Web Page, you'll need to alter the defaults set in Visio.

The first thing you can alter is the title of your document. The title of your HTML document is displayed in the titlebar of the browser whenever anyone opens up your diagram. You can change the title of your document before you save it as HTML by clicking the Change Title button on the Save As window. This opens a small dialog box allowing you to enter a new title.

To get to where the rest of the defaults are set, choose File | Save As Web Page. The Save As window opens as shown in Figure 7-4. Click the Publish button. This opens the Save As Web Page window shown in Figure 7-5.

There are three tabs in the Save As Web Page window. This section helps you understand how to use each of them.

General Tab, Save As Web Page window. The General tab opens when you launch the Save As Web Page window, shown in Figure 7-5. It handles the settings affecting how and what Visio exports when you choose to Save As Web Page.

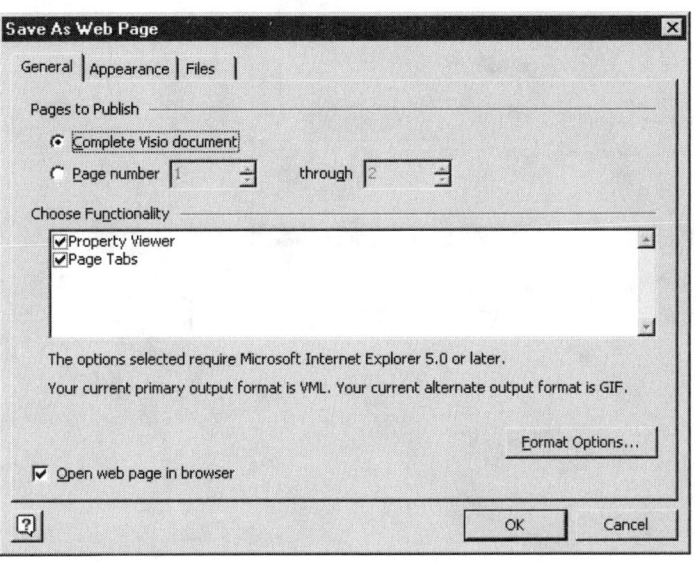

FIGURE 7-5   Save As Web Page

- **Page to Publish**   Allows you to select to save every page in the diagram as a Web page, or you can choose to only save a sub-set of the pages in your diagram.

- **Choose Functionality**   Lets you choose the added functions that Visio includes in your HTML files. The most common are a Custom Properties window that appears beside the diagram in the Web browser and lists the custom properties of all the shapes, and page tabs that allow your readers to move between the pages of your diagram using tabs like the ones in Visio.

- **Format Options**   Opens the Format Options window, which sets the type of image Visio exports to. Setting the Format Options window is covered later in "Selecting Graphic Types".

- **Open Web page in browser**   Sets whether or not the browser automatically opens when Visio finishes saving your pages as HTML.

Appearance Tab, Save As Web Page window   The Appearance tab, shown in Figure 7-6, sets formatting for how your page looks to your readers.

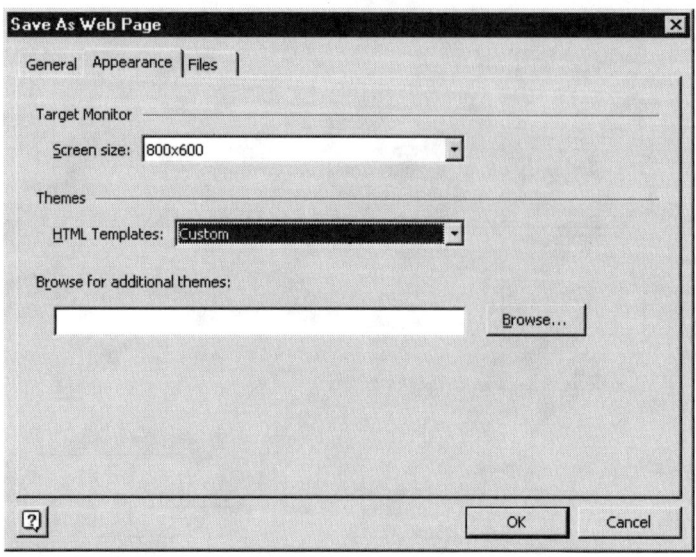

Save As Web Page window, Appearance tab

- ■ **Target Monitor**   Sets the maximum size for the images you export from Visio. This maximum is set by defining the size of the monitor since the images shouldn't be larger than the monitor they are optimized for. The default is 800x600 pixels, since this is the smallest type of monitor you can expect in today's Internet workplace.

- ■ **Themes**   Sets the default template used to create your Web pages. Choose a template to use from the list. If you choose Custom Visio, enable the browse feature so you can point to it. You can create your own Web page templates using Visio's basic template as a model. For more information about using and changing templates, see "Altering or Creating a Visio HTML Template" later in this chapter.

Files tab, Save As Web Page window   There are only two options on the Files tab, shown in Figure 7-7.

- ■ **Use long filenames whenever possible**   Lets you choose to use either the 8.3 convention for filenaming (if you uncheck the box) or to use long filenames like those used in Microsoft Windows.

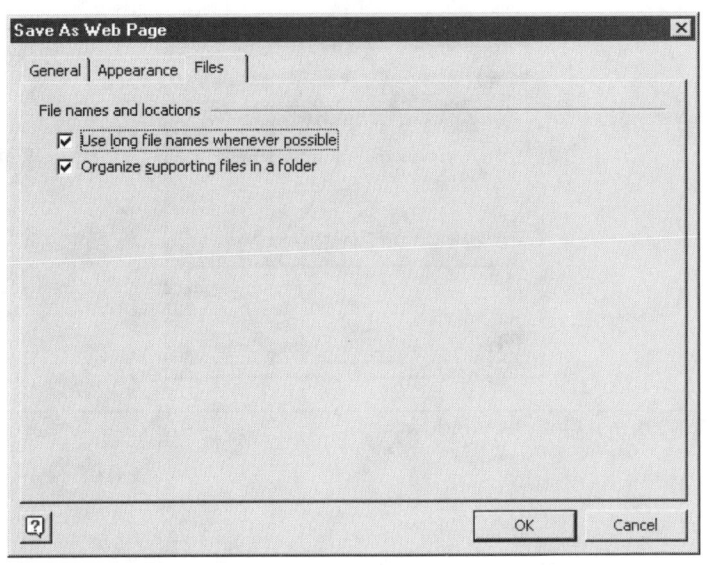

FIGURE 7-7   Save As Web Page window, Files tab

- **Organize supporting files in a folder**   When checked, puts all the image files, cascading style sheet files, and HTML files into one folder. When you uncheck this box, you will get every file that comes with the HTML version of your diagram loose in the diagram folder itself, and this can be quite a mess.

Once you've set all the HTML options, select OK on the Save As Web Page dialog box (Figure 7-5). Visio displays a progress bar to let you know it's generating files, then it displays the pages in your default Web browser, if you have left that option checked on the General tab.

Selecting Graphic Types

On the General tab of the Save As Web Page window you have the option of changing your diagram's format in HTML. This means you can alter the graphic type Visio uses to save your diagram. Alter your image by choosing Format Options on the General tab of the Save As Web Page window, this displays the Format Options window shown in Figure 7-8.

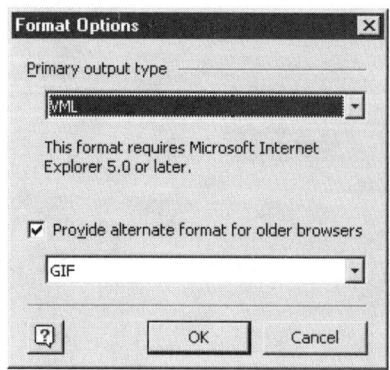

Format Options window

You can use these four formats:

- Graphic Interchange Format (.gif)
- Joint Photographic Experts Group Format (.jpg)
- Portable Network Graphics Format (.png)
- Vector-Based Markup Language (.vml)

Visio uses a primary output of VML by default with GIF as a backup. This means Visio exports both VML and GIF images for your diagram, but gives preference in its HTML files to the VML images. If your reader doesn't have the option of using VML, they will be pointed to the GIF files.

You may or may not want to change these defaults. GIF or JPEG formats are the most widely-used formats on the Web, so one of them should certainly be your backup choice, but what you choose as your primary has a great deal to do with your requirements for the files. VML is discussed in length in the next section.

TIP *You can see what your primary and secondary choices are on the General tab without going to the Format Options window. They are listed just under the Choose Functionality section in text.*

Using VML

VML is a special graphic format available in Visio and several other Microsoft products. VML is a special implementation of XML, the Web standard. VML stands for Vector-Based Markup Language—a format developed by Microsoft, Visio, Autodesk, and Hewlett-Packard to display vector-based drawings. Until now, vector-based drawings were converted into one of several types of bitmaps for use on the Web. Consequently, they lost the scalability and preciseness available in vector diagrams. VML allows the browser to zoom in on the page without losing graphic quality, making it a very valuable tool, even for complex Visio diagrams.

> NOTE   *Only Internet Explorer, version 5.0 and later, can handle VML files. If you translate to VML files, you need to choose an alternate graphic for all other browsers.*

7

If you select VML from the list of graphic types on the Format Options window (in Figure 7-8), make sure to choose either JPG or GIF in the Format Options window as your secondary choice. This guarantees that your page will be able to be seen by everyone no matter which browser they have.

Understanding the Pages Produced by the Save As Web Page

The pages produced by Visio's Save As Web Page feature can be difficult to sort out. There are at least 15 pages produced for even the simplest diagrams, and for multipage complicated diagrams there can be more than 50 pages. Table 7-2 describes the file types you're going to receive and where they fit into the page that displays in the browser. First, before you look at the file types themselves, you need to understand where Visio puts the files and why.

Visio places all the files in the directory you select, and it uses the name provided for the first part of every filename. If you move the files outside the folders Visio places them in, you'll break a link and your pages might not work. The most important part of this process is the link between the front page and the folder full of images and supporting pages. You will know the front page because it is the only one outside the folder, saved in the location you indicated on the Save As window. The folder full of supporting files is saved in the same place. If you move the file or the folder in relation to each other you'll break links and your pages won't display as you expect.

Once you know how the front page uses the supporting files, you'll be better able to move the files around if you need to. Table 7-2 walks you through each type of file created.

In Table 7-2, {filename} is a placeholder for the name you gave the file when you saved it as HTML and Visio uses it to preface the filenames for most of the files it generates.

For a drawing with more than one page, Visio generates at least 10 files for the drawing, plus at least three files for every page. If you need to change their location, you need to move all these files together, and they must all stay within

Filename	File Type	Function
{filename}.htm	HTML file	Your homepage, identifiable by the fact that it is simply the filename with no modifying text and also by the fact that it is outside the folder created in the same directory.
{filename} files	folder	A folder holding all the supporting files for your web page. If you unchecked this option on the Files tab, you won't have this folder.
{filename}.css	Cascading Style Sheet	The template Visio uses display your web page, and has been customized for these pages alone.
{filename}_util.js or {filename}_vml.js	Java Script file	A pseudo-programming language document that tells your Web browser what to do when you click on any of the special parts of the page that Visio generates, and also how to handle the VML information.
{filename}_*.htm	HTML files	These are the files that create the parts of your diagram that Visio has turned into the Web page. They can have almost anything after the underline, but they always start with the filename and then an underline character.
{filename}_gif_1.gif, {filename}_jpg_1.jpg, or lt_off.gif, or rt_over.gif	Graphics files	Any file that ends in .gif or .jpg, is a graphics file and they are called from the HTML files that make up the body of your Web pages.
{filename}_vml_1.emz	VML file	Contains the VML information required for the vector-drawn functions.
{filename}.xml	XML file	XML information about each shape on the Visio page.

TABLE 7-2 Files Generated with your Save As Web Page

one directory. If you change the relationship of any of the file's nesting the links will break, and you won't be able to display the pages properly.

 *Before you start, create a folder to keep all your Save As Web Page files together. That way, you can move them as one compact group without worrying about breaking links.*

Altering or Creating a Visio HTML Template

Visio uses a template every time it saves your drawing as a Web page. Controlling that template means you control the look of your Web pages. There is only one default template in Visio for saving as Web pages, the basic.htm template, found in the Visio Extras folder in the Solutions folder with the Visio program files. This section helps you understand how to use the templates that come with Visio and how to create templates of your own.

Altering a Template   Visio's template is a text page with standard HTML tags and special codes that correspond to elements from the drawing, such as page number, graphics, and links (or anchors) to other HTML pages or files. When you save your diagram as HTML, drawing elements are substituted for the codes.

You can get the best of both worlds by creating a custom template for saving and formatting HTML pages by modifying the Visio default template, found in the Visio Extras folder in the Visio program files. This allows you to include standard substitution codes with your own HTML tags and formatting. When you save a drawing as an HTML file, you can choose which template you want to use, so you can even create more than one custom template.

To create a simple custom template, use the Notepad program that comes with Microsoft Windows to open the basic.html file found in the Visio Extras folder. It contains this code:

```
<html>
<head>
<title></title>
<script>
<!--
var appVer = navigator.appVersion;
var msie = appVer.indexOf( "MSIE " );
var msieWin31 = (appVer.indexOf( "Windows 3.1" ) >= 0);
var isMac = (appVer.indexOf("Macintosh") >= 0);
var ver = 0;
if( msie >= 0 )
```

```
      ver = parseFloat(appVer.substring(msie + 5,
appVer.indexOf(";", msie)));
else
      ver = parseInt(appVer);
if( msie < 0 && ver < 5 )
      window.location.replace("%%VIS_SAW_FILE%%");
//-->
</script>
</head>
<IFRAME src="%%VIS_SAW_FILE%%" width="100%" height="100%"
frameborder="1" scrolling="auto">
      <!-- No IFRAMEsupport -->
</IFRAME>
</html>
```

This code may look confusing at first, but a few small changes to this file can create major layout differences for your pages. You can mostly ignore the section between the <!— and —> at the start of the code. Between these is a script telling Visio and the browser what to do with the different versions of browsers. Altering this script isn't suggested unless you are familiar with Web programming languages.

Alterations to the basic.htm should be in the IFrame section: the height, width, and frame settings. This affects the floating frame that appears as the majority of Web pages you create.

Creating a New Template

Making a template completely from scratch isn't something you should attempt on a whim. You'll need to recreate the syntax used by Visio in its translation of the files into HTML and VML documents. Use the basic.htm as a guideline to create your own template, remembering to use the "%%VIS_SAW_FILE%%" file reference.

For more information about creating your own templates, see the Microsoft Knowledge Base at www.microsoft.com/visio.

Saving as an Image

There are times when you don't want Visio to translate your files into image maps, or when you don't want to use Save As Web Page to create HTML pages for you. If you simply want a Web-ready version of your Visio diagram, you need to save the diagram as a standard Web image.

 *All links in your diagram are lost when you translate them as images.*

Saving a Visio diagram as an image follows the same basic pattern. First, you create the diagram, and then you select the part you wish to export as an image. If you wish to export the entire page, click on the page where there are no shapes to make sure no individual shape is selected.

Once you have the correct part of the diagram selected, choose Save As from the File menu. A Save As dialog box appears. Choose either GIF or JPG from the "Save as type" drop-down list and click OK. One of the dialog boxes shown in Figures 7-9 and 7-10 appears. The type of dialog box depends on the type of image you select.

For a GIF image, you can decide how your image is translated, including setting the image's resolution and size. For a JPEG image, you also need to decide how your image is translated. You can set options including color format and image quality. For both GIF and JPEG images, Visio has a standard set of protocols you can use to export your images. You only need to change the options manually if you have specific needs or if the standard translations don't work well on your system.

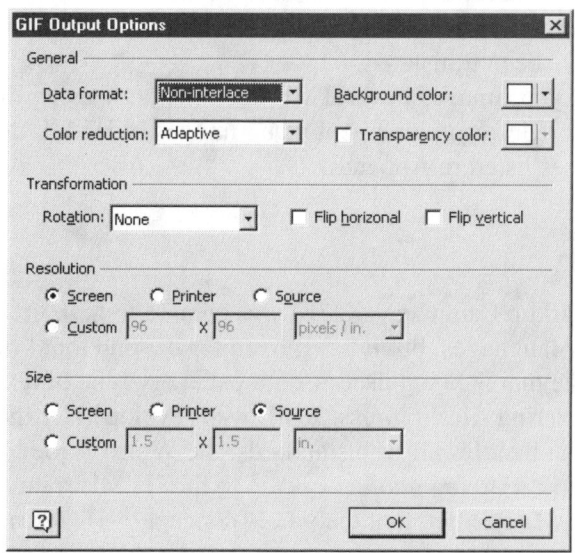

FIGURE 7-9 GIF Output Filter setup

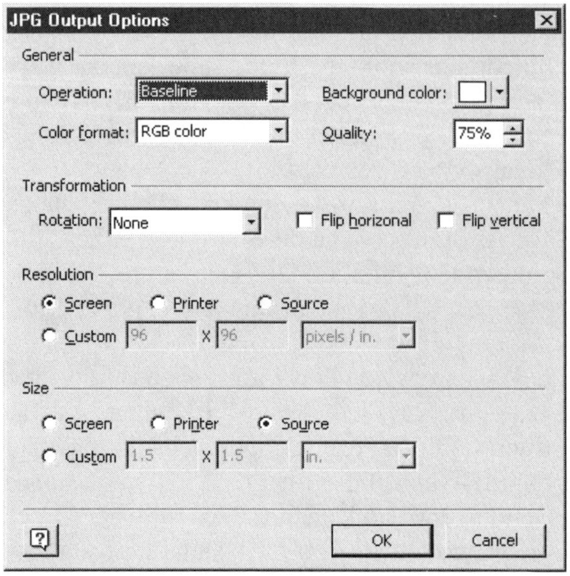

FIGURE 7-10 JPG Output Filter setup

When you've finished with the filter settings, click OK. Visio displays a progress bar to let you know it's translating the files. The progress bar vanishes after your files have been translated.

You can insert your images into HTML documents by using the tags set aside for images. For more information about using images in HTML documents, see the HTML resources listed in Appendix B.

XML

The Extensible Markup Language (XML) was created to give greater flexibility to web-based display languages, but it has moved far beyond that limited scope. XML is so versatile that is being used for almost every type of text delivery, up to and including delivering files to press. XML was developed by the same governing body that handles all web standards, the World Wide Web Consortium, called W3C for short. Forcing another update to the HTML standard had become so difficult, that it was decided that the whole concept of HTML needed an overhaul, and XML was the result.

XML is a relatively new development in the world of text delivery, and Visio 10 is the first version of Visio that has a native translator allowing you to create XML files. The bonus of having this translator is that XML is so portable, and your XML documents can be used everywhere, from the World Wide Web to publishing software to printed documentation. This means you need only develop your document once in Visio and then it can be used in all the different ways you need.

Why Use XML With Visio?

Visio has its own standard format, one accepted throughout the software world. So why change to XML? Because it is becoming a standard not only for Visio, but for text and information delivery packages worldwide.

The transformation to XML and other sophisticated content delivery methods began with VML and other vector graphics formats. It allowed the power of scaling and altering that vector graphics have to be widely distributed over the Internet. XML is doing the same with every type of information delivery package. It is like an expansion of the single formats for each software package that we are accustomed to using. Now, instead of simply saving your new document in the format created for the software package, you can save it as XML giving it the ability to be used in more places and in more ways than ever before.

What software could benefit more from this than Visio? The ability of Visio to diagram and display information is unmatched, and using the power of XML, you can deploy your diagrams in every way possible, without needing to reimport the diagram and save it another way. As the format of XML used in Visio becomes more accepted, you'll be more and more able to use your diagrams everywhere without alteration.

The power of XML and Visio doesn't stop with deployment of diagrams, it is also a powerhouse when it comes to importing diagrams into Visio that have been created using XML. When you import a diagram that's used the Visio XML, you can open that document and alter it as a standard Visio document, including moving and resizing shapes. This is amazing because the diagram could have been created in any program, the creator didn't need to use Visio.

XML takes Visio diagrams to a new level, allowing a free flow of information without the constraints of software packages or development platforms. It's the next step in information exchange.

Using XML

Using XML is simple in Visio. You'll save and alter Visio documents as you would normally, only you'll do so with everything in XML. This section walks you through the process.

Saving and Opening as XML

Saving your files as XML is easier than saving your files as a Web page, and it is almost as easy as saving your files in the Visio formats you're used to using.

To save your diagram as a Visio XML document, choose XML Drawing (*.vdx) from the Save As list, and click OK. Visio saves your files as XML, and returns you to your document. If you are trying to save something in your diagram that Visio can't save as XML, Visio will warn you before saving and let you know that not all the changes may make it into the XML document.

> TIP *It's a good idea to save your files in both XML and Visio formats.*

Visio not only writes files to XML, it opens documents that have been created in the Visio XML format as well. Since this format is easy to get, and since the documents are simply text outlining Visio standard, it is easy to convert or create XML documents for Visio.

XML Stencils and Templates

XML depends on templates and other settings to display its information. This is part of the power of XML. For Visio to take full advantage of the power of XML it needs to create stencils and templates in XML as well as in the standard digital format.

To harness the power, you can also save any of your documents as XML templates (*.xtx) or a stencil as a XML stencil (*.vsx). These give you the ability to create XML documents in a totally XML native platform.

The XML document

Unlike other ways of saving Visio diagrams, you can take a look at your Visio diagram that's been saved as XML in any text viewer you like. You can open and alter the XML document without opening Visio, and you can even change how the XML displays without using Visio as the intermediary. After you have created the document in Visio, you can simply use text editors to continue to alter it.

Reading an XML document may not be as simple as reading an HTML document, but it's close. For more information about using XML in Visio, or about XML in general, see Appendix B, "Resources".

Summary

In this chapter, you learned how to work with Visio to create HTML files, XML files, and Web-ready images of your diagrams.

In the next chapter, you'll learn how to use project-scheduling templates to create timelines and calendars. You'll also learn how to work with the Office Layout template, using it to create diagrams of your office space, and to generate inventory and ownership reports.

7

Chapter 8

Using Visio with Microsoft Office XP

How to...

- Link to Visio diagrams
- Using Visio with other Microsoft Office XP Programs
- OLE and Visio
- Troubleshooting linked documents

In the last chapter, you learned how to create flowcharts using Visio, as well as how to import and export data into and out of your Visio diagrams.

In this chapter, you'll learn how to use Microsoft Office XP software and Microsoft Visio together. You'll see how to include Microsoft Office XP documents in your Visio diagrams, how to include Visio diagrams in your Microsoft Office XP documents, and how to link two documents to create automatic updates. You'll also learn the most common ways Microsoft Office XP programs are used with Visio.

Using Visio with Other Software

During the business day, you need to accomplish tasks that require many different kinds of software, of which Visio is only one. One task alone—creating a report, for example—may require several programs working together to generate text, diagrams, and tables. Collecting all the information into a presentation requires yet another program. For many businesses, the standard business productivity programs are Microsoft products. Businesses use Microsoft Office XP to create the text and tables and to collect the data from different programs into unified documents. Many businesses also use Microsoft Outlook and Exchange for e-mail. All these products work with Visio to create a seamless environment for accomplishing tasks.

Visio was designed to work with these other programs, allowing you to use data and diagrams created in Visio in other programs and allowing information from other sources to be added to Visio documents. There are many ways you can use Visio with Microsoft products.

NOTE *Many of the figures in this chapter use Microsoft Word 2002 as an example. Most other Microsoft products work similarly.*

New Integration with Microsoft Office

Earlier versions of Microsoft Visio worked well with Office, but the integration wasn't seamless. Now, with its full addition into the Microsoft product family, Visio is completely integrated into the information sharing that makes working with Microsoft software so powerful.

If you've used Visio with Microsoft products before, you'll find the process much easier and with better results than before. The Object Linking and Embedding is smoother and produces a better image. The copy and paste feature works between Visio and other Office products like it does internally in any of the products. Overall, the addition of Visio to Microsoft's product family has made the interaction better, faster, and more productive.

NOTE   *Microsoft Visio 2002 is primed to work with Microsoft Office XP. The techniques discussed in the chapter will work with some older versions of Microsoft Office software, but for best results, use Microsoft Office XP.*

8

Understanding Object Linking and Embedding

When a Visio diagram is included in whole, or in part, in another program, it is done in one of three ways:

- As an image saved in Visio and inserted into the new document.

- As an embedded object included in the new document but editable as if it were in Visio.

- As a linked object included in the new document in such a way that changes are reflected, no matter where you edit the diagram.

The first of these options requires saving your file as an image and then inserting it in a different documents in another piece of software. Saving your diagrams is covered in Chapter 2, "Your First Visio Diagram."

These last two options require the use of Object Linking and Embedding.

Object Linking and Embedding, or OLE, is the main way Visio is designed to work with Microsoft Office XP. OLE allows programs to "speak the same language" when they exchange data. Microsoft first incorporated a common language for programs to exchange data when it developed Windows 3.1. Since then, OLE has become an industry standard, greatly increasing the productivity of business software by allowing different programs to work together seamlessly.

 *Visio uses an updated version of OLE, specifically OLE2. Only OLE2-compliant programs can use some of the features discussed in this chapter. Some of the OLE functions discussed here may not work with older versions of Microsoft products (for example, Word for Windows 95).*

Visio has a complete set of OLE functions that allow you to trade Visio information between it and other OLE-compliant programs. Programs in the Microsoft Office XP Suite are the most widely used products with which Visio can interact, and OLE operations are almost identical between all the members of Microsoft Office XP.

Creating Visio Drawings in Other Programs

The best way to see OLE in operation is to create a Visio diagram right inside another program. OLE embeds a Visio diagram when you do this.

When you install Visio, Visio tells other programs installed on your system about itself. It notifies them what type of program Visio is, what Visio is capable of, and how to interact with Visio if they require its services.

NOTE *Many of the figures in this chapter use Microsoft Word 2002 as an example. Other Microsoft products work similarly.*

To create a Visio diagram in the document of another product (for example, Microsoft Word 2002), first place the cursor where you'd like the Visio diagram to appear. Then choose Insert | Object. The Object dialog box opens, as shown in Figure 8-1.

Choose Visio Drawing from the list of object types, and click OK. The Choose a Drawing Template dialog box appears, as it does when you start Visio (see Figure 8-2).

The program inserts a Visio drawing page, opens the selected Visio template, and replaces the program's standard toolbars with Visio's standard toolbars. You can create the diagram as you would any new diagram in a Visio window, including drawing and dropping shapes, adding text, and even adding connections.

When you're done editing the Visio drawing, click somewhere on the document outside the embedded Visio window. This closes Visio and restores the program's standard toolbars. After Visio has closed, you're able to move the diagram around as you would any inserted image

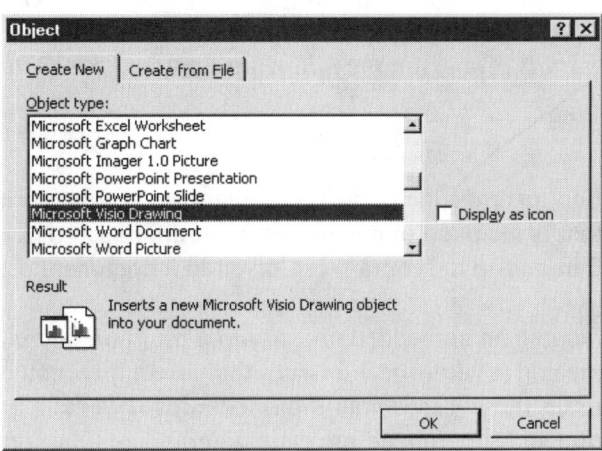

FIGURE 8-1   Microsoft Word 2002 Insert Object window, Create New tab

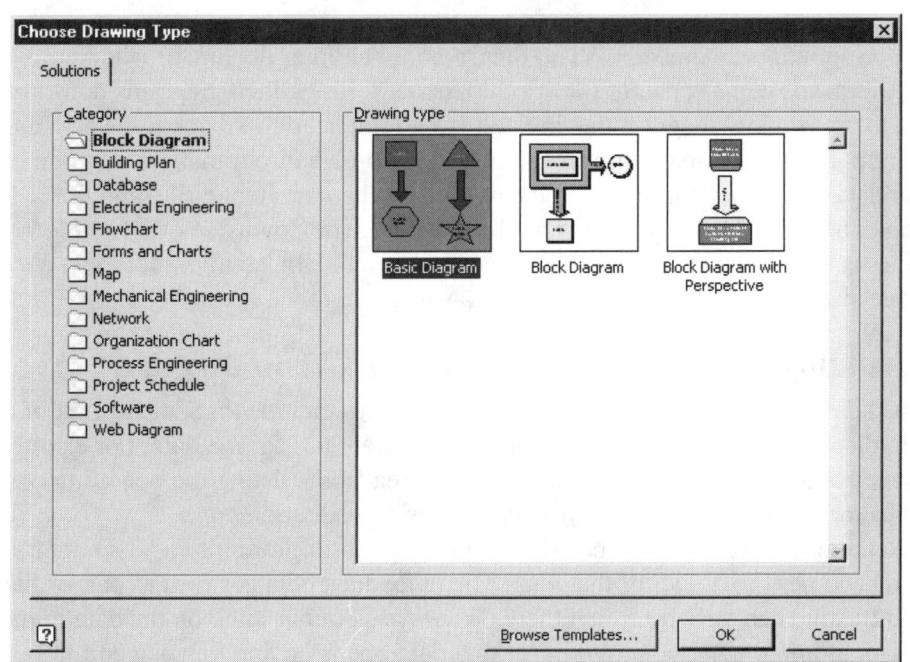

FIGURE 8-2   Microsoft Word 2002 Insert new Visio Object, Choose Drawing Type window

 *If you accidentally close Visio while editing a linked or embedded drawing, double-click on the drawing to open Visio again. You'll learn more about this process in the following section, "Embedding."*

Embedding

As explained earlier, an embedded object is data created by one program (the *native* program) that is included in the document of another program in such a way as it can be edited in its native program but saved in a document created in the new program.

When you're adding an embedded object into a program, there are several ways it can be done and several special issues that affect how you edit the object. This section discusses these issues both for embedding data from other programs into a Visio diagram and for embedding Visio diagrams in other programs

 *Remember, when you embed data into another program, it becomes part of that program's file, and you can only edit it as an embedded object from then on.*

You should only embed a Visio diagram into another document when you don't want to keep a separate file for the diagram. Embedded diagrams don't refer back to the original diagram that created it, and it has no link back to its original program. Embedded diagrams are useful when you want to transfer a diagram or other data to another computer; you can send all the data in one file, and the receiver need not have Visio to view the diagram. The downside of embedded images is that they can increase the file size dramatically, so make sure you check the file size before sending the document over a network.

Embedding Another Program's Data in a Visio Diagram

Embed data from other programs when you want to include that data as part of a Visio diagram but don't want to maintain a separate file for the data. For example, you may want to include a Microsoft Excel spreadsheet listing the operating costs of a factory under the shape for that factory on a production chart.

Remember, when you embed data from another program into a Visio diagram, Visio becomes the holder of that data. The embedded data is saved as part of the Visio file and can only be edited there. When you double-click on the data in the Visio diagram, the native program for that data opens up and you can edit it, but any change you make exists only in the Visio diagram. This may make it easier for you since you need not keep track of a separate file. The data doesn't exist as a separate file; it's incorporated into the Visio document. Figure 8-3 shows a Microsoft Excel spreadsheet that's embedded in a Visio diagram.

> **NOTE**   *Sometimes Visio wants to paste Excel spreadsheet data as plain text. To get around this choose Edit | Paste Special and then tell Visio to paste it as Excel spreadsheet data.*

To embed another program's data into a Visio diagram, first open the file that has the data you want to include in the Visio diagram. Copy the data out of the file, usually by selecting it and then choosing Edit | Copy. This copies the data to the clipboard.

With the data on the clipboard, open the Visio diagram into which you want to embed it. To make sure nothing in the diagram is selected, click on a blank portion of the drawing page, and then choose Edit | Paste (or click the Paste button on the Visio toolbar).

The data appears in the center of your Visio window as an embedded object. Move the object as you would any Visio shape, placing it wherever you want on the drawing page.

8

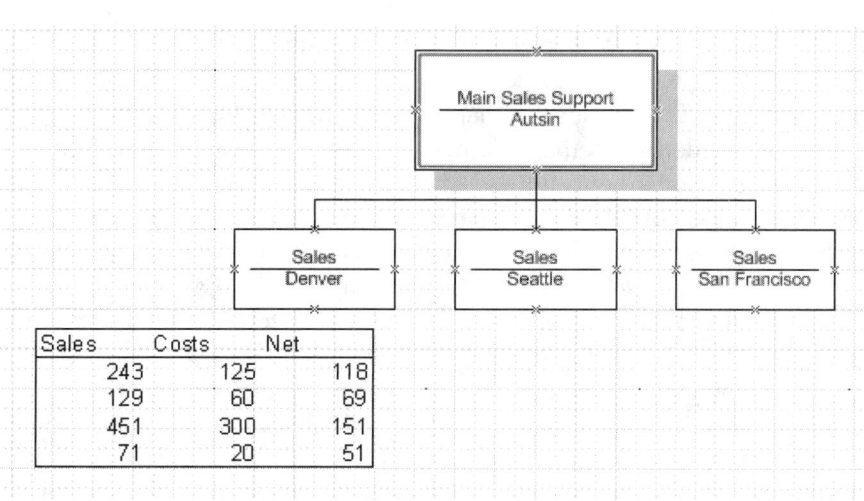

FIGURE 8-3   Microsoft Excel spreadsheet in a Visio Diagram

 *Always save the file before and after embedding an object. The process can be memory-intensive and if there are any computer problems, you want to make sure you don't lose data.*

Embedding Visio Shapes in Another Program's Document

There are two ways to include Visio shapes in the documents of other programs: you can drag the shapes or you can copy and paste the shapes. Both methods work in a similar manner.

To drag a Visio shape into another program's document, first make sure both the Visio diagram and the document into which you will embed the shape are open and visible on the Windows desktop.

 *To arrange the programs so both are visible, launch both programs and then right-click on the Windows taskbar. Select one of the options for tiling the windows, either horizontally or vertically.*

With both programs open and visible, select the shape in the Visio diagram and drag it to the new document. This *moves* the shape, deleting it from the Visio diagram and placing it in the new document. If you want to *copy* the shape, select it in the Visio diagram and hold down CTRL as you drag the shape to the new document. This leaves a copy of the shape in the Visio diagram and embeds a copy in the new document.

To copy and paste Visio shapes into another document, first make sure both Visio and the other program are open. Then select shapes in the Visio diagram and choose Edit | Copy. This copies the shapes to the clipboard. While the shapes are still on the clipboard, display the document in which you want to place them. Move the cursor where you want the shapes to appear in the new document and then paste the shapes, usually by choosing Edit | Paste.

To move a shape from a Visio page to another document, use the same process as for copying and pasting, but instead of choosing Edit | Copy, choose Edit | Cut. This places the shape on the clipboard and removes it from the Visio diagram. Then paste the shape in the document.

No matter how you embed the shapes, the Visio window opens inside the other program. When you're done placing the shapes, click outside the box containing the embedded Visio shapes, and the Visio toolbars and rulers disappear. Remember to save the new document after embedding the Visio shapes.

Embedding a Many Shapes or Whole Visio Page in Another Program's Document

What if you want to embed more than one or two shapes from a Visio diagram? You can embed an entire Visio drawing page in another document by using the Select All feature.

First, open the Visio diagram that contains the page you'd like to copy. Then open the document you'd like to copy the page into. Remember to save your diagram and the document first. In the Visio window, display the page you want to copy and click on a blank portion of the page to be sure nothing on the page is selected. Then, in your Visio diagram, choose Edit | Select All, this chooses every shape on the Visio drawing page. You can deselect any shape you don't want to copy by holding down SHIFT and clicking on it. Once you are happy with the shapes to be copied, choose Edit | Copy. This places the selected shapes onto the Windows clipboard.

With the shapes on the clipboard, click on the document into which you'd like to insert the page. Place the cursor where you want to embed the Visio drawing page and paste the Visio data, usually by selecting Edit | Paste.

Editing Embedded Visio Data in Another Program

Once you've placed your Visio diagram into a document in another program, the beauty of OLE becomes apparent when you need to edit that data. No matter what type of data you've embedded—one shape, a drawing page, or an entire diagram—the editing process is the same.

First, open the document containing the embedded Visio data. Then double-click on the data, which usually appears inside its own box. When you double-click on your embedded Visio data, OLE automatically opens Visio and temporarily replaces the toolbars of the new program with the Visio standard toolbars. If the data is a drawing page or a whole Visio diagram, Visio also opens any stencils attached to the original drawing. Figure 8-4 shows a Visio diagram embedded in a Microsoft Word document.

When you edit the Visio data in the new document, the Visio rulers appear on two sides of the Visio diagram, indicating that you're editing the diagram in Visio running inside the other program. Also, the menus and toolbars temporarily become Visio menus and toolbars.

NOTE *If you need a stencil in the new program, use the Open Stencil button on the Visio toolbar, which temporarily replaces the program's toolbar.*

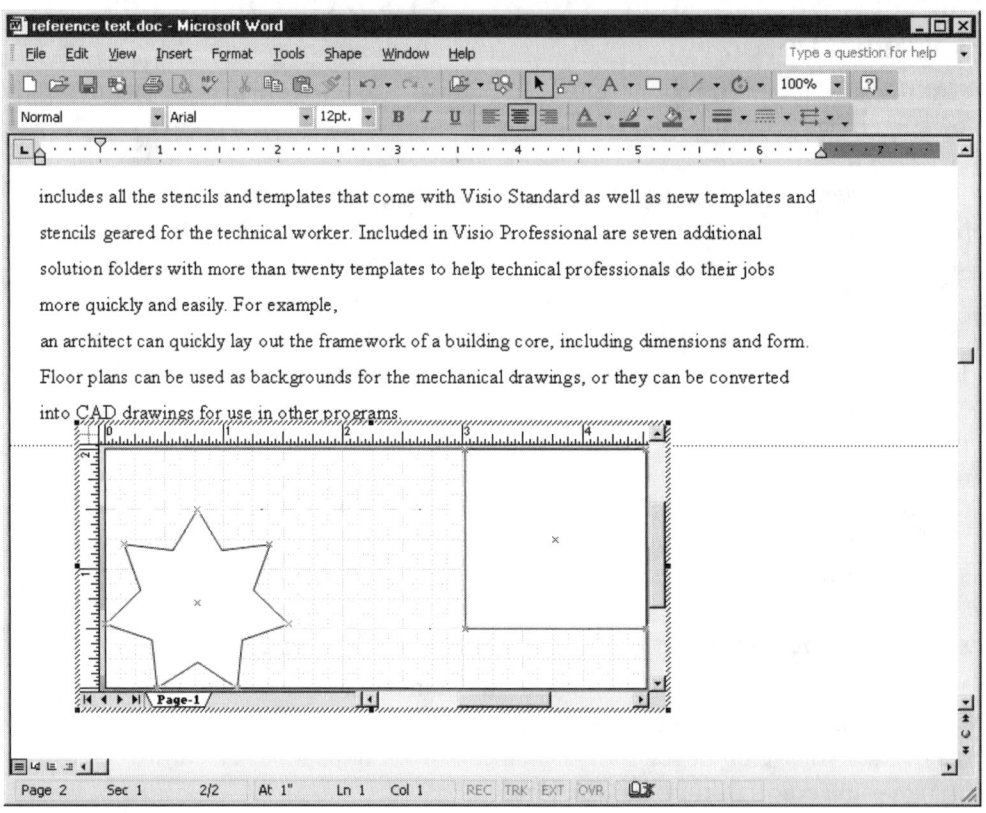

FIGURE 8-4   Visio Diagram Embedded in Microsoft Word 2002

Edit the Visio diagram as you would if it were running in the main Visio window. If you need more space or a larger drawing page, resize the drawing by moving the cursor to the bottom-right corner of the diagram until it turns into a double arrow, then click and drag the corner until the drawing page is the correct size.

When you're satisfied with your changes to the diagram, click on the new document's page somewhere other than on the embedded diagram. This restores the native program's toolbars and removes the Visio rulers and stencils.

TIP   *If you accidentally click outside the embedded diagram, you can return to the editing function by double-clicking on the embedded diagram.*

After you've restored the native program's toolbars, remember to save the document. Because your diagram only exists as part of the new document, if you don't save the new document, you'll lose all changes.

Managing the Space Around Embedded or Linked Visio Diagrams

Because the program into which you embed a Visio diagram sees the diagram as a type of image, by default, a blank border exists around the diagram. This space is free of text and other data to avoid crowding the diagram, but you may want to set the amount of white space yourself for a couple of reasons.

■ For small diagrams or single shapes embedded as Visio diagrams, the white space is too little and the shape becomes crowded when other text or data is added to the document. You may need to add a white border shape around your shape to compensate for this.

■ When you copy and embed an entire drawing page into another program, extra white space can appear around the Visio diagram. You may need to remove some of the white space around your diagram so it doesn't cover part of the new document.

To adjust the amount of white space around your embedded or linked Visio diagram, first select the diagram in the new document. Do not double-click to open the Visio editing capability, but instead edit the Visio diagram in a Visio window. To edit the diagram in the Visio window, you need to choose Edit | Visio Object | Open after you've selected the embedded diagram on the drawing page. This opens the diagram in an independent Visio window like the one shown in Figure 8-4.

Once you have the diagram open in a Visio window, you can change the amount of white space around the diagram by changing the size of the page.

To change the size of the Visio page, choose File | Page Setup and select the Page Size tab, shown in Figure 8-5.

Choose the page size and orientation that most fits your needs. Here are the options available on the Page Size tab:

■ **Same as printer paper size**   Sets the drawing page size to be the same as the paper size set in the printer.

■ **Pre-defined size**   Sets the drawing size to one of four standard page-size sets: Standard U.S. sizes, Standard E.U. sizes, Architectural sizes, or

8

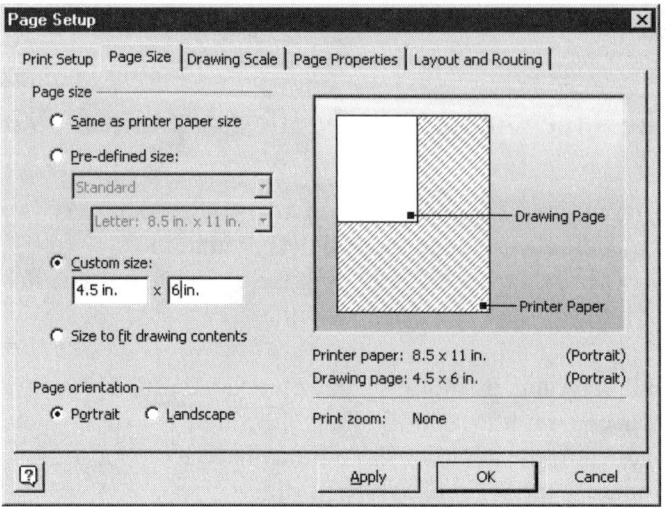

FIGURE 8-5   Page Size tab of the Page Setup window

Engineering sizes. Once you choose the page-size set, then the second drop-down menu allows you to choose the exact page size.

- **Custom size**   Sets the exact size of the page. This is one of the two most useful settings for managing white space.

- **Size to fit drawing contents**   Shrinks the drawing page to include only the shapes with no white space outside them. This setting is also very useful for handling white space.

- **Page orientation**   Changes the orientation of the drawing page to have the long side vertical (portrait) or the long side horizontal (landscape).

 *There is more discussion of page size and printer settings in Chapter 1, "Visio Basics."*

Once you've selected the drawing page size, click OK and the Page Setup window closes. Visio changes the drawing page containing your embedded diagram according to your choice.

TIP

You can alter the diagram in any way you like in the Visio main window, because it is actually open in Visio. You can open and close stencils and add shapes and text. Also, while you have the diagram open in the Visio window, you can save a copy of the diagram in Visio file format or as an image by choosing File | Save Copy As.

When you're finished altering the page size of your diagram, and you're ready to return to your document, choose File | Exit and Return to (document). This closes the Visio window and returns you to the document in the main window of its resident program. Remember to save the document as soon as you close the main Visio window.

NOTE

For advice on troubleshooting problems with embedded data, see "Troubleshooting Linking and Embedding Problems" at the end of the next section.

8

Linking

A linked object is data created in one program (the native program) that is included in a file of another program in such a way that the data can be edited both in the original file *and* in the file of the other program. Both files (the original and the one containing the linked data) reflect changes to the data regardless of where those changes are made.

NOTE

Linking data can happen between more than two programs. You can link to the same data from as many programs as you like. However, only linking between two programs will be covered in this chapter. For more information about linking, see the online help for your OLE-compatible program.

Link data when you want to be able to update the information from both programs. Data included via linking can be altered in its original document in its original program, and the link updates the data and incorporates the change when the new document is opened again.

For example, if you have text describing the confidentiality of company data that you'd like to include at the bottom of your Visio diagram, you can create that data in another OLE-compatible program, then link to the data. If you later need to change the wording of the text, simply alter it in its original program, and Visio automatically updates the data on the diagram page.

One of the biggest benefits of linking to data instead of embedding it is that when you link to data from another program, Visio only keeps a reference to the data instead of containing it. This lack of inclusion in the new document means that linking to data doesn't increase file size, so your documents remain small.

 *Because linking adds a reference to the data via the filename and location, if you change the filename or move the files related to each other, you'll break the link. If you need to move linked files you must move them all together.*

The advantage of linking is that files are updated no matter where the data is changed. This ability can be a huge time-saver, but adding links to data and managing linked data has its own special procedures. This section explains how to add links, change them, edit the data, and make sure they're updated correctly.

Preparing Documents to Be Linked

You need to make some preparations before you can add linked data to a document. Make sure you have completed all of these steps before you begin the linking process.

- Make sure the document containing the data you're linking to has been saved.

- Make sure that both programs—the native program and the one in which you're creating the link—are installed on your computer system.

- Make sure the two files are saved in the same locations, or at least in the same relative locations, where they will reside when you have finished editing them.

Inserting Linked Data into a Visio Diagram

There are two ways to add linked data to the drawing page. One is to insert the data as an object, and the other is to create a link while copying the data. This subsection explains how to insert the data as an object. The next subsection explains how to link data while copying it.

To insert linked data into a Visio diagram using the first method, make sure your Visio diagram is saved. Because linking involves adding a reference to another document, both documents must be saved to create the reference.

After you've saved both documents, you're ready to create the link. On the Insert menu in the main Visio window, select Object | Create from File. The Insert Object window opens, as shown in Figure 8-6.

Select the checkbox for Link to File, setting the object to be inserted to automatically update as the file changes. Click Browse to display the Browse dialog box, shown in Figure 8-7. Browse to the file, select the filename, and then click Insert. The file path you select appears in the File Name text box of the Insert Object window.

NOTE   *In the Insert Object window, you can also select to display the object as an icon. This choice puts a placeholder in your diagram instead of displaying all the data in the document you link to.*

When you're satisfied with the path and options set in the Insert Object dialog box, click OK. The Insert Object dialog box closes, and Visio places a copy of the first page of the linked data in the center of your drawing page. Remember to save your diagram after setting a link.

Copying Linked Data into a Visio Diagram

To copy linked data into the drawing page, first make sure both the Visio document and the document containing the data are saved.

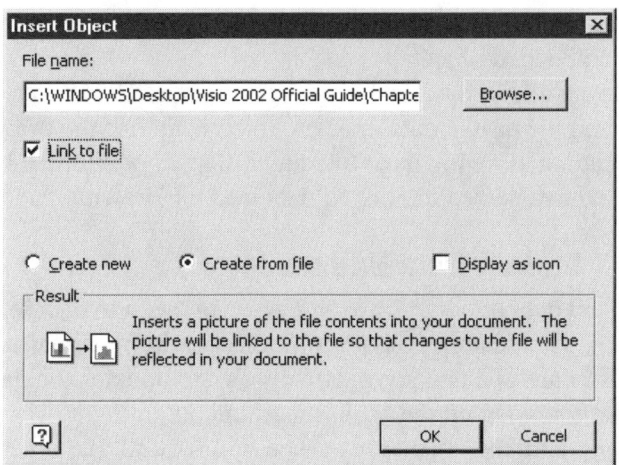

FIGURE 8-6   Insert Object window

8

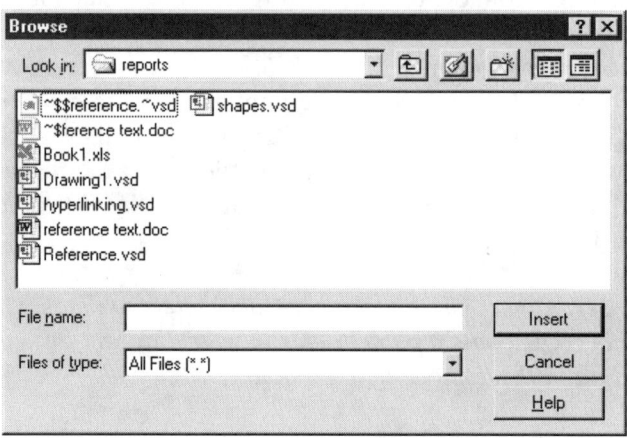

FIGURE 8-7 Browse window

In the document containing the data, copy the data to the clipboard, usually by selecting it and then choosing Edit | Copy.

After you have the data on the clipboard, open the Visio diagram you wish to add the data to and choose Edit | Paste Special. The Paste Special window appears, as shown in Figure 8-8.

Choose to paste the data in any format you wish, but make sure to select the Paste Link option button. This option pastes the data on the clipboard as a link instead of as an embedded object.

When you've set all the options for the your data, click OK. The Paste Special window closes, and the pasted data appears in the center of the drawing page. You can move it around the drawing page like any other shape. Remember to save your diagram after you have pasted the linked data into the drawing page.

Deciding How Linked Data Updates

After you've linked data on your drawing page, you need to decide how Visio updates those links. There are two types of link updating: manual and automatic. By default, all links are updated automatically. Visio updates the data in a linked object every time you open up the Visio diagram containing it. Manual updating changes the data in a linked object only when you request that it be updated.

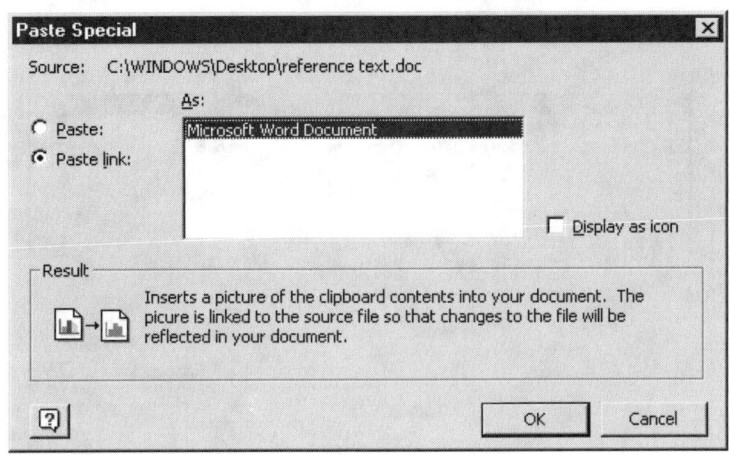

FIGURE 8-8   Paste Special window, Pasting Microsoft Word text

8

Usually, automatically updated links work well. When you use automatic updating, you can still manually update links without closing and reopening the file. If a link is set to be updated automatically and Visio cannot find the linked file when you open the diagram, Visio prompts you for the file's location. If you plan to do a lot of editing on a diagram and won't have consistent access to the linked document, it's best to use manually updated links.

To change the update method for a linked object, select it on the drawing page. Then choose Edit | Links. The Links window appears, as shown in Figure 8-9. The Links window shows the file paths for all the linked objects on the drawing page. The path for the selected link is highlighted. Below the list of links, the Source field shows the path for the highlighted link, and the Type field shows what kind of file it is.

To set the update method, select either the Automatic or the Manual option button at the bottom of the Links window. (In the next section, you'll learn how to use the other options available on the Links window.) After you've selected the update method, click OK. The Links window closes, and Visio uses the new update method for the linked data.

Managing Linked Data in Visio 2002

In addition to the setting that determines how linked data is updated, there are several other settings you can adjust using the Links window. If you have set

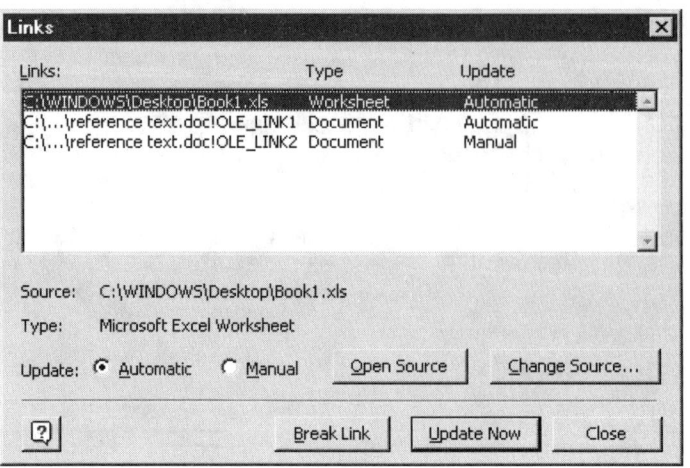

Links window

linked data to be manually updated, it's important to know how to use these settings. These settings are also important if the data is set to automatically update and you later move or rename the original files.

NOTE *If you open a drawing containing linked data and Visio cannot find the original file, Visio asks you to update links manually.*

All settings for your linked data are set on the Links window. To open the Links window, choose Edit | Links. The Links window appears, as shown in Figure 8-9.

Here's a list of the available settings on the Links window:

■ **Links List**   Lists all linked data on the current page. This area of the window lists the path, type, and update method for each link.

■ **Source**   Shows the file path for the highlighted link in the Links list.

■ **Type**   Shows the file type for the highlighted link in the Links list.

■ **Update**   Shows the setting for updating the link selected on the Links list, which can be either manual or automatic. Automatic is the default.

■ **Open Source**   Launches the original program for the linked data selected in the Links list and opens the file containing the linked data.

> **NOTE**   *If you click the Open Source button and the native program for the linked data is not available on your computer, Visio displays an error message telling you that the link is not working.*

■ **Change Source**   Opens the Change Source dialog box, which looks very similar to the Browse dialog box shown earlier in Figure 8-7. The Change Source dialog box allows you to reset the path for the link selected in the Links list.

■ **Break Link**   Removes the link between the linked data's original document and the Visio drawing page. This turns the linked data into embedded data. When you select to break a link, Visio displays a dialog box telling you that this action will disconnect the linked data from its source and asks if you want to continue. Click Yes and the link is broken.

■ **Update Now**   Forces a manual update of the linked data selected in the Links list.

> **NOTE**   *You can also open the source file by selecting the linked data and then choosing Edit | Linked Object | Open.*

When you're done updating the information for your linked data, click Close. Visio applies the new settings to the data. Remember to save the diagram after changing any linked data settings.

Linking to a Visio Diagram from Another Program

Just as you can insert linked data into a Visio diagram, you can insert Visio data into the files of another program. First, however, you must make sure that both documents have been saved. Because linking involves setting up a relationship between the documents based on their relative paths, the documents must have full path names to have a linking relationship.

To link Visio diagrams into another Office product by inserting an object, you'll need to open the document where you want to place the linked Visio diagram, and then choose Insert | Object. Choose to create the object from a file, and choose to link to it. The Object window with all the settings for Microsoft Word 2002 is shown in Figure 8-10.

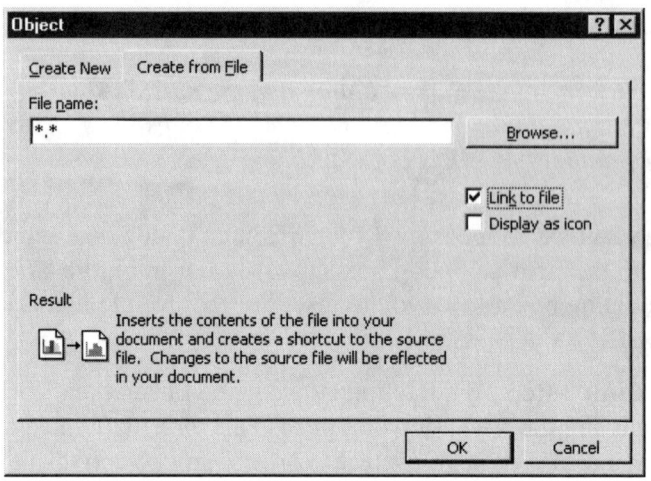

FIGURE 8-10   Link to Object window for Microsoft Word 2002

The Object window in some Microsoft Office XP programs looks like the one for Visio, shown in Figure 8-9. Figure 8-10 shows only the object window for Microsoft Word 2002

Just as with linking in Visio itself, you can choose to include the link as an icon instead of as an image. Once you browse to locate your Visio diagram, and finish with the link settings, click OK. Your Visio diagram inserts in your document as a linked diagram.

To link Visio diagrams into another Office product by copy and pasting, once the documents are saved, select the data you want on the Visio drawing page and then choose Edit | Copy. This copies all the data from the page to the clipboard.

In the document where you want to link to the Visio data, choose Edit | Paste Special. Make sure the diagram is placed as a Microsoft Visio Drawing Object, and then choose to paste the data as a link.

Once the linked data has been pasted in the new document, remember to save it.

Troubleshooting Linking and Embedding Problems

Because embedded data requires two programs working together, problems sometimes occur that would not happen if just one program were used to create a document. No matter if you're inserting other program data into Visio, or Visio data into another program, editing that data can be problematic.

The most common error message you'll see is one indicating you cannot edit the data; the message might not give a reason for the error. This message appears when the source file for the data or source program containing the document can't be opened for some reason.

Here are some reasons you might encounter an error while editing (and some ways to resolve such problems):

- The program used to create the document is not loaded on your computer.

- Your computer cannot open both Visio and the new program at the same time.

- The program that created the data is not responding.

- The data is already being edited.

- The filename has changed on the linked file.

Using Visio with Specific Microsoft Products

Visio is designed to work seamlessly with Microsoft products, especially the products in Microsoft Office XP. You can include a Visio drawing page in your Microsoft PowerPoint presentations, import Microsoft Excel data to create a flowchart, and you can include Visio diagrams in your Microsoft Front Page web pages. You can even create new Microsoft Exchange routing slips from inside Visio. This section discusses some of the most common uses of Visio with Microsoft Office XP.

 *This section just covers specialized issues with each Microsoft product that has particular uses with Visio. For standard Linking and Embedding in any Microsoft product, see the appropriate section earlier in this chapter.*

Adding Visio Hyperlinks to Microsoft Office XP Documents

In Chapter 7, "Linking and the Internet," you will learn how to add hyperlinks to your Visio shapes. Microsoft Office XP documents can also have hyperlinks, and you can paste a hyperlinked Visio shape into one of these documents.

To paste a hyperlinked Visio shape into your Microsoft Office XP document, first set the hyperlink for the shape in Visio. Then select the hyperlinked shape in Visio and copy the shape by choosing Edit | Copy. This copies the shape to the clipboard.

After the hyperlinked shape is on the clipboard, open the Microsoft Office XP document to where you would like to include it. Then, to paste the entire shape and its hyperlink, choose Edit | Paste. If you want to use the hyperlink alone, choose Edit | Paste as Hyperlink.

 *Versions of Microsoft programs older than Microsoft Office 97 do not support the Paste as Hyperlink feature.*

Adding Graphics to Microsoft Word

Using Visio graphics in Microsoft Word can really enhance your Word documents. There are three standard ways to include a Visio diagram in Microsoft Word:

- Saving the diagram as an image
- Embedding the diagram
- Linking to the diagram from Word

Saving the Diagram as an Image

This process allows you to place your diagram into your Microsoft Word document as you would a piece of clip art, moving and resizing as needed. Also, the copy of the diagram is saved with the Word document. Unfortunately, you may lose resolution when you save the diagram as an image, and you lose the ability to continue to change the diagram. For more information about how to save Visio diagrams as images, see Chapter 2, "Creating Your First Diagram."

Embedding the Visio Diagram

Embedding allows you to continue to edit the diagram as a Visio document and saves the image data with the document. You can also move embedded images around on the drawing page, but Microsoft Word can be a little picky about how text wraps around embedded documents. If necessary, you can also convert embedded data into standard images. For more information about embedding Visio documents, see the section "Embedding" earlier in this chapter.

Linking to the Diagram from Microsoft Word

Linking allows you to continue editing your diagram no matter where you change it, and both your Microsoft Word document and your Visio diagram will reflect the change. Unfortunately, the relationship between the files must stay the same or the link breaks. For more information about linking to Visio documents, see the section "Linking" earlier in this chapter.

Importing and Exporting Data from Microsoft Excel and Microsoft Access

Several different Visio macros and templates are designed to import and export data to and from Microsoft Excel and Microsoft Access. This section briefly discusses the most commonly used features.

Importing or Exporting Flowchart Information

The Organizational Wizard and the Import Flowchart Data Wizard can use data from Microsoft Excel and Microsoft Access to create an organizational chart. Both templates can also export data based on the charts you create to these formats. For more information, see Chapter 5, "Creating Flowcharts."

Updating Automatically from Databases

Several Visio macros were created to help you keep a Visio diagram and Microsoft databases in sync. The Database Wizard can help you set up the relationship; open it by choosing Tools | Macros | Database Wizard. The Macros menu also includes database export, refresh, settings, and update tools.

Creating Presentations Using Visio Diagrams in Microsoft PowerPoint

Visio and PowerPoint work so well together, it's as if they were made for each other. Microsoft PowerPoint enables you to use your Visio diagrams to make your point and to strengthen your presentations.

Because PowerPoint is an OLE-compatible program, you can link and embed your Visio diagram if you choose, or even create a completely new Visio diagram right in PowerPoint. You can also copy and paste your Visio diagram into PowerPoint. You can even just drag all or part of a Visio diagram into an open presentation in PowerPoint, and it is incorporated quickly and easily.

One feature that helps Visio and PowerPoint work well together is *color schemes*. The color schemes you set in Visio are the same as those that come with PowerPoint, allowing you to choose a color scheme for your PowerPoint presentation and then apply it to all parts of your Visio diagram that you wish to include.

If you want, you can even include PowerPoint clip art in Visio diagrams, helping you to create a cohesive theme within diagrams, just as you would throughout a presentation.

To include your Visio diagram in your PowerPoint presentation, follow these steps:

1. Open both PowerPoint and Visio to the documents you want to alter.

2. Copy all or part of your Visio diagram by choosing the shapes and then clicking Copy.

3. In PowerPoint, position your cursor where you'd like the Visio diagram to appear.

4. Click Paste.

This will give you an embedded copy of your Visio diagram. If you want to have a linked Visio diagram follow the same steps as listed earlier in the "Linking" section of this chapter.

Displaying Diagrams in Microsoft Internet Explorer

Microsoft Internet Explorer and Visio also work very well together. To open a Visio diagram within Internet Explorer, choose File | Open. In the Open dialog box, click Browse. Then select the All Files file type and locate the Visio diagram.

When you open a Visio diagram, the Visio menus, toolbars, and stencils appear. You're able to edit your Visio diagram in Internet Explorer just as you can in the main Visio window. You can also use the Internet Explorer navigation buttons and menus (such as the Forward and Back buttons) to move between Visio diagrams, Microsoft Office XP documents, and World Wide Web pages.

Sending a Diagram as an E-Mail Message with Microsoft Exchange

E-mail has become a major tool for conducting business, and Visio diagrams often need sent through e-mail. Visio has included three options to make this process easier, all of which are accessed by choosing File | Send To. The options are as follows:

- **Mail Recipient**   Opens your Microsoft mail program, starts a new message, and adds the current Visio drawing as an attachment.

- **Routing Receipt**   Opens Microsoft Exchange and creates a routing slip with the current Visio drawing attached. You select the address for the document to be routed to, the order in which it is routed, and you can track the status of the diagram at any time. You can also add message text to the routing slip and send it, or you can continue to edit the drawing and send it later.

- **Exchange Folder**   Allows you to save your Visio drawing as an embedded object in a Microsoft Exchange folder you select.

NOTE   *You can also include your Visio file in an e-mail message by saving it as an image (a .GIF or .JPG file) and then add it to the body of your message. It may make the message a bit large, but the graphic impact is impressive.*

8

Summary

In this chapter, you learned how to include Microsoft Office XP documents in your Visio diagrams and how to include Visio diagrams in your Microsoft Office XP documents. You also learned how to link the two documents together to create automatic updates, as well as finding out the most common ways to use Microsoft Office XP software with Visio.

In the next chapter, you'll learn how to create your own shapes and solutions in Visio using advanced Visio features and Visual Basic for Applications.

Chapter 9

Creating Custom Shapes and Solutions

How to...

- Modify Shapes
- Make New Shapes
- Use Operations to Change Shapes
- Define Custom Properties for Shapes
- Use ShapeSheets
- Use the Pencil Tool to Alter Shapes

In the last chapter, you learned how to use Visio with other Office Products.

In this chapter, you'll learn how to create original shapes, both by modifying existing shapes and by creating new shapes from scratch. You will also learn how to define custom properties for shapes, and how to use and alter ShapeSheets.

In Chapter 4, "Using Stencils and Templates," you learned how to move shapes from one stencil to another and how to create new stencils by adding shapes from other stencils. This section explains how to create entirely new shapes for stencils.

Occasionally, you cannot find a shape to meet your special needs in the thousands of shapes that come with Visio. You might need a custom shape of some kind. Simple company logos, unique professional shapes, and combined groups of standard shapes are all good candidates for new master shapes. Making a new master shape allows you to create the shape once, and then pull it from a stencil over and over and be assured that the shape will always look and act the same.

There are two ways to create new shapes: modifying shapes that already exist on stencils, and creating new shapes using the drawing tools. Both methods produce fully functional master shapes, complete with custom properties if you wish.

Modifying Existing Shapes

If you find yourself modifying the same shape over and over, you can save time and energy by creating a custom shape that already has the modifications. The fastest way to create a new shape is to modify an existing master shape. There are two major benefits of modifying an existing master shape. First, it's quick and easy. Second, the new shape can inherit the custom properties of the original master shape, including resizing and double-click functions.

To modify an existing shape, you can use the format and other options that you can set for any shape. Once you have modified a shape you can drag it back onto an editable stencil and you will have a master shape with all the modifications ready to drag to your drawing page. This section outlines all the different preferences, formats, and settings you can change on a shape.

> **NOTE** *This section lists only the most popular changes to existing shapes, but you can create a new master with almost any change you can make to a Visio shape. Feel free to play around with creating new masters out of existing shapes that have been altered and placing them on your own new stencil.*

Adding Text, Color, or Line Options for New Master Shapes

Some of the most common changes people make to Visio shapes are to add text, change the color, or alter the line of the shape. When you find yourself making the same changes over and over to the same shape, it's time to make a new master of that shape with the changes already applied.

The process for adding these simple changes to a master shape is the same. First, drag the shape you want to modify to the drawing page. Alter the shape, and then drag it back onto an editable stencil. Rename the new master shape from the default name to something you'll remember. Now you can pull the shape from the stencil and skip a step when you need the shape with the text.

> **NOTE** *If the stencil isn't set to be edited, Visio asks if you would like to open the stencil to edit it when you drop a shape on the stencil. Always make sure you've opened a copy of the stencil. Don't overwrite the stencils that come with Visio.*

Here are some specific hints on altering shapes in these simple ways:

- **Adding Custom Text**   One of the quickest and easiest changes is to create a new master twith text that you add to the same shape over and over. To create a shape with custom text already added, move the shape you want to modify to the drawing page, and using the text tool, add the text. Using the text rotation tool, move the text around in the shape until you are happy with its position. When you are finished adding text, move the shape onto an editable stencil to make it a new master shape.

- **Adding Color** Creating a new master shape with the color already applied saves time and ensures consistency when you need the same shape repeatedly. Just as with adding text to make a new master, to add color to a shape simply drag it to the drawing page. Use the drop-down color list, or choose Format | Fill to choose a new color for the shape. After you are done altering the shape, drag it back to your alterable stencil and you have a new master shape that will always be the same color.

- **Changing Line Weight or Pattern** Altering the outline of a shape, or its line, can be a subtle or massive change to a shape. If you find you need new shape with a heavier outside line or a patterned exterior, you can alter the line weight or pattern in much the same way as adding color. Drag the shape to the drawing page and then use the drop-down line weight and pattern buttons (or choose Format | Line) to alter the shape. When you are done, drag it back onto your editable stencil.

 *For more information about editing stencils, see chapter 4, "Using Stencils and Templates."*

Altering Shape Functions for New Master Shapes

There are many shape functions that we take for granted, for example, connection points. But you may find that you need a new master that is the same as a standard shape but has connection points in a different place. You can change almost anything about a shape's functions fairly easily by setting shape properties or functions.

These changes to shapes follow the same steps as any other modification to a shape. The steps are (1) make the stencil editable, (2) move the shape to the drawing page, (3) make the alterations, (4) move the shape back onto the stencil, (5) rename the new master to something logical.

- **Moving a Connection Point** If you need a shape that connects in a different way, or if you have created a shape and need to set its connection points, select the Connection Point tool after you've dragged the shape to the drawing page. With the Connection Point tool you can move or add connection points. Then drag the shape back to the editable stencil for a new master shape. For more information about using the Connection tool, see Chapter 2 "Creating Your First Diagram."

■ **Protecting Size and Rotation**   Altering a shape over and over for size and a particular rotation isn't necessary. You can make all of these alterations once and then create a new master where the size and rotation are protected and cannot be changed. To do this, alter your shape and then select Format | Protection. On the Protection window select to protect the Width, Height, and Rotation, or any one of them. Now you can move your new master back to the editable stencil.

Several of the options available on the Protection window will not work for a new master, for example, start and end point. As a general rule, only width, height, and rotation are useful for new masters.

■ **Adding a Note**   Any shape can have a hidden note added that pops up when the cursor is held over the shape. You can create a master shape with a note by using the Insert | Comment option. Then move the shape back to the editable stencil.

Using the Pencil Tool

9

If you want to do more than simply add or alter shape properties of an existing shape—for example, if you want to change the contour of a shape—you need to use a more powerful tool than setting dialogs. To alter the geometry of a shape, the best tool is the Pencil tool. With the Pencil tool, you can change the arc of individual lines that make up the shape arc, and you can change the shape's vertices. Figure 9-1 shows a hexagon shape before and after it was modified with the Pencil tool.

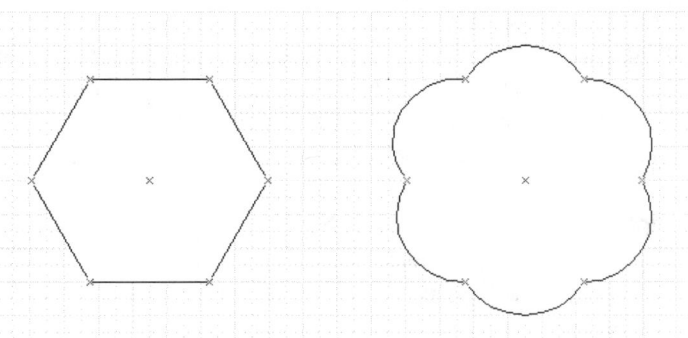

FIGURE 9-1   A hexagon shape modified with the pencil tool

In Figure 9-1, you can see how the Pencil tool was used to pull the sides of the hexagon into arcs. The Pencil tool allows you to draw line and arc segments to whatever length or arc you might need, singly or in groups. It also allows you to edit any shape in Visio no matter how it was created.

To edit existing shapes with the Pencil tool, make sure the part of the shape you wish to edit has an endpoint, a control point, or a vertex. If it doesn't have a vertex or control point you can add one by using the Pencil tool. Move the Pencil tool over the line you want to add a control point or vertex to and then hold down CTRL while you click with the mouse. Visio adds a control point.

Once you have a control point, move the Pencil tool over the control point; the cursor turns into a cross with arrows at the tips. Click and hold on the control point and move it where you'd like it to be. If you pull the control point directly away from the center of the shape, Visio creates straight lines on the sides that are connected to the control point. If you pull in any other direction than straight from the center, Visio creates an arc on the sides that are connected to the control point.

NOTE   *It helps when using the Pencil tool to understand that the tool works on gesture recognition and creates lines or arcs depending on how you move the cursor once you start drawing.*

For an explanation of how the Pencil tool works, see Chapter 2, "Creating Your First Diagram."

After you've modified a shape using the Pencil tool, you can convert it into a master shape by adding it to a stencil. To add a shape to a stencil, make sure the stencil is set to be edited, and then drag the modified shape to the stencil. After you've modified the stencil, save it in a folder within the Solutions folder.

Defining Custom Properties

Custom properties are the pieces of information you add to a shape after you have moved it to the drawing page. But what custom information you are asked for, and when you are asked for it, are defined in the shape attributes. You can make a new master by adding custom property fields to an existing shape and then moving it back to the stencil.

Custom properties are important because the information you can add to a shape can be exported into a database report and it can even be used as a selection criteria. The information doesn't show up on the page, but for large diagrams especially, it can be vital.

Some shapes come with custom properties already included; for example, the furniture shapes on the Office Layout Shapes stencil come with an option to include the inventory number and owner. Most shapes in Visio don't include custom properties by default. However, you can add a custom property to any shape.

To define custom properties for a shape, select the shape and choose Shape | Custom Properties. If a shape already has a custom property defined, the Custom Properties window opens. In the Custom Properties window, click Define to open the Define Custom Properties window, shown in Figure 9-2. If the shape has no Custom Properties defined, Visio will ask you if you want to define some; click Yes and the Define Custom Properties window opens.

Use the Define Custom Properties dialog box to add custom property fields to a shape. There are five pieces of information you need to supply to create a custom property field:

- ■ **Label**   Type the name for the custom property into Label. This name appears on the Custom Properties window for the shape. Every custom property for the same shape must have different labels.

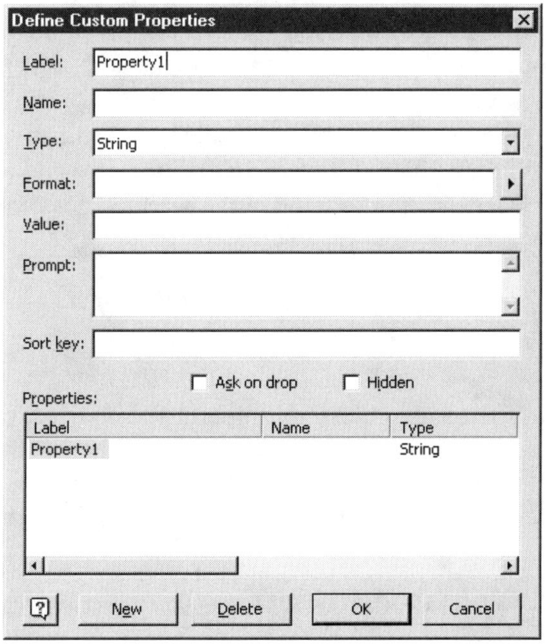

FIGURE 9-2   Define Custom Properties window

■ **Type**   Use the drop-down list to select the Type. Type sets the kind of information that will be entered into the custom property field. There are eight types of data Visio can accept: String (plain text), Number, Fixed List (a list of values you define), Variable List (a list you define or for user-entered information), Boolean (either TRUE or FALSE), Currency (displayed using the Regional Settings), Date (includes seconds, minutes, hours, and days), and Duration (elapsed time).

■ **Format**   Depending on the choice you make in the Type field, Format could be very different. For some Type values, the arrow on the side of the Format field allows you to select a standard format for the added custom property. For the list of values in the Type field, you'll need to include a list in the Format field, a list that becomes the drop-down selection list for the user. For the Boolean Type, the Format field is disabled. For all other Type values choose a Format type from the list.

■ **Value**   Enter the starting data into the Value field. The data in the Value field will be overwritten by any data entered by the user, even if the Value is protected.

■ **Prompt**   Enter the text that you want to display at the bottom of the Custom Properties dialog box when someone adds data to the field.

Use the Properties area of the window to select and edit any of the custom properties already set for a shape. Click the New button to add a new custom property. Click the Delete button to remove the selected custom property from the Properties list.

NOTE   *If you're in Developer Mode, there will be several more fields to complete on the Define Custom Properties dialog box.*

After you've finished adding custom properties to a shape, click OK. If you want to use the custom properties of this shape again when you pull it from the stencil, you need to save the shape as a master shape. To save a shape as a master shape, drag it to a stencil that's set to be edited, and then save the stencil.

Creating an Entirely New Shape

There may be times when simply modifying an existing shape will not give you the results you're looking for. When that's the case, you can create an entirely new shape.

There are two ways to create a new shape. You can combine parts of shapes that already exist, or you can use the drawing tools to create a shape from scratch. Combining shapes uses *shape operations,* which are discussed in detail later in this section. To use the drawing tools, you first need to understand shape architecture—that is, how shapes are defined in Visio.

Understanding Shape Architecture

Shape architecture is how Visio defines the way shapes look on the drawing page. Visio defines shapes as sets of vertices and arcs that work together. Figure 9-3 shows a shape that has been selected with the Pencil tool, illustrating its vertices, segments (also called arcs), and control points.

You can edit the vertices and arcs with the Pencil tool, but no matter how a shape is created, it still has vertices and arcs. A shape is defined as closed—and therefore able to be filled—when the last segment ends on the first vertex.

When you create a new shape using a drawing tool, you can modify the shape architecture by using the Pencil tool to alter the location of vertices or the curvature of the shape's segments. The control points, located around the shape, are the mechanism that allows you to alter the curvature of segments.

9

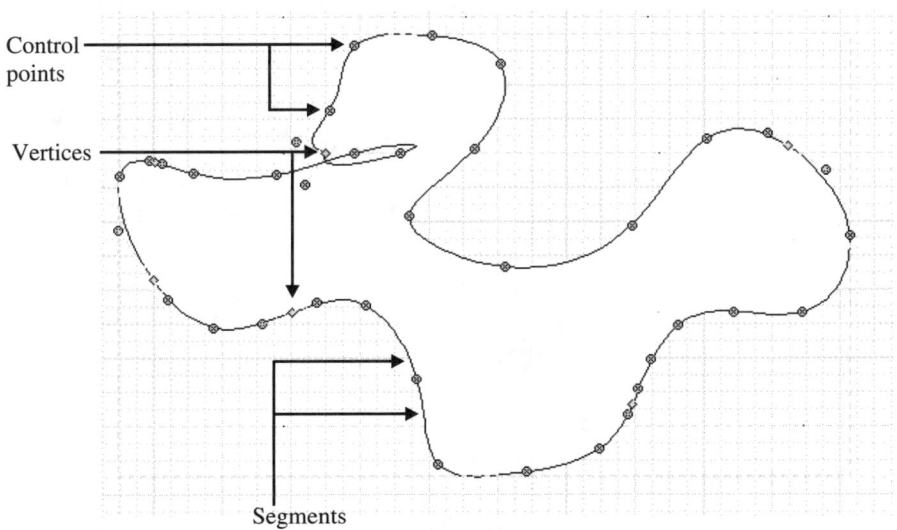

FIGURE 9-3   Vertices, segments, and control points of a shape

To change the arc of a segment using the Pencil tool, first select the shape with the Pencil tool. (Figure 9-3 shows an example of a shape that has been selected.) Then move the Pencil tool over a control point until it turns into a cross with arrows on all ends. Click and drag the control point, noticing as you do that the shape changes as you drag the control point. There are also special control points that extend from vertices, allowing you to change the angle the arcs use to connect at the vertices. These special control points, called *eccentricity handles*, appear as green, dotted lines.

You can add a vertex anywhere on the outline of the shape by holding down the CTRL key and clicking with the Pencil tool where you want to add the vertex. This adds not only a vertex, but also control points on either side of it. There is always at least one control point between vertices.

You can alter a shape's architecture beyond recognition by using the Pencil tool to move control points. Figure 9-3 demonstrates just the beginning of what you can accomplish by modifying shape architecture.

NOTE   *Some shapes on Visio's stencils are locked, and you cannot alter their shape architecture.*

Using Shape Operations

Visio has thousands of shapes, including everything from simple shapes for children's drawings to complex shapes for network architecture diagrams. However, sometimes these shapes aren't exactly what you need. You might need to create a shape using parts from several existing shapes. Or you might need to create a complex shape comprised of many individual shapes you've drawn with the Pencil tool. *Shape operations* were created for just these kinds of cases. Figure 9-4 shows a shape from the Basic Shapes stencil that has been modified using shape operations.

There are 11 different shape operations that modify or merge together shapes in various ways. To use shape operations, all the shapes you wish to modify or merge must exist on the drawing page. Most operations require selecting more than one shape. For such operations, the resulting shape will have the formatting of the shape that was selected first.

NOTE   *When you select multiple shapes, the first shape selected has green handles, and all other shapes have blue handles. The resulting shape often takes the properties of the first shape selected.*

FIGURE 9-4   Interlaced seven-pointed stars created with shape operations

The following 11 shape operations are available by choosing Tools | Operations.

Update Alignment Box

Resizes the box and control handles that surround a shape. Typically, you use this operation *after* you have finished modifying a shape's geometry. When you change the geometry of a shape, the alignment box doesn't automatically resize. You need to use this operation to resize the alignment box.

It's a good idea to update the alignment box of any shape that has been created from one or more shapes, or that has had any significant portions removed. This operation can also help you with imported objects that have alignment boxes that don't seem to fit the object.

Reverse Ends

Reverses the start and end settings. One-dimensional shapes have two endpoints—a start and an end. Normally, when you rotate a shape, the endpoints stay positioned in the same orientation with respect to one another.

Reverse Ends allows you to flip a shape inside its alignment box, switching the start and end. Use the Reverse Ends operation only after you have finished modifying a shape's geometry, because there are creation operations you can run that flip the orientation. This operation is particularly useful when it comes to lines, or any shape with a definite start and end, and not as useful on two dimensional objects.

Union

Union creates a single shape out of all selected shapes. Figure 9-5 shows three shapes before and after using Union.

Union creates the new shape from the exterior outline of the existing selected shapes. This means the new shape includes all the spaces, or mathematical points, that were in any of the original shapes. If the shapes you select don't overlap, the resulting shape will not look different from the original shapes, but it will behave as a single shape; they will act almost as if they are a grouped, but they cannot be separated in any way.

Union can be used only on 2-D shapes.

NOTE   *Using the Combine or Union operations is not the same as grouping shapes. When you group shapes, you can still edit the grouped shapes individually. When you use the Combine operation, you create a single shape; the original shapes can no longer be edited separately.*

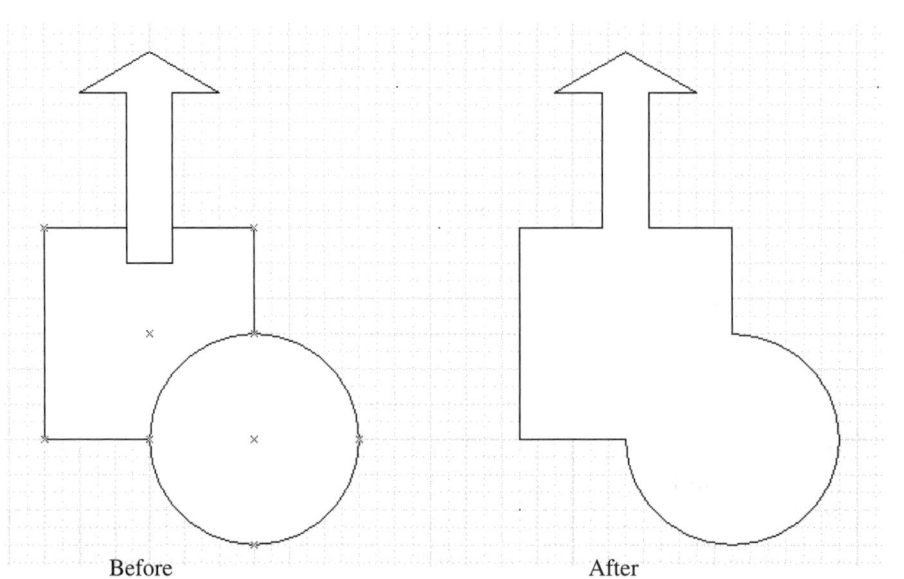

Before   After

FIGURE 9-5   Shapes merged using the Union operation

Combine

Combine creates a single shape out of all selected shapes and deletes the area where the original shapes overlap. Figure 9-6 shows three shapes before and after using the Combine operation.

Combine is the reverse of Union, which joins any shared space. Combine removes all shared spaces and then creates a new shape from the exterior outline of the shapes with holes where they overlap. Combine is particularly useful for making frames of shapes. The first step for the example shape shown in Figure 9-4 was made by using Combine on two seven-pointed star shapes stacked exactly one on top of the other, one slightly smaller. This created a seven-pointed star frame that could then be copied to create the second star frame.

You can use the Combine operation on both 1-D and 2-D shapes.

Fragment

Fragment breaks overlapping shapes into pieces along their original exterior lines. This means overlapping shapes get as many pieces as they have overlaps. Figure 9-7 shows shapes before and after using the Fragment operation.

9

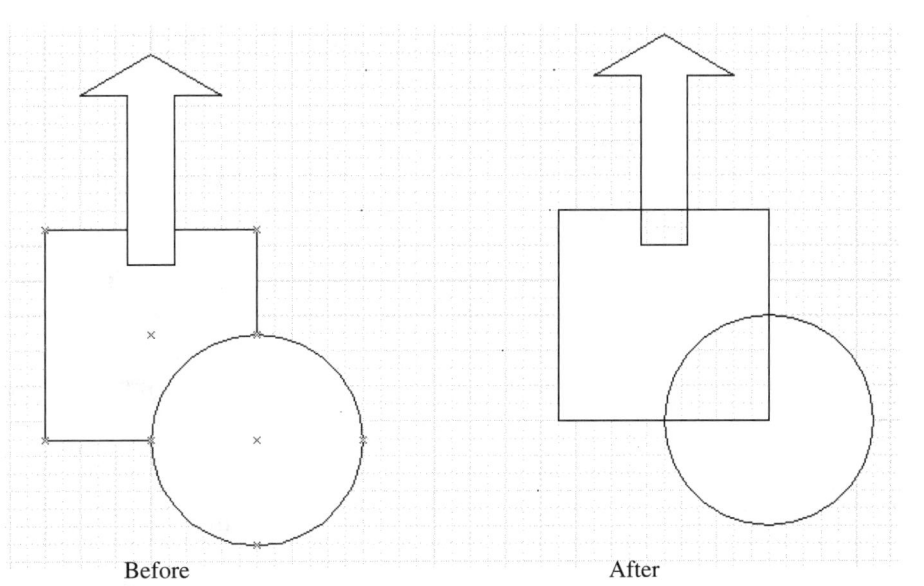

Before   After

FIGURE 9-6   Shapes merged using the Combine operation

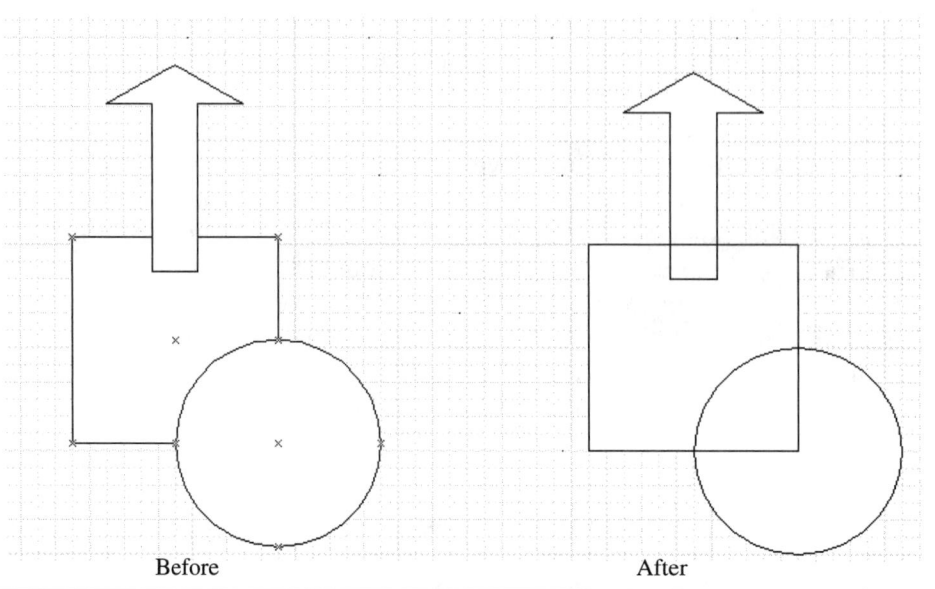

Before   After

FIGURE 9-7   Shapes created using the Fragment operation

This operation creates new shapes where the original shapes intersect, resulting in smaller pieces of the original shapes. You can then use the pieces individually, or you can use Union to merge some of them together. Fragment is especially useful when you need only part of a shape. You can use Fragment with a standard shape (such as a rectangle) to break off pieces of other shapes. The pieces can then be added to other shapes using Combine and Union.

You can also use a line and shape with Fragment to slice the shape into pieces. Since all Fragment looks for is where shapes intersect, you can use a line as a knife to cut a 2-D shape. Several lines that spider-web over a shape would give you wedges of a shape you could use.

Using three or more straight lines together, depending on their layout, gives you several shapes defined by the intersection of the lines. If, for example, the lines are laid out such that they define a triangle, then when you use Fragment the lines disappear and in their place Visio creates a triangle. This can be especially useful if you want to create several boxes. Lay out the lines in the form of a grid and you'll get as many boxes as there are spaces in the grid.

The example seven-pointed star, shown in Figure 9-4, was copied and then rotated until two seven-pointed stars sat on top of each other. Then they were fragmented. The fragments were then rejoined, using Union, to create one shape out of the pieces of each star.

Fragment makes pieces of 2-D shapes, and uses 1-D shapes as knives or dividers.

Intersect

Intersect creates a single shape out of the area where two or more shapes intersect. It is like the opposite of Combine. Figure 9-8 shows shapes before and after using Intersect.

Intersect only works on shapes that intersect. If you try to use Intersect on shapes that don't intersect, the result will be no shape at all. This operation also doesn't work on 1-D lines, because it uses combined surface areas and 1-D lines have no surface area.

However, Intersect can be very useful when you want to slice off part of a shape. Since it only allows you to take the part of shapes that overlap, you can get just part of one 2-D shape by using another 2-D shape like a knife to slice it off. In Figure 9-8, a square was used to slice off part of a seven-pointed star, but any shape can act as a knife with Intersect. Also, since Visio only takes the common area of two shapes with Intersect, it doesn't matter which shape you choose first before using it.

9

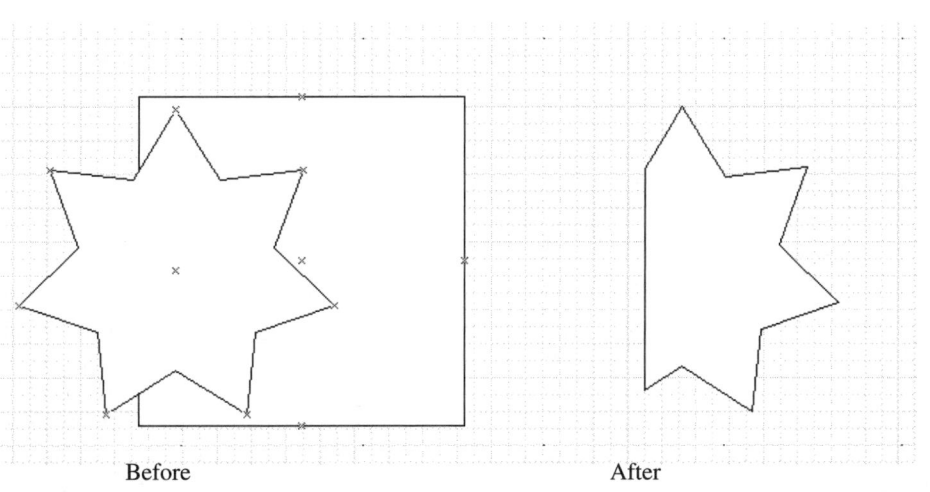

Before   After

FIGURE 9-8   A shape created using the Intersect operation

 *If your shapes don't overlap, and you use Intersect, Visio removes both shapes and leaves you with nothing at all on the page.*

Subtract

Subtract removes the area where one shape overlaps another. Figure 9-9 shows shapes before and after using Subtract.

Subtract is useful when you want most of a shape, but need to remove a part of it. This operation was designed to slice out a piece of a shape, and only that.

The order in which you select shapes is very important when using Subtract. The shape you select first remains, and the shape you select second—the "cutting shape"—disappears completely. In the middle shape shown in figure 9-9 the square was selected first, and the circle was the cutting shape. In the example on the right, the circle was selected first, and the square was the cutting shape.

Join

Join creates a new shape out of straight-line or arc segments. To use Join, first create the line segments, second arrange the segments however you want the shape to, and last use Join to merge them into a single shape. If you place all the segments start to end, Join creates a complete 2-D shape.

It can be difficult to see if the lines truly start and end in the same place. Increasing to maximum magnification can be helpful.

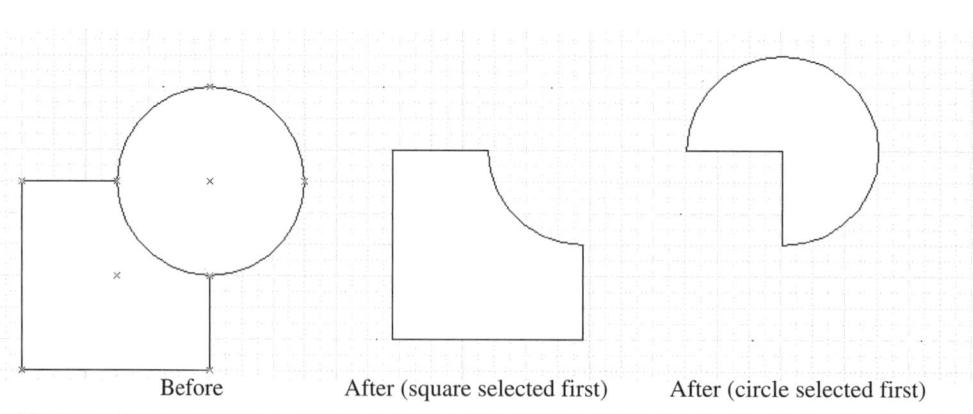

| Before | After (square selected first) | After (circle selected first) |

FIGURE 9-9   Shapes created using the Subtract operation

Trim

Trim separates any shape when it intersects itself. It turns a 2-D object into connected 1-D objects based on the outline of the selected shape. Trim can also turn a set of 1-D lines into four smaller lines, using their intersection point as a break point.

Generally, once you use Trim on a shape you can no longer fill the shape, because it no longer functions like a 2-D shape. Instead it behaves as a series of connected 1-D shapes. Trim acts like the opposite of Join, turning shapes into lines instead of the other way around. If you choose to trim two or more 1-D shapes that intersect, the result is several line segments outlining the shapes and separated at all points of intersection.

> NOTE   *Visio's Trim functions like the AutoCAD function Trim.*

Offset

Offset creates two or more new shapes at a specified distance from the original shape. Figure 9-10 shows a line, circle, and five pointed star that have used Offset.

9

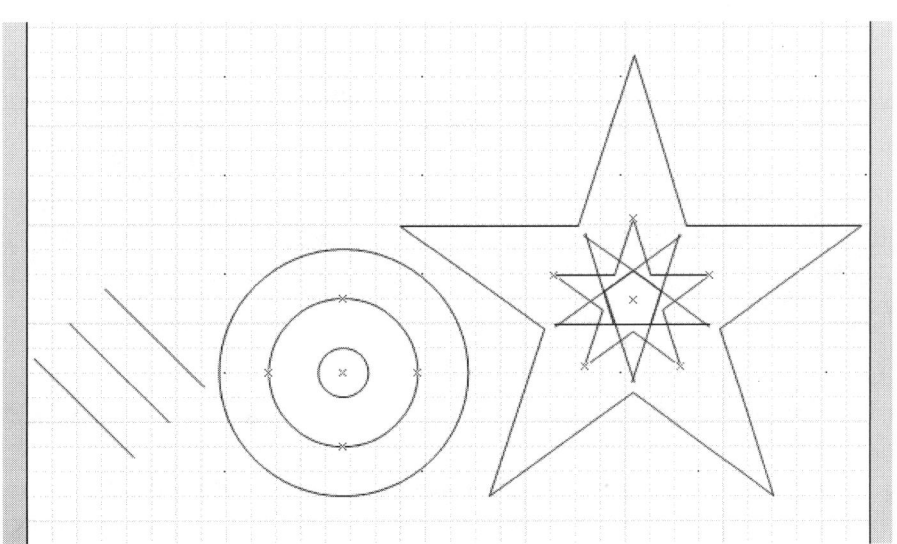

FIGURE 9-10   Shapes creating using the Offset operation

Offset is most often used with 1-D lines. Creating two lines that are centered on your first line could be a road, or anything else that has a measured distance and a center point. Offset is also very useful with simple 2-D shapes, like the circle. The bull's eye effect would make a nice addition to your drawing. Since Offset uses the exterior line of the shape as its starting point, when you use Offset on closed, simple, 2-D shapes you generally get one smaller version of the shape on the inside, and one larger version on the outside.

But as you can see in Figure 9-10, Offset can give some very interesting and unexpected shapes with more complicated 2-D shapes. The shapes generated by using Offset on the five-pointed star are actually a series of unconnected angles and lines, but it is a very interesting set of lines and angles. The more angles and points a shape has, the more complicated the shapes resulting from Offset.

To use Offset, first move the shape onto the page, then select Tools | Operations | Offset. Visio displays the Offset dialog box appears, as shown here:

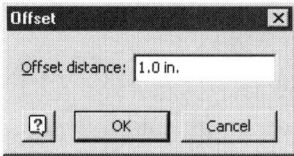

Choose the distance between the original shape and the new shapes, and then click OK.

If you want the small shape inside the original 2-D shape, you'll need to choose the offset to be less than half the size of the shape.

If the original shape is a 1-D line, Visio creates lines on both sides of the original line at the distance you specify. If the original object is 2-D shape, Visio creates 1-D lines around the shape in such a way that the new shapes do not intersect with the original shape.

Fit Curve

Fit Curve creates an arc wherever a straight line appears in the selected shape. Figure 9-11 shows a cross shape before and after using Fit Curve.

Fit Curve turns all straight lines into arcs that have the same vertices as the original line segments. If the shape you start with is a closed 2-D shape, the new shape will also be a closed 2-D shape. Fit Curve doesn't work on simple 1-D lines,

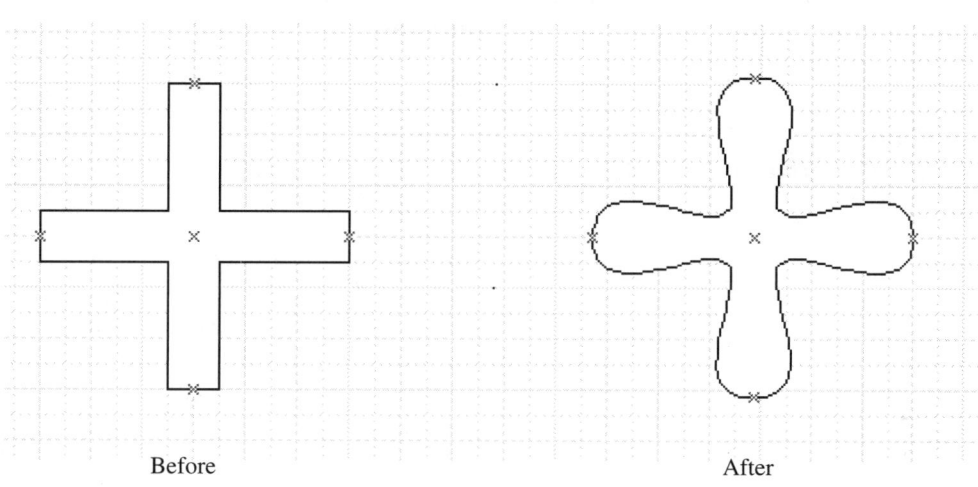

Before   After

FIGURE 9-11   A cross shape before and after using the Fit Curve operation

but it does work on a series of 1-D lines as long as they are attached to each other and are at an angle to each other.

A square ia a good example of how Fit Curve affects 2-D shapes. When you Fit Curve a square you create a circle with the same radius as the distance from the center of the square to the corner of the square. The circle also has connection points where the old square's corners were instead of at the top, bottom, and sides like on the circle shape you can drag from the stencil.

To use Fit Curve, drag the shape you want to curve onto the drawing page, then select Tools | Operations | Fit Curve. Visio opens the Fit Curve dialog box shown here:

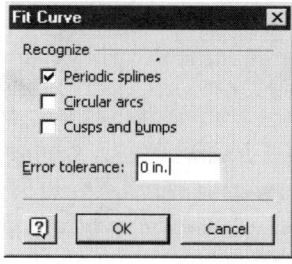

The settings in the Fit Curve dialog box set how close your new shape will be to the old shape.

■ **Periodic Splines**   Sets that if you started with a closed 2-D shape, you'll end with a smoother variation on that closed 2-D shape.

■ **Circular Arcs**   Sets that intersections in your old shape are replaced with arcs.

■ **Cusps and Bumps**   Retains the angles inherent in the design, when checked.

■ **Error Tolerance**   Sets how different from your old shape you want the new shape. The larger the number, the more different the new shape. If you enter 0, the new shape will have the exact same vertices, and go through as many of the points of the old shape as possible.

NOTE   *The more vertices a shape has, the smaller the apparent change when you use Fit Curve.*

Understanding ShapeSheets

Chapter 4 introduced the idea that ShapeSheets are the power behind Visio. As you alter and create shapes you may wonder how Visio keeps track of all the information inherent in a shape, or you may want to know how to control a shape beyond the alterations available with the Pencil tool or with the operations. ShapeSheets allow you to modify the formulas that affect how a shape behaves in Visio.

All the shapes that come with Visio already have ShapeSheets attached, and every shape you create in Visio automatically has a ShapeSheet as well. This section walks you through basic ShapeSheets—the one for a square and for a more complicated shape—and shows you how to alter the ShapeSheet to change how a shape looks or behaves.

Then this section introduces you to using Visual Basic for Applications (VBA) to alter the way your shapes or documents behave, and addresses creating and adding Add-ins created in other languages.

TIP   *You can right-click and select to see a ShapeSheet for any shape if you are in Developer Mode. You also have access, in Developer Mode, to the developer documentation, which can be invaluable for working with ShapeSheets or VBA. To get to Developer Mode, select Tools | Options. On the Advanced Tab, under Developer Settings, check the box next to Run in Developer Mode, then click OK.*

Basic ShapeSheets

The simple ShapeSheet for a square, shown in Figure 9-12, has 15 tables.

Though the parts of a ShapeSheet look like tables, Visio refers to them as sections. Sections is a better name since it implies a group of like information instead of simply rows and cells.

> **NOTE** *A great deal of information about ShapeSheets is in the developer documentation that comes with Visio. If you haven't selected to install the developer documentation when you installed Visio, you will be prompted for your Visio disk when you select Developer Reference from the Help menu.*

The 15 sections in the square ShapeSheet are present in almost every different shape in Visio by default, though for a square more than half of them are effectively blank. Table 9-1 lists all the sections in a ShapeSheet for a square, and the parts of shape behavior they control.

Drawing1:Page-1:Square <SHAPE>

Shape Transform

Width	1.5 in.	PinX	2.5 in.	FlipX	FALSE
Height	1.5 in.	PinY	6.5 in.	FlipY	FALSE
Angle	0 deg.	LocPinX	Width*0.5	ResizeMode	0
		LocPinY	Height*0.5		

User-defined Cells

	Value	Prompt
User.visKeywords	"Square,Four,sided,customized,drag	No Formula
User.visVersion	10	No Formula

Connection Points

	X	Y	DirX / A	DirY / B	Type / C
1	Width*0.5	Height*0.5	No Formula	No Formula	No Formula
2	Width*1	Height*0	No Formula	No Formula	No Formula
3	Width*0	Height*0	No Formula	No Formula	No Formula
4	Width*1	Height*1	No Formula	No Formula	No Formula
5	Width*0	Height*1	No Formula	No Formula	No Formula

Geometry 1

	Geometry1.NoFill	FALSE		Geometry1.NoLine	No Formula		Geometry1.NoShow	No Formula		Geometry

	Name	X	Y	A	B	C	D
1	MoveTo	Width*0	Height*0				
2	LineTo	Width*1	Height*0				
3	LineTo	Width*1	Height*1				
4	LineTo	Width*0	Height*1				
5	LineTo	Geometry1.X1	Geometry1.Y1				

Protection

	LockWidth	0		LockBegin	0		LockTextEdit	0

FIGURE 9-12 ShapeSheet for a square

Section Name	Information the section controls
Shape Transform	The first table in every ShapeSheet is Shape Transform. This table lists and controls how the shape appears on the page. It lists current values for height and width as well as position markers.
User-defined Variables	This is one of the most changed sections in any ShapeSheet. This contains not only the keywords set for any shape, but also any new or special behaviors for a shape are defined here. When you are adding behavior to a ShapeSheet, this is the section you'll likely add them to. Calls to added programs, or the passing of information to Add-ins generally happens here.
Connection Points	The definitions for where connection points are on the shape are kept in this section. As a general rule connection points are some formula based on width or height.
GeometryX	There can be more than one Geometry section, and the X can be any number from 1 to 100, but the numbering always starts at 1. This section controls the geometry settings for the shape. This is where the Visio shape's look is defined. When you need to alter how something looks, alter the formulas for Geometry.
Protection	This controls which of the shape attributes is protected and therefore unchangeable. The options here are the same as they are in the Shape | Protection window. When something has been locked, the value is set to 1.
Miscellaneous	Sets the options that don't fit into any of the above sections. If you want to turn off control handles, or the alignment box, this section is where you do it. Something in this section is turned on if it's set to TRUE.
Line Format	Controls how the line displays, including it's pattern, weight and color.
Fill Format	Controls the color and fill pattern for the shape, as well as any shadow settings.
Character	Sets how any text attached to the shape behaves. You can see in a new square that all text is set to 8pt. type by default.
Tabs	Sets any tabs for the text attached to the shape.
Text Block Format	Sets the margins and text background for the text block attached to the shape, as well as the default tab stop to use if there are not settings in Tabs.
Events	These are the possible actions that could trigger something to happen with your shape. The most commonly-used is the double-click action, listed here as: EventDblClick. For most shapes, that event calls OPENTXTWIN() or opens the text editing window. All the events listed in this section can have actions they call. If you need a new event, you'll add a row to this section.
Image Properties	These are the properties set for any shape that is an image, but is also included on many basic ShapeSheets.
Glue Info	Sets the gluing options for 1-D shapes.
Shape Layout	These settings control how other shapes treat this shape, and how layout happens around this shape. Many of these settings are the same as the ones on the Placement tab of the Behavior window.

TABLE 9-1   Sections in the ShapeSheet for a square

You can control the display of sections by clicking on their titlebars. When you click on a displayed section's titlebar it hides all the rows of that section. You can see the rows again by clicking on the titlebar again.

Altering ShapeSheet cells

Of the 15 sections in the square ShapeSheet, only about three or four are often altered, and usually for a relatively small set of reasons, like changing the geometry or adding a function. This section addresses the most common changes, namely those to the geometry of a shape. By examining how to change the geometry using ShapeSheet, you'll see how to alter the formulas, add functions, and even add a section to your ShapeSheet.

Before you can alter the ShapeSheet cells, however, you first need to learn your way around the ShapeSheet. Figure 9-13 shows the complete Visio window with a ShapeSheet for a square open.

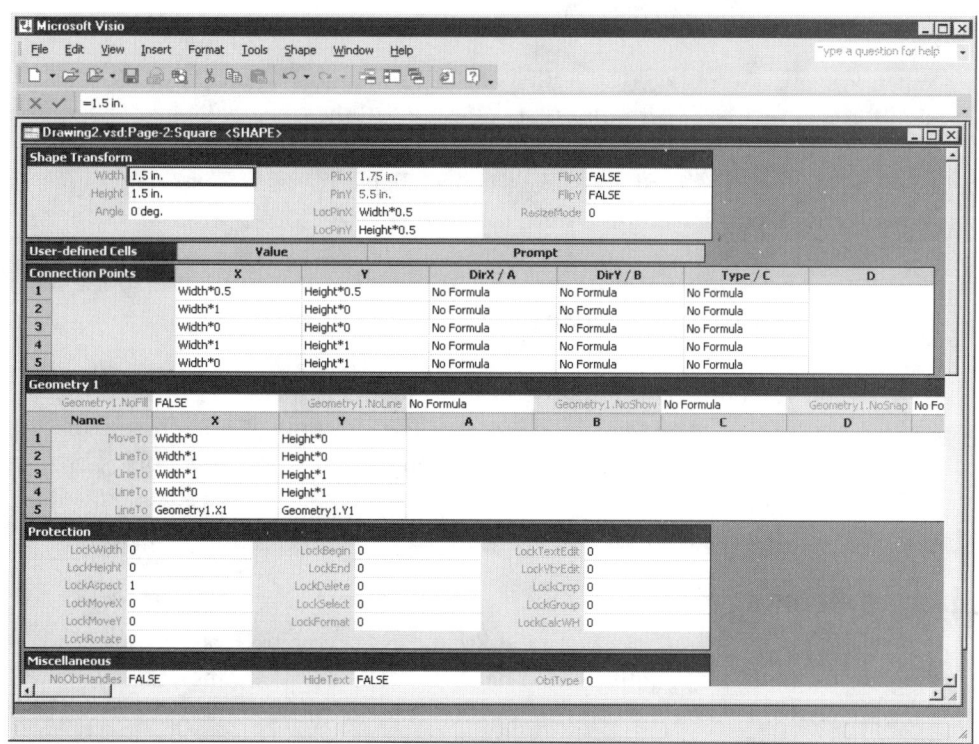

FIGURE 9-13   Visio window with ShapeSheet open

As you can see in Figure 9-13, Visio alters the toolbars and menus when it opens a ShapeSheet, and includes a new toolbar at the bottom, the formula bar. This formula bar operates like the similar bar in Microsoft Excel. Information that Visio displays here will be a value if it is a defining value for the shape, like a position or height number, but most of the time the information you'll see here will be formulas. These formulas control how the shape behaves and looks. To alter a formula, click on the cell you want to change, and then type over the old formula in the formula bar.

> **NOTE** *To display values for all the cells in a ShapeSheet, choose View | Values. To view Formulas choose View | Formulas. When you select a cell with values displayed, Visio displays the formula in the formula bar.*

The formulas in Visio operate much the same as in any other desktop program. An asterisk (*) means something is multiplied, a plus sign (+) means something is added, and a back slash (/) means something is divided. Any word generally refers to another cell in the ShapeSheet, but can also refer to Add-Ins or other code inside Visio.

When you are altering cells in a ShapeSheet, remember the basics of formulas, and don't create recursive formulas that call on a cell that then calls back on the original cell. Also don't forget to save your shape by dragging it back to a stencil once you have changed the ShapeSheet for that shape. If you forget to drag your shape back, you won't have it as a master to use later.

> **TIP** *A good reference for writing formulas for Microsoft Excel is also useful when you are creating formulas in Visio.*

Also, when you click on a cell to see its formula, Visio draws a black box around the part of the shape that cell describes. For example, if you clicked on the cell for X coordinate for the first connection point, Visio would put a black box around that connection point. This helps you see which part of the shape you are dealing with.

Altering Geometry

Now that you know your way around the ShapeSheet, you are ready to start altering the formulas that control shape behavior. The most common change is how the shape displays on the drawing page, or the shape's geometry.

The GeometryX sections control the look of a shape. In theory there can be almost an infinite number of Geometry sections, but they always start with the number 1 and work their way up. The square only has one Geometry section, shown in Figure 9-14.

For a simple, rectangular shape, the geometry is fairly easy to understand. The first row tells Visio to start at Width*0 and Height*0, which means directly at the same point that defines width and height, which for a square is the lower left-hand corner. You can verify that this is the point of origin by clicking on either of the cells in row 1 and Visio will put a black box around that point on the shape.

The next row in the geometry is a LineTo row, which means that it instructs Visio to draw a line from the last defined point to another point, defined by Width*1 and Height*0. This means the new point is over one width value to the positive, but is the same height. This point is the lower right-hand corner of the square.

The next row works the same way, drawing a line from the last point to Width*1 and Height*1, or the upper right-hand corner. Then row 4 tells Visio to draw a line to Width*0 and Height*1, the upper left-hand corner.

Finally row 5 tells Visio to go back where it started by referencing the first cells in this section. The section is identified by name, and so is each cell. Geometry1.X1 means the first row, in the X column, on the Geometry1 table. Visio guarantees that the shape is closed by drawing a line back to the beginning by referencing its name instead of by giving its location.

If you want to alter the geometry of a shape in a way that you can't using any other way in Visio, you can almost certainly do it by altering the GeometryX section for the shape. You can remove vertices by removing rows, you can add vertices by adding rows, and you can even alter where vertices happen by altering the formulas already there. Figure 9-15 has a standard square and two with altered geometry. The first altered square has had the first cell in row 2 altered to read Width*.5.

NOTE   *The other columns on a GeometryX section control how arcs and other complicated lines behave between the points defined in the X and Y columns. View the ShapeSheet for a circle to see these columns in use.*

Connection Points	X	Y	DirX / A	DirY / B	Type / C	D
1	Width*0.5	Height*0.5	No Formula	No Formula	No Formula	
2	Width*1	Height*0	No Formula	No Formula	No Formula	
3	Width*0	Height*0	No Formula	No Formula	No Formula	
4	Width*1	Height*1	No Formula	No Formula	No Formula	
5	Width*0	Height*1	No Formula	No Formula	No Formula	

FIGURE 9-14   Geometry1 for a square

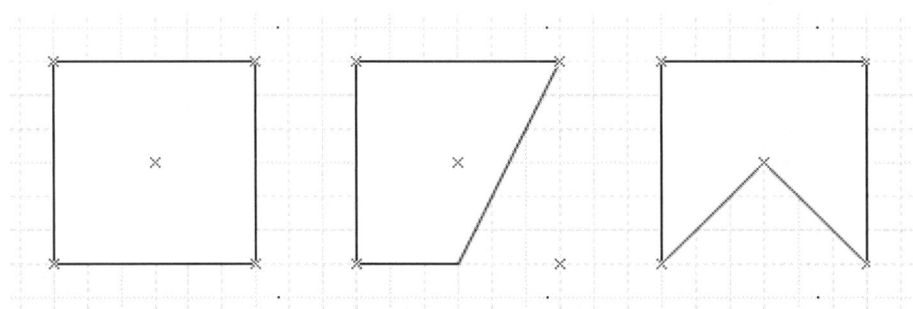

FIGURE 9-15 Standard square and two with altered geometry

You can also alter how the line between two points is drawn by altering the row type that contains those points. You could make the line between two shapes an arc instead of a straight line if those points are not perfectly horizontal or vertical. The second altered square shown in Figure 9-15 is a square that's had a row added before the old row 2. This was a ArcTo row type instead of simply a LineTo like all the others in Geometry1. The X and Y were set to Width*0.5 and Height*0.5 receptively.

To change a row type, select the row by clicking on the row number. Then right-click on the row and select Change Row Type from the right-click menu (or select Edit | Change Row Type). Visio displays the Change Row Type window, shown in Figure 9-16.

To change the type of row, select a different one from the list and then click OK. Visio automatically redraws the shape to conform to the new row settings. You can also use the same right-click menu to add or delete rows in the section.

NOTE *Not all sections have row types you can change, and the window shown in Figure 9-16 is only for the geometry rows.*

As you might imagine, by adding, subtracting, and changing rows you can significantly alter the look of a shape. If you want to use this method for changing the look of a shape, take a few moments and look at the geometry sections of several shapes that look similar to the one you are trying to achieve. Using the settings from shapes that are close saves you a lot of time when you try to alter the formulas for geometry to get the look you are after.

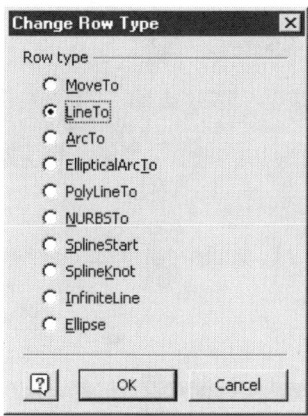

FIGURE 9-16   Change Row Type window for a geometry row

Adding a Function

Changing the geometry by adding or changing rows works well for simple shapes that have straight lines or simple arcs. But if your shape needs to change dynamically in response, or if your shape's geometry is defined by trigonometric functions, you'll need to add a function to your cells.

Visio comes with some 150 functions you can add to your ShapeSheet cells. They include all the major trigonometric functions, basic algebraic functions, and even functions to include the time and date currently set on the computer. Within these 150 functions you'll use some 30 or so for most geometric changes.

The best example of a simple shape that has functions included in the geometry section of the ShapeSheet is the rounded square. The Controls, Geometry1, and Scratch sections for the ShapeSheet are shown in Figure 9-17.

If you look at the first row in the Geometry1 section, you'll see that the cells include far more complicated text than the simple width and height references in the square. There is a control point on a rounded square that sets the amount of curvature in the corners. Since Visio can't know what the curvature will be set at for the shape, functions are needed to compute the settings for the sides, and where all the angles meet up.

It can be a little difficult to follow, but basically the settings for the geometry are set by comparing the value of the height or width of the square with the distances the control is set from zero. The control value is kept in the Control section. It is compared to the value in the Scratch section, which limits the control

9

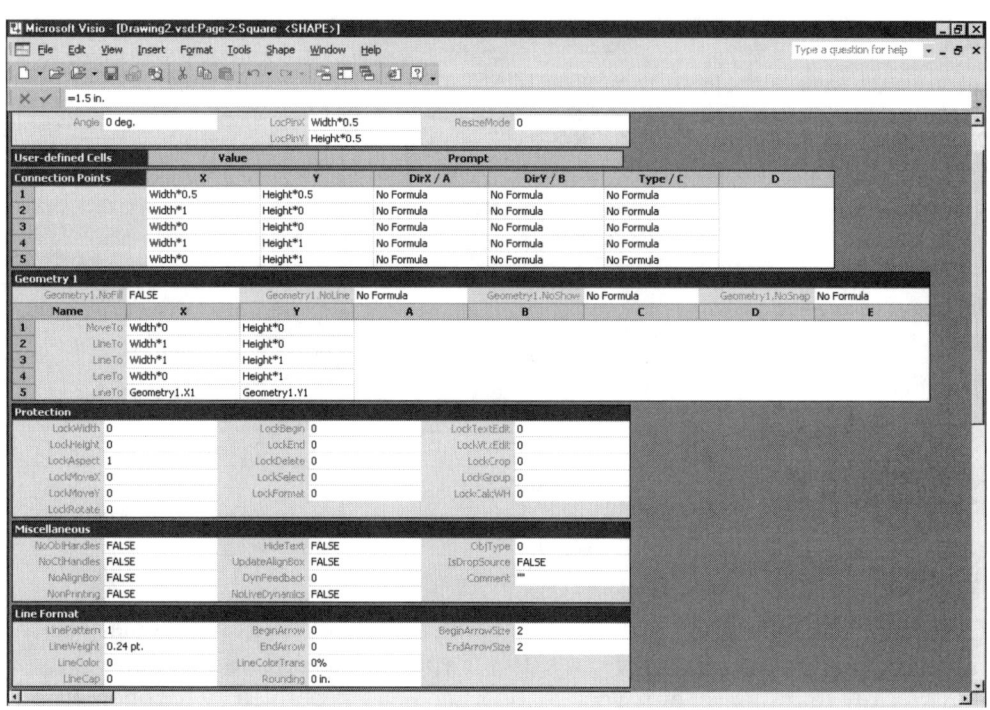

FIGURE 9-17   ShapeSheet for a rounded square

value so it remains positive and not more than half the width of the shape. Then the rows in the Geomerty1 section take the minimum or maximum of these reference numbers and uses them as settings for height and width.

If you need to include functions in your formulas, you'll need to follow these simple steps.

1. Select the cell in which you want to include the function.

2. Place your cursor where you want the function to be in the cell on the formula bar.

3. Choose Insert | Function. Visio displays the Function window, shown in Figure 9-18.

4. Choose the function you'd like to include, and then click OK.

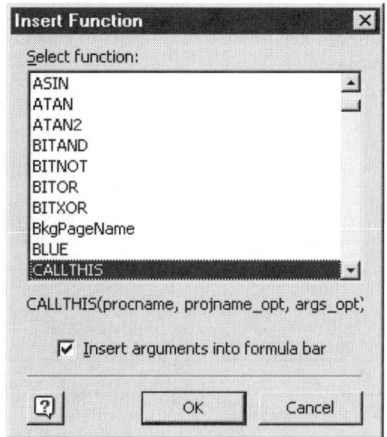

FIGURE 9-18   Insert Function window

5. Visio includes the function and leaves places for you to include the variables and references you need to make the function work.

TIP   *The Developer's Reference that comes with Visio lists all the available functions, the variables they call, and their intended use.*

Adding Sections

Once you have added rows, and then functions, you may find that you are trying to squish too much information into one section. Adding a section is a quick process.

First, open the ShapeSheet you want to add to. Then select Insert | Section. Visio displays the Insert Section window, shown in Figure 9-19.

Choose the type of section you need to add. Remember, not all kinds of sections are available for every ShapeSheet because some are only allowed once and already exist, and some are just not available for some shapes.

TIP   *As with functions, all the available types of Sections are listed in the Developers Reference that comes with Visio.*

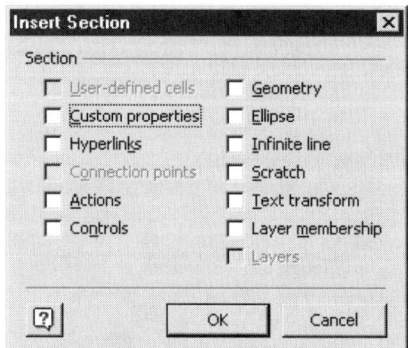

Insert Section window

Programming Visio to Create Solutions

Beyond all the alterations to shapes, there are times you need Visio to act in a new way, or you simply need a custom behavior for Visio. These customized needs are called Solutions. This section walks you through the most common way of programming Visio solutions, Visual Basic for Applications (VBA), but also briefly discusses using other Automation-ready programming languages with Visio.

Creating Add-ons and Working with VBA

With all the operations, the ShapeSheet options, and every other way you can alter a shape in Visio, there are still times when Visio can't do what you need it to do. For example, if you need to have a message display when a shape is dragged to the drawing page, there is no way to accomplish this with a ShapeSheet alone.

This is the time to resort to the Visual Basic Editor that comes with Visio. Visio also takes other types of Add-ons as well, but let's leave those until later in this chapter.

NOTE   *The Visio Developers Reference has a special section for add-ons, called Automation Reference.*

The Visual Basic Editor helps you add new behavior to your documents to respond to events. As with most Microsoft applications, Visual Basic for Applications is how macros and more complicated behaviors are created in Visio. Access the Visual Basic Editor for Visio by choosing Tools | Macros | Visual

Basic Editor. Figure 9-20 shows a Visual Basic Editor screen for a Visio document.

View all the Visual Basic code in your document by double-clicking on the document icon in the upper left-hand window called the Project window. This gives you a new window (called the Code window) in the main section of the editor listing all the VBA in the document, like the example shown in Figure 9-20.

When you want to create a new behavior for a shape, or when you want to have Visio start a process when you alter your document in some way, you need to have Visio act on an event. Visio triggers events when something happens, such as opening a new document, adding a shape, or even deleting a page. These events can be captured by VBA which lets you identify an action and link it to the event. An action is a type of method, and is launched by Visio when the event takes place.

To add an action, first you need to select the event. You can select an event to respond to in your document by first choosing Document from the left drop-down list in the Code window. Then the right drop-down menu lists all the available

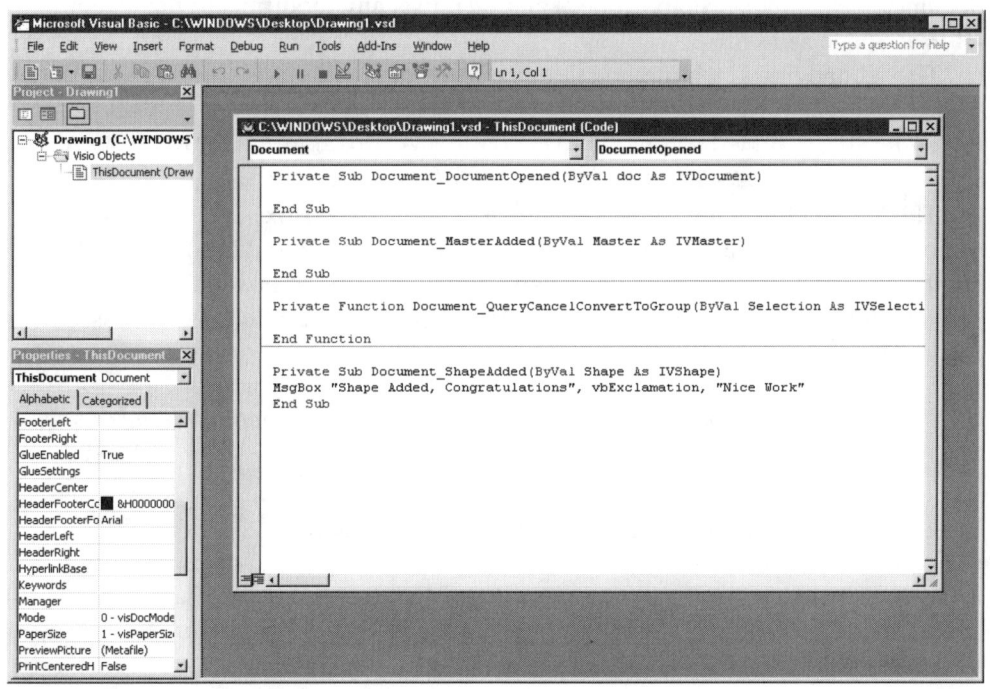

FIGURE 9-20   Visual Basic Editor

events that Visio can capture. Select an event from the right drop-down list, and Visio adds code signifying the event to the Code window.

Now that you have a selected an event, you can add the action Visio is supposed to take when this event occurs. You can look at all the available methods, including actions, by opening the Object Browser library. Access the library by choosing View | Object Browser.

> TIP　*If you plan to edit the VBA for your Visio documents, a good VBA reference is almost a requirement.*

The example shown in Figure 9-20 has a Message Box method launched by adding a shape to the page. The syntax works like this:

The first line shows the event you are using to trigger the method:

```
Private Sub Document_ShapeAdded(ByVal Shape As IVShape)
```

This first line lists that you are triggering an event when a shape is added to the document (Document_ShapeAdded) and then lists any modifiers to that event (ByVal Shape as IVShape).

The second line is the method that is triggered:

```
MsgBox "Shape Added, Congratulations", vbExclamation, "Nice Work"
```

This second line calls the Message Box method (MsgBox) and then lists the options that define the message box. "Shape Added, Congratulations" is the text displayed in the message box. vbExclamation is the type of box, and will give a exclamation point in a yellow triangle. "Nice Work" is the title for the message box.

> TIP　*You can see what options are available for a given method in the Object Browser.*

The third line ends the event trigger, and the method:

```
End Sub
```

Figure 9-21 shows the message box created by this method.

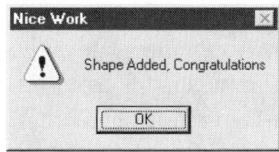

| FIGURE 9-21 | Example message box |

Going Further with VBA

So far in this section, you've seen the most basic kind of VBA programming. VBA is a powerful tool that can totally reformat how Visio works for you. VBA is a complete programming language on its own, and is used primarily with Microsoft products and similar desktop programs.

To get the most out of creating custom solutions with Visio, you'll need to learn more about VBA. Events, methods, objects, and properties are all under the purview of VBA, and you'll likely need a book all about Visual Basic for Applications.

Also, don't forget the extensive documentation available with Visio in the Developers Reference. There you'll find the object model for Visio, as well as all the events, objects, methods, and properties particular to Visio's needs of VBA.

9

Using COM, C++, and VB to Create Solutions

If you don't want to create your solution by programming in VBA, or if you want to create a stand-alone program instead of nesting your solution inside Visio, you'll need to use another programming language. As stated in Visio's developer help documentation, you can create your own solutions in any of the languages that adhere to the COM standards, in other words, any programming language that supports Automation.

Both C++ and VB are common languages to produce programs that support the Automation standards. This means you can create your own custom solutions that interact with Visio. It also means you can use your new program with other COM-based programs. Most of the Microsoft Office Suite uses these same COM standards.

TIP

For more information about COM, see "Inside COM" by Dale Rogerson. For information about creating VB for application use, see "VB COM" by Thomas Lewis.

Summary

In this chapter, you learned how to create your own shapes both by modifying existing shapes and by creating new shapes from scratch. You also learned how to alter ShapeSheet and create custom solutions with VBA. You are encouraged to use Visio's online help to further explore these topics.

In the next chapter, you will learn how to use the Microsoft Visio Professional Manufacturing and Building Plan solutions.

Chapter 10

Engineering, CAD, and Building Planning Diagrams

How to...

- Understand Visio Professional
- Use Precision Drawing Tools
- Creating Engineering Diagrams
- Using Facility Management Templates
- Creating Mechanical Engineering Drawings
- Working with CAD drawings

In the last chapter, you learned how to create custom shapes and solutions with Visio. You learned how to integrate newly created masters into your creation process, and you learned how to add programming into your solution creation process.

In this chapter, you'll learn about Visio Professional. You'll learn how to make the most of the precision drawing tools, how to work with CAD drawings, and how to create engineering drawings. You'll also learn about the facilities management tools that come with Visio Professional.

Understanding Visio Professional

Visio Professional was created for advanced business, network design, engineering, development, architectural, and drafting users. This chapter deals with the engineering and drafting uses of Visio Professional, and Chapter 11 handles the advanced business and computer network designer uses. Visio Professional includes all the stencils and templates included with Visio Standard and has additional templates and stencils geared for the technical worker. Visio Professional includes eight additional solution folders with more than forty additional templates.

Most basic users won't need Visio Professional, but if you need to take your drawings farther, or if you need to work with precise complicated diagrams, then Visio Professional is for you. For example, an architect can quickly lay out the framework of a building core, including dimensions and form. Floor plans can be used as backgrounds for the mechanical drawings, or they can be converted into CAD drawings for use in other programs.

Visio Professional also includes easy-to-use tools for the general business user to create detailed floor plans even if they don't know anything about architecture or space planning. For example, you could use Visio Professional to design new shelves for your garage. With Visio Professional you could quickly lay out the garage space, add new cabinets, drop in a car shape and see how much space is left over for golf clubs or a lawn mower.

The following table lists the additional solution folders and templates in Visio Professional.

NOTE   *The first four solutions listed in Table 10-1 are covered in this chapter. The second four are covered in Chapter 11.*

Exploring Precision Drawing Tools

The precision drawing tools are included in Visio Standard; however, they are used to their fullest with the Visio Professional. Often, engineering and architectural drawings require accurate, precise measurements. Visio Professional provides drawing and positioning tools that are easy and powerful for the most complex drawing types.

10

Solution Folder	Templates
Building Plan	Electric & Telecom, Floor Plan, Home Plan, HVAC Control Logic Diagram, HVAC Plans, Office Layout, Plant Layout, Plumbing & Piping Plan, Reflected Ceiling Plan, Security and Access Plan, Site Plan, Space Plan.
Electrical Engineering	Basic Electrical, Circuit & Logic, Industrial Control Systems, Systems.
Mechanical Engineering	Part & Assembly Drawing, Fluid Power.
Process Engineering	Piping and Instrumentation Diagram, Process Flow Diagram.
Database	Database Model Diagram, Express-G, ORM Diagram.
Network	Logical Network Diagram, Visio Network Equipment Sampler, Basic Network Active Directory, LDAP Directory, Novell Directory Services.
Software	UML Model Diagram, Data Flow Model Diagram, Enterprise Application, Windows User Interface, Jackson, ROOM, Program Structure, COM and OLE.
Web Diagram	Conceptual Web Site, Web Site Map.

TABLE 10-1   Visio Professional Solutions

Understanding Drawing Scale and Diagram Size

In drawings that depict abstract concepts (for example, in flowcharts and organization charts), the scale of the drawings often isn't important. Plan shapes, on the other hand, represent real-world objects, which rarely are depicted at full size, and so drawing scale and page size can become very important.

The drawing scale and dimensioning tools can help you set up your Visio drawings with the drawing scale and units to create a wide range of engineering and architectural drawings. Both Visio Standard and Visio Professional use the same two ways to establish scale: drawing units and page units. *Drawing units* are measurements in the real world, while *page units* are measurements on the printed page. Scale is the ratio of the page units to the drawing units.

 *Scale is represented by two numbers in comparison with one another; for example 1/4" to 1' means a quarter inch on the drawing page equals one foot in real life.*

All templates in Visio open with a default scale. For example, the Floor Plan template opens with an architectural scale of 1:96. Some schematic drawings, such as electrical schematics, have a scale of 1:1. You can change the drawing scale at any time, and each page can have its own scale.

To change the scale of a drawing, first make sure the page you want to change the scale of is open. When the page is ready, choose File | Page Setup, and then choose the Drawing Scale tab, as shown in Figure 10-1

You can choose three types of scale on the Drawing Scale tab:

- **No Scale**   Sets the scale as 1:1.

- **Pre-Defined Scale**   Lists standard scales. Choose one of the types of scale from the first box, and then choose one of the different settings for that type.

- **Custom Scale**   Allows you to set any scale you choose. The first box represents the size on the page; the second box represents the size in real life.

 *You can change the units for the page on the Page Properties tab. Doing this also affects how the ruler displays.*

When you're done setting the drawing scale, click OK. Visio automatically updates the drawing page and resizes all the shapes that have a preset real size.

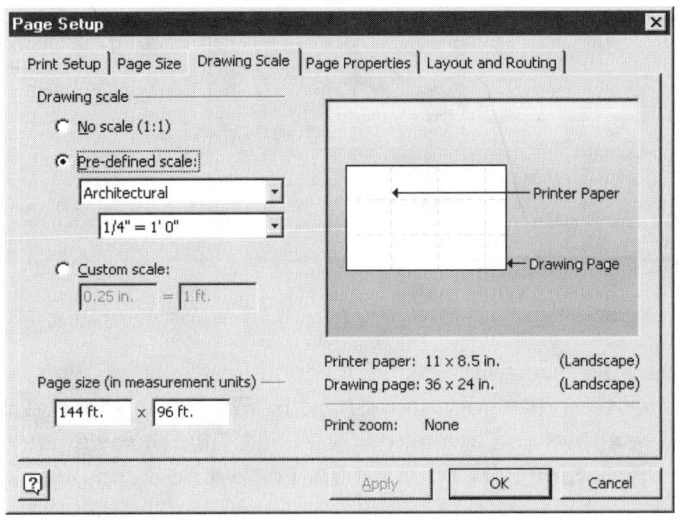

FIGURE 10-1 Page Setup window, Drawing Scale tab

Locating Shapes Precisely

In Chapter 3 you were introduced to the concept of grid lines, guidelines, and guides, as well as the tools for snapping and gluing. In Visio Professional, these tools become even more valuable, and they have additional functions that can help you create drawings faster and with greater ease.

Using Exact Coordinates to Position Shapes

Sometimes you need to know the exact coordinates of a shape. Every shape has a pin through its reference point that anchors the shape on the drawing page. The location of this pin is listed as a set of X and Y coordinate values, giving the location of the shape relative to the page coordinate system. For example, the pin point of a chair could be the center point, and where the center point is located is the X, Y coordinate pair.

To locate or move a shape by using exact coordinates, first drag or move the shape to the approximate location on the drawing page. Then choose View | Size & Position. This displays a set of values for the shape, including the coordinates, as shown in Figure 10-2. To move a shape to an exact location, enter values for the new location in the X and Y boxes. Click somewhere else on you Visio diagram when you're satisfied with the values, and Visio positions the shape.

X	720 in.	
Y	660 in.	
Width	4 ft.	
Height	1 ft.	
Angle	0 deg.	
Pin Pos	Center-Cente	

FIGURE 10-2   Size and Position window

Because the reference point sets the location for the shape, you may need to change where the reference point for a shape is. The Pin Pos box on the Size & Position window allows you to alter the position to one of several preselected places on the shape. Simply click on the Pin Pos box, and choose from the drop-down list.

> **TIP** *You can also make the Size and Position window Autohide by clicking on the pushpin icon on its toolbar.*

Visio also has is the ability to move shapes using the arrow keys. This feature is commonly known as *nudging*. Nudging allows you to select a shape and then change its position by very small increments using the arrow keys on the keyboard. Visio also give you the ability to nudge objects one pixel at a time by holding down SHIFT as you use the arrow keys.

If you need to move a shape a specific distance, use the Move command. This command allows you to specify the distance along the X and Y-axes, or the distance and the angle to move a shape.

> **TIP** *The Move command only exists in Visio Professional.*

To move a shape a specified distance:

1. Select the shape to move.

2. Choose Tools | Macros | Visio Extras | Move Shape. The Move dialog box appears, as shown here:

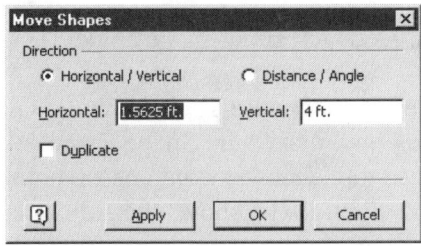

3. Choose either to move the shape by Horizontal and Vertical or by Distance and Degrees.

4. Enter the distances or degree settings into the dialog box.

5. Decide if you want to leave a copy of the shape in its original location, which you can do by selecting to duplicate.

6. Click OK to move the shape.

NOTE   *Clicking the Apply button allows you to see the impact of the move before you close the dialog box.*

Snapping to Points on Shapes

Snapping can be enhanced by deciding where and how you snap. You can snap to geometric points on shapes-such as endpoints, tangents, and intersections-for more accurate designs. This is very useful when you want to place a shape on another shape without knowing the exact coordinates of either one.

NOTE   *Snapping to geometric points in Visio Professional is similar to the object snaps used in CAD packages.*

To set snap settings, choose Tools | Snap & Glue. Under Currently Active, make sure that Snap is checked. Under Snap To, check Shape Handles, Shape Vertices, and Connection Points, and then click OK.

Using Advanced Snapping

When drawing in Visio, it's sometimes necessary to specify additional snap-to points. Visio includes shape extensions to give you maximum control over how your shapes snap. Extension lines appear when you position your pointer near the target point of the shape, allowing you to span to it there instead of just at a control point. You can draw shapes with exacting precision using shape extension lines,

10

since they provide visual feedback about shape angles, tangents, and other useful geometric relationships.

To turn on shape extensions, choose Tools | Snap & Glue. On the General tab of the Snap & Glue dialog box, make sure Shape Extensions is checked under Snap To. On the Advanced tab, choose the geometric options you want under "Shape extension options. Figure 10-3 shows the Advanced tab for the Snap & Glue dialog box:

The shape extension options are:

- **Alignment box extension**   Draws a line extended from the shape's alignment box.

- **Center alignment axes**   Draws a line extended from the center of the shape's alignment box.

- **Curve interior tangent**   Illustrates the curve's tangent at the midpoint of the arc segment when you move the cursor over an arc segment.

- **Segment endpoint**   Highlights the endpoint when you move the cursor over a line segment or arc segment. A line segment can include line shapes and lines used to create the sides of a polygon.

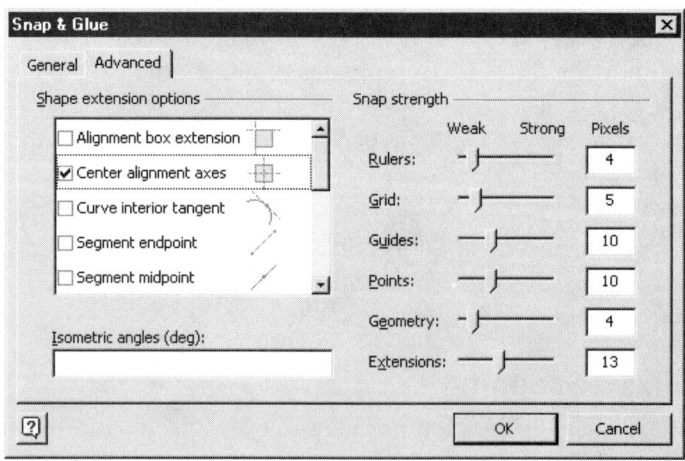

FIGURE 10-3   Snap & Glue, Advanced Tab

■ **Linear extension**   Draws a line segment from the nearest endpoint when you move the cursor over a line segment. A line segment can include line shapes and lines used to create the sides of a polygon.

■ **Curved extension**   Illustrates how an arc would look as an ellipse when you move the cursor over an arc segment. For freeform shapes, it extends the curve at the endpoint that you're near.

■ **Endpoint perpendicular**   Draws a line perpendicular to the nearest endpoint when you move the cursor over a line segment or arc segment. A line segment can include line shapes and lines used to create the sides of a polygon.

■ **Midpoint perpendicular**   Draws a line illustrating a perpendicular line on the line segment or arc's midpoint. A line segment can include any edge of a polygon.

■ **Horz line at endpoint**   Draws a line illustrating a horizontal line on the nearest endpoint when you move the cursor over a line or arc segment. The line is horizontal to the screen, not the page, so it's not affected by page rotation. A line segment can include line shapes and lines used to create the sides of a polygon.

■ **Vert line at endpoint**   Draws a vertical line on the nearest endpoint when you move the cursor over a line or arc segment. The line is vertical to the screen, not the page; it is not affected by page rotation. A line segment can include line shapes and lines used to create the sides of a polygon.

■ **Ellipse center point**   Highlights the ellipse's center point when you move the cursor over an ellipse.

■ **Isometric angle lines**   Draws a line extended at the angles specified in the Isometric Angles (Deg.) box. You can enter up to 10 angles in degrees, separated by commas. This option is most useful if you're creating an isometric drawing.

While drawing, move the cursor toward or along a shape to see a shape extension. Shape extensions work with the Line, Arc, Freeform, Pencil, Ellipse, Rectangle and Connection tools.

10

Using the Dynamic Grid

The Dynamic Grid gives you the ability to align a single shape with any horizontal or vertical edge. The Dynamic Grid provides visual cues onscreen and intelligent object-snapping to automatically place shapes in an evenly distributed and aligned order. To do this as you place shapes, Visio gives you extra guides to move the shapes around, as shown in Figure 10-4.

NOTE *Make sure you've turned Dynamic grid on in the Tool | Snap & Glue window before you attempt to use it.*

To dynamically align a shape with other shape edges, first start to drag the shape as normal. Then tell Visio that you want to consider another of the shape's

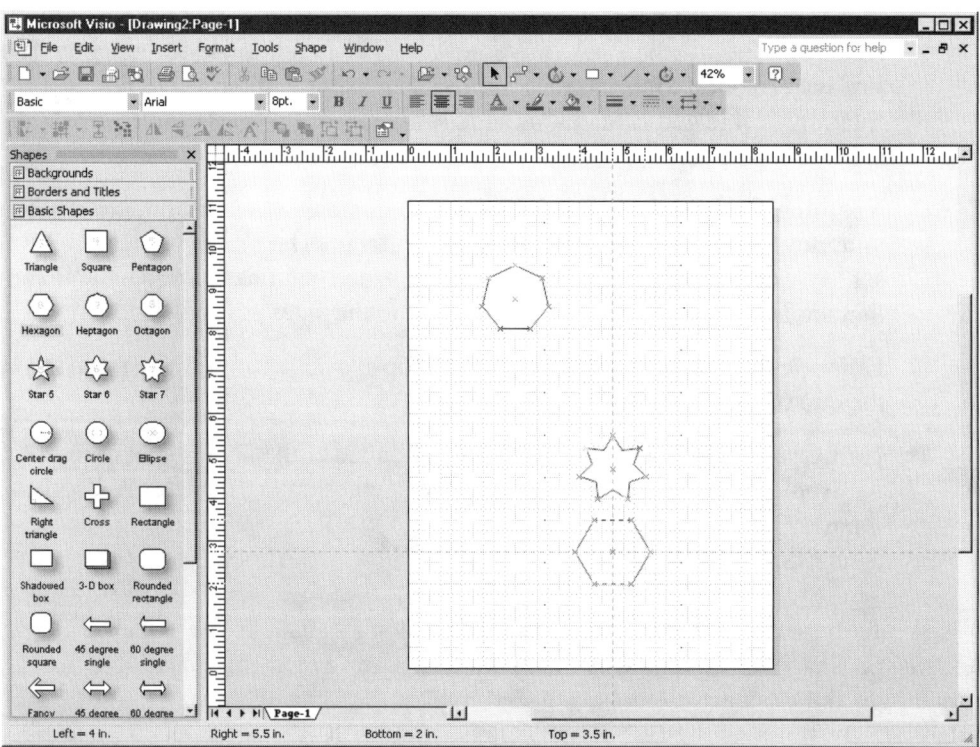

FIGURE 10-4   Dynamic Grid example

edges for alignment by pausing over the target shape for about two to three seconds. Once paused, the target shape's geometry is examined for horizontal and vertical lines. Visio places a dotted line on the shapes, allowing you to position and align shapes quickly and accurately.

A dotted line will show you the most desirable position of a shape in relation to the nearest shape. The dotted lines show the center points of the shapes. For example, if you were locating a PC shape on a desk, the Dynamic Grid will show you the center of the two shapes when they're aligned.

Using Pan & Zoom

Many of the drawings created in Visio Professional are large and contain hundreds of shapes, and moving around the diagram can get very confusing where there are so many shapes on the page.

Visio provides a tool that lets you easily navigate around a diagram: the Pan & Zoom window. To open the Pan & Zoom window, choose View | Pan & Zoom. Figure 10-5 shows an example of a Pan & Zoom window for a large facilities management drawing.

Pan & Zoom shows a miniaturized overview of the current page. Manipulate the red rectangle to zoom and pan in the drawing. The window stays open, allowing you to maintain a bird's-eye view of your drawing no matter how closely zoomed in you are.

You can customize how the Pan & Zoom window works, as follows:

- To hide the Pan & Zoom window, click the pushpin icon on the toolbar to enable AutoHide. When the Pan & Zoom window is hidden, move your pointer over its title bar, and the window will reappear.

- To make the Pan & Zoom window float, right-click inside the Pan & Zoom window, and then choose Float Window. Or you can click the Pan & Zoom window's title bar and drag it away from its docked position.

- To dock the Pan & Zoom window, right-click inside the Pan & Zoom window, and then choose Anchor Window.

NOTE   *You can drag the Pan & Zoom window to the location you want, including in the same column as the stencils.*

10

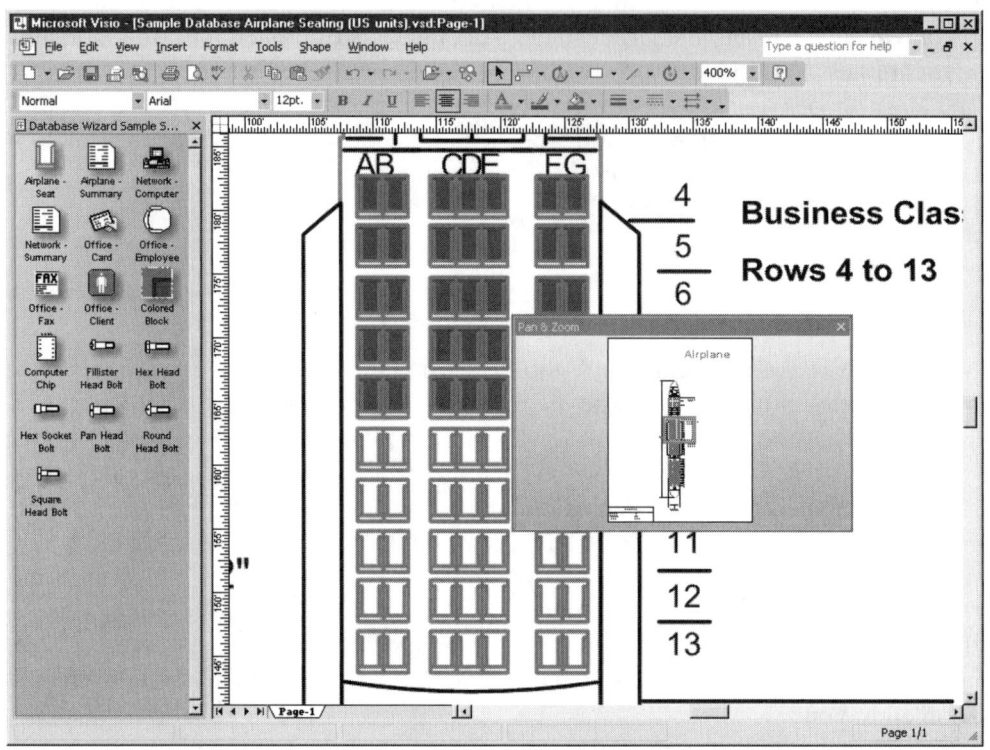

FIGURE 10-5   Pan & Zoom window

Creating Engineering Diagrams in Visio Professional

Once you have mastered the art of precise drawing in Visio, you are ready to start tackling the complicated Engineering diagrams for which Visio Professional was designed.

The key to Visio Professional's ease of use is SmartShapes technology. Included are intelligent shapes designed to behave like pipes, valves, pumps, and other real-world objects. Engineers can easily assemble drawings by dragging and dropping these industry-standard shapes onto a page. They can even store data in shapes, link them to databases or spreadsheets, and automatically generate detailed reports.

Process Engineering

With Visio Professional you can create piping and instrumentation diagrams (P&IDs) and process flow diagrams (PFDs) that show how industrial process equipment is interconnected by a system of pipelines. P&ID schematics also show the instruments and valves and monitor and control the flow of materials through the pipelines.

Draw P&IDs and PFDs by dragging process engineering equipment shapes onto the drawing page and connecting them with "smart" pipelines. Then drag components, such as valves and instruments, onto the pipelines. You can add data to components in your diagrams by entering the data specifications you want for a component into its custom properties.

To identify components in your diagram you can add custom properties information. This custom properties information identifies the components. Some custom property information is automatically entered when you drag the shape onto the drawing, and the name or number for the component may be displayed in the Visio drawing page in the form of a tag.

> TIP *You can hide tags by right-clicking and choosing Hide Tag from the menu.*

10

From the data in the custom properties, you can generate lists of equipment, pipelines, valves, and instruments. As you modify diagrams, you can generate a new list from the updated reports.

> NOTE *Visio Professional includes a sample Process Engineering project. This project includes P&IDs, datasheets, and lists. This is a great way to learn more about the Process Engineering solution. Open the example by choosing Open from the File menu and then browse to File | New | Browse Sample Drawings | Process Engineering | P & ID (US Units).vsd and click Open.*

Visio 2000 used a very different model for Process Engineering diagrams, including a Project Explorer and datasheets. These have been updated in this version of Visio, now reports raise the use of your information above datasheets, and custom property information is more available. When you open your Visio 2000 Process Engineering diagrams in newer version of Visio you'll need to convert them. Each Process Engineering diagram is converted to its own Visio file, and all the datasheet and tag information will be converted to custom property information.

Visio also adds new ways to handle your Process Engineering diagrams with the use of the Component and Connectivity Explorer. To use the explorers, choose them from the Process Engineering menu.

Using the Component Explorer

To help you manage your Process Engineering diagrams better, Visio has the Component Explorer. It opens up with your stencils, as shown in Figure 10-6.

The Component Explorer gives you a hierarchical view of your process engineering components, like pipelines or valves, grouped by category. The Component Explore displays each category of components, each type component in the diagram, and the shapes that make up that component. The tag number identifies components in a category. Shapes that belong to a component are identified by their name.

Using the Connectivity Explorer

You can also view your process engineering diagram by using the Connectivity Explorer, which like the Component Explorer also appears with your stencils. The Connectivity Explorer shows pipelines and all components to which the pipeline is connected. The Connectivity Explorer is shown in Figure 10-7.

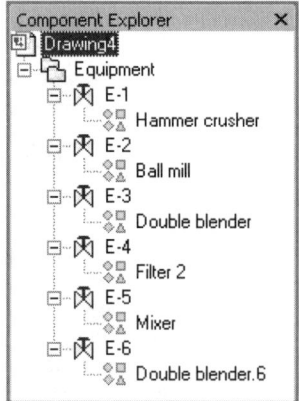

FIGURE 10-6   Component Explorer

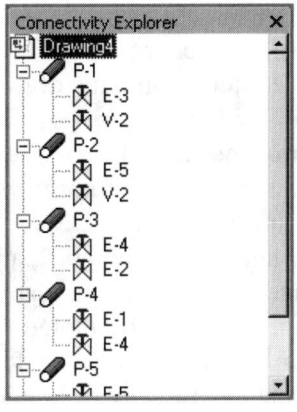

FIGURE 10-7   Connectivity Explorer

If you display the Connectivity Explorer and Component Explorer at the same time, they occupy the same space in the stencil part of your window with tab to help you move between them.

10

Mechanical Engineering

The Mechanical Engineering solution contains templates for both Parts and Assembly drawings and Fluid Power diagrams.

Visio Professional supplies shapes that let you create part and assembly drawings to provide information needed for manufacturing a product. Part drawings are created in order to show each individual part that makes up a product. Assembly drawings show how all the parts fit together.

Visio Professional also provides the tools and shapes for creating hydraulic and pneumatic circuit diagrams. You can use the valve shapes provided with Visio Professional or create your own valve shapes by using the Valve Builder.

Creating Part and Assembly Drawings

Start by opening the Part and Assembly Drawing solution, located in the Mechanical Drawing solutions folder.

The Part and Assembly Drawing drawing page appears in landscape orientation and has no scale. The ruler and the grid are set to Fine resolution, and the ruler zero point and the grid origin are at the lower-left corner of the drawing page. You can change these settings at any time by using the features described in Chapter 3.

To create a title block, drag shapes from the Title Blocks stencil. Drag shapes from the Drawing Tool Shapes stencil onto the drawing page to draw outlines of objects. You can configure many of the shapes by right-clicking on them and choosing the appropriate command from the shortcut menu as well as using the control handles. To display a screen tip explaining what the control handle does, hover the pointer over the control handle.

Drag shapes from the Fasteners 1, Fasteners 2, and Springs and Bearings stencils onto the drawing page. When you drag many of these shapes from these stencils onto the drawing page, you'll be prompted for information about the shape's characteristics. Fill in the appropriate data to configure the shape. You can change custom property data at any time by right-clicking on the shape and choosing the appropriate command from the shortcut menu.

In order to complete your drawing, you now need to add the following:

- Dimensions

- Datum feature symbols and feature control frames from the Geometric Dimensioning and Tolerancing stencil

- Welding symbols from the Welding Symbols stencil

- Callouts and other reference notes from the Annotations stencil

Creating Fluid Power Drawings

To create a new Fluid Power diagram, open the Fluid Power template, located in Mechanical Engineering solutions folder. Then drag equipment and valve shapes from the Fluid Power – Equipment, Fluid Power – Valve Assembly, and Fluid Power – Valves stencils onto the drawing page. You can configure many fluid power shapes by right-clicking on them and choosing the appropriate command from the shortcut menu.

Now use the Connector tool to connect the components. Remember that there are additional connectors located in the General Connectors stencil in the Annotation folder. Add interest to your drawing by adding text, labels, callouts, and other reference notes from the Annotations stencil.

Creating Electrical and Electronic Drawings

With Visio Professional you can create electrical and electronic schematic diagrams, as well as wiring diagrams. You can also generate a netlist file from your drawing that can be used to input information into a circuit analysis program, such as SPICE.

You can create a number of different types of electrical or electronic drawings. The following table lists the templates included andtheir intended use.

Working with CAD Drawings

Visio delivers CAD compatibility for those who need to work with DWG and DGN drawings. You can open CAD drawings in Visio to use as background images, enlarged plans, or as details. When you open CAD files as backgrounds, shapes will automatically snap to the underlying CAD geometry for faster and more accurate placement. For example, furniture shapes, equipment shapes, electrical outlets, and HVAC ducts automatically rotate and snap into place. You can pan and zoom drawings with background CAD files as quickly as you can move your mouse.

10

Working with CAD Legacy Data in Visio

Visio Professional provides the capability to open CAD drawings in Visio as a background page or a reference layer. After opening the CAD file, you can drag shapes onto it, add notes, and control the way the layers display. Visio shapes will snap to objects that reside on the CAD drawing.

Template	Intended use
Circuit & Logic	Integrated circuit and logic circuit schematics
General	General electrical diagrams (schematics, one-line, and wiring)
Industrial Control Systems	Control system schematics
Systems	Printed circuit boards

TABLE 10-2   Electrical Engineering templates

 *A CAD drawing inserted into a Visio document is a copy of the original CAD drawing. Changes made to the drawing within Visio do not alter the original.*

When you use Visio Professional, you have the additional capability to convert CAD entities into Visio shapes.

To open a CAD drawing as a background image in Visio, first start Visio, and choose to Open Existing File and click OK. The Open dialog box is shown in Figure 10-8

Under Files of Type, use the drop-down list to select a CAD drawing file format—AutoCAD Drawing (.dwg, .dxf) or MicroStation drawing (.dgn). Then browse to the file location and click Open. Visio opens CAD Properties window shown in Figure 10-9.

The CAD Drawing Properties window is used for sizing and scaling the CAD drawing on the Visio page as well as setting up the drawing page. The General Tab graphically illustrates how the CAD drawing will fit on the Visio page. Visio fits the CAD drawing onto the page and gives them both the same scale. You can drag Visio shapes onto the drawing, hide layers or levels, redline drawings, and add

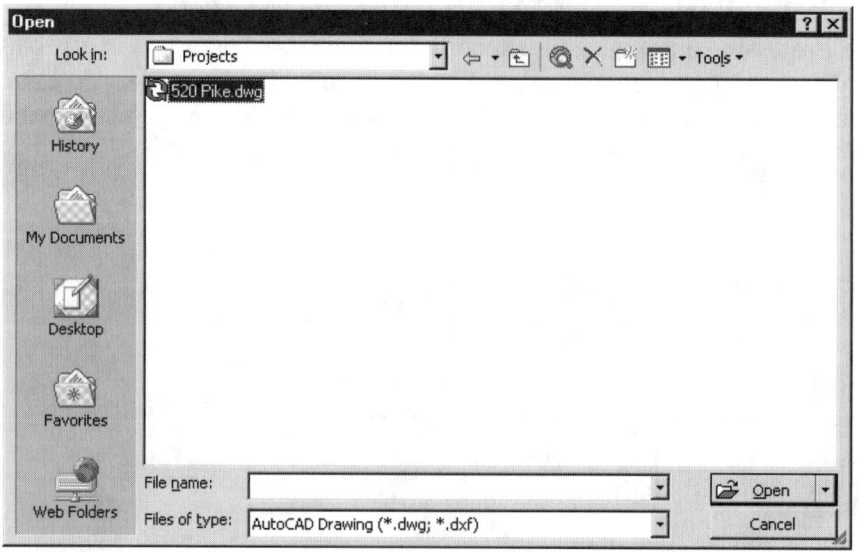

FIGURE 10-8 Opening a CAD diagram

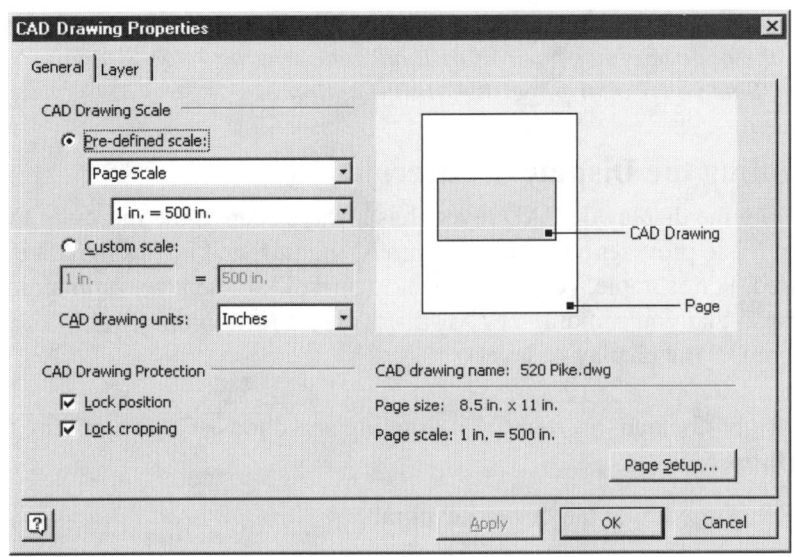

FIGURE 10-9   CAD Drawing Properties window

comments. Visio shapes will snap to objects on the background CAD drawing. The Layer tab allows you to choose which of the CAD Drawing's layers you want to open.

Whenever possible, you should work with opened CAD drawings. Working "over" opened CAD drawings is faster and generally gives better visual results. In particular, if you work with CAD drawings that are frequently updated, you should open the CAD drawings so that they can be easily updated with newer versions.

Locking the CAD Layer

In order to facilitate selecting and moving the shapes you drag onto a CAD drawing, you should lock the Visio layer that contains the CAD drawing. This guarantees that you do not accidentally select and move the CAD drawing instead of the Visio shapes.

To lock the Visio layer, first open the CAD drawing. Then right-click on the CAD drawing and choose View | Layer Properties. Click Lock Column for the CAD Drawing layer, and then click OK.

10

 *You may need to rotate the drawing page for your CAD drawing. To do so, choose File | Page Setup. On the Print Setup tab, set the orientation of the page to either portrait or landscape. On the Page Size tab, select the "Same as printer page size" radio button.*

Controlling the Display of Layers

Controlling the display of CAD layers has always been at the mercy of the CAD operator. Visio provides a tool for accomplishing this, and no prior CAD experience is required. For example, you might want to turn off all the layers containing office furniture so that you can drag HVAC ducts onto a floor plan.

To control the display of layers:

1. Right-click an inserted CAD drawing and choose CAD Drawing Object | Properties.

2. Click the Layer tab or the Level tab.

3. To hide a layer or level, uncheck it in the Visible column.

4. Click OK to accept your changes.

 *You can click Apply instead of OK to keep the dialog box open as you see how the changes affect the drawing. Then click OK to close the dialog box.*

Snapping to CAD Geometry

Drag a shape from the template and drop it onto the Visio drawing. As you position the shape near something on the background CAD drawing, your cursor will display "Snap to Geometry." This functionality allows shapes to automatically rotate, align, and snap to each other intelligently for faster layout. Shapes will automatically snap to the underlying DWG geometry for faster and more accurate placement. For example, electrical outlets, HVAC ducts, and furniture shapes automatically rotate and snap into place.

Saving Visio Drawings into CAD Format

It's possible to convert Visio Professional drawings into CAD format by choosing Save As from the File menu. Converting drawings works best when done in only one direction: from CAD format into Visio format, or from Visio format into CAD format. It's very hard to maintain data integrity when files are going back and forth. The best way to maintain the data is to convert only once.

Visio Professional converts the current Visio drawing page into CAD format. If you're working with a multiple-page drawing, you must convert each page separately.

To convert a Visio page, first open the drawing containing the pages you wish to convert. Then choose Save As from the File menu. Select the CAD drawing format from the Save As Type box and then click OK.

Converting CAD Entities into Visio Shapes

If you need to delete or modify objects in the CAD drawing, you must first convert the layers containing those objects into Visio shapes. This process provides you with an outline shape that you use with Visio Professional, and if necessary turn it into a Visio shape.

To convert CAD objects into Visio shapes:

1. In Visio, right-click the CAD drawing and choose CAD Drawing Object |
    Convert. The conversion dialog box appears, as shown here:

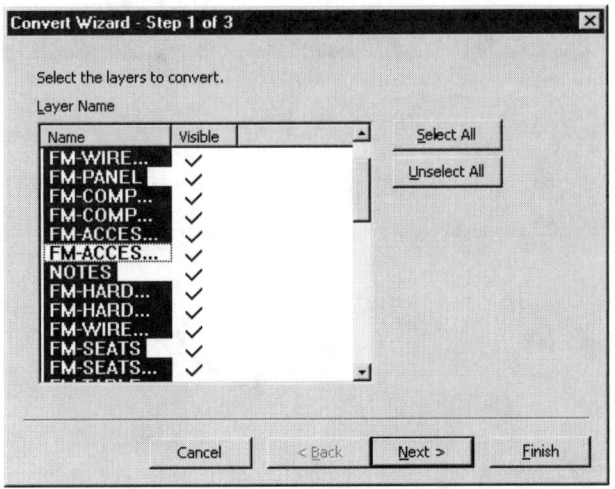

2. When the Convert Wizard opens, it assumes that you want to convert all
    visible layers. Click the Unselect All button; then hold CTRL while you
    click to select the layers or levels containing the objects you want to
    convert. Click Next, and the second box for the Convert Wizard appears, as
    shown next:

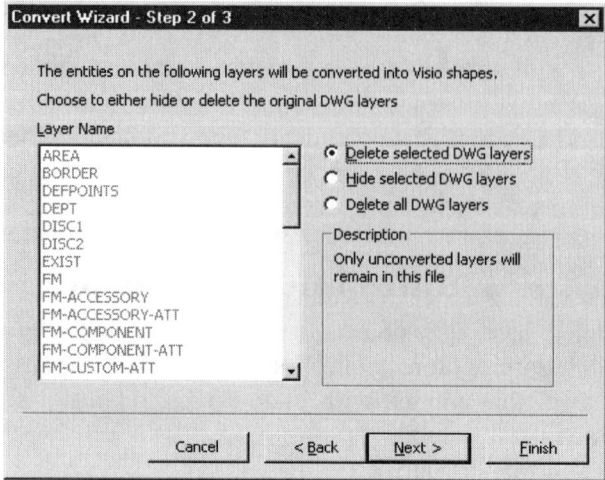

3. Choose whether to delete selected layers or levels, hide the selected layers or levels, or delete all layers or levels. Click Next, and the third box for the Convert Wizard appears:

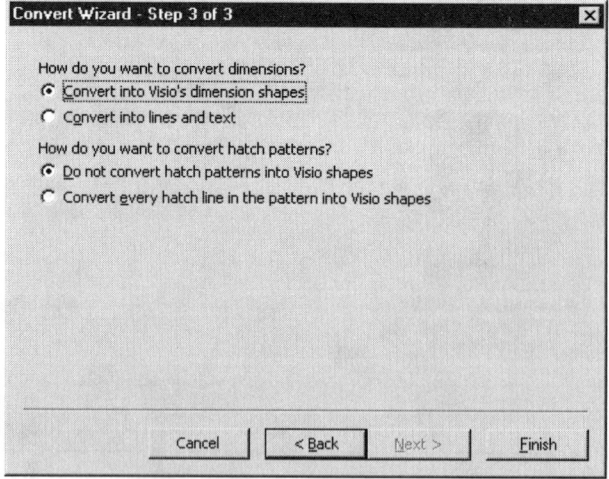

 *For DGN files, you can't specify to delete only selected layers.*

4. If you're converting DWG files, you need to specify how you want to convert dimensions. Select "Convert into Visio's dimension shapes" for dimensions that update when you resize the associated Visio shapes. Select "Convert into lines and text" to preserve the CAD formatting.

> **NOTE** *For DGN files, you can't specify how dimensions are converted.*

5. Click Finish. Visio now goes through the process of converting the objects on the selected CAD layers or levels into Visio shapes.

6. These shapes can now be added to stencils. You can add custom properties—in effect turning them into SmartShapes objects.

For the CAD User

Seasoned CAD users typically look for their favorite CAD commands in Visio. It's fair to say that some CAD commands don't exist, while others will be slightly different and even easier than their CAD equivalents.

The Table 10-3 lists some favorite CAD commands and their Visio Professional equivalents.

CAD Command	Visio Professional
Copy an object	Select the shape, hold the CTRL key while you drag a copy to the new location.
Move an object	With the Pointer tool, select the shape and drag it.
Move an object a specific distance	Select the shape and choose Tools | Add Ons | Visio Extras | Move Shape.
Add Hatching to an object	Select the shape and choose Format | Fill. The options are Color, Pattern, and Pattern color. You can also create your own patterns.
Create a block/cell	Use the Visio drawing tools to draw the shape, and then drag the shape to a stencil.
Object Snaps	Choose Tools | Snap & Glue and check Shape Extensions. On the Advanced tab, check the shape extensions you need.
Set drawing scale	Choose File | Page Setup, select the Drawing Scale tab, then select the scale.

TABLE 10-3   CAD commands in Visio

Managing Your Facility

Facilities managers have traditionally relied on CAD and proprietary CAFM (computer-aided facilities management) tools to create space plans, track and manage physical assets, and move facilities. These tools often cost thousands of dollars, require extensive training, and make it hard to share data with others. Visio Professional combines the aspects of CAD and database-oriented tools with core Microsoft technologies.

The facilities management solution combines space-planning and asset-tracking capabilities. This offers you two different views of your facility information: a spatial view when using the facilities plan, and an organizational view when using the Categories and Space Explorers.

There are five major facilities management solutions in Visio Professional for creating your initial floor plans or space plans. They are listed in Table 10-4 with their intended use.

In addition to facilities plans, Visio Professional offers other drawing types, such HVAC, security systems, and network diagrams that can be used in conjunction with the facilities plans.

With Visio, you can link to and work with the data from any SQL-compliant database for which they have 32-bit ODBC drivers, such as Oracle, SQL Server, dBase, and Access. ODBC (Open Database Connectivity) is a Microsoft standard with which programs can access, view, and modify data from the database.

Template	Intended use
Floor Plan	This is the basis template meant to help you create your layout and design as well as to help with your facilities management. You can use most other Building Plan templates to build on diagrams created in this template.
Office Layout	Used to create single offices with all the furniture laid out. You can create a series of offices together and it may look like a floor plan.
Plant Layout	Meant to be used to diagram and design shipping and receiving centers, as well as storage and production of manufactured goods.
Site Plan	Use this template to design the outside of any facility. These are stencils and macros designed to be used with landscaping of all kinds.
Space Plan	Meant to be used in conjunction with Floor Plans to identify and organize spaces within a office.

TABLE 10-4 Facilities Management templates

 *You must have the appropriate ODBC components and database drivers installed on your computer. To find out if your database program is ODBC-compliant, check the program's documentation.*

Creating Facilities Management Drawings

When you first start a facilities plan you can connect your drawing to a facilities database, if the information you need is already resident in a database. This database contains the information you want to track for your organization. That way, the drawings you create act as a "visual database" and have asset-tracking capabilities added to them. These capabilities are information about resources and assets, specifically spaces, boundaries, people, furniture, fixtures, and equipment.

Connecting Your Drawings to a Database

Linking your facilities management data to your Visio diagram is a powerful way to manage your space and equipment needs. Visio has the power to become dynamically linked to databases so that the shapes you see on the page are visual representations of the data in the database.

If you want your diagram to pull information from a datasource, such as a Microsoft Excel spreadsheet or another ODBC database, you'll need to use either the Import Data Wizard or the Database Wizard.

The Import Data Wizard is the most useful when you simply want to import data that will stay in Visio and not be exported back to a spreadsheet or other simple database. The Database Wizard is far more powerful and lets you read ODBC databases and create new masters based on their data.

You can also dynamically link your drawing to a database using some of the other Database options that come in the Visio Extras folder, such as Link to Database. To access them, choose Tools | Macros | Visio Extras. Once you create this link you can keep the data in your Visio diagram synchronized with the database.

If you simply want to export raw data from your facility management diagram into a database, you can use the Export to Database wizard on the Tools menu.

Creating a Floor Plan

Each page in your Visio drawing can represent a floor or a portion of a floor. You cannot represent more than one floor on the same page, though you can have many pages as part of one diagram. The creation of the plan can be accomplished one of three ways:

■ Use the shapes on the Walls, Shell and Structure, and Building Core stencils

■ Insert a floor plan from a CAD program

■ Use an existing plan created in Visio

Sizing Walls in Visio

Visio Professional has automated the process of dimensioning with the use of room and space shapes. Simply select a group of walls to be dimensioned, right-click and select Add Dimension from the shortcut menu.

With space shapes, convert the space shape to walls. Right-click on the space and select Convert To Walls. The Convert to Walls dialog box appears, as shown here:

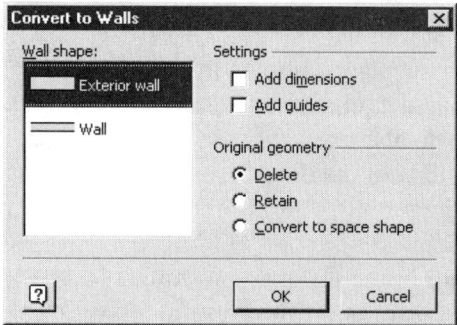

Be sure to select Add Guides and Add Dimensions in the Convert to Walls dialog box, then click OK. Visio Professional automatically reforms the shape as a space shape with walls, including dimensions and connected wall shapes.

When dimensions are connected to a shape, they'll stay with the shape even as you move or resize it. You can glue the dimension lines to the connection points of shapes or wall shapes. You can choose from a wide variety of dimensioning shapes, including horizontal and vertical baselines, horizontal and vertical outside dimensions, and diameter and radius dimensions.

Using the Categories and Space Explorers

Just like their cousins, the Category and Connectivity Explorers in the Mechanical Engineering diagrams, the Categories and Space Explorers help you keep the organization of your space plan neat, as well as helping you rearrange the diagram quickly and easily. They are available in Space diagrams and display all the spaces you've created and their various information. Figure 10-10 shows the two explorers with the Spaces explorer on top.

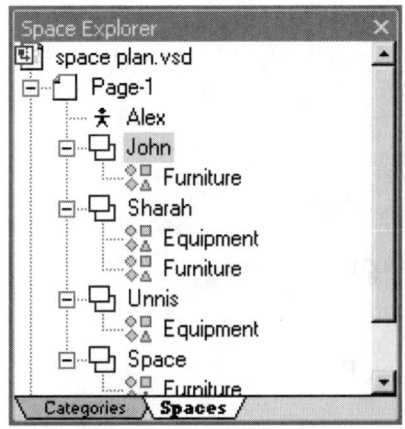

FIGURE 10-10   Categories and Spaces Explorers

To display the Categories and Spaces Explorers, select Explorer from the Plan menu in your Space Plan diagram.

The Spaces Explorer shows a complete list of all the spaces you've placed on your diagram. If these spaces have the name category entered in their custom properties, the Spaces Explorer lists them by name of occupant. Under each space is a list of all the furniture and other equipment that the space contains. You can move the furniture from space to space by clicking on the furniture and dragging it to another space.

The Categories Explorer shows all the different categories that are possible for anything added to your space diagram. This includes all types of assets, furniture, and even people. There are nine categories in all. This explorer is used to help you keep track of how many of each category you have placed in your space diagram.

> **TIP** *As a general rule, you'll create a diagram starting first with a floor plan, add any mechanical or facility specific information, and then start attributing spaces using the Space Plan.*

HVAC, Electrical, and Plumbing Drawings

Visio Professional provides you with shapes to create building services diagrams of HVAC control systems, basic duct layouts, fire and security plans, and lighting and electrical layouts. All these drawing types can be created on a blank drawing

10

page or as a layer in an existing floor plan. You can create the floor plan with Visio or bring it in from CAD.

The templates for creating these drawing types are found in the Building Plan Solution folder. The templates are:

- Electric & Telecom Plans

- Fire & Security Systems

- HVAC Control Logic Diagrams

- HVAC Plans

- Plumbing & Piping Plans

Tracking Assets

Visio Professional has the ability to help you not only create spaces but keep track of how those spaces are used. You can assign information to your facilities management diagrams, allowing you to run reports to show how the space is allocated. The ability to track assets is part of all facilities management diagrams.

After you complete the floor plan, you can start assigning information for spaces, areas, or departments. You can assign people to the spaces and calculate the square footage each person takes up or that is allocated to each department.

Tracking Assets requires several steps:

1. Designating spaces

2. Designating boundaries

3. Assigning people to spaces

4. Assigning assets to spaces

5. Designating categories

6. Assigning a category to a shape

7. Working with databases to retrieve and update data

Each step is important, and all are outlined in detail in this section.

Designating Spaces

If you have created a floor plan by using one of the Building Layout solutions, it might already contain space shapes. In that case, you can begin assigning assets to spaces. Otherwise, you need to drag shapes to the drawing page before you can assign them to a person or department.

> **NOTE**   *If you drag walls to the drawing page and create a room out of them, Visio Professional will automatically size a space shape to them. First, you need to make sure your room is closed by gluing all the walls together, then drop the space shape on them.*

To specify custom properties for a space, right-click on the shape and choose Properties from the menu. In the Properties window, fill in the appropriate information in the Value column. Values in the Properties dialog box are saved as soon as you change them.

Designating Boundaries

In addition to designating spaces, you can also designate areas or departments by using the Boundary shape on the Resources stencil. This shape creates a boundary around an area. This is used only for square-footage totals; you can't associate people or assets to a boundary.

To create a Boundary, drag the Boundary shape from the Resources stencil onto the drawing page near a collection of offices. Size the shape so that it encompasses all the offices you wish. Then right-click on the Boundary shape and select Properties. The Boundary window appears. Fill in the required values in the Boundary window. Then click OK.

> **TIP**   *For irregular shapes, you can modify the Boundary shape the same way you modify a Space shape.*

Assigning People to Spaces

You can also assign people to spaces and associate them with that location. You can assign a person to more than one space, and you can assign more than one person to a single space.

To assign a person to a space, drag a Person space from the Resources stencil and place it onto a Space shape. When you want to move a person to a different office or location, simply drag the Person shape onto the new location. When a resource or asset is dragged onto a space shape, it becomes associated with that space. You have to associate resources and assets with Space shapes if you want to use the Find command on the Edit menu to locate them by their space. To specify information about a person, double-click the Person shape. Fill out the information on the Properties dialog box.

TIP *You can use the Space Explorer to organize people within departments or areas.*

Assigning Assets to Spaces

To associate an asset with a space, drag an asset shape (desk, chair, filing cabinet, etc.) from the stencil onto a Space shape. Right-click on the asset and choose properties from the menu. Fill out the Properties dialog box, making sure to double-check the information before you click OK. Any asset not assigned to a space will be associated with the floor or page.

NOTE *Remember to save your drawing frequently so that your drawing and the database are synchronized.*

Designating Categories

Facilities information is organized into *categories* and *properties*. Categories are groups that shapes belong to. Properties are information you track for a given category.

Many of the shapes in the Building Plan solutions are assigned to a category. Every category has a name, a reference word or number (called *ref*), note properties, and other properties specific to that category.

You can customize the default categories by adding your own properties or by adding your own subcategories and properties. A subcategory is a category based on a default category. When you add a subcategory, it will inherit the properties of the categories it was based on. After you add subcategories, you must assign the subcategory to the appropriate shape.

Assigning a Category to a Shape

You can assign categories to shapes you create, as well as change or assign a category to any shape. You can also assign a category to one or more shapes. Remember, if you change the category of a shape on the drawing page, only that particular shape will have that change. On the other hand, if you change the category of a shape on a stencil, every time you drag that shape onto the drawing page it will have the new category.

FIGURE 10-11   Assign Category window

To assign a category to a shape on a stencil, first make sure nothing is selected on the drawing page, then select Assign Category from the Plan menu. The Assign Category window opens as shown in Figure 10-11.

Choose the category for your shape, and then click OK.

If you want more control over how the categories are handled, choose Properties on the Assign Category window. This launches the Properties window, shown here in Figure 10-12.

In the Properties window, you can choose how the information you enter into the Custom Properties fields for your shapes changes how they are listed in your reports and how they are displayed in the Space and Floor Plan diagrams.

To change a relationship between a Custom Properties field and a Category, choose the Custom Property from the first list and then the new Category from the second list. You'll see the effect of the changes in the Results lists, usually listed as a new formula.

10

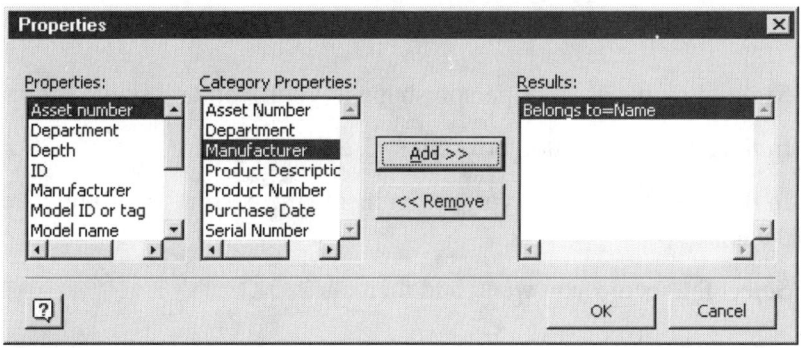

FIGURE 10-12   Properties window

 *Remember, when you alter the properties or category this way you are only altering it for one shape on the drawing page at a time. If you want to make a more permanent change, you can drag your shape back onto the stencil to make a new master with the new changes intact.*

Working with Data from an Existing Database

You can link properties in your facilities plan to fields in existing databases so that you don't need to reenter existing data into your plan. When the external database is updated, your plan will also be updated. To access an external database you must know its name, user name, and (if it's protected) the password. You also need to know enough about the database tables in order to select the data you need.

Here's the process for connecting to a database:

1. Select Plan | Import Data.

2. Choose the Category of data you want to add from the database.

3. Select the type, and location of your database.

4. Identify the columns that contain the relevant information, including name, Space ID, and Building ID.

5. Choose the fields you want to add in the Custom Properties field of the new shapes.

6. Add a building ID for the drawing, and indicate which pages are to be updated with the imported data.

7. Click Finish.

After the link has been set up, you can use the data in the plan:

1. Right-click the asset or person shape in your plan and select Properties.

2. In the Properties dialog box, click Use Existing Item.

3. In the Search For box, type text to locate the correct record in the external database.

4. Select the record you want, and then click OK.

At this point, any property that is linked to a database field is automatically filled in. Linked properties are unavailable for editing in the Properties dialog box. Click OK to save the changes and close the Properties dialog box.

Locating Assets in Your Facilities Plan

The Categories Explorer is a tool for listing people, assets, spaces and boundaries, and then locating them in your facilities plan. It offers a hierarchical view of the facilities data. It is a great holding place for information about resources or assets. By default, the Category Explorer displays the facilities information you entered in your facilities plan. Each Facilities Management shape in the plan is represented as an item.

To start the Category Explorer, choose Plan | Explorer. This launches the Category and Space Explorer, with it docked on the side of the window. You can use the Find command on the Edit menu to locate specific shapes.

Summary

In this chapter, you learned about Visio Professional. You learned how to make the most of the precision drawing tools, how to work with CAD drawings in Visio, and how to create engineering drawings in Visio Professional. You also learned about the facilities management tools that come with Visio Professional.

In the next chapter, you'll learn about the other added solutions that come with Visio Professional, including tools to help you diagram you network and map your web sites.

10

Chapter 11

Network, Software, Web Diagrams, and Reports

How to...

- Create Network Diagrams
- Use Visio Professional with Software Development
- Map Web Sites
- Manage Web Sites
- Use the Added Reports in Visio Professional

In the last chapter, you learned how to use the engineering diagrams in Visio Professional.

In this chapter, you'll learn how to use the advanced computer templates in Visio Professional, including the network and software development templates. You'll also learn how to diagram your web site, and manage web site design, using Visio Professional templates. Lastly, you'll learn about the reports that have been added to Visio Professional to help you manage all the added templates.

Creating Network Diagrams

Managing a large computer network, or even a very small network, can be a complicated and annoying task, especially when you can't have the visual tools you need. Visio Professional comes with an invaluable tool to help you manage your networks. The Network templates are meant to help you create visual diagrams of your computer networks, complete with everything from token rings to printers. You can create complete diagrams with manufactures part numbers and inventory tracking numbers, and you can display the network diagram one level at a time to help you understand how it operates. Networking diagrams can be a vital tool to help you create or manage your network.

TIP   *It helps to have information about all the parts of your network before you start attempting to diagram it.*

The Basic Network template comes with Visio Standard; however, Visio Professional has five additional Networking diagrams. This section covers all of these networking diagrams.

Networking Diagrams, accessible under the Network solutions folder, are meant to help you design and diagram your network. There are six networking templates in Visio Professional:

- Basic Network

- Active Directory

- LDAP Directory

- Logical Network Diagram

- Novell Directory Services

- Visio Network Equipment Sampler

Each template has a different use. This section discusses each template so you know which you'll need for your diagram.

Using the Basic Network Template

The Basic Network template is the simplest of the networking templates in Visio Professional, and this is the only networking template that comes with Visio Standard. It is meant to be used to diagram smaller, simpler networks. It has the capability to identify pieces of your network by manufacturer and by use.

Use the Basic Network template to:

- Assemble a graphical representation of your network.

- Track hardware properties, including serial number, location, manufacturer, and description.

- Sort equipment by manufacturers or type.

- Create a networking plan to include in a presentation document.

- Export hardware information from your diagram to a database.

NOTE   *Before you use the Basic Network template, make sure you have a good grasp on the general use of Visio.*

The Basic Network template includes many added features beyond those in basic diagrams. There are five stencils with more than a hundred shapes, six layers

11

added by default (each listing a different computer manufacturer or type of computer), and most shapes have an extensive list of custom properties already added. Figure 11-1 shows the main Visio window with the Basic Network template open.

To make the most of any networking diagram, it helps to follow these four basic steps for creating a network diagram.

1. Create a list of all networking hardware you want to diagram, including owner, manufacturer, product ID, and location.

2. Drag a network ring or network backbone to the drawing page.

3. Add hardware to the ring or backbone by using the extra control handles.

NOTE *You can add only eight shapes to a ring. If you want more shapes on a ring than that, drag another ring shape onto the first and use it as more "arms."*

4. Add custom property information to each piece of hardware on the ring.

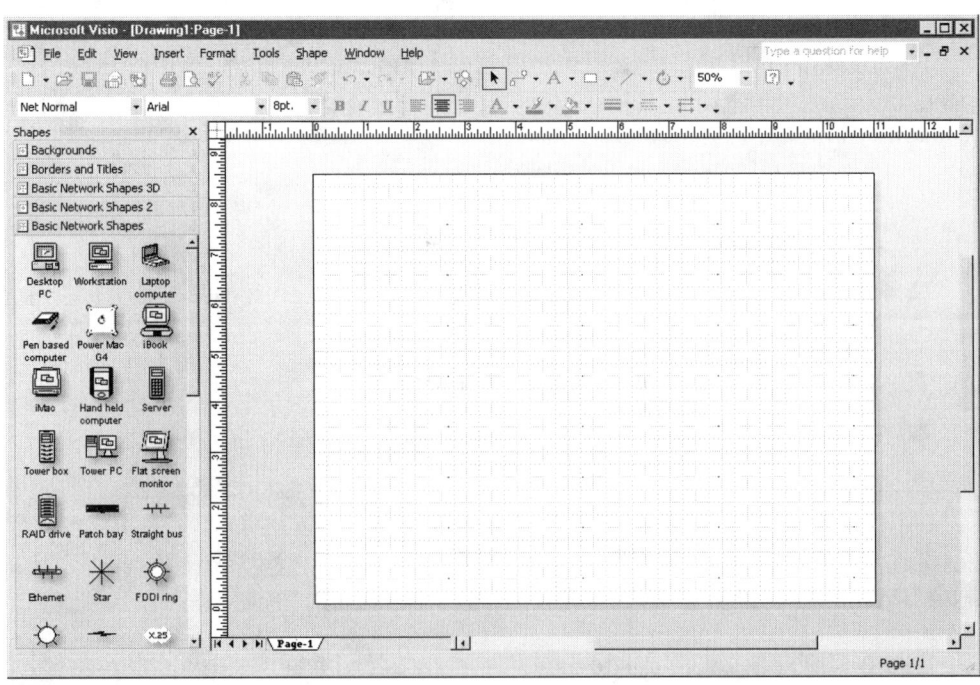

FIGURE 11-1   Basic Network Template

After you've added the custom property information, save your diagram. Then you're ready to use it for any purpose you like, including generating reports, adding it to presentations, or even using it to view your network based on hardware type.

To generate a report with your diagram, use one of the Reports discussed later in this chapter.

To link your diagram to a database, use the Database Wizard (choose Tools | Add Ons | Visio Extras | Database Wizard). Then use the Database Export, Database Refresh, and Database Update macros to keep the diagram and database working together.

As you work with your network diagram, you may need shapes off stencils that aren't on the network template. Feel free to open any stencils that might help you complete the diagram. For example, the Off Page Reference shape on the Basic Flowchart Shapes template has the option to keep text synchronized across pages, a useful tool when a networking diagram spans several pages.

Creating a Logical Network Diagram

After a Basic Network Diagram, a Logical Network diagram is next more complicated diagram. The Logical Network Diagram template is meant to help you diagram either the physical layout of your network , or to show the virtual connections between parts of your network and how they interrelate.

The Logical Network Diagram opens with only one layer, but seven stencils open. Each template contains a different type of computer part. The Stencils are:

- Generic Manufacturing Equipment

- Internet Symbols

- Logical Symbols

- Network Devices

- PC & Peripherals

- Printers & Scanners

- Telecom

Figure 11-2 shows the Visio main window with the Logical Network Diagram template open.

11

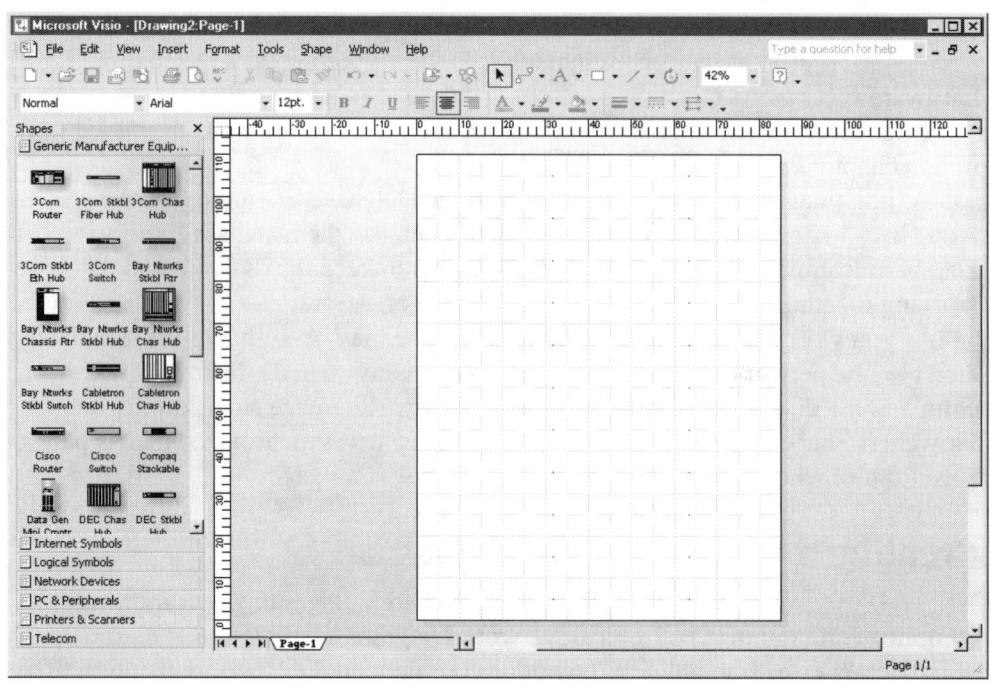

FIGURE 11-2 Logical Network Diagram template

How you use the Logical Network Diagram template depends on what you are attempting to diagram with it.

Diagramming your Logical Network

To diagram you logical network, start with a list of all your routers, servers, and clients, as well as any other hardware, such as switches, modems, or even printers. Make sure your list includes any inventory numbers or tracking information so you can use your new diagram to create reports.

Once you have assembled the information about your network, start by dragging a center shape onto your diagram, such as a token ring shape, onto the drawing page. Once you have the center of your network set, drag all the different types of computer shapes that attach to that center to the drawing page. Don't forget to add printers, and other less used peripherals. Figure 11-3 shows an example of a logical network diagram created for a small network connected by Ethernet.

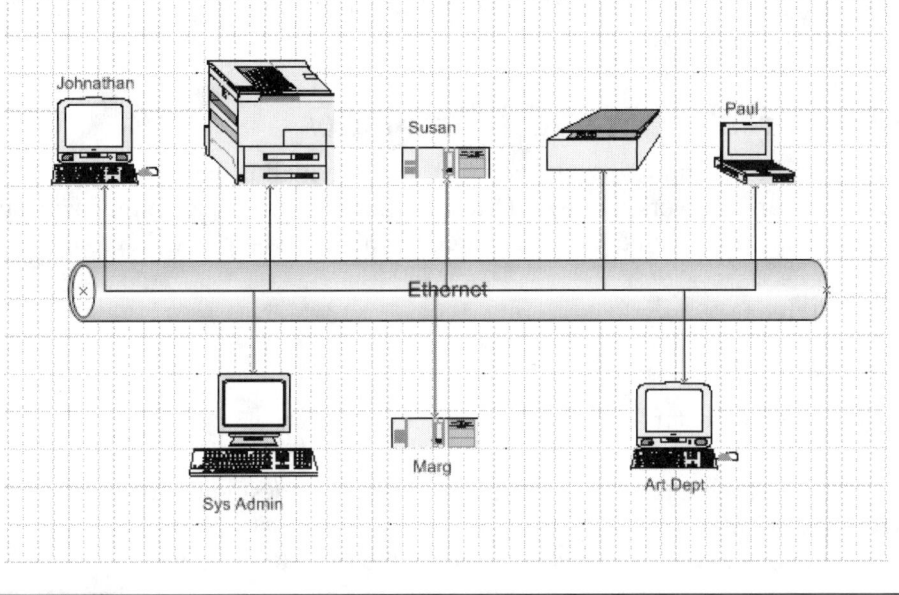

FIGURE 11-3   Example Logical Network diagram

Diagramming your Physical Network

Visio can be a powerful tool to help you design and diagram a network as it exists in a physical space. By combining in the power of the Building Plan templates with the Logical Network template, you can diagram exactly how your network is arranged in a space.

To diagram your physical network, first you'll need the physical location for the computer shapes. Use the Building Plan templates to create a physical space diagram.

> NOTE   *The Building Plan templates are discussed in detail in Chapter 10 "Engineering, CAD, and Building Planning Diagrams."*

Once you have a physical space laid out, start dragging your computer shapes onto the drawing page and arranging them in the space. After you have them all laid down on the drawing page make sure to select them all and add them to their own layer. Using layers in Building Plan diagrams makes it harder to accidentally move a shape, and helps you quickly identify what each type of object is on the drawing page.

11

 *It's a good idea to save your Building Plan diagram to another name before you start adding computer shapes. That way you'll have a clean diagram for any building needs.*

Using Directory Services Templates

Another way to diagram your network is to show how it is handling network information and networking tasks. Directory Services has become the mainstay of network management, and Visio has three templates to help you diagram it.

- Active Directory

- LDAP Directory

- Novell Directory Services

All three of these templates are meant to help you design or document directory services.

As with other types of network diagram, the first step is to identify all the systems attached to your network. Make sure to find inventory or other identifying numbers as well as the system's make and model.

Once you have collected all the information about your network, you are ready to start identifying which groups, or directories each piece belongs too.

TIP   *You can also use the Organizational Chart template to create a theoretical diagram of your directory services before you start diagram the actual network.*

There are three templates included to diagram your Active Directory network, and each is intended for a different type of network and has specialized stencils included.

- **Active Directory**   Diagrams Microsoft Active Directory networks. It opens three stencils: Active Directory Objects, Active Directory Sites and Services, and Exchange Objects.

- **LDAP Directory**   Diagrams a transition from a non-LDAP network to one based on Directory Services. It only opens one stencil with conceptual shapes to help you identify groups.

- **Novell Directory Services**   Diagrams NDS networks. It opens five stencils: NDS ZENworks, NDS GroupWise, NDS Partitions, NDS Objects, NDS Additional Objects.

Schema and Directory Navigator

Each of the templates also has a default scheme set in place, and you'll see a window telling you Visio is opening the default scheme when you start any of these templates. This scheme has all the classes and properties you're likely to need to complete your Active Directory network diagram.

There is also a Directory Navigator that opens with each of these templates. The Directory Navigator for a Novel Directory Services diagram is shown in Figure 11-4.

The Directory Navigator gives you a look at your network from a hierarchical perspective so that no matter how the shapes are laid out on the page, they are still easily viewed from a top down perspective. The Directory Navigator also has the scheme outlined for you, including the classes and properties.

11

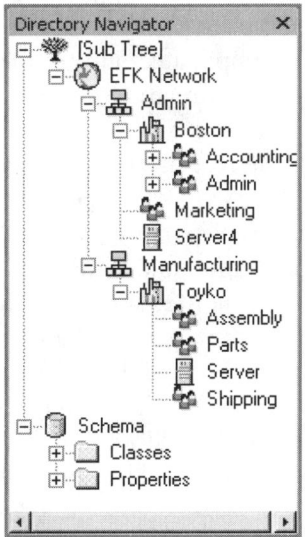

FIGURE 11-4   Directory Navigator

The Visio Network Equipment Sampler

Visio also includes a small sampling of shapes that already have their model and make numbers set. The Visio Network Equipment Sampler template opens one stencil filled with dozens of computer shapes with their manufacture information already attached in the Custom Properties field. All you'll need to do is attach the part of inventory number for the piece.

> **NOTE** *Instead of using the Visio Network Equipment Sampler alone, you'll find it useful to open up the Visio Network Equipment Sampler stencil in other network diagrams.*

Designing Your Web Site using Visio Professional

The tool most people are excited about using in Visio Professional is the web site mapping. Visio Professional includes two templates that handle web sites.

The Conceptual Web Site template allows you to create a diagram of a web site without using the actual pages. The Web Site Map automatically indexes all the web pages and creates a Visio diagram of them for you.

Using the Conceptual Web Site Template

Creating a web page can be a complicated and complex process. The obvious first step in creating web sites that are a dream to manage is to create a diagram of the site before you even start. But, even if you haven't pre-planned your web site, having a diagram of how it is interconnected is a vital part of quick and easy management.

The Conceptual Web Site template comes with three stencils: Web Site Map Shapes, Conceptual Web Site Shapes, and Callouts.

To use the Conceptual Web Site Map template, first draw a Main Page shape from the Conceptual Web Site Shapes stencil. Identify this as the home page by dragging a Home shape, from the Web Site Map Shapes stencil to the main page shape. Next draw on more pages and with the connector tool attach them to the main page. Use the shapes on the Web Site Map Shapes to identify what type of information each page contains. Continue this process until you have a completed web site diagram.

Mapping A Web Site

What if you have inherited a web site and don't have the diagram for how it's connected? Or what if you don't have a current diagram to your web site and you know there have been changes? Visio Professional has an automatic diagramming option to help you diagram a web site you don't have a visual representation for, called the Web Site Map template.

> NOTE
> *The Web Site Map template only shows how a web site is connected, it cannot update a web site with changes you make on the Visio drawing page.*

The Web Site Map comes with Visio Professional and it automatically maps any web site and gives you a graphical representation of the web site, complete with information about every page, link, and detail it found.

> TIP
> *You can also access the Web Site Map crawler by choosing Tools | Add-ons | Web Diagram | Web Site Map.*

Understanding Web Site Mapping

The Web Site Map template opens up with a dialog box asking you for a web address. This is the start of the mapping functions. This dialog box launches a web crawler. Several of the internet search services are crawlers as well, but instead of indexing the entire web, the Visio Web Mapper index starts at the web page you point it at and goes down as many levels as you tell it. It makes a temporary database for every link from the pages as well as every graphic, audio, movie, and scripting file. Then it creates a Visio graphical element for each one and positions them on the Visio drawing page, interlocked like an organizational chart.

The crawler is looking at the HTML text of every page it finds and then sifting through the code looking for the standard link references like HREF and SRC, and then looking for the referenced file. If it doesn't find the file, it decides the link is broken and displays it that way. Figure 11-5 shows a completed Web Diagram created by Visio Professional's web crawler.

You can choose to have it look for the different types of files or links, or you can let it find everything on the page. Once you have it all on the Visio page you can use it any way you like, including adding it to other documents about your web site.

Visio also creates a memory model of everything it finds and uses that to store the data it gleaned from the code on the pages. The memory model allows you to run reports and also allows you to compare the changes you made on the Visio

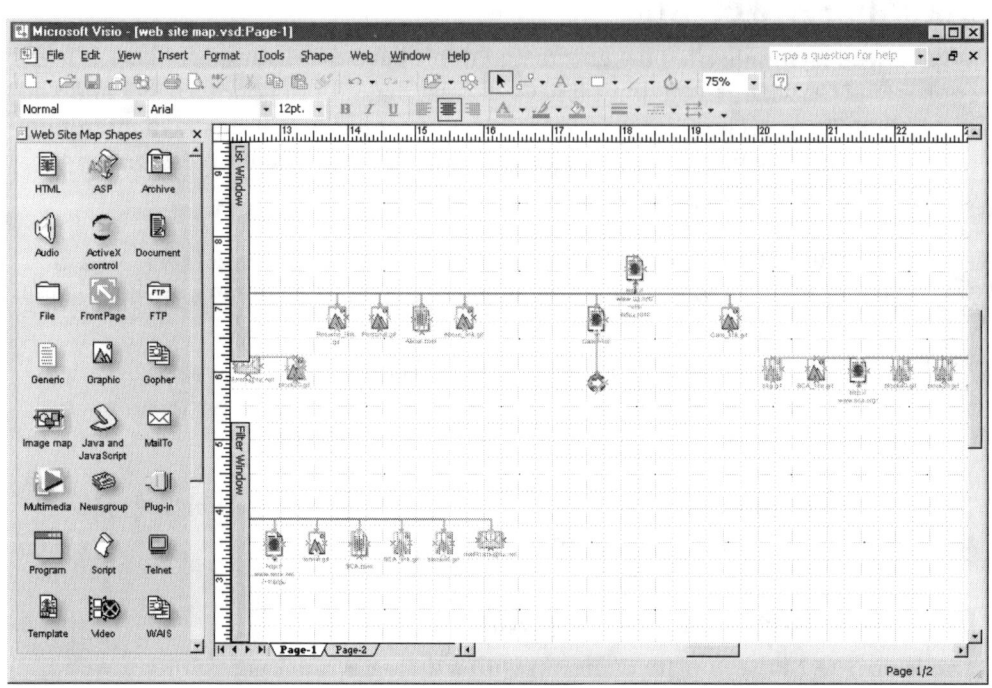

FIGURE 11-5   Visio Main window with Web Site Map

page to the original web site you mapped. But, the most powerful part of Memory Mapping is that it allows you to display and hide parts of your diagram without actually loosing the data.

The Memory model for your web sites is new in Visio Professional 2002, and any older diagrams you open will create a new memory model when you open them up in Visio 2002.

Creating Your First Mapped Web Site

Now that you understand what the Web Site Map tool is doing, you're ready to map a web site. First, start Visio Professional and select to open Web Diagram | Web Site Map. This opens a Web Site Map template.

As soon as Visio has opened the template a dialog box appears, like the one shown in Figure 11-6, asking you for the web site address of the site you want to

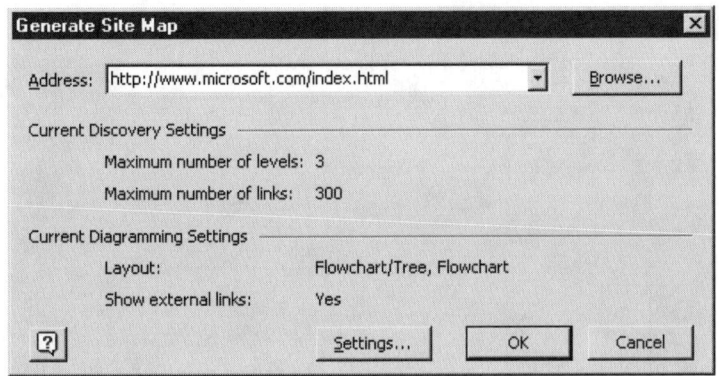

FIGURE 11-6   Generate Site Map dialog box

map. Make sure you have access to the web site you want, which may mean connecting to the internet if you want to map a live site.

The Generate Site Map dialog box has many defaults you can change by selecting the settings button, but for your first web site simply enter the address of the first page in the hierarchy you want to map and click OK.

Visio maps the web site from the top down, showing you a dialog box listing all the pages it indexing. When it has all the data, it creates the memory model, and then creates the diagram on the page for you.

NOTE   *Even a simple site can create a very complicated and large Visio diagram since it includes not only all the pages, but all the images and references as well.*

Setting Web Crawler Options

When you first mapped a web site, you probably used the crawler options set by default in Visio Professional. You can choose from several dozen options for the Visio crawler to use.

To change the options and generate a new web site map, start a new Web Site Map template with a clean drawing page. Do this by opening a new template from the New button. Click on Settings when the Generate Web Site Map dialog box opens. This brings up the Web Site Map Settings window shown in Figure 11-7.

11

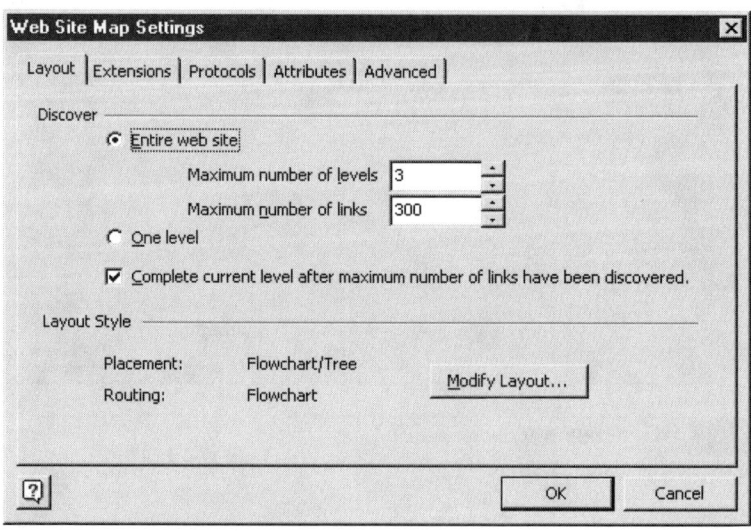

Web Site Map Settings window

The Web Site Map Settings window has five tabs, and each handles a different type of crawler setting. The first is the layout tab.

Setting the Layout Tab on the Web Site Map Settings window

On the Layout tab you can select the number of levels the crawler will search down (the default is 3) and how many total links it will investigate before stopping (the default is 300). The number of levels defines how many links down from the first page you want the crawler to go. You can make sure the crawler only goes one level down by using the One Level button to override this option entirely. The total number of links is the total number of shapes on the Visio drawing page, usually one page for each link set on the web page. You can also make sure Visio doesn't stop while investigating a level by checking the Complete current level after maximum number of links have been discovered.

You can also set the layout options by using the Modify Layout button on the Layout tab. This opens the Lay Out Shapes window shown in Figure 11-8.

The Lay Out Shapes window lets you set how the shapes appear on the page when Visio goes to layout the shapes it find when it maps you web site. There are a few different layout options, and you need to know how the documents will be used before you can choose between them.

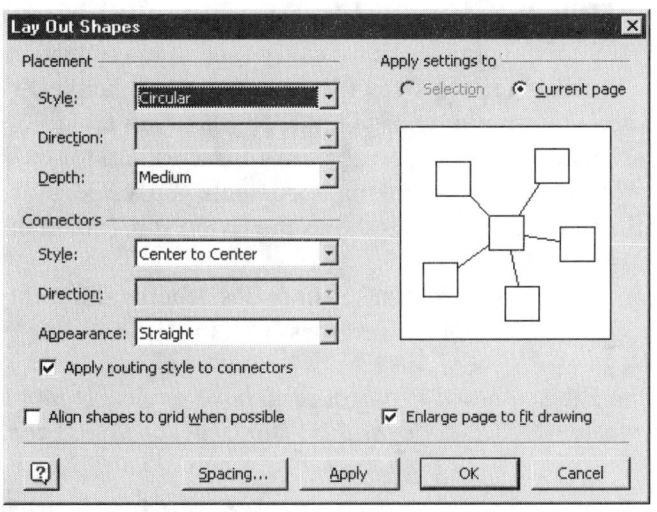

FIGURE 11-8   Lay Out Shapes window

By default, the shapes are laid out like you would expect in a flowchart, but you can also use Radial and Circular styles. Each has it own set of options for depth of connector and type of connection. Radial is great for web sites with lots of back links, or links between pages that go back and forth between pages on the same level. Flowchart is good for web sites with a very top down structure, where the only back links are those back to the homepage. Circular is good for sites that have a complicated link structure, or for web sites that have links to all pages from all pages.

In the Lay Out Shapes window you can also choose how the lines that connect the shapes behave (using the connectors options), and how the shapes behave on the drawing page. By selecting or deselecting to align the shapes with the grid, you can let Visio help you arrange your diagram. The last option, whether or not the drawing page expands to contain the diagram, should always be selected. That way you can be assured that you will always be able to print the whole diagram.

When you are finished setting the layout options for your web site map, click OK and Visio closes the Lay Out Shapes window and returns you to the Web Site Map Settings window.

11

Setting the Extension Tab on the Web Site Map Settings window

By default, Web Site Mapping looks for every type of every kind of link possible in HTML. The Extension tab lets you turn some or all of them off. This can be very helpful when you want only page links, or when you are trying to sort out some linking problem (when your image links are working, for example). You can also use this tab to add types for linking documents you've developed that use a non-standard file types. Figure 11-9 shows the Extension Tab on the Web Site Map Settings window.

Using the Extension tab, you can select or deselect the different types of files as you choose, or add and remove file types from the list.

NOTE *Both the Extension and Protocols Tab have an Add button that allows you to create new HTML code for the Visio Crawler to look for.*

Setting the Protocols Tab on the Web Site Map Settings window

Not only does Visio Professional look for every type of web document by default, it also looks for every possible type of link, including FTP, GOPHER, and mailTo. You can choose to leave these options intact or you can remove them by using the Protocols tab, shown in Figure 11-10.

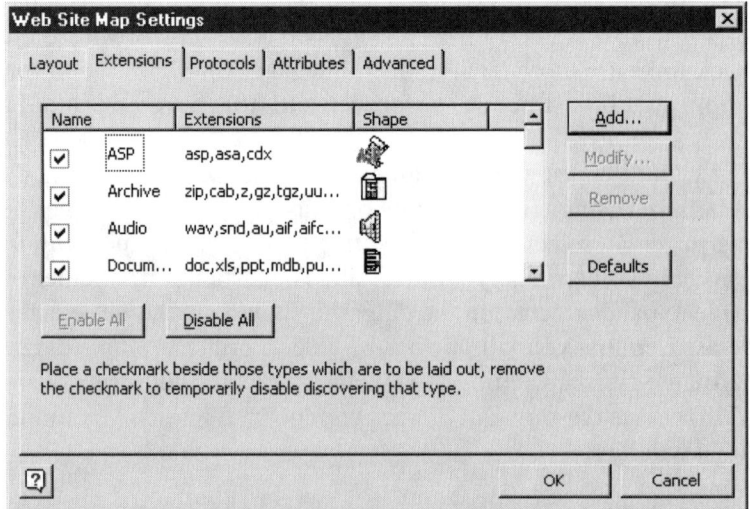

FIGURE 11-9   Extension Tab on the Web Site Map Settings window

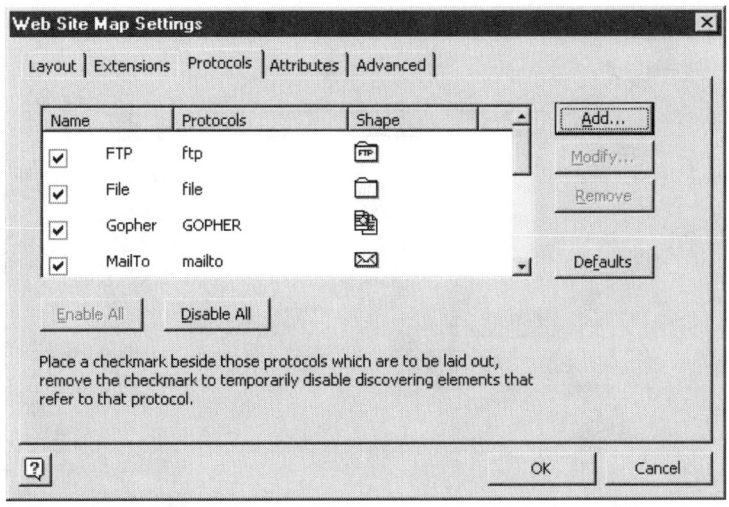

FIGURE 11-10   Protocols Tab on the Web Site Map Settings window

Using the Protocols tab you can add or remove the options to search for these protocols from the Web Site Map crawler.

Setting the Attributes Tab on the Web Site Map Settings window

The Attributes tab gives the means to tell the crawler what you want to display in your diagram. Since the crawler sifts though your HTML code, you can identify which of the code triggers it looks for and force it to ignore others. By default all the triggers (such as HREF and SRC) are set to create a link and a shape in your diagram.

You have the choice to tell the Web Site Mapping to ignore any of the triggers it is programmed to find. The Mapper is set to find a link based on: HREF, SRC, BACKGROUND, ACTION, and CODE attributes. You can turn this off in the Attributes Tab on the Web Site Map Settings window, so for example it does not search the CODE parts of your HTML documents. Figure 11-11 shows the Attributes tab on the Web Site Map Settings window.

Uncheck the boxes on the Attributes tab to remove them as search criteria. Use the Edit button to change the attribute you have selected. Also, you can disable or enable all of the attributes by using the buttons at the bottom of the window. The Defaults buttons returns the window to the default, which is to search for all the listed criteria.

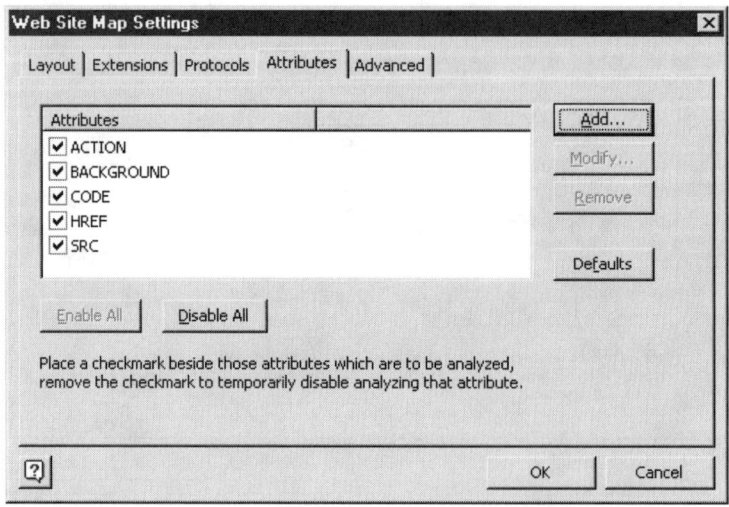

FIGURE 11-11 Attributes Tab on the Web Site Map Settings window

NOTE *You cannot turn off the option to search HREF attribute. Visio always searches for this.*

Setting the Advanced Tab on the Web Site Map Settings window

As you might expect, the Advanced tab contains the most complicated settings for you Web crawler. Figure 11-12 shows the Advanced Tab on the Web Site Map Settings window.

There are six options at the top of the window called the Search Criteria options.

You can choose how the crawler looks for pages on the Search Criteria section. The first three options listed are radio buttons, and you may choose one of the three:

- **Analyze all files discovered** is the broadest criteria you can give the crawler. It tells Visio to show the links for any page you link to within the level limits you've set, no matter where that page resides.

- **Analyze files with a specified domain** is the default and tells Visio to only analyze pages that stay within the same directory as the pages to which you have pointed it.

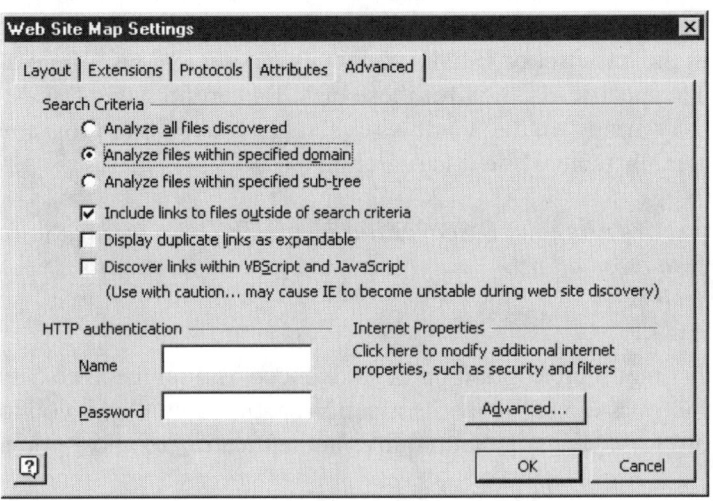

FIGURE 11-12   Advanced Tab on the Web Site Map Settings window

■ **Analyze files with a specified sub-tree** is the most stringent criteria and tells Visio to only look in the pages directly under the page you specified.

The next three options tell Visio what else to look for and display.

■ **Include link to files outside of search criteria** shows the links to pages outside the search criteria set above, but does not search those pages for more links, even if they are within the limits set on the Layout tab. Visio ignores links to other sites when you uncheck this box.

■ **Display duplicate links as expandable** tells Visio that you want to include links to the same page from several different pages on the site you are diagramming. By default, this is set to be on since you probably want Visio to show you all the links on your site. This means that if you have a link to your home page from several places on the page Visio will show each one individually. Generally this option is checked, but it can give you a huge number of links on the page if you have used the link over and over, (a graphic link, for example) so you may want to turn it off to avoid unnecessarily cluttering up your diagram.

11

■ **Discover links with VBScript and JavaScript** tells Visio to look for links embedded in code on the web page. Since this code is generally removed from the basic set of HTML code with a comment tag, Visio needs to be told to specifically look for these tags. Be careful using this options since, as the warning on the window says, it can make other programs on your system unstable while it is searching.

 *If you are using the Discover links with VBScript or JavaScript option it is best to close all other programs on your computer before you start the search.*

The only other major option on the Advanced Tab on the Web Site Map Settings window is the HTTP authentication section that allows you to set a name and password for a web site that requires authentication to allow you access.

 *Visio erases the HTTP information when you close the Web Site Map template.*

Just as with the basic site map, when you are done with the more advanced setting options, click OK until you are back to the main window and run the Web Site Mapping tool.

Using the List and Filter Windows

A new addition in this version of Visio Professional is the List and Filter windows in the Web Site Map. These windows give you two other ways to shows your diagram beyond the standard flowchart layout of the Visio drawing page.

 *For both types of lists, you can remove the page or file type from your Visio drawing page by unchecking the check box. Then later, due to the power of memory mapping, you can add them back by rechecking the box.*

The List window lists all the pages from the top down and lists all the links inside each page. Figure 11-13 shows the List window. The list shows all the broken links and all the off site links.

The Filter window shows each types of page Visio found and shows the types in a list format. Figure 11-14 shows the Filter window. The types of files are the same as the ones set in the Extensions and Protocols tabs on the Web Site Map Settings window.

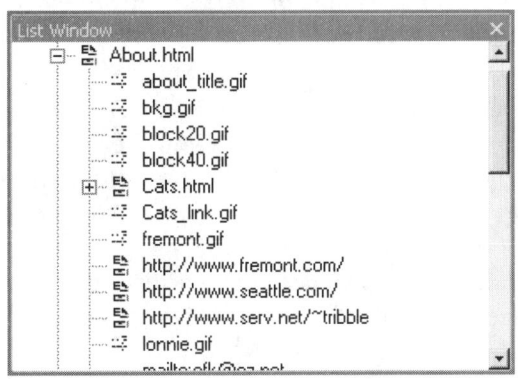

FIGURE 11-13   Lists window for Web Site Map

Printing Web Site Maps

Once you have generated the shapes, and Visio has placed them on the drawing page, you'll notice that several hundred shapes on one page can look very unmanageable. You can choose layouts that favor your type of diagram, but in the end, it is still several hundred shapes, at least. For most web sites, this generates a very wide and very short document, looking something like a long strip of paper.

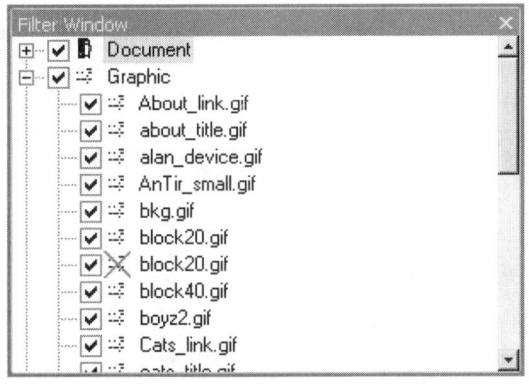

FIGURE 11-14   Filter window for Web Site Map

 *You can choose the complete options for laying out your web site map in the layout setting options discuss earlier in this chapter*

No matter what your layout options are, most web site maps will be too large to show reasonably on one page. This means you'll either want to shrink the diagram (which can get unreadable) or move some of the links to another page. Visio has a quick way to do this. Go back to the drawing page and right click on one of the web page shapes. Select Make a Subpage. Visio moves that web page and all its corresponding links on a new, standard sized, page. The page also has a copy of the web page shape that the moved page links to, helping you keep track of the interrelationships of your web site.

As a general rule, moving web page shapes and links to a new page gives you a far more manageable diagram, one that will print happily across pages and gives you shapes you can read. If you do not want to add more shapes to new pages, you can always just print the document as it is and Visio automatically tiles the diagram to print across several pages. If you like, you can tape the pages back together. All of this gets a lot easier if you have a printer that can handle large size paper and allows you to print the large diagram out all at once.

 *Don't forget to save your web site map.*

Using Visio Professional with Software Development

Visio Professional comes with eight templates to help you create and manage software. Software development has become a huge part of how business is done with computers, and almost every office will eventually need some sort of advanced software solution. The eight templates that come with Visio Professional are designed to help the software developer create new software better and easier. The eight templates are:

- COM and OLE
- Data Flow Model Diagram
- Enterprise Application
- Jackson

- Program Structure

- ROOM

- UML Model Diagram

- Windows User Interface

NOTE *All of the software templates are in the Software solutions folder.*

Application Modeling with Visio Professional

Of the eight templates that come with Visio Professional Software solution, seven of them are for modeling applications. This section walks you though the uses for each type of templates. Table 11-1 lists all the modeling templates and their uses.

NOTE *Software modeling is complex and you'll need more information than simply the templates in Visio to create good and workable software models.*

Template	Type of Software or Method
COM and OLE	COM allows applications to be written in several different languages and still speak to each other, of which Object Linking and Embedding (OLE) is an example. This template has COM objects and interfaces, as well as references, to help you diagram how an application that uses COM functions.
Data Flow Model Diagram	This is a Gane-Sarson notation way to model data in an application. Creating a Data Flow Model requires a few simple shapes: Process. Interface, and Datastore; the main information in a Data Flow Model is in the connections. The Visio Data Flow Model Diagram shows not only the data flow, but also shows the hierarchical view of the model using the Model Explorer and the Output screen helps you identify the errors in your Model.
Enterprise Application	Applications that span a network or set of networks are called Enterprise Applications. This template helps you diagram how they will happen, where their data is stored, and how the different parts will interrelate. It also lists all the physical or logical parts of the network to help you diagram the work of a enterprise application.
Jackson	As with Data Flow Models, Jackson diagrams are made up of a few simple shapes and connections. These connections show how a piece of information works its way though the system in a software application. Visio includes a template with all the rules for Jackson diagrams included. Simply start dragging the procedure shapes to the drawing page and use the Tree Connector shape to create a logical diagram.

TABLE 11-1   Software Modeling templates

11

Template	Type of Software or Method
Program Structure	Before creating software applications, you need to understand the structure and memory objects. The Program Structures template helps you understand that gives you shapes to help show how functions and memory work within the application.
ROOM	Meant to be used as a model for the ROOM language for software development. You can create models of data flow, or behavior of a part of the program, you can also illustrate the relationship between major parts of the software.
UML Model Diagram	UML modeling has gained great popularity in the last several years, and the UML Modeling template is a fully functioning diagramming tool to help you create a UML Model of your software.
	Included in the UML Model Diagram template are eight stencils, a Model Explorer and a blank drawing page. It also includes menu options to help you make the most of your model diagram.

TABLE 11-1   Software Modeling templates *(continued)*

Using the Windows User Interface Template

The majority of the eight templates help when diagraming the flow of your software. However, one template is used for something else: the Windows User Interface template. The Windows User Interface template helps you create mock-ups of Windows user interfaces. Figure 11-15 shows the Visio main window with the Windows User Interface template open.

The Windows User Interface template has two stencils: Window User Interface and Office User Interface.

Create a mock-up of a Microsoft Windows window or interface by dragging the body of it to the drawing page. You can then drag buttons, list boxes, and other windows parts onto the drawing page to create a Windows interface. You can also include several parts of Microsoft Office interface by using the shapes on that stencil.

> **TIP**
> *You can copy and paste your interface mock ups into any OLE compliant software to include your designs with a report, spreadsheet, or presentation.*

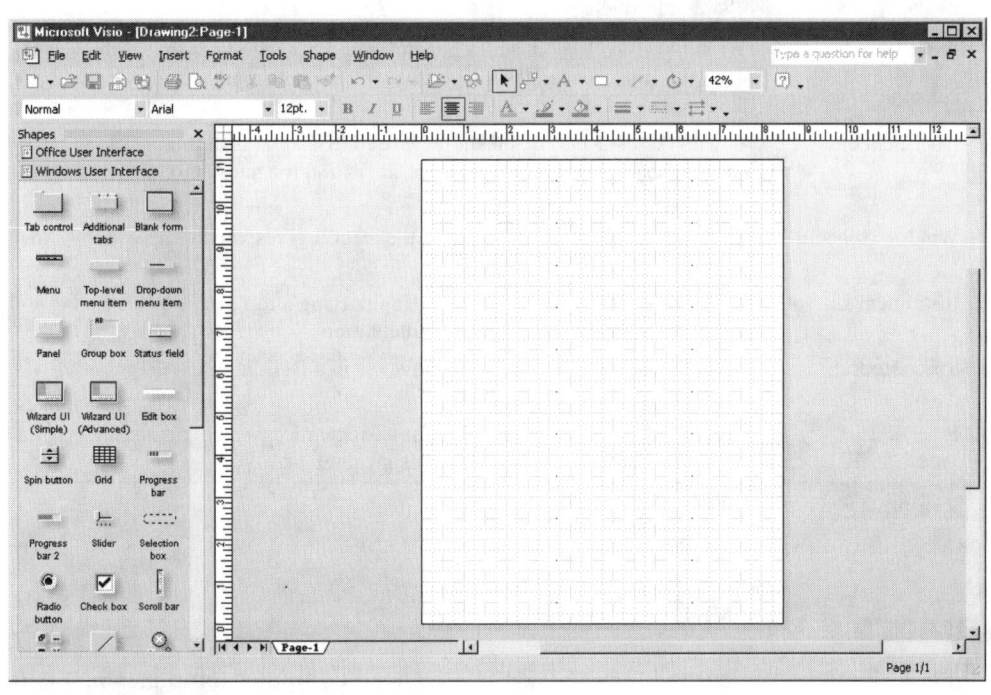

FIGURE 11-15   Windows User Interface template

Using Visio Professional Reports

In Chapter 5 you were introduced to using the basic Visio reports. Visio Professional has an additional six pre-created reports that help you get the information you need out of your diagrams. Table 11-2 lists all the new reports and their intended purpose.

Also, as described in Chapter 5, you can create any report you need using the Report Definition Wizard. Creating a report specially designed to list your computer or network components would help you in managing many of the diagrams in this chapter.

Report Name	Intended Purpose
Asset Report	Use with Office Layout and other Building Plan templates that allow you to place furniture. Generates a report of all the assets represented in these diagrams.
Door Schedule	As with Assest Reports, meant to be used in diagrams outlining a living or working space. Lists all the types of doors and the number of each type required.
Window Schedule	Similar to the Door Schedule report, except it gives you all the windows in a diagram including their type.
Instrument List	Meant to be used with the Process Engineering template. Lists all the tag and descriptions for each type of instrumentation.
Space Report	Lists all the different spaces you have set in a Building Plan diagram, including the room information.
Pipeline List	Lists all the pipeline information for a Process Engineering diagram, including their tag, line size, and design settings.

TABLE 11-2   Visio Professional Reports

Summary

In this chapter, you learned how to use the advanced computer templates in Visio Professional, including the network and software development templates. You also learned how to diagram your web site, and manage web site design, using Visio Professional templates. Lastly, you learned about the reports that are new to Visio Professional to help you manage all the added templates.

Appendix A lists all the templates and stencils in Visio Standard and Visio Professional.

Appendix A

Stencils and Templates

This appendix lists all the templates and stencils that come with Visio 2000 Standard Edition, as well as all the shapes that come with each stencil.

Visio Standard

Visio Standard comes with dozens of templates, and hundreds of shapes. This section outlines each template, its attached stencils, and then lists the stencils and each shape it includes.

Templates

This section lists all the templates that come with the U.S. version of Visio Standard by category.

Block Diagrams

The following table lists the basic Visio diagrams, meant for simple charts.

Template	Stencils Opened	Template Description
Basic Diagram	Basic Shapes, Borders and Titles, Backgrounds	Contains 2-D geometric shapes and directional lines for feedback loops and for functional decomposition, hierarchical, data structure, data flow block, and data block diagrams.
Block Diagram	Blocks Raised, Blocks, Borders and Titles, Backgrounds	Contains 2-D and 3-D shapes and directional lines for feedback loops and annotated functional decomposition, data structure, hierarchical, signal flow, and data flow block diagrams.
Block Diagram with Perspective	Blocks with Perspective, Borders and Titles, Backgrounds	Contains 3-D geometric shapes, directional lines, and a vanishing point for changing depth and perspective. Use for functional decomposition, hierarchical, and data structure diagrams.

Flowcharts

These are the most used standard Visio templates. The following table lists all the templates that come with Visio standard meant for creating flowcharts.

Template	Stencils Opened	Template Description
Audit Diagram	Audit Diagram Shapes, Borders and Titles, Backgrounds	Create auditing flowchart diagrams for accounting, financial management, fiscal information tracking, money management, decision flowcharts, and financial inventories.
Basic Flowchart	Basic Flowchart Shapes, Borders and Titles, Backgrounds	Create flowcharts, top-down diagrams, information tracking diagrams, process planning diagrams, and structure prediction diagrams. Contains connectors and links.
Cause and Effect Diagram	Cause and Effect Diagram Shapes, Borders and Titles, Backgrounds	Create cause-and-effect diagrams (also known as fishbone or Ishikawa diagrams) to systematically review factors that might affect or contribute to a given situation.
Cross-Functional Flowchart	Cross-Functional Flowchart Shapes Vertical, Cross-Functional Flowchart Shapes Horizontal, Basic Flowchart Shapes	Show the relationship between a business process and the organizational or functional units, such as departments, that are responsible for steps in that process.
IDEF0 Diagram	IDEF0 Diagram Shapes	Create hierarchical diagrams using IDEFO process charting models for model configuration management, need and benefit analyses, requirements definitions, and continuous improvement models.
Mind Mapping Diagram	Mind Mapping Diagram Shapes, Borders and Titles, Backgrounds	Create mind maps (graphical representations of thought processes) for planning, problem solving, rational analysis, decision making, and brainstorming, using Buzan's creativity techniques.
Work Flow Diagram	Work Flow Diagram Shapes, Borders and Titles, Backgrounds	Create diagrams representing information flow, business process automation, business process re-engineering, accounting, management, and human resources tasks.
TQM Diagram	TQM Diagram Shapes, Borders and Titles, Backgrounds	Create cause-and-effect, top-down, and cross-functional process flow diagrams for business process re-engineering, Total Quality Management (TQM), and continuous improvement.

A

Forms and Charts

The following table lists the 3 templates you can use for creating marketing diagrams and forms.

Template	Stencils Opened	Template Description
Charts and Graphs	Charting Shapes, Borders and Titles, Backgrounds	Contains chart and graph shapes for financial and sales reports, profit and loss statements, budgets, statistical analyses, accounting tasks, market projections, and annual reports.
Form Design	Forms Shapes	Create inventories, invoices, order forms, business records, timesheets, personnel reports, transaction sheets, certificates, registers, memos, rosters, expense reports, and schedules.
Marketing Charts and Diagrams	Marketing Shapes, Marketing Diagrams, Charting Shapes, Borders and Titles, Backgrounds	Use for process diagramming, benchmarking, simulation, path routing, resource or what-if analyses, deployment charts, targets, sales pyramids, activity-based costing, and task management.

Map

The following table lists the map templates. Map templates are used to create diagrams showing a specific area or landscape.

Template	Stencils Opened	Template Description
Directional Map	Landmark Shapes, Metro Shapes, Recreation Shapes, Road Shapes, Transportation Shapes	Contains transportation and mass transit shapes, such as highways, parkways, intersections, road and street signs, routes, railroad tracks, transit terminals, rivers, and buildings.
Directional Map 3-D	Directional Map Shapes 3-D	Contains transportation shapes such as roads, vehicles, intersections, and building landmarks.

Network and Office Layout

Visio Standard comes with one each network template and office layout template, listed in the following table. If you need more stencils to diagram your computer network or office environment, see Visio Professional.

Template	Stencils Opened	Template Description
Basic Network	Basic Network Shapes 2, Basic Network Shapes D, Basic Network Shapes, Borders and Titles, Backgrounds	Contains basic network and computer equipment shapes for network architecture diagrams, network design and documentation, and networked structures.

Template	Stencils Opened	Template Description
Office Layout	Cubicles, Office Accessories, Office Equipment, Office Furniture, Walls, Doors and Windows	Create floor charts, plans, and blueprints for facilities management, move management, office supply or assets inventories, office space planning, and cubicle layout.

Organizational Charts

The following table lists the Organizational template and the wizard. Use the template to create charts from scratch and the wizard to create them from a database.

Template	Stencils Opened	Template Description
Organization Chart	Organization Chart Shapes, Borders and Titles, Backgrounds	Create diagrams for human resources management, staff organization, office administration, and management structures.
Organization Chart Wizard	Organization Chart Shapes, Borders and Titles, Backgrounds	Using this wizard, create diagrams for human resources management, staff organization, office administration, and management structures.

Project Schedule

The following table lists the templates created to help you manage and illustrate the timeline of a project.

Template	Stencils Opened	Template Description
Calendar	Calendar Shapes	Create and format a calendar for any month. Add shapes to annotate the calendar.
Gantt Chart	Gantt Chart Shapes, Borders and Titles, Backgrounds	Create Gantt charts for project management, task management, schedules, timetables, agendas, project lifecycles, and goal setting.
Pert Chart	Pert Chart Shapes, Borders and Titles, Backgrounds	Create PERT charts for project or task management, schedules, timetables, agendas, work breakdown structures, critical path method, project lifecycles, goal setting, and timelines.
Timeline	Timeline Shapes, Borders and Titles, Backgrounds	Create linear timelines with milestones and interval markers.

A

Other Templates

The following table lists Visio documents that aren't opened by any templates shown in the categories window, but are useful for either creating new templates or as stencils after you open another template.

Template	Stencils Opened	Template Description
Blank Drawing	None	A completely empty template meant as a basis for building your own templates.
None	Callouts, Connectors, Symbols, Embellishments, Miscellaneous Flowchart Shapes	These Stencils Appear in none of the standard templates, but are accessible though the Visio Extras folder.

Stencils

Dozens of stencils come in Visio Standard. This section lists each stencil in the category you are most likely to use it.

Most Used Shapes

The following table lists the most used stencils in Visio. They are opened with almost every template.

Stencil	Shapes
Basic Shapes	3-D box, 45 degree tail, 45 degree double, 45 degree single, 60 degree tail, 60 degree double, 60 degree single, Center drag circle, Circle, Cross, Double flexi-arrow, Dynamic connector, Ellipse, Fancy arrow, Flexi-arrow 1, Flexi-arrow 2, Flexi-arrow 3, Heptagon, Hexagon, Line-curve connector, Octagon, Pentagon, Rectangle, Right triangle, Rounded rectangle, Rounded square, Shadowed box, Square, Star 5, Star 6, Star 7, Triangle
Backgrounds	Background city, Background clouds, Background compass, Background cosmic, Background expedition, Background geometric, Background high-tech, Background horizon, Background leaf, Background mountains, Background none, Background orbit, Background rain, Background steel, Background stripes, Background tranquil, Background web, Background world
Borders and Titles	Border binder, Border classic, Border contemp., Border elegant, Border graduated, Border graphic 1, Border graphic 2, Border modern 1, Border modern 2, Border neon, Border retro, Border small, Border technical 1, Border technical 2, Border triangles, Hyperlink button, Hyperlink circle 1, Hyperlink circle 2, Note box classic, Note box contemp., Note box deco, Note box file, Note box neon, Note box triangles, Title block bold, Title block classic, Title block compass, Title block contemp., Title block corporate 1, Title block corporate 2, Title block deco, Title block elegant, Title block geometric, Title block horizon, Title block jagged, Title block notepad, Title block retro, Title block sphere

Block Diagrams

Block Diagram stencils, listed in the following table, contain the most basic shapes in Visio. Simple squares, circles, and other enclosed shapes, as well as simple lines. They also include some common 3-D shapes.

Stencil	Shapes
Blocks	1-D double, 1-D single, 1-D single, open, 2-D double, 2-D single, 2-D single, open, 3-D box, Arced arrow, Arrow box, Auto-height box, Auto-size box, Box, Button, Circle, Concentric center, Concentric layer 1, Concentric layer 2, Concentric layer 3, Curved arrow, Diamond, Dot & arrow, Dotted line, Double arrowhead, Double tree sloped, Double tree square, Dynamic connector, Line-curve connector, Mid-arrow, Mid-arrow dotted, Multi-tree sloped, Multi-tree square, Open/closed bar, Partial layer 1, Partial layer 2, Partial layer 3, Partial layer 4, Single arrowhead
Blocks Raised	Circle, Down arrow, Down arrow, open, Elbow 1, Elbow 2, Elbow 3, Elbow 4, Frame, Horizontal bar, Left / right arrow, Left arrow, Left arrow, open, Right arrow, Right arrow, open, Square block, Up / down arrow, Up arrow, Up arrow, open, Vertical bar
Blocks with Perspective	1-D Left / right arrow, 1-D Up / down arrow, Arrow, down, Arrow, left, Arrow, right, Arrow, up, Block, Circle, Elbow 1, Elbow 2, Elbow 3, Elbow 4, Hole, Left / right arrow, Shallow block, Up / down arrow, Vanishing point, Wireframe block 1, Wireframe block 2

Flowchart

Flowchart stencils contain connector shapes and shapes to represent steps in a process. The following table lists all the flowchart specific templates that come with Visio Standard.

Stencil	Shapes
Audit Diagram Shapes	Check 1 (audit), Check 2 (audit), Compare 1, Compare 2, Data transmission, Database, Decision, Disk storage, Diskette 1, Diskette 2, Display, Divided event, Divided process, Dynamic connector, Event, I/O, Line-curve connector, Lined document, Lined/Shaded process, Magnetic tape, Manual file, Manual input, Manual operation, Multi document, Multi proc/doc, Note block, Off-page reference, On-page reference, Reference point, Tagged document, Tagged process, Terminator, Title block
Basic Flowchart Shapes	Annotation, Auto-height box, Card, Control transfer, Data, Decision, Direct data, Display, Document, Dynamic connector, Flowchart shapes, Internal storage, Line-curve connector, Loop limit, Manual input, Manual operation, Off-page reference, On-page reference, Paper tape, Parallel mode, Predefined process, Preparation, Process, Sequential data, Stored data, Terminator

A

Stencil	Shapes
Cause and Effect Diagram Shapes	Category 1, Category 2, Effect, Fish frame, Primary cause 1, Primary cause 2, Secondary cause 1, Secondary cause 2, Secondary cause 3, Secondary cause 4, Secondary cause 5, Secondary cause 6
Cross-Functional Flowchart Shapes Horizontal	Functional band, Separator
Cross-Functional Flowchart Shapes Vertical	Functional band, Separator
Mind Mapping Diagram Shapes	Apple, Arrow, Arrow2, Auto-size box, Big cloud, Brain, Bulb, Central theme, City, Clock, Coins, Cross, Cube, Curve, Curvy arrow, Drink, Exclamation, Exclamation point, Factory, First tier line, Food, Fourth tier line, Frowning face, Growing bubble, Heart, Hourglass, House, Inner branch, Knight, Large character, Lightning, Moon, Ordering idea, Ordering theme, Outer branch, Pencil, Planet, Question mark, Rainbow, Raindrop, Rounded stamp, Scales, Second tier line, Small cloud, Smiling face, Star, Stop, Storm, Sun1, Sun2, Third tier line, Tree, Wavy
Miscellaneous Flowchart Shapes	And gate, Bordered rectangle, Branch: no return, Branch: return, Check, Check 2, Collate, Create request, Data store, Data store 3, Database, Deck of cards, Delay, Divided process 2, Drum storage, Duplicating, Dynamic connector, Ellipsis, External control, External entity 1, External entity 2, Extract, Feedback, File of cards, Framed rectangle, Interrupt, Line-curve connector, Lined document, Lined/Shaded process, Merge, Message from user, Message to user, Microform, Microform processing, Microform recording, Off-line storage, Open rectangle, Or, Or gate, Output, Primitive from call control, Primitive to call control, Process (circle), Refinement, Rounded process, Sort, Sort 2, Summing junction, Tagged document, Tagged process, Transmittal tape, Variable procedure, Variable start, Vertical P And, Vertical XOR, XOR (Exclusive Or)
TQM Diagram Shapes	2-part function, 2-part metric, Branch: no return, Branch: return, Category, Cause 1, Cause 2, Cause 3, Connected issues, Connector (TQM), Decision 1 (TQM), Decision 2 (TQM), Delay, Dynamic connector, Effect, External control, External organization, External process, Fabrication, Feedback arrow, Fish frame, Force-field analysis, Inbound goods, Inspection, Inspection/ measurement, Interrupt, Issue, Line connector, Line-curve connector, Metric, Move, Multi in/out decision, No result, Off-page reference, Operation, Operation/ inspection, Organization function, Procedure, Refinement, Result, Selectable process, Storage, Store, System database, System function, System support, Text block 8pt, Transportation, Work flow loop 1, Work flow loop 2, X-function-horiz, X-function-vert

Stencil	Shapes
Work Flow Diagram Shapes	Accounting, Accounts payable, Accounts receivable, Bank, Board of directors, Copy center, Customer service, Distribution, Dynamic connector, Finance, Information systems, International division, International marketing, International sales, Inventory, Legal department, Line-curve connector, Mailroom 1, Mailroom 2, Management, Manufacturing, Marketing, Motorpool, Off-page reference, On-page reference, Packaging, Payroll, Person 1, Person 2, Personnel/ Staff, Publications, Purchasing, Quality Assurance, Receiving, Reception, Research & Development, Sales/PR, Shipping, Suppliers, Telecom, Treasurer, Warehouse

Forms and Charts

Forms and Charts stencils, listed in the following table, contain shapes to help you create marketing diagrams and forms. They contain many graphs and charts that automatically update to your input.

Stencil	Shapes
Charting Shapes	1-D word balloon, 2-D word balloon, 3-D axis, 3-D bar graph, Annotation, Bar graph 1, Bar graph 2, Column header, Data point, Deployment chart, Divided bar 1, Divided bar 2, Exponential curve, Feature comparison, Feature on/off, Graph scale, Graph line, Horizontal callout, Horizontal text 3-D bar, Line graph, Normal curve, Pie chart, Pie slice, Process chart, Row header, Special pie slice, Table, Text block 10pt, Text block 12pt, Text block 8pt, Vertical text 3-D bar, X axis, X-axis label, X-Y axis, X-Y-Z axis, Y axis, Y-axis label, Yes/No box, Z axis, Z-axis label
Forms Shapes	10-Column, 10-Log lines, 10pt Arial text block, 18pt Arial text block, 2 mm Border, 4 mm Border, 5-Column, 8pt Arial text block, Arrow, Business card, Business card 2, Check box, Checkmark, Creator / Company, Data boxes, Date / Time / Page, Date box, Dotted line, Double line, Drawing scale, FAX 2, FAX cover, Filename, Horizontal callout, Info box, Info line, Info line 2, Logo Placeholder, Reversed text, Right-angle horizontal, Rounded border, Shaded box, Single line, Table, Title, Today's date, Triple line
Marketing Diagrams	3-D box, 3-D circle, 3-D matrix, 3-D matrix with labels, 3-D pyramid, Add-on step, Adoption process, Ansoff matrix, Boston matrix, Circle, Circle-spoke diagram, Circular arrows, Colored block, Divided 3-D box, Dynamic connector, Market share, Market analysis, Marketing mix, Matrix, Normal curve, Patterned block, PLC, Position map, Rectangle, Scope 1, Scope 2, Step chart, SWOT, Triangle, Venn diagram

A

Stencil	Shapes
Marketing Shapes	1st place, Access, Airplane, American Express, Award circle, Aztec label, Barbells, Building block, Cash cow, Check box, Check/ Cross, Clipboard, Coin, Consumer, Crystal ball, Cylinder, Dart/ Pushpin, Delta, Diamond label, Diners Club, Dog, Empty box, Euro, Eurocard, Extend-o hand, Factory, Financial institution, Full box, Globe, Growing flower, House, House 2, MasterCard, Money bag, NO sign, Oil barrel, Oil well, Pencil, People, Person, Pound, Puzzle corner, Puzzle middle 1, Puzzle middle 2, Puzzle middle 3, Puzzle side, Question mark, Retailer, Rocket, Scales, Ship, Shopping cart, Shopping cart 2, Sign post, Stack of papers, Star, Stop sign, Stretchable dollars, Stretchable pounds, Sunglasses, Switch, Target, Television set, Thermometer, Tombstone, Train, Train car, Tree, Truck, Truck 2, U.S. dollar, Umbrella, Variable building, Variable smoke, Variable stack, VISA, Warning sign, Wholesaler, Wooden barrel, Yen, Yin Yang

Map

The following table lists the stencils that open with the Map templates. Map shapes in Visio are meant to help you diagram a place or landscape.

Stencil	Shapes
Landmark Shapes	Airport, Building 1, Building 2, Callout, Cathedral, City, Curiosity, Direction, Factory, Ferry, Fire station, Hospital, House, Lake, North, Ocean, Park, Petrol station, Public house, River, Scale, School, Shopping centre, Shrine, Skyscraper, Stadium, Temple, Text block 10pt, Text block 18pt, Text block 8pt, Town hall, Train station, Train Station2, Tree, Warehouse
Metro Shapes	Flexible metro, Metro curve 1, Metro curve 2, Metro Line, Rounded metro, Station, Stop callout, Transfer station
Recreation Shapes	Amphitheater, Boat launch, Campfire, Campground, Canoe access, Climbing, Cross-country skiing, Downhill skiing, Fishing, Golf, Hiking, Horseback riding, Kayaking, Marina, Parking, Potable water, Racquetball/handball, Restroom, RV, SCUBA diving, Shower, Skating, Snowboarding, Snowmobile, Supplies/store, Swimming, Tennis, Volleyball
Road Shapes	3-way, 4-way, Bridge, Cloverleaf interchange, Corner, Curve 1, Curve 2, Diamond interchange, Flexible road, Road round, Road square, Roadway break, Roundabout, Thin road
Transportation Shapes	Alignment road, Arrow, Arrow sign, City/Town dot, EU country designation, Forbidden, Give way, Hazard warning, Information, Junction number, Motorway, Motorway services, No access, No Entry, No Parking, One way, Parking, Railway, Railway curve, Route number 1, Route number 2, Smart junction 1, Smart junction 2, Smart road (distance), Smart road 1, Smart road 2, Smart road 3, Stop, Traffic light

Network

The one network template in Visio standard opens 5 stencils, 3 or which are network shapes, as listed in the following table.

Stencils	Shapes
Basic Network Shapes	ASCII Printer, Bridge, CD burner, Cell phone, City, Cloud, Comm-link, Database, Desktop PC, DVD drive, Dynamic connector, Ethernet, Fax, FDDI ring, Firewall, Flat screen monitor, Floppy drive, Hand held computer, Hub, iBook, iMac, Keyboard, Laptop computer, Line connector, Line-curve connector, Modem, Monitor, Mouse, MUX / DEMUX, Optical drive, Patch bay, Pen based computer, Plotter, Power Mac G4, Printer, Printer 2, Printer 3, RAID drive, Removable storage, Scanner, Server, Star, Straight bus, Tape drive, Telephone, Token-ring, Tower box, Tower PC, Workstation
Basic Network Shapes 2	10BASE-T wall plate, A-B switchbox, Acoustic coupler, Answering machine, Cable, Comm. hub, Cray, CRT projector, Custom equipment, Digitizing pad, Disk array, Fiber optic xmitter, Host, IBM AS/400, IBM PS/2, Link builder, LocalTalk, Long card, Mainframe, Micro VAX, Minicomputer, Network Controller, Network processor, Oscilloscope, PBX / PABX, Power strip, Processor, Public switch, Punchdown block, Rack mount, Radio tower, Repeater, Router, Satellite, Satellite dish, Screen, Short card, Synchronous host, Tape, Television, Terminal server, VAX, Video
Basic Network Shapes 3D	Bottom to top angled, Bridge, Bus network, Card, City, Color box, Comm. tower, Comm-link, Fax, Firewall, Hub / switch, Keyboard, Laptop, Mainframe, Mini computer, Modem, Mouse, Multiplexer, PBX / comm. hub, PDA, Personal computer, Plotter, Printer, Repeater, Ring network, Room, Router, Satellite, Satellite dish, Scanner, Server, Side to side angled, Telephone, Terminal server, Town, WAN, Workstation

Office Layout

The one office layout template in Visio standard opens 5 stencils as listed in the following table. Use these shapes to create your office or home as a Visio diagram.

Stencil	Shapes
Office Accessories	Coat rack, Desk lamp, Large plant, Marker board, Paper tray, Plant, Round waste can, Small plant, Square waste can, Table lamp, Tackboard
Office Equipment	Copier, Desktop copier, Document shredder, Duplicator, Fax machine, Hub, Keyboard, Overhead projector, PBX, PC, PC monitor, Plotter, Power point, Printer, Projection screen, Projector, Scanner, Switch, Telephone, Telephone jack, Terminal, Tower PC, Typewriter

A

Stencil	Shapes
Office Furniture	1-arm seat module, 2 seat sofa, 2-arm seat module, 45° table, 90° table, Boat shape table, Bookshelf, Chair, Corner surface, Corner table, Credenza, Desk, Desk chair, File, Flat file, High stool, Lateral file, Multi-chair boat shape, Multi-chair racetrack, Multi-chair rectangle, Multi-chair round table, Racetrack table, Round corner, Round table, Seat 30° in-module, Seat 30° out-module, Seat module, Side chair w/o arms, Side chair with arms, Sofa, Stool, Storage unit, Swivel tilt chair, Table, Work surface
Cubicles	Corner surface, Council workstation, Cube workstation, Curved panel, L shaped workstation, L workstation, Panel, Panel post, Pedestal, Round corner, Storage unit, Straight workstation, Susp coat bar / shelf, Susp open shelf, Suspended lateral file, U shaped workstation, Work peninsula, Work surface
Walls, Doors and Windows	Callout, Controller dimension, Corner pilaster, Curved wall, Door, Double door, L Room, Opening, Pilaster, Room, Room measurements, Space, T Room, Wall, Window

Organizational Chart

Both the Organizational Chart and the Organizational Chart Wizard open the same stencils, the Background stencil, the Borders stencil, and the Organizational Chart Stencil in the following table.

Stencils	Shapes
Organization Chart Shapes	Assistant, Consultant, Dynamic connector, Executive, Manager, Multiple shapes, Position, Staff, Team frame, Three positions, Title, Title/Date, Vacancy

Project Schedule

The four templates in Project Schedule open several different stencils, listed in the following table. Shapes on these stencils automatically update to your input.

Stencil	Shapes
Calendar Shapes	Arrow, Circle label, Date frame, Large month, Moon phases, Small date frame, Small month, Square label, Star label, Timeline, Yearly calendar
Gantt Chart Shapes	Column, Gantt Chart frame, Horizontal callout, Legend, Link lines, Milestone, Right-angle horizontal, Row, Task bar, Text block 10pt, Text block 12pt, Text block 8pt, Title

Stencil	Shapes
PERT Chart Shapes	Dynamic connector, Horizontal callout, Legend, Line connector, Line-curve connector, PERT 1, PERT 2, Right-angle horizontal, Summarization structure
Timeline Shapes	1-D timeline, 2 triangle milestone, Block interval, Block timeline, Bracket interval 1, Bracket interval 2, Chiseled interval, Chiseled timeline, Circle milestone, Cylindrical interval, Cylindrical milestone, Cylindrical timeline, Dagger milestone, Diamond milestone, Divided timeline, Elapsed time, Line milestone, Ruler timeline, Today marker, Triangle milestone, X milestone

Other Stencils

The stencils listed in the following table are stencils that come with Visio Standard, but do not open up with any template by default. They are generally for a very specific purpose and are meant to be opened when you need then in any template, and they are kept in the folder labeled Visio Extras.

Stencil	Shapes
Callouts	2-D word balloon, Angled stamp, Annotation, Automatic dimension, Balloon horizontal, Balloon vertical, Bend callout, Blunt starburst, Box callout, Braces with text, Button, Centre text callout, Custom callout 1, Custom callout 2, Custom callout 3, File, Full bracket text, Line with text, Mid box callout, Mid elbow box, Mid elbow callout, Mid line callout, Mid line elbow, Mid text callout, Oval callout, Partial bracket text, Rounded stamp, Sharp starburst, Side box callout, Side brace, Side bracket, Side elbow box, Side elbow callout, Side line callout, Side line elbow, Side parenthesis, Side text callout, Tag, Window, Yellow note
Connectors	1-D double, 1-D open end, 1-D single, 2 lines, 2-line elbow, 4 lines, 4-line elbow, Angled connector, Arced arrow, Bottom-top, Bottom to side 1, Bottom to side 2, Bottom to side 3, Bottom to top 1, Bottom to top 2, Bottom to top fixed 1, Bottom to top fixed 2, Bus, Comm-link 1, Comm-link 2, Control transfer, Curve connect 1, Curve connect 2, Curve connect 3, Directed line 1, Directed line 2, Dot & arrow, Dotted line, Double arrowhead, Double tree sloped, Double tree square, Dynamic connector, Elbow 1, Elbow 2, Ethernet, Flexi-arrow, Flow director 1, Flow director 2, Hollow connect 1, Hollow connect 2, Hollow connect 3, Jumper, Layout connector, Line connector, Line-arc connector, Line-curve connector, Mid-arrow, Mid-arrow dotted, Multi-tree sloped, Multi-tree square, One to many, Side-side, Side-top/bottom, Side to side 1, Side to side 2, Side to side fixed 1, Side to side fixed 2, Side to top, Side to top/bottom, Sides, Single arrowhead, Square loop, Star, Top/bottom-side, Top/bottom to side, Tops or bottoms, Universal connector, Wavy connector 1, Wavy connector 2

A

Stencil	Shapes
Embellishments	Arc ornament, Art deco circle, Art deco frame, Art deco tile, Braid corner, Braid end-cap, Braid section, Button ornament, Celtic ornament, Checker section, Chiseled frame, Classic frame, Cross corner, Cross end-cap, Cross section, Diamond tile, Egyptian corner, Egyptian end-cap, Egyptian section, Fun frame, Graphic tile, Greek border, Greek corner, Greek section, Jewel frame, Multi line frame, Op-art tile, Photo frame, Roman section, Single line frame, Square frame, Star section, Triangle section, Wave corner, Wave corner 2, Wave corner 3, Wave section, Wave section 2, Wave tile, Weave tile, Zigzag tile
Symbols	Airport, Bicycle, Biohazard, Bus station, Cloudy, Coffee, Deutsche Mark, Dining, Drinks, Euro, First aid, Fragile, Franc, Handicap, Information, Lightning, Lodging, Men, NO sign, No smoking, Park, Partly cloudy, Post, Pound, Radioactive, Rail transportation, Rain, Recycle 1, Recycle 2, Service station, Square box, Stair, Storm, Sunny, Telephone, Trash Bin, U.S. dollar, Warning sign, Women, Yen, Zone
Annotations	12pt. text, 15 ruled column, 5 ruled column, 6pt. text, 8pt. text, Benchmark, Box callout, Break line, Callout-bent, Callout-curved, Callout-straight, Ceiling, Circle callout, Datum, Drawing scale, Info. line, Level, North arrow 1, North arrow 2, North arrow 3, North arrow 4, North arrow 5, Note symbol, Oval callout, Reference callout 1, Reference callout 2, Reference circle, Reference hexagon, Reference oval, Reference plane (site), Reference plane 1, Reference plane 2, Reference rectangle, Reference triangle, Revision cloud, Scale symbol, Section 1, Section 2, Section 3
Dimensioning – Engineering	Aligned even, Aligned out even, Aligned out uneven, Aligned uneven, Angle center, Angle even, Angle outside, Angle uneven, Arc radius, Centerline, Diameter, Diameter outside, Horizontal, Horizontal baseline, Horizontal outside, Ordinate horizontal, Ordinate multi-horz., Ordinate multi-vert., Ordinate vertical, Radius, Radius outside, Room measure, Special characters, Vertical, Vertical baseline, Vertical outside, Circle, ellipse, Rt. triangle: angle, hyp.
Drawing Tool Shapes	Arc-graphical, Arc-numeric, Arc tangents, Arc: 3pt., Chamfered corner, Chamfered rectangle, Circle-diameter, Circle-radius, Circle tangent, Circle tangents, Circle: 3pt., Circles, Diagonal rectangle, Line with extensions, Multigon center, Multigon edge, Opposite tangent, Perpendicular angle, Perpendicular lines, Rectangle, Rounded rectangle, Rt. triangle: 2 legs, Sector-graphical, Sector-numeric, Triangle: base, height, Triangle: free
Title Blocks	15 ruled column, 5 ruled column, Block-side label, Block-top label, Contin. sheet large, Contin. sheet small, Date, Description, Drawn by, File/path, Filename, Frame, Page#, Parts list block, Projection symbol, Revised, Revision large, Revision small, Revision zone large, Revision zone small, Revisions block, Scale, Section header, SI symbol, Title, Title block large, Title block small, Zones-4, Zones-8

Stencil	Shapes
Custom Line Patterns	Border, Border2, BorderX2, Center, Center2, CenterX2, Dashdot, Dashdot2, DashdotX2, Dashed, Dashed2, DashedX2, Divide, Divide2, DivideX2, Dot, Dot2, DotX2, Hidden, Hidden2, HiddenX2, Pattern help, Phantom, Phantom2, PhantomX2
Custom Patterns– Scaled	Ar-B816, Ar-B816C, Ar-B88, Ar-Brelm, Ar-brstd, Ar-hbone, Ar-rshke, Brick, Brstone, Pattern help
Custom Patterns– Unscaled	ACAD_ISO02W100, ACAD_ISO03W100, Angle, ANSI31, ANSI32, ANSI33, ANSI34, ANSI35, ANSI36, ANSI37, ANSI38, Ar-Conc, Ar-parq1, Ar-Rroof, Box, Brass, Clay, Cork, Cross, Dash, Dolmit, Dots, Earth, Escher, Flex, Grass, Grate, Hex, Honey, Hound, Insul, Line, Mudst, Net, Net3, Pattern help, Plast, Plasti, Sacncr, Square, Stars, Steel, Swamp, Trans, Triangle, Zigzag

Visio Professional

Visio Professional comes with more than twenty templates, almost a hundred stencils, and thousands of shapes. This section outlines each template, its attached stencils, and then lists the stencils and each shape it includes.

Templates

This section lists all the templates that come with Visio Professional by category.

Block Diagram

These are the exact same templates and stencils that come with Visio standard in the same category.

Building Plan

These are what used to be called Office Layout templates in earlier version of Visio. The next table lists all the Building Plan templates.

Template	Description	Stencils Opened
Floor Plan	Create commercial building designs, space plans, architectural layouts, construction documents, structural diagrams, and facilities plans. Uses a scale of 1/8 = 1' (1:96).	Building Core, Dimensioning Architectural, Drawing Tool Shapes, Electrical and Telecom, Walls, Shell and Structure

A

Template	Description	Stencils Opened
Home Plan	Create kitchen, bathroom, and interior designs, architectural and construction documents, space plans, home layouts, and plans for remodeling and additions. Uses a scale of 1/4:1' (1:48).	Annotations, Appliances, Bath and Kitchen Plan, Building Core, Cabinets, Dimensioning-Architectural, Drawing Tool Shapes, Electrical and Telecom, Furniture, Garden Accessories, Walls, Shell and Structure
Plant Layout	Create plant layouts for production, storage, distribution, transport, shipping, and receiving of manufactured goods. Uses a scale of 1/8=1' (1:96).	Annotations, Building Core, Dimensioning-Architectural, Drawing Tool Shapes, Electrical and Telecom, Shop Floor-Machines and Equipment, Shop Floor-Storage and Distribution, Vehicles, Walls, Shell and Structure, Warehouse-Shipping and Receiving
Reflected Ceiling Plan	Create commercial building ceiling tile and lighting panel layouts, and HVAC grille and diffuser layouts. Uses a scale of 1/8=1' (1:96).	Building Core, Drawing Tool Shapes, Electrical and Telecom, Registers, Grills and Diffusers, Walls, Shell and Structure
Site Plan	Create residential and commercial landscape designs, parks plans, yard layouts, plat maps, outdoor recreational facilities plans, and irrigation systems. Uses a scale of 1=10' (1:120).	Annotations, Dimensioning-Architectural, Drawing Tool Shapes, Garden Accessories, Irrigation, Parking and Roads, Planting, Sport Fields and Recreation, Vehicles, Site Accessories
Electric and Telecom Plan	Create plans for internal and external security systems, security control systems, security control monitoring, security system blueprints, and wiring diagrams.	Drawing Tool Shapes, Electrical and Telecom, Walls, Shell and Structure
HVAC Control Logic Diagram	Create HVAC systems and controls diagrams for heating, ventilation, air conditioning and distribution, refrigeration, automated building control, environmental control, and energy systems.	Annotations, HVAC Controls, HVAC Controls Equipment
HVAC Plan	Create annotated diagrams of heating, ventilation, air conditioning and distribution, and refrigeration systems for automated building control, environmental control, and energy systems.	Drawing Tool Shapes, HVAC Ductwork, HVAC Equipment, Registers, Grills and Diffusers
Plumbing and Piping Plan	Create annotated diagrams or schematics of waste water disposal systems, hot and cold water supply systems, water lines, and plumbing layouts for plumbing systems and waste water engineering.	Drawing Tool Shapes, Pipes and Valves-Pipes1, Pipes and Valves-Pipes2, Pipes and Valves-Valves1, Pipes and Valves-Valves2, Plumbing

Template	Description	Stencils Opened
Security and Access Plan	Create plans for internal and external security systems, security control systems, security control monitoring, security system blueprints, and wiring diagrams.	Alarm and Access Control, Initiation and Annunciation, Video Surveillance
Space Plan	Create space plans to track the locations of people, offices, and equipment. Uses a scale of 1/8 = 1' (1:96).	Annotations, Building Core, Cubicles, Dimensioning-Architectural, Electrical and Telecom, Office Equipment, Office Furniture, Resources, Walls, Shell and Structure

Database

The following table lists the templates meant to help you diagram your database.

Template	Description	Stencils Opened
Database Model Diagram	Design and generate new databases, and document and update existing databases. Supports IDEF1X and relational notations.	Entity Relationship, Object Relational
Express-G	Create entity level and schema level diagrams, and product data models, using the Express-G notation. Meets STEP (Standard for the Exchange of Product Model Data) interface specifications.	Express-G
ORM Diagram	Contains shapes for objects, constraints, connectors, predicates, and relationships. Use for object-relationship models and static diagrams in object-oriented analysis and design.	ORM Diagram

Electrical Engineering

The templates listed in the next table are meant to help you design and diagram your Electrical Engineering system.

Template	Template Description	Stencils Opened
Circuits and Logic	Create annotated circuit and printed circuit board diagrams, integrated circuit schematics, and digital and analog logic designs. Contains terminal, connector, and transmission path shapes.	Analog and Digital Logic, Integrated Circuit Components, Terminals and Connectors, Transmission Paths

A

Template	Template Description	Stencils Opened
Basic Electrical	Create schematic, one-line, and wiring diagrams and blueprints. Contains shapes for switches, relays, transmission paths, semiconductors, circuits, and tubes.	Fundamental Items, Qualifying Symbols, Semiconductors and Electron Tubes, Switches and Relays, Transmission Paths
Industrial Control Systems	Create annotated diagrams of industrial power systems. Contains shapes for rotary machines, semiconductors, solid-state devices, switches, relays, and transformers.	Fundamental Items, Rotating Equip and Mech Functions, Switches and Relays, Terminals and Connectors, Transformers and Windings, Transmission Paths
Systems	Create annotated electrical schematics, maintenance and repair diagrams, and utilities infrastructure designs. Contains shapes for static, communications, and solid-state devices.	Composite Assemblies, Maintenance Symbols, Maps and Charts, Switches and Relays, Telecoms Switch and Peripheral Equip, Terminals and Connectors, Transformers and Windings, Transmission Paths, VHF-UHF-SHF

Flowchart, Forms and Charts, and Map

These are the same templates as come with Visio Standard, listed earlier in this chapter.

Mechanical Engineering

The templates listed in the next table are the templates meant to help you create diagrams of complicated mechanical systems.

Template	Template Description	Stencils Opened
Fluid Power	Create annotated drawings of pneumatic and hydraulic systems, fluid power assemblies, flow control, flow path, valves and valve assemblies, and fluid power equipment.	Annotations, Connectors, Fluid Power-Equipment, Fluid Power-Valve Assembly, Fluid Power-Valves
Part and Assembly Drawing	Create annotated mechanical engineering and technical drawings, diagrams, blueprints, and schematics to design machine tools and mechanical devices.	Annotations, Dimensioning-Engineering, Drawing Tool Shapes, Fasteners 1, Fasteners 2, Geometric Dimensioning and Tolerancing, Springs and Bearings, Title Blocks, Welding Symbols

Network

The templates listed in the next table are meant to help you diagram your computer network.

Template	Template Description	Stencils Opened
Logical Network Diagram	Contains network and computer equipment shapes for detailed physical, logical, and network architecture diagrams, network design and documentation, and networked structures.	Generic Manufacturer Equipment, Internet Symbols, Logical Symbols, Network Devices, PC & Peripherals, Printers & Scanners, Telecom
Visio Network Equipment Sampler	Contains a sample of manufacturer-specific Visio Network Equipment shapes used in the creation of network diagrams.	Visio Network Equipment Sampler
Basic Network	Contains basic network and computer equipment shapes for network architecture diagrams, network design and documentation, and networked structures.	Basic Network Shapes 2, Basic Network Shapes 3D, Basic Network Shapes, Borders and Titles, Backgrounds
Active Directory	Document Active Directory services using shapes that represent common Active Directory objects, sites, and services.	Active Directory Objects, Active Directory Sites & Services, Exchange Objects
LDAP Directory	Contains shapes that represent common LDAP (Lightweight Directory Access Protocol) objects used to document directory services.	LDAP Objects
Novell Directory Services	Document Novell Directory Services (NDS) using shapes that represent common NDS objects and partitions.	NDS Additional Objects, NDS Objects, NDS Partitions, NDS GroupWise, NDS ZenWorks

Organizational Chart

These are the same templates, in the same category, listed earlier in this chapter under Visio Standard.

Process Engineering

The templates listed in the next table are meant to help diagram complicated piping and other systems.

Template	Template Description	Stencils Opened
Piping and Instrumentation Diagram	Create P&IDs for piping systems (industrial, process, vacuum, fluids, hydraulics, and air and gas), piping supports, materials distribution, and liquid transfer systems.	Equipment-General, Equipment-Heat Exchangers, Equipment-Pumps, Equipment-Vessels, Instruments, Pipelines, Process Annotations, Valves and Fittings

A

Template	Template Description	Stencils Opened
Process Flow Diagram	Create PFDs for piping systems (industrial, process, vacuum, fluids, hydraulics, and air and gas), piping supports, materials distribution, and liquid transfer systems.	Equipment-General, Equipment-Heat Exchangers, Equipment-Pumps, Equipment-Vessels, Instruments, Pipelines, Process Annotations, Valves and Fittings

Project Schedule

These are the same templates listed earlier in this chapter under Visio Standard.

Software

The templates listed in the following table are meant to help you design and diagram parts of the software design process.

Template	Template Description	Stencils Opened
UML Model Diagram	Create UML models and static structure (class and object), use case, collaboration, sequence, component, deployment, activity, and statechart diagrams, using the UML notation.	UML activity, UML collaboration, UML component, UML deployment, UML sequence, UML statechart, UML static structure, UML use case
Data Flow Model Diagram	Create dataflow diagrams using the Gane-Sarson (DFD) notation.	Gane-Sarson
Enterprise Application	Create enterprise architecture diagrams using shapes representing PCs, mainframes, and architecture layers.	Enterprise Application
Windows User Interface	Contains user interface elements, controls, buttons, and clip art for conceptual screen shots and diagrams of Windows and Office applications.	Windows User Interface, Office User Interface
Jackson	Create data structure diagrams for program design using the Jackson methodology.	Jackson
ROOM	Model real time systems based on timeliness, dynamic internal structure, reactiveness, concurrency, and distribution, using the ROOM notation.	ROOM
Program Structure	Create structural diagrams, flowcharts, and memory diagrams.	Language Level Shapes, Memory Objects

Template	Template Description	Stencils Opened
COM and OLE	Create systems, COM, and OLE diagrams, or diagrams of public exposed interfaces, COM interfaces, and OLE interfaces in object-oriented programming.	COM and OLE

Web Design

Web design templates, listed in the next table, are meant to help you design and document your web site.

Template	Template Description	Stencils Opened
Conceptual Web Site	Design conceptual diagrams and high-level architectures of home pages, Web sites, and hyperlinked documents.	Conceptual Web Site Shapes, Web Site Map Shapes, Callouts
Web Site Map	Design diagrams of home pages, Web sites, hyperlinked documents and networked information for the Internet, intranets, computer communications, and the World Wide Web.	Web Site Map Shapes

Stencils

This section lists all the stencils, by category, which are included with the U.S. version of Visio Professional.

Most Used Stencils

These are the same stencils listed earlier in this chapter under Visio Standard.

Block Diagram

These are the same stencils listed earlier in this chapter under Visio Standard.

Building Plan

Building Plan stencils, listed in the following table, contain walls, rooms, structural shapes, furniture, wiring, and even plants to help you diagram or design your environment.

A

Stencil	Shapes
Office Accessories	Coat rack, Desk lamp, Large plant, Marker board, Paper tray, Plant, Round waste can, Small plant, Square waste can, Table lamp, Tackboard
Office Equipment	Copier, Desktop copier, Document shredder, Duplicator, Fax machine, Hub, Keyboard, Overhead projector, PBX, PC, PC monitor, Plotter, Power point, Printer, Projection screen, Projector, Scanner, Switch, Telephone, Telephone jack, Terminal, Tower PC, Typewriter
Office Furniture	1-arm seat module, 2 seat sofa, 2-arm seat module, 45° table, 90° table, Boat shape table, Bookshelf, Chair, Corner surface, Corner table, Credenza, Desk, Desk chair, File, Flat file, High stool, Lateral file, Multi-chair boat shape, Multi-chair racetrack, Multi-chair rectangle, Multi-chair round table, Racetrack table, Round corner, Round table, Seat 30° in-module, Seat 30° out-module, Seat module, Side chair w/o arms, Side chair with arms, Sofa, Stool, Storage unit, Swivel tilt chair, Table, Work surface
Cubicles	Corner surface, Council workstation, Cube workstation, Curved panel, L shaped workstation, L workstation, Panel, Panel post, Pedestal, Round corner, Storage unit, Straight workstation, Susp coat bar / shelf, Susp open shelf, Suspended lateral file, U shaped workstation, Work peninsula, Work surface
Walls, Doors and Windows	Callout, Controller dimension, Corner pilaster, Curved wall, Door, Double door, L Room, Opening, Pilaster, Room, Room measurements, Space, T Room, Wall, Window
Appliances	Built-in Refrg, Chest freezer, Coffee maker, Combo W/D, Cooker 1, Cooker 2, Cooker 3, Dishwasher, Food cooler, Microwave, Range, Refrg 1, Refrg 2, Refrg 3, Refuse compactor, Stacked W/D, Television, Tumble dryer, Vending machine, Video game, Wall oven, Washing machine, Water cooler, Water heater
Bath and Kitchen Plan	Basin, Bath 1, Bath 2, Bidet, Corner bath, Corner shower, Countertop sink, Double basin, Medicine cabinet 1, Medicine cabinet 2, Oval bath, Pedestal sink 1, Pedestal sink 2, Shower, Sink 1, Sink 2, Sink 3, Squat wc, Toilet, Towel rack, TP dispenser, Wall toilet
Building Core	Calculated stairs, Chute, Corner hand rail, Corner landing, Countertop sink, Elevator, Escalator, Freight elevator, Guard rail, Hand rail, Loading dock, Ornamental stair, Ramp, Scissor staircase, Spiral staircase, Stair direction, Stair landing, Stair section, Straight staircase, Toilet, Toilet Stall, Urinal, Vault, Washroom counter 1, Washroom counter 2
Cabinets	Base 1, Base 2, Base blind corner, Base corner, Base end angle, Base end-shelf, Base peninsula 1, Base peninsula 2, Locker, L-shaped countertop, Peninsula end-shelf, Track 45 deg., Track corner, Track end-bevel, Tray track, Utility cabinet 1, Utility cabinet 2, Wall corner, Wall 1, Wall 2, Wall angle cabinet, Wall blind corner 1, Wall blind corner 2, Wall blind peninsula, Wall end-shelf, Wall peninsula 1, Wall peninsula 2

Stencil	Shapes
Furniture	Adjustable bed, Bookcase, Chair, Chest, Circular dining table, Circular table, Couch, Desk, Double dresser, Grand piano, House plant, Large plant, Lounge chair, Night stand, Oblong dining table, Oval dining table, Ping-pong table, Recliner, Rect. table, Small plant, Sofa, Spinet piano, Square table, Stool, Triple dresser
Garden Accessories	Brick pathway, Chain link fence, Chain link gate, Concrete pathway, Driveway, Flagstone, Hex stone, Masonry fence, Masonry post/pillar, Metal post, Patio, Round stone, Square stone, Stone fence, Wood fence, Wood gate, Wood post
Irrigation	Backflow preventor, Controller, Drip line, Hose bib, Lateral line, Main line, Valve, Valve key symbol, Var. circ. spray head, Var. rect. spray head, Water meter
Parking and Roads	Center island 1, Center island 2, Corner curb 1, Corner curb 2, Curb with ramp, Driveway beveled, Driveway rounded, End island 1, End island 2, Intersection, Parking lane 1, Parking lane 2, Parking stall 1, Parking stall 2, Parking strip 1, Parking strip 2, Radial strip 1, Radial strip 2, Sidewalk ramp, Wrap-around island
Planting	Broadleaf evrg. shrub, Broadleaf evrg. tree, Broadleaf hedge, Cactus, Conifer hedge, Conifer shrub a, Conifer shrub b, Conifer shrub c, Conifer shrub d, Conifer tree A, Conifer tree B, Conifer tree C, Conifer tree D, Decid. shrub a, Decid. shrub b, Decid. shrub c, Decid. shrub d, Decid. shrub e, Decid. tree A, Decid. tree B, Decid. tree C, Decid. tree D, Groundcover, Ornamental grass, Palm tree, Perennial border, Plant callout, Potted plant 1, Potted plant 2, Succulent
Shop Floor-Machines and Equipment	Centre lathe, CNC lathe, Compressor, Drill press, Drilling machine, Fire extinguisher, First aid cabinet, Folding machine, Generator, Hand roller press, Horz. band saw, Horz. milling machine, MIG welder, Mobile tool box, Operator, Platform trolley, Sawing machine, Shaping machine, Shearing machine, Standard box, Surface grinder, TIG welder, Turret milling machine, Vert. band saw, Vert. milling machine, Work bench
Shop Floor-Storage and Distribution	Angled roller, Bridge crane, Conveyor belt, Diesel forklift, Drive-in rack, Electric forklift, Floor crane, Freestanding shelf, Gantry crane, Manual pallet truck, Mezzanine floor, Mobile shelf, Order picker, Overbrace jib crane, Powered pallet truck, Push back rack, Rack section, Rising cab forklift, Roller conveyor, Sloped rack, Stacking forklift, Standard pallet, Standard rack, Standard shelf, Storage drum, Underbrace jib crane, Wall jib crane
Site Accessories	Barbecue, Bench, Bike rack, Bird bath, Bollard, Bollard line, Boulder, Collection box, Drain, Dumpster, Fire hydrant, Handicapped sign, Lamp post, Lawn chair, Light, Lounge chair, Manhole, Outdoor Bench, Picnic table, Security booth, Security gate, Site light 1, Site light 2, Table, Trash can, Umbrella
Sport Fields and Recreation	Badminton court, Baseball diamonds, Basketball 3-pt, Basketball court, Basketball hoop, Basketball key, Competition pool, Diving board, Football field, Kidney-shaped pool, Lap pool, Oval pool, Play structure, Rectangular pool, Soccer field, Spa, Swing set, Tennis court, Volleyball court

A

Stencil	Shapes
Vehicles	Articulated metro bus, Box van, Bus turn, Compact car, Compact pickup, Fire Truck, Full-size car, Full-size pickup, Full-size van, Large semi turn, Large semitrailer, Large tractor, Limousine, Med. tractor, Metro bus, Mid-size car, Minivan, School bus, Semi trailer, Small semi turn, Small semitrailer, Small tractor, Streetcar, Tour bus, Truck, Truck turn, X-large semi turn
Walls, Shell and Structure	Beam, Bi-fold, By-pass, Casement, Circular column, Controller dimension, Corner pilaster, Curtain wall, Curved wall, Door, Door schedule, Double, Double bi-fold, Double hung, Double pocket, Exterior wall, Garden window, Glider window, Grid line, Grid origin, L Room, L Space, Opening, Opposing, Overhead door, Pilaster, Pocket, Rectangular column, Revolving, Room, Room measurements, Slab, Sliding glass, Space, T Room, T Space, Uneven, Wall, Window, Window schedule, Window wall
Warehouse-Shipping and Receiving	Compactor, Container crane, Container ramp, Dock leveller, Dock-side crane, Gas cage, Gate, Insulated door, Loading bay, Loading dock, Oil tank, Roller shutter, Security barrier, Security office, Shipping container, Skip, Swing door 1, Swing door 2, Wheel guards
Electrical and Telecom	Batten fluores, Ceiling fan, Detector, Dimmer switch, Down lighter, Emerg. light, Emerg. sign, Encl ceiling lum, Fire alarm, Ground, Hold open unit, Lum. ceiling mount, Main control, Modular fluores, Multi-light bar, Office fluores, Outdoor lighting, Pull-cord switch, Service panels, Socket outlet, Stereo outlet, Switches, Telephone outlet, Television outlet, Thermostat, Wall light
Registers, Grills and Diffusers	Circular outlet, Grille, Grille (side), Grille diffuser, Linear outlet, Rectangular inlet, Rectangular outlet, Troffer inlet, Troffer outlet
Alarm And Access Control	Biometric access, Camera with card reader, Camera with intercom, Camera with keypad, Card access, Card reader with keypad, Card reader with time, Electronic lock, Exit device, Keypad device, Revolving door, Security window screen, Traffic arm, Turnstile, Vehicle loop detector
HVAC Controls	Actuator, Air quality, Connection line, Current, End switch, Enthalpy, Flow, General, Humidity, I/O point, Label, Level, Light, Power, Power connection, Pressure, Rotation, Smoke, Temperature, Timer, Velocity, Vibration, Voltage, Wire note
HVAC Controls Equipment	Air flow station, Boiler, Centrifugal fan, Chiller, Converter, Cooling tower, Damper, DD-VAV box, Duct, Duct extension, Equipment, Fan coil housing, Filter, Heat exchanger, Htg/clg coil, Humidifier, Multi fan section, Pipe flow arrow, Propeller fan, Pump, Return duct, Side to bottom pipe, Side to side pipe, Starter, Supply duct, Top to bottom pipe, Unit heater, Valve, Vane axial fan, VAV box, VSD, Water flow meter
HVAC Ductwork	3 Way Junction, Beveled Junction, Branch Duct, Dampers, Duct, Flexible connection 1, Flexible connection 2, Flexible duct 1, Flexible duct 2, Flexible duct pattern, Flexible duct pattern.14, Junction, Miter bend, Offset transition, Return, Sliding damper, Straight Duct, Supply, Tee junction, Transition, Variable bend, VAV Box, Vertical Duct, Y Junction

Stencil	Shapes
HVAC Equipment	Access door, Air filter, Axial fan, Centrifugal fan, Centrifugal pump, Chiller, Condenser 1, Condenser 2, Drier, Fan blades, Moisture eliminator, Pipe coil, Propeller fan, Pump, Reciprocating pump, Refrigerant receiver, Rotary pump, Screw pump, Silencer
Initiation and Annunciation	Audio device, Control panel, CPU, Document destroyer, Intercom, Keyboard, Multiplex panel, Printer, Two way radio
Pipes and Valves-Pipes 1	Access points, Anchor, Basic support, Bellows, Capillary line, Cross, Crossings, Double branch, Elbow 45, Elbow 90, Electric line, Electrical device, Expansion loop, Flexibility provision, Flexible hose, Flow restrictor, Guide 1, Guide 2, Hangers, Heated or cooled, Hydraulic line, Indication of flow, Internal connection, Jacketed, Junctions, Lagged, Mechanical linkage, Pipe bore change, Pneumatic line, Reducer, Rotary motion, Route radiation, Signal line, Sleeve extension, Sleeved, Spray device, Stirring /Fan, Stopper, Supports/ Anchor, Traps, Vibratory device, Weight device
Pipes and Valves-Pipes 2	Bell mouth, Bursting disc, Butt welds, Drain silencer, Electrically bonded, Electrically insulated, End caps 1, End caps 2, End caps 3, Exhaust head, Exhaust silencer, Flame arrester, Flanged/ bolted, General joint, Hydrant, Liquid seal open/closed, Open vent, Screwed joints, Separator, Sleeve joints, Socket and Spigot, Socket welds, Soldered/ solvent, Strainer, Swivel joints, Syphon drain, Tundish, Y strainer
Pipes and Valves -Valves 1	3-Way plug valves, Angle valves, Ball valves, Butterfly valves, Character. port, Check valves, Diaphragm valves, Flanged valve, Float operated, Gate valve, Globe valves, In-line valves, Mixing valve, Needle valves, Plug valves, Powered valves, Reducing valves, Relief (angle), Relief valves, Screw-down valves, Wedge/ Parallel
Pipes and Valves -Valves 2	Chain operated, Connecting units, Dash-pot/ piston, Diaphragm, Float operated, Gear operated, In-line Valves, Manual isolation, Motor elements, Power signal, Quick- open/close, Regulating, Remote control, Solenoid, Spring loaded, Statically loaded, Weight loaded
Plumbing	Basin, Basin(side), Bath, Bath (side), Boiler, Convector, End view, Heater / cooler, Heating / cooling coil, Pipe coils, Pump, Radiant panel (plan), Radiant panel(face), Radiator, Shower head, Sink unit, Tank open/closed, Toilet (side), Toilet 1, Toilet 2, Towel rail, Water surface
Video Surveillance	Bi-static beam sensor, Camera, Camera P/T/Z, Glass break sensor, Monitor, Motion detector, Push button, Recorder, Screening device, Security window screen w/ alarm, Switch-automatic, Switch-manual, Video keyboard, Video motion detector, Video multiplexer
Resources	Asset, Asset report, Boundary, Computer, Equipment, Fixture, Furniture, Person, Printer, Space, Space report, Title block

A

Database

Database stencils, listed in the following table, contain shapes to help you diagram the relationships between pieces of data or even table of data.

Stencil	Shapes
Entity Relationship	Category, Category to child, Dynamic connector, Entity, Parent to category, Relationship
Express-G	Base types, Boundary, Cardinality, Defined type, Entity, Enumerated type, From-page reference, Inverse cardinality, Label, Normal r'ship, Page reference, REFERENCED entity, Relationship pointer, Schema, Select type, Subtype/ supertype, To-page reference, Tree structure, USED entity
Object Relational	Category, Category to child, Dynamic connector, Entity, Parent to category, Relationship, Table inheritance, Type, Type inheritance
ORM Diagram	Binary, Constraint Connector, Entity, Equality Constraint, Exclusion Constraint, Ext. Freq. Constraint, Ext. Mand. Constraint, Ext. P Constraint, Ext. Uniq. Constraint, Frequency Constraint, Index Annotation, Left Uniqueness Constraint, Mand. Role Connector, Mandatory Constraint, Middle Uniqueness Constraint, P Constraint, Quaternary, Right Uniqueness Constraint, Ring Constraint, Role Connector, Subset Constraint, Subtype connector, Ternary, Unary, Uniqueness Constraint, Value, Vertical Binary

Electrical Engineering

Electrical Engineering stencils, listed in the following table, contains shapes for all your electrical diagramming or designing needs.

Stencil	Shapes
Analog and Digital Logic	Amplifier, Analog symbol, Buffer, Clock, Converter, Crystal, Delay element, Digital symbol, Divider, Flip-flop, Function generator, Function generator 2, Generalized integrator, I/O port, Integrator, Inverter, Logic gates 1, Logic gates 2, Multiplier, Negative logic dot, Operational amplifier, Operational amplifier 2, Positional servo, Potentiometer, Signal waveforms, Summing amplifier, Three-state buffer
Composite Assemblies	1-way repeater, 2-way repeater, 2-way repeater 4-wire, 2-way repeater bypass, Amplifier, Amplifier external DC control, Amplifier with bypass, Bridge rectifier, Chopper, Controlled rectifier, Converter, Demodulator, Fire ext. actuator, Fire ext. double, Gyro, Gyro 2, Heat source, Magnetic amplifier, Negative impedance both-way amp, Network low voltage, Phase shifter, Position indicator inductor, Position indicator synchro, Position transmitter Desynn, Position transmitter inductor, Proximity sensor, Rectifier, Rectifier bridge

Stencil	Shapes
Fundamental Items	AC source, Accumulator, Alternating pulse, Antenna, Antenna 2, Attenuator, Battery, Bell, Buzzer, Capacitor, Chassis, Circuit breaker, Crystal, DC source, Delay element, Equi-potentiality, Explosive squib, Ferrite core, Fluorescent lamp, Fuse, Generic component, Ground, Half inductor, Ideal source, Igniter plug, Indicator, Inductor, Lamp, Lamp 2, Magnet core, Material, Microphone, Microphone 2, Oscillator, Permanent magnet, Pickup head, Pulse, Resistor, Saw tooth, Sensing link squib, Speaker, Squib igniter, Step function, Surge protectors, Surge protectors 2, Thermal element, Thermocouple, Thermopile, Transducer, Transducer 2
Integrated Circuit Components	1X Building block-base, 1X Building block-complete, 1X Building block-middle, 1X Building block-top, 2-4 decoder, 3-8 decoder, 4-bit a/d converter, 4-bit counter, 4-bit d/a converter, 4-bit register, 4X Building block-base, 4X Building block-complete, 4X Building block-middle, 4X Building block-top, 8-bit a/d converter, 8-bit counter, 8-bit d/a converter, 8-bit register, Analog switch 2, Analog switch 4, Board, Driver, Ground, Horizontal extension, MUX 2, MUX 4, MUX 8, Negative logic dot, One shot, Preload counter 4, Preload counter 8, PWM, Switch point, Vertical extension, Voltage converter
Maintenance Symbols	Amplifier, Composite circuit, Energize relay signal, Feedback, Linear element, Reference signal, Relay coil, Relay contacts, Signal code, Signal generator, Switch, Test signal, Transmitter pulse
Maps and Charts	Coal fueled station, Controlling station, Converting station, Direction finding, Earth tracking station, Elec/heat station, End station, Generating station, Geothermic station, Hydroelectric station 1, Hydroelectric station 2, Hydroelectric station 3, Hydroelectric station 4, Mobile station, Nuclear station, Oil/gas fueled station, Passive relay, Plasma station MHD, Portable station, Prime mover, Radio station 1, Radio station 2, Radio relay station, Rectifier substation, Solar station, Space station, Subscriber equipment, Substation, Switching station, Telegraph equipment, Telegraph equipment qualifiers, Telegraph repeater, Telegraph repeater qualifiers, Telephone, Thermoelectric station, Wind station
Qualifying Symbols	2-phase 3-wire, 2-phase 4-wire, 3 separate windings, 3-phase delta 1, 3-phase delta 2, 3-phase delta 3, 3-phase delta 4, 3-phase zigzag, 3-Phase (T), 3-phase (V), 3-phase 4-wire, 3-phase star, 4-phase, 6-phase fork, 6-phase double delta, 6-phase double star, 6-phase polygon, Coaxial symbol, Electret, Multiple-phase, Negative polarity, Neutral symbol, Positive polarity, Radiation, Special connector
Rotating Equip and Mech Functions	Armature, Automatic return, Blocking device, Brake, Brush, Clutch, Clutch 2, Delayed action, Detent, Field, Gearing, Latching device, Manual control, Mechanical interlock, Permanent magnet, Rotating machine, Rotation, Synchro, Winding connection

A

Stencil	Shapes
Semiconductors and Electron Tubes	Backward diode, Bipolar, Breakdown diode, Controlled rectifier, Controlled switch, Darlington, Diac, Diode, Four layer diode, IGFET N-type, IGFET P-type, Junction, Latch, LED / photo-diode, MOSFET, Ohmic, Transverse, Triac, Tube diode, Tube pentode, Tube tetrode, Tube triode, Tunnel diode, Turn off rectifier, Turn-off triode, Unijunction, Varactor, Zener diode
Switches and Relays	2 position switch, 3 position switch, 4 position switch, Break contact, Change-over contact, Circuit breaker, DPDT, DPST, Flow actuated, Fuse, Gas flow actuated, Inertia switch, Isolator, Limit switch, Limit switch n/c, Limit switch n/o, Liquid level actuated, Liquid level actuated 2, Make contact, Manual switch, Mercury switch, Mercury switch 2, Passing make-contact, Pilot light, Pressure actuated, Proximity limit switch, Pushbutton 2-circuit, Pushbutton break, Pushbutton make, Relay, Relay coil, Relay contacts, Safety interlock, Selector switch, Shorting selector, SPDT, Spring return, Spring return 2, Spring return 3, SPST, Stay put, Switch disconnector, Temperature actuated, Temperature switch, Thermostat, Time delay break, Time delay break 2, Time delay make, Time delay make 2, Two way contact
Telecoms Switch and Peripheral Equip	Amplified circuit, Changer, Concentrating, Connecting stage, Disc type, Drum type, Erasing, Filter, Frequency band, Frequency spectrum element, Guided light transmitter, Magnetic type, Marking stage, Modulator, Moving coil type, Moving iron type, Networks, Pulse modulation, Recorder / reproducer, Recording / reproducing, Reproducing, Stereo type, Switching equipment 1, Switching equipment 2, Switching stage, Tape/Film type, Terminating sets, Transducer head
Terminals and Connectors	2-conductor jack, 2-conductor jack 2, 2-conductor plug, 2-conductor plug 2, AC out, Adapter, C header connector, Cable termination, Center cond. coax., Circuit terminal, Coaxial jack/plug, F/M 2-conductor 1, F/M 2-conductor 2, F/M 2-conductor 3, F/M 3-conductor 1, F/M 3-conductor 2, F/M 3-conductor 3, F/M 3-conductor 4, F/M 3-conductor 5, Large D connector, M/F contact, M/F contact 2, Normalled jack, Normalled jacks, Outside cond. coax., Shielded jack/plug, Small D connector, Terminal board
Transformers and Windings	1-phase induction volt. reg., Adjustable transformer, Choke, Coaxial choke, Current trans. 1, Current trans. 2, Current trans. 3, Induction voltage regulator, Inductor, Linear coupler, Magnetic core, Outdoor metering device, Pot. trans. 3 windings, Potential transformer, Potential transformer 2, Saturating transformer, Transductor, Transformer, Transformer 2, Triplex induction volt. reg., Variometer
Transmission Paths	2-line bus, 2-line bus elbow, 3-line bus, 3-line bus elbow, 4-line bus, 4-line bus elbow, Anticreepage device, Bus width, Cable group, Direction of flow, Elbow bus 1, Elbow bus 2, Junction, Junction/ crossing, Label, Lead group, Line / cable, Line concentrator, Optical fiber, Overground enclosure, Straight bus, Terminal, Terminal 3-phase, Test point, Transmission path

Stencil	Shapes
VHF-UHF-SHF	Balun, Capacitive reactance, Capacitive susceptance, Circulator fixed, Circulator reversible, Conductance, Directional coupler, Discontinuity, E-H tuner, Equivalent series, Equivalent shunt, Ferrite bead ring, Field polarization amp., Field polarization rotator, Frequency filter, Gyrator, Inductance capacitance 1, Inductance capacitance 2, Inductance capacitance 3, Inductance capacitance 4, Inductive reactance, Inductive susceptance, Isolator, Laser/Maser, Line stretcher, Mode filter, Mode suppressor, Multistub tuner, Phase shifter, Phase shifter (matched), Resistance, Resonator, Rotary joint, Ruby laser, Slide screw tuner

Flowchart, Forms and Charts, and Map

These are the same stencils listed earlier in this chapter under Visio Standard.

Mechanical Engineering

Mechanical Engineering stencils, listed in the following table, contain shapes for diagramming a process to create something, or detailed shapes to design or diagram parts that already exist.

Stencil	Shapes
Fasteners 1	Cheese head (slotted), Cheese head top, Countersunk (posidriv), Countersunk (slotted), Countersunk top, Fillister (slotted), Fillister top, Hex shoulder, Hex cap nut, Hex head, Hex head top, Hex jam nut, Hex nut, Hex nut top, Hex socket, Hex socket top, Panhead (posidriv), Panhead (slotted), Panhead top, Posidriv top 1, Posidriv top 2, Raised ck. (posidriv), Raised ck. (slotted), Raised ck. top, Roundhead (slotted), Roundhead top, Shoulder (slotted), Square head, Square head top, Square nut, Square nut top, Wing nut 1, Wing nut 2, Wing nut top, Wing screw, Wing screw top
Fasteners 2	Ball plunger, Collar head rivet, Countersunk rivet 1, Countersunk rivet 2, Flat head rivet, Fluted head set, Fluted set top, Hex head set, Hex set top, Hex-bevel head set, Hex-bevel set top, Pan head rivet, Round head rivet, Slotted head set, Slotted set top, Spring lock washer, Spring lock washer top, Square head set, Square set top, Stud, Taper pin, Thin round head rivet, Truss head rivet, Washer, Washer (chamfer), Washer top, Washer top (chamfer)
Geometric Dimensioning and Tolerancing	1 datum frame, 2 datum frame, 3 datum frame, All around callout, Angularity, Arc length, Basic frame, Box callout, Callout, Circular runout, Circularity, Concentricity, Conical taper, Counterbore/ spotface, Countersink, Cylindricity, Datum (new), Datum (old), Datum symbol, Datum targets, Depth, Diameter, Flatness, Line profile, Material condition, Parallelism, Perpendicularity, Position, Simple frame, Slope, Statistical tolerance, Straightness, Surface finish, Surface profile, Symmetry, Text block, Total runout

A

Stencil	Shapes
Springs and Bearings	Angular cont. (dbl.), Angular contact, Centering bore, Chamfer, Countersunk hole, Cutaway, Cylindrical roller, Cylindrical roller (dbl.), Deep groove, Gear, General, Helical spring, Keyway, Needle roller, Round key, Self aligning (double), Spherical roller (dbl.), Spindle end, Spring hook, Taper roller, Tapered key, Tapered shaft, Threaded hole 2, Threaded hole 1, Through hole, Thrust, Undercut
Welding Symbols	Additional arrow, Arrow, Arrow with bend, Backing, Backing/ spacer, Bevel groove, Contours, Contours-angled, Field weld, Fillet, Flange corner, Flange edge, Flare bevel groove, Flare V groove, Insert, J-groove, Melt thru, Resistance seam, Scarf, Slot/plug, Spot, Square groove, Stud, Surfacing, Text block, U-groove, V-groove
Fluid Power – Equipment	Accumulator, Actuator, Actuator (semi-rotary), Actuator/ intensifier, Air receiver, Air compressor, Air dryer / lubricator, Air service unit, Double-acting, Double- ended, Double-act. magnetic, Drain, Drive unit, Energy source, Energy source 1, Filter, Flow- meter, Flow indicator, Heat exchanger, Intensifier, Pressure gauge, Pulse counter 1, Pulse counter 2, Pump/ motor 1, Pump/ motor 2, Pump/motor (simple), Sealed reservoir, Separator, Silencer, Single-acting, Switch/ transducer, Tachometer, Telescopic, Thermometer, Vented reservoir
Fluid Power- Valve Assembly	2 position 5 port, 2 position 2,3,4 port, 2-port, 2-port closed, 3 position 5-port, 3 position 2,3,4 port, 3-port, 3-port crossover, 4 position 5-port, 4 position 2,3,4 port, 4-port, 4-port open, 4-port closed, 4-port tandem, 4-port crossed, 4-port crossover, 4-port semi-conn., 5-port, 5-port closed, 5-port crossover, Air bleed, Air exhaust port, Arrow, Box, Closed path, Closed path (double), Curved arrow, Detent, Electric, Electric rotor, Electric (linear), Flexible line, Fluid flow, Fluid energy, Junction dot, Junction/ crossing, Latch, Lever, Manual override, Over-center, Pedal/ treadle, Pilot-operated, Plunger, Pull/push button, Restriction, Rod, Roller, Rotary connection, Shaft, Spring, Temperature, Variable arrow
Fluid Power – Valves	2/2 valve, 3/2 valve, 4/2 valve, 4/3 valve, 5/2 valve, 5/3 valve, Cartridge valve, Coupling (connected), Coupling (disconn.), Flow control, Flow divider, Gate-valve, Non-return, One-way restrictor, Pressure reducing, Pressure relief, Pressure relief (E), Pressure relief 2, Quick exhaust, Restrictor valve, Shuttle valve

Network

Network stencils, listed in the next table, contain all types of computers and connective systems to help you diagram or design your network.

Stencil	Shapes
Basic Network Shapes	ASCII Printer, Bridge, CD burner, Cell phone, City, Cloud, Comm-link, Database, Desktop PC, DVD drive, Dynamic connector, Ethernet, Fax, FDDI ring, Firewall, Flat screen monitor, Floppy drive, Hand held computer, Hub, iBook, iMac, Keyboard, Laptop computer, Line connector, Line-curve connector, Modem, Monitor, Mouse, MUX / DEMUX, Optical drive, Patch bay, Pen based computer, Plotter, Power Mac G4, Printer, Printer 2, Printer 3, RAID drive, Removable storage, Scanner, Server, Star, Straight bus, Tape drive, Telephone, Token-ring, Tower box, Tower PC, Workstation
Basic Network Shapes 2	10BASE-T wall plate, A-B switchbox, Acoustic coupler, Answering machine, Cable, Comm. hub, Cray, CRT projector, Custom equipment, Digitizing pad, Disk array, Fiber optic xmitter, Host, IBM AS/400, IBM PS/2, Link builder, LocalTalk, Long card, Mainframe, Micro VAX, Minicomputer, Network Controller, Network processor, Oscilloscope, PBX / PABX, Power strip, Processor, Public switch, Punchdown block, Rack mount, Radio tower, Repeater, Router, Satellite, Satellite dish, Screen, Short card, Synchronous host, Tape, Television, Terminal server, VAX, Video
Basic Network Shapes 3D	Bottom to top angled, Bridge, Bus network, Card, City, Color box, Comm. tower, Comm-link, Fax, Firewall, Hub / switch, Keyboard, Laptop, Mainframe, Mini computer, Modem, Mouse, Multiplexer, PBX / comm. hub, PDA, Personal computer, Plotter, Printer, Repeater, Ring network, Room, Router, Satellite, Satellite dish, Scanner, Server, Side to side angled, Telephone, Terminal server, Town, WAN, Workstation
Generic Manufacturer Equipment	3Com Chas Hub, 3Com Router, 3Com Stkbl Eth Hub, 3Com Stkbl Fiber Hub, 3Com Switch, Bay Ntwrks Chas Hub, Bay Ntwrks Chassis Rtr, Bay Ntwrks Stkbl Hub, Bay Ntwrks Stkbl Rtr, Bay Ntwrks Stkbl Swtch, Cabletron Chas Hub, Cabletron Stkbl Hub, Cisco Router, Cisco Switch, Compaq Stackable, Data Gen Mini Cmptr, DEC Chas Hub, DEC Mini Computer, DEC Stkbl Hub, Hitachi Chassis Sw, HP Bridge/ Router, HP Chassis Hub, HP Mini Computer, HP Stckbl Hub, HP Switch, IBM Chas Hub, IBM Mainframe, IBM Mini Computer, IBM Stkbl Hub, IBM Token Ring Hub, Nortel Switch
Internet Symbols	Firewall w/hole, Firewall w/tunnel, Generic Firewall, Hardware Firewall, Smartcard, Secure ID Card, Virtual web site (root), WWW Cluster, WWW Server

A

Stencil	Shapes
Logical Symbols	100BaseT Hub, ATM Router, ATM Switch, ATM/FastGB Etherswitch, Bridge, Bus, CDDI/FDDI Concentrator, Certificate Server, Cloud, Coaxial line tag, Comm Server, Comm-link, Curved bus, DSU/CSU, Dynamic connector, Ethernet, FDDI ring, Fiber optic line tag, Gateway, Government, Headquarters, Home Office, Host, House Regular, ISDN Switch, Key, Line connector, Line-curve connector, Lock, Lock and Key, Medium Building, Microphone, Network Connector, Peer-to-peer, Probe, Public/Private Key Server, Relational Database, Router, Small Business, Small Hub, Speaker, Star, Telecommuter House, Terminal Server, Token-ring, Twisted pair line tag, University, WAN, Workgroup Switch
Network Devices	Bridge/Router, Chassis 5 Slot, Department/Workgroup Server, Ethernet Hub, Generic File Server, Generic UPS, Layer 3 Switch, Media Converter, Meter, Network Attached Storage (NAS), Patch Panel, Print Server, Raid Drives Storage Tower, Remote Access Server (RAS), Repeater Hub, RMON Probe, Sniffer, Thin-client, Token Ring Hub, UPS -Rack, UPS-Standalone Large, UPS-Standalone Small/Medium, VPN Access Router
PC & Peripherals	CD Burner, CD Tower, CE Device/Jupiter/Subnotebook, Digital Camera, DVD Player, Flat Screen Monitor, Generic Desktop, Generic Laptop, Generic Terminal, Generic Tower, iMac, PalmPilot, PCMCIA Card/Device, Portable Mass Storage Device, PowerMac G3, Projection System, SwitchView PC Switch, Tape Backup (DLT and DAT)
Printers & Scanners	BubbleJet Printer, Flatbed Scanner, Generic Dept Laser, Generic Dot Matrix, Generic Line Printer, Generic Plotter, Generic Prsnl Prntr, Generic Scanner, Label Printer
Telecom	Cable Modems, Cell Phone, IP Phone, Modem Bank, Pager
Active Directory Objects	Certificate Template, Directory Connector, Domain, Organizational Unit
Active Directory Sites and Services	Application 3D, Client, Comm-link, Database, Domain 3D, Domain contrl. 2D, Domain contrl. 3D, Replication connection, Site link 3D, Site link bridge 3D, Site or subnet, Site or subnet 2D, WAN
LDAP Objects	Alias, Application entity, Application process, Country, cRL distribution point, Device, Directory connector, dmd, dSA, Generic Object, Group of names, Locality, Organization, Organizational person, Organizational role, Organizational unit, Person, Residential person, Unknown
NDS Additional Objects	Auditing, Bindery Object, Bindery Queue, Broker, CommExec, Device, Directory Map, Distribution List, DNS-DHCP, External Entity, Key Material, LAN Area, LDAP Group, LDAP Server, License, License count, License Server, Msg Routing Grp, NDPS Manager, NDPS Printer, NDSCat: Catalog, NDSCat: Master, NDSCat: Slave, Organizational Person, Profile, SAS: Service, Security, SLP Directory Agent, SLP Scope Unit, Template

Stencil	Shapes
NDS Objects	[ROOT], AFP Server, Alias, Computer, Country, Directory connector, Group, Locality, Messaging Server, Organization, Organization unit, Organizational Role, Print Server, Printer, Server, Unknown, User, Volume
NDS Partitions	Bus network, Comm-link, Database, Partition 1, Partition 2, Partition 3, Partition 4, Replication connection, Server, Smart partition, WAN, 3Com Chas Hub, 3Com Router, 3Com Stkbl Eth Hub, 3Com Stkbl Fiber Hub, 3Com Switch, Bay Ntwrks Chas Hub, Bay Ntwrks Chassis Rtr, Bay Ntwrks Stkbl Hub, Bay Ntwrks Stkbl Rtr, Bay Ntwrks Stkbl Swtch, Cabletron Chas Hub, Cabletron Stkbl Hub, Cisco Router, Cisco Switch, Compaq Stackable, Data Gen Mini Cmptr, DEC Chas Hub, DEC Mini Computer, DEC Stkbl Hub, Hitachi Chassis Sw, HP Bridge/ Router, HP Chassis Hub, HP Mini Computer, HP Stckbl Hub, HP Switch, IBM Chas Hub, IBM Mainframe, IBM Mini Computer, IBM Stkbl Hub, IBM Token Ring Hub, Nortel Switch

Organizational Chart

These are the same stencils listed earlier in this chapter under Visio Standard.

Process Engineering

Process Engineering stencils, listed next, contains shapes to help you diagram or design a process for manufacturing.

Stencil	Shapes
Equipment – General	Ball mill, Blender, Boom loader, Breaker, Briquetting machine, Centrifuge 1, Centrifuge 2, Conveyor, Conveyor wheel, Crusher, Cyclone 1, Cyclone 2, Double blender, Dryer, Electric motor, Electromagnet, Elevator 1, Elevator 2, Filter 1, Filter 2, Fluid separators, Hammer crusher, Hoists, Kneader, Mixer, Overhead conveyor, Prill tower, Roll crusher, Rotary filter, Scraper conveyor, Screen, Screw conveyor, Skip hoist, Tank car, Tank truck, Various crushers 1, Various crushers 2, Various kneaders, Various mills, Various mixers
Equipment-Heat Exchangers	Air cooling evaporator, Air-blown cooler, Autoclave, Automatic stoker, Boiler, Chilling evaporator, Condenser, Condenser (air cooled), Cooling tower, Cooling tower 1, Cooling tower 2, Double pipe type, Evaporative Condenser, Extractor hood, Fan blades, Finned tube, Fired heater, Heat exchanger1, Heat exchanger2, Kettle reboiler, Oil burner, Oil separator, Plate type, Refrigerators, Shell and tube, Triple fan blades, Tube bundle 1, Tube bundle 2

A

Stencil	Shapes
Equipment – Pumps	Axial flow fan 1, Axial flow fan 2, Centrifugal fan, Centrifugal pump, Compressor / turbine, Ejector / injector, Fan blades, In-line pump, Motor driven turbine, Positive displacement, Proportioning pump, Reciprocating pump 2, Reciprocating pump/compr., Rotary compressor, Rotary pump 1, Rotary pump 2, Selectable compressor1, Selectable compressor2, Selectable compressor3, Selectable fan 1, Selectable fan 2, Selectable pump 1, Selectable pump 2, Selectable pump 3, Spray, Triple fan blades
Equipment – Vessels	Access point, Autoclave, Bag, Barrel, Branch fitting, Carrying vessel, Clarifier, Closed tank, Column, Covered tank, Flanged access point, Fluid contacting, Gas cylinder, Gas holder, Open tank, Reaction vessel, Storage sphere, Tank, Tray (dashed), Tray (solid), Tray column, Vessel, Water surface
Instruments	AND gate, Capillary Tube, Computer, Computer 2, Converter, Correcting element, CRT, CRT 2, Dashed mid-line, Data, Diamond, Double, Electric, Electric 2, Electric 3, Electric Binary, Electric Binary 2, Electromagnetic, Electro- magnetic 2, Flowmeter, Flowmeters, Generic Utility, Heat Trace, Heated / Cooled, Hydraulic, Hydraulic 2, Indicator, Indicator 2, Indicator/ recorder, Level Meter, Level meters, Light, Mechanical, Mechanical 2, NOT gate, Operator Box, OR gate, PID Capillary Tube, PID Data, PID Electric, PID Electric 2, PID Electric Binary, PID Electrical 3, PID Electrical Binary 2, PID Electromagnetic, PID Electro-magnetic2, PID Heat Trace, PID Heated / Cooled, PID Hydraulic, PID Hydraulic 2, PID Mechanical, PID Mechanical 2, PID Pneumatic, PID Pneumatic 2, PID Pneumatic Binary, PID Signal, PLC, PLC 2, Pneumatic, Pneumatic 2, Pneumatic Binary, Pressure gauges, Propeller meter, Rotameter, Signal, Steam traced, Thermometers, Venturi, Vortex sensor
Pipelines	Major Pipeline, Major PipelineL, Major PipelineR, Minor Pipeline, Minor PipelineL, Minor PipelineR
Process Annotations	10pt. text, 10pt. text & Line, 6pt. text, 6pt. text & Line, 8pt. text, 8pt. text & Line, Callout 1, Callout 2, Callout 3, Callout 4, Callout 5, Callout 6, Interface Point 1, Interface Point 2, Off-Sheet Label 1, Off-Sheet Label 2, Off-Sheet Label 3, Slope
Valves and Fittings	3-way Plug Valve, Angle valve, Ball valve, Bell mouth, Bursting disc, Butt weld, Butterfly valve, Character. port, Check valve, Diaphragm valve, Drain silencer, Electrically bonded, Electrically insulated, End caps 1, End caps 2, Exhaust head, Exhaust silencer, Flame arrester, Flanged valve, Flanged/ bolted, Float operated, Gate valve, General joint, Globe valve, Hydrant, Liquid seal open/closed, Mixing valve, Needle valve, Open vent, Plug valve, Powered valve, Reducer, Reducing valve, Relief (angle), Relief valves, Screw-down valve, Screwed joints, Separator, Sleeve joint, Socket w/ spigot, Socket weld, Soldered/ Solvent, Stop check valve, Strainer, Swivel joint, Syphon drain, Tundish, Valve Manifold, Wedge / Parallel, Y strainer

Project Schedule

These are the same stencils listed earlier in this chapter under Visio Standard.

Software

Software stencils, listed next, contain shapes to help you design or document either a piece of software or the software development process.

Stencil	Shapes
COM and OLE	Boundary, COM object, Connector, Data store, Document/ file, Embedded document, Folder, Interface, Object Hierarchy, Object model, OLE server/app., Open folder, Process boundary, Reference, Vtable, Weak reference
Enterprise Application	Boundary, Communication Link, Component, Datastore, Document, Interface, Label, Laptop, Laptops, Mainframe, Mainframes, Object, Process, Server, Servers, Spare, User, Workstation, Workstations
Gane-Sarson	Data Flow, Data Store, Interface, Process
Jackson	Logical connector, Procedure, Procedure 2, Process, Tree connector
Language Level Shapes	Bracket, Cloud, Conditional invocation, Data flow, Flag flow, Flowchart shapes, Function / subroutine, Function w / invocation, Invocation, Invocation w / jump, Lexical inclusion, Switch
Memory Objects	3D stack middle, 3D stack top, Array, Byte or variable, Data block, Data chunk, Data store, Double link. list node, Pointer, Pointer (1-D), Range label, Single link. list node, Stack or heap, Stack pointer
Office User Interface	Control toolbox icons, Forms icons, Toolbar, Visual basic icons, Web icons, WordArt icons
ROOM	Actor class, Actor reference, Binding, Choicepoint, End ports, Group transition, Internal self-transition, Layer/Export connections, Modified actor ref., Reference ports, Relay ports, State, State context, Textual definitions, Transition, Transition points, Transition to history
UML Activity	2-element Constraint, Action State, Constraint, Control Flow, Decision, Final State, Initial State, Note, Object Flow, Object In State, OR Constraint, Signal Receipt, Signal Send, State, Swimlane, Transition (Fork), Transition (Join)
UML Collaboration	2-element Constraint, Association Role, Association Role, Classifier Role, Composite, Constraint, Multi-Object, Note, OR Constraint
UML Component	2-element Constraint, Component, Constraint, Dependency, Interface, Node, Note, OR Constraint, Package
UML Deployment	2-element Constraint, Component, Component Instance, Composition, Constraint, Dependency, Interface, Node, Node Instance, Note, Object, OR Constraint, Package
UML Sequence	2-element Constraint, Activation, Constraint, Left Asynchronous, Lifeline, Message, Message (async.), Message (call), Message (call), Message (return), Message (return), Note, Object Lifeline, OR Constraint

A

Stencil	Shapes
UML Statechart	2-element Constraint, Composite State, Constraint, Decision, Deep History, Final State, Initial State, Note, OR Constraint, Shallow History, State, Transition, Transition, Transition (Fork), Transition (Join)
UML Static Structure	2-element Constraint, Association Class, Binary Association, Binding, Bound Element, Class, Constraint, Data Type, Dependency, Exception, Generalization, Generalization Arrow, Interface, Interface, Metaclass, N-ary AssocClass, N-ary Association, N-ary Link, Note, Object, OR Constraint, Package, Parameterized Class, Refinement, Signal, Subsystem, Trace, Usage, Utility
UML Use Case	2-element Constraint, Actor, Communicates, Constraint, Extends, Generalization Arrow, Interface, Note, OR Constraint, Package, System Boundary, Use Case, Uses
Windows User Interface	Additional tabs, Blank Form, Blank Toolbar Button, Button, Check Box, Combo Box, Combo Box Pull-down, Corner Resize Handle, Dialog Icons, Dir List Box, Drive List Box, Drop-Down Menu Item, Edit box, File List Box, Grid, Group box, Line, List Box, Menu, Mouse pointer, Panel, Progress bar, Progress bar 2, Radio Button, Scroll Bar, Selection Box, Slider, Spin button, Status bar, Tab control, Text Box, Toolbar, Toolbar Buttons, Toolbar Separator, Top-Level Menu Item, Tree nodes, Tree View, Windows Buttons, Wizard UI (Simple), Wizard UI: Welcome, Toolbar Separator

Web Design

Web Design stencils, listed next, contain shapes to help you design, or document a web site.

Stencil	Shapes
Conceptual Web Site Shapes	Dynamic connector, For creation, Gateway, Legend, Main page, Page, Page component, Page groups, Related pages, Similar pages
Web Site Map Shapes	ActiveX control, Archive, ASP, Audio, Document, Download file, Dynamic connector, File, Form, FrontPage, FTP, Generic, Gopher, Graphic, Home, Home page, HTML, Image map, Java and JavaScript, Line-curve connector, MailTo, Multimedia, Newsgroup, Off-page connector, Page jump, Plug-in, Program, Script, Search, Telnet, Template, Title, Title 2, Video, WAIS, XML

Appendix B Resources

This appendix contains a selection of online resources, phone numbers, and addresses to help you get more information about Microsoft Visio.

Microsoft Visio Address and Phone Numbers

Corporate Headquarters
Microsoft Corporation
One Microsoft Way
Redmond, WA 98052-6399
(425) 882-8080

Sales Support
(800) 426-9400
5:00AM - 5:30 PM PST, Mon- Fri, excluding holidays

Product Support
(800) 936-3500

Online Resources

The Microsoft web site has a Visio section filled with information and useful links for any Visio user.

- Microsoft's main front page can be reached at: http://www.microsoft.com

- Information for all Microsoft Office products can be reached at: http://www.microsoft.com/office

- Resource information for Microsoft Visio can be reached at: http://www.microsoft.com/office/visio

- Visio Smart Pages, a bi-monthly e-newsletter about Visio solutions, can be registered for at: http://register.microsoft.com/regsys/custom/newslettersdk/officenews.asp

- Resources to help design and learn Visio can be found at: http://www.microsoft.com/office/visio/resources.htm

- Visio Training can be reached at: http://www.microsoft.com/trainingandservices

■ To be matched up with a Microsoft Corporate Sales Executive, go to http://www.microsoft.com/USA/

■ To contact Visio consulting services, known as VisioPartners, for a project or question, go to: http://www.visiopartners.com/. You can also list yourself as a VisioPartner at the same web site

■ To find international Microsoft offices, go to http://www.microsoft.com/worldwide/

Developer Resources

The Microsoft Knowledge Base and the Microsoft Technical web sites hold an almost limitless amount of information for the Visio developer. This is an overview of many of the developer options for Visio.

■ For developer tours of Microsoft Visio at: http://www.microsoft.com/office/visio/evaluation/IT

■ Access the Visio Developer web site at: http://msdn.microsoft.com/visio/

■ For a technical exchange of ideas, go to: http://www.microsoft.com/technet/visio/

■ For Microsoft Visio tips and tricks, go to: http://www.microsoft.com/technet/visio/tips.asp

■ For developer-level information relating to Microsoft and Visio products, go to http://search.support.microsoft.com/kb

■ For Visio case studies, go to: http://www.microsoft.com/technet/visio/case.asp

■ Access others who want to talk about Visio technical issues at: http://www.microsoft.com/technet/discuss/default.asp

■ For online classes and seminars, go to: http://msdn.microsoft.com/visio/

■ The Visio Developer's Forum is available at: http://www.microsoft.com/technet/chats

■ Visio Developer Support is available at: http://support.microsoft.com/support

B

HTML and XML Resources

■ http://www.ncsa.uiuc.edu/Indices/Resources/html-resources.html.
National Center for Supercomputing Applications page for HTML
Resources. A great site for those new to HTML.

■ http://www.w3.org/MarkUp/. The World Wide Web consortium home
page for HTML. You can find links to specifications, pointers, tutorials,
bulletin boards, mailing lists, and more at this site.

■ http://www.w3.org/Style/XSL/. The World Wide Web consortium home
page for XML. You can find links to learning XML from this page.

Index

INTERNATIONAL CONTACT INFORMATION

AUSTRALIA
McGraw-Hill Book Company Australia Pty. Ltd.
TEL +61-2-9417-9899
FAX +61-2-9417-5687
http://www.mcgraw-hill.com.au
books-it_sydney@mcgraw-hill.com

CANADA
McGraw-Hill Ryerson Ltd.
TEL +905-430-5000
FAX +905-430-5020
http://www.mcgrawhill.ca

**GREECE, MIDDLE EAST,
NORTHERN AFRICA**
McGraw-Hill Hellas
TEL +30-1-656-0990-3-4
FAX +30-1-654-5525

MEXICO (Also serving Latin America)
McGraw-Hill Interamericana Editores S.A. de C.V.
TEL +525-117-1583
FAX +525-117-1589
http://www.mcgraw-hill.com.mx
fernando_castellanos@mcgraw-hill.com

SINGAPORE (Serving Asia)
McGraw-Hill Book Company
TEL +65-863-1580
FAX +65-862-3354
http://www.mcgraw-hill.com.sg
mghasia@mcgraw-hill.com

SOUTH AFRICA
McGraw-Hill South Africa
TEL +27-11-622-7512
FAX +27-11-622-9045
robyn_swanepoel@mcgraw-hill.com

**UNITED KINGDOM & EUROPE
(Excluding Southern Europe)**
McGraw-Hill Education Europe
TEL +44-1-628-502500
FAX +44-1-628-770224
http://www.mcgraw-hill.co.uk
computing_neurope@mcgraw-hill.com

ALL OTHER INQUIRIES Contact:
Osborne/McGraw-Hill
TEL +1-510-549-6600
FAX +1-510-883-7600
http://www.osborne.com
omg_international@mcgraw-hill.com